# THE ROYAL HOSPITAL CHELSEA AT WAR

The East Wing Long Ward accommodation block of the Royal Hospital Chelsea suffered bomb damage after an air raid during the First World War. The North-East Wing was severely damaged in the same raid. (RHC Archives)

# THE ROYAL HOSPITAL CHELSEA AT WAR

MARTIN CAWTHORNE

**Dedicated to**
Private Arthur Walter Cattell, King's Own Yorkshire Light Infantry, killed in action on 1 July 1916, the first day of the Battle of the Somme – my great-grandfather.

First published 2024

The History Press
97 St George's Place, Cheltenham,
Gloucestershire, GL50 3QB
www.thehistorypress.co.uk

© Martin Cawthorne, 2024

The right of Martin Cawthorne to be identified as the Author of this work has been asserted in accordance with the Copyright, Designs and Patents Act 1988.

All rights reserved. No part of this book may be reprinted or reproduced or utilised in any form or by any electronic, mechanical or other means, now known or hereafter invented, including photocopying and recording, or in any information storage or retrieval system, without the permission in writing from the Publishers.

British Library Cataloguing in Publication Data.
A catalogue record for this book is available from the British Library.

Hardback ISBN 978 1 80399 745 2
Paperback ISBN 978 1 80399 599 1

Typesetting and origination by The History Press
Printed and bound in Great Britain by TJ Books Limited, Padstow, Cornwall.

Trees for Life

# Contents

Foreword 7
Preface 9
Introduction 13

1   Pre-War Civil Defence Planning 19
2   The Royal Hospital Prepares for War 29
3   The Munich Crisis 43
4   War Clouds Over Europe 56
5   The Outbreak of War 69
6   The Phoney War 87
7   Dunkirk and the Threat of Invasion 101
8   The Battle of Britain 113
9   The Blitz 129
10  A Winter of Bombs 143
11  The Bombing of the Royal Hospital's Infirmary 175
12  The Bombing of Chelsea Old Church 193
13  Aftermath 208
14  Out-Stations 227
15  Dispersal and Demolition 247
16  Post-War Planning 261
17  Peace Returns to Chelsea 281

| | |
|---|---|
| Epilogue | 299 |
| Notes | 301 |
| Bibliography | 325 |
| Acknowledgements | 331 |
| Index | 333 |

# Foreword

We owe Martin a debt of gratitude for the story you are about to read, *The Royal Hospital Chelsea at War*. The story has not been previously told. Martin has searched through our archives, delved into unopened boxes lying in the back of long forgotten cupboards, painstakingly sifted official documents, uncovered remarkable pictures and first-hand diary accounts. He has assembled and presented them in a way that shows his deep love of this subject, respect for accuracy and authenticity, and passion in telling a story waiting to be told. Underpinned by rigorous academic research, he has crafted a highly readable narrative which brings to life the characters, the events and the dilemmas facing the authorities, and the enduring resilience of the Royal Hospital's Pensioners. I am immensely grateful to Martin and to The History Press for bringing this story to a wider audience.

It tells the tale of a nation, city and community under fire, of sadness and loss, hope and rebirth, ingenuity and courage. It will take you to those critical moments, guide you through complex official decisions and dilemmas, the preparations for war and aerial bombardment, the construction of air-raid shelters (some of which exist to this day) and share with you a minute-by-minute account of the fateful night of 16–17 April 1941, when the infirmary sustained a direct hit and was destroyed, and the remarkable rescue operation that followed.

You will also discover another remarkable rescue operation that took place at the Hospital at the end of the war, when the Commissioners found themselves once again on the front line. This time against officialdom who eyed up the Hospital, itself wounded by war, and wondered if it was time for it to be pensioned off.

*The Royal Hospital Chelsea at War*, told so faithfully and with so much affection by Martin Cawthorne, demonstrates the values and proud heritage of the British Army: service, discipline, bravery, courage under fire, endurance in privation and resilience. We continue to draw on those same values today, discovering new ways that we can share community, comradeship and care with the wider veteran community, and opening our doors to welcome more visitors to share this wonderful heritage that I and my colleagues here are privileged to serve.

There will be future stories to be told. Enjoy reading this one.

General Sir Adrian Bradshaw, KCB, OBE, DL<br>
Governor, Royal Hospital Chelsea

# Preface

The archives of the Royal Hospital Chelsea have an interesting history. Over the centuries of the Hospital's existence, literally tons of internally generated paperwork were routinely destroyed as there was simply not the space to store the physical documents. That is, until the overwhelming bulk of the surviving archives (estimated as still consisting of around 1 million documents) was sent to the Army Records Office at Hayes in 1974. From here, they were transferred to the Public Record Office and are now held by The National Archives in Kew. There remained, however, an overlooked, small and eclectic collection of material stored in boxes in an attic at the Royal Hospital.

In 2013, the Hospital authorities decided to investigate these documents and digitise their contents to preserve the material for future generations. There was also the hope that the Hospital might find out a little more about itself and its history from the contents of these boxes. Regimental Quartermaster Sergeant John Rochester was given the task of organising this project and chose to recruit some volunteers to assist him. So it was that, in 2014, I officially joined the ranks of the Royal Hospital Chelsea volunteer militia attached to the Quartermaster's Department.

During this project, I happily worked with John and his other volunteers as we opened archive boxes and investigated their contents. The documents were subsequently digitised, with complex material sent off-site to specialist facilities and simple documents scanned using equipment brought in-house. As a result of our detective work during this preservation project, we uncovered a myriad of different stories about the Hospital and I enjoyed writing a couple of articles for the in-house magazine, *The Tricorne*. One of these covered the loss of much of the Hospital's original endowment fund during the South Sea Bubble, which appealed to my finance background. We also uncovered some fascinating but contradictory material about the Second World War history of the institution.

As a home for retired soldiers, the Royal Hospital Chelsea has always been associated with warfare. The Second World War, however, represents a unique chapter in its history when the institution itself was in the line of fire for a sustained period in a way hitherto unknown. Its wartime experience is remarkably under-researched, with very little of any substance written about this period.

Captain C.G.T. Dean, in his 300-page definitive work, *The Royal Hospital Chelsea*, devotes little more than a page and a half to the war years. To some extent, this can be attributed to the fact that for Dean, writing in 1949, the war represented recent news rather than a unique historical era. It was also a time that he himself had lived through and many of his experiences were unquestionably traumatic, such that he may not have wished to revisit them while the scars were still fresh. But this does not explain the lack of substantive coverage of the war years in the work of the Hospital's subsequent historians. However, the previous lack of readily available source material about the Royal Hospital during the Second World War may explain why this period has to date attracted so little attention.

The clues we uncovered during our digitisation work suggested a fascinating and previously untold wartime story which deserved further investigation. Rather than simply writing another short magazine article, I determined that I wished to attempt something more substantial and embarked upon a two-year Master's degree course in Historical Studies at the University of Oxford which enabled me to conduct my research under the guidance of some exceptional academic supervision. My intimate familiarity with the archives held in Chelsea ensured that when I visited the National Archives I knew immediately where to start looking among the wealth of material held in Kew and had a reasonable idea of what I was hoping to find. In the event, I found much more than I expected.

I completed two dissertations during my studies. My first-year dissertation covered the question of how the Royal Hospital prepared for war, and in my second year I covered the war years themselves. I investigated the role and nature of evacuation strategies, which represent an ever-present but constantly evolving theme in the Hospital's wartime story. The overwhelming majority of wartime evacuation historiography focuses on the experiences of young children and their guardians. The elderly and infirm, although in principle eligible for publicly funded assistance, were, in practice, more usually overlooked and hence have been largely ignored in the historiography of war on the Home Front. The Royal Hospital's archives, by contrast, provide a uniquely detailed archive record of the challenges and experiences of a specific cohort of elderly and infirm: Chelsea Pensioners, recording their lives and lived experience during an exceptional period in our collective history.

The completed dissertations were considered to be of publishable quality given the depth of research and the weight of original source material used. One of the biggest challenges I faced was trying to squeeze the story I wanted to tell into available word count limits.

The wartime story of the Royal Hospital is more than simply a historiographical investigation into an overlooked chapter in the history of a nationally significant institution. It is also about the personal stories of individuals whose ordinary lives were impacted by extraordinary events during exceptional times; the people who lived, worked, and in some cases died, at the Royal Hospital during the Second World War. This is as much their story as it is the wartime history of a national institution and the neighbouring district of Chelsea. This book is my attempt at telling the wartime story of the Royal Hospital and its residents and I hope that its publication adds a little to our collective understanding of a unique chapter in the history of such a remarkable and worthy institution.

Martin Cawthorne

On the outbreak of war, a requisition order was served on the Royal Hospital for the use of part of the grounds for the installation of this searchlight unit. Two barrage balloons were also operated from the Royal Hospital grounds. (IWM Collections)

# Introduction

The Royal Hospital Chelsea (RHC) opened its doors in 1692 as a retirement home for British Army veterans, one of a number of such institutions founded in the seventeenth century.[1] Others included L'Hôtel des Invalides in Paris, founded in 1670 by Louis XIV as a home for French Army veterans; the Royal Hospital Kilmainham in Dublin, established in 1675; and the Royal Hospital Greenwich, opened as a retirement home for Royal Navy veterans at around the same time as RHC.[2]

The impetus for the establishment of these retirement institutions for ex-military personnel can be traced to the increasing prevalence of standing armies as a feature of the military landscape in Europe during the seventeenth century. In the United Kingdom, the success of the Parliamentarian New Model Army and the decisive role it played in the English Civil Wars demonstrated the advantages of a professional force of full-time soldiers trained in the skills necessary for the successful prosecution of military campaigns.

The Declaration of Breda in 1660, eleven years after the execution of Charles I, is notable for setting in train the restoration of the monarchy, with the subsequent coronation of Charles II ending the period most often referred to as the Interregnum. The Declaration, however, also contained provisions, which in effect formalised the continuation of a standing army, as Charles II proclaimed:

> We do further declare, that we will be ready to consent to any Act or Acts of Parliament [...] for the full satisfaction of all arrears due to the officers and soldiers of the army under the command of General Monk; and they shall be received into our service upon as good pay and conditions as they now enjoy.[3]

This opened the way for soldiers of the New Model Army to join the remnants of the Royalist Army, which had escaped into exile with the king. However, in the spirit of the Declaration of Breda, the Bill of Rights of 1689 and the Claim of Right Act of 1689 enshrined in law the requirement for parliamentary consent for the Crown to maintain these regular armed forces. By the second half of the seventeenth century, a professional standing army, swearing allegiance to the Crown but answerable to Parliament, had become a permanent feature of the United Kingdom's military landscape.

This new British Army was soon in action. In 1661, Charles II married Catherine of Braganza and the accompanying marriage treaty provided an alliance with the kingdom of Portugal. The treaty also resulted in the Portuguese ceding control of the important port and fortress of Tangier.

This strategically located anchorage on the coast of North Africa afforded the Royal Navy the opportunity to extend its reach into the Mediterranean and provided a base for disrupting the activities of Barbary pirates. These marauding corsairs had terrorised coastal communities throughout the reign of Charles I, carrying off men, women and children to be sold into slavery. In 1625, the year of Charles I's coronation, Salé corsairs had occupied the island of Lundy in the Bristol Channel and used it as a base to conduct raiding expeditions throughout the West Country and coastal regions of the Irish Sea.[4]

Tangier offered Charles II the opportunity to take the fight to the Barbary pirates and in the summer of 1661 the army dispatched a newly formed Tangier Regiment to garrison the fortress and protect the anchorage for the navy's warships. On their departure, the troops were assured by the king, 'lett those honest men knowe, who are along with you, yet they shall allwayes be in my particular care and protection, as persons yet venture themselves in my service'.[5]

Putting boots on the ground, however, inevitably provoked a response and the garrison at Tangier was in continuous action throughout the period of occupation until the fortress and anchorage were finally abandoned in 1684. Tangier was subsequently recognised as the first Battle Honour of the newly constituted British Army.[6]

Casualties were incurred throughout the course of the campaign and the twenty-three-year occupation of Tangier resulted in a steady stream of wounded soldiers returning to the British Isles. Soldiers' discharge papers increasingly reported 'worn out' as the principal reason given for a veteran leaving the regimental colours. Soldiering was hard and took its toll on the health of those in the service, and regardless of some modest financial provision provided under statutes for maimed soldiers, aged and disabled veterans became a regular sight throughout the country.

Discontent soon grew among both the military and wider population at the inadequate provision afforded to those who had served in uniform. It was increasingly clear that a regular standing army, while affording opportunities to the monarch and Parliament, also created obligations. Something needed to be done to support old soldiers who were 'broken by age or war'.

Inspiration for how best to accommodate the needs of the increasing numbers of aged and infirm veterans came from the Continent. In 1670, Louis XIV of France founded L'Hôtel des Invalides in Paris as a home for 5,000 so-called '*ineffectives*' of the French Army, and in 1672 the site was inspected by the Duke of Monmouth, Charles II's illegitimate son.[7] Les Invalides is subsequently cited as the institution from which 'the notion of building the like [...] was happily entertained'.[8]

With the king's approval, in the summer of 1679 funds were obtained via deductions from the pay of serving soldiers and thus was founded the Royal Hospital Kilmainham, on the outskirts of Dublin. Its immediate success in providing succour to the growing ranks of previously destitute former soldiers, who had become a common sight throughout Ireland, soon prompted calls in London for similar treatment to be afforded to other military veterans.

The growing clamour for action resulted in Charles purchasing the buildings and grounds of an abandoned theology college on the banks of the River Thames in the district of Chelsea. The eminent architect

Christopher Wren was appointed by the king's agent, Sir Stephen Fox, to design a suitable home for retired soldiers, and construction started soon after the purchase of the site. After Charles' death, work continued under James II and his successors until, in 1692, the first veterans entered the doors of the newly opened Royal Hospital Chelsea.

A similar institution to the east of London was founded as a home for ex-sailors – the Royal Hospital Greenwich opened at about the same time. The most notable difference between these two royal Hospitals was one of scale, with Chelsea designed to accommodate around 500 residents, whereas Greenwich was built to house multiple times this number. Although the difference in scale reflected the relative size of the army compared to the navy in 1692, it was also a gross underestimate of precisely how many former soldiers were eligible for entry into the Royal Hospital Chelsea. The result of this miscalculation led to Chelsea reaching its full occupancy almost as soon as it opened, which in turn raised the question of what should happen to those who were eligible for entry, but for whom no berth was immediately available.

Charles II did not live long enough to witness the opening of the Royal Hospital Chelsea, but even during its construction it became apparent that it would be sub-scale relative to the role envisaged for it. Consequently, when James II inherited the project he issued a Royal Warrant in 1686, addressing the issue of how to alleviate the condition of old soldiers who were congregating in the inns, taverns and boarding houses in the village of Chelsea in anticipation of being offered a berth in the Hospital on its completion. The warrant decreed soldiers 'that are or shall be disabled by wounds in fight or other accidents in the service of the Crown, are to be provided for in the Royal Hospital [...] in such manner as his Majesty shall hereafter direct; and in the meantime are to receive [...] allowances' to be paid from Hospital funds.[9]

The amount of each allowance was determined by rank and length of service, together with an assessment for any disabilities incurred while in the army. The recipients of these pension payments were restricted to the rank and file and did not extend to the officer class, because from its foundation, the Royal Hospital was always intended to provide succour and relief for the enlisted ranks only.

Thus, a system of pension payments was established, administered from Chelsea and paid either in person at the Royal Hospital or via agents acting as intermediaries. Army pensions consequently became known colloquially as 'Chelsea pensions' and old soldiers referred to as 'Chelsea Pensioners'.

On becoming eligible for a Chelsea pension, ex-soldiers not residing at RHC were recorded as 'Out-Pensioners'. However, when a berth became vacant, on condition an Out-Pensioner had no immediate dependents and was deemed to be 'unencumbered by spouse', they could move into the Royal Hospital. On doing so, Out-Pensioners surrendered or 'commuted' their pension on entry into the Hospital, whereupon they became known as 'In-Pensioners'. Their army pension was henceforth paid to the Hospital authorities and used to provide three meals a day and a berth in one of the Long Ward accommodation blocks. This remains the modus operandi of the institution to this day, with the exception that army pensions are no longer administered from the Royal Hospital but are instead the direct responsibility of the Ministry of Defence.

However, by the late-nineteenth century, these symbols of benevolence towards retired military personnel had fallen from favour. The Royal Hospital Greenwich closed for financial reasons in 1869 after a series of parliamentary inquires into its cost-effectiveness, with some of the buildings later used by the National Maritime Museum.[10] Les Invalides ceased to perform its original function before the outbreak of the First World War as the French moved to a conscript army and fewer soldiers attained the twenty years of service necessary for entry.[11] Some of the buildings are now home to the Musée de l'Armée.

In Dublin, Kilmainham closed after Irish Independence in 1922, with the last residents moving out in 1927, and part of the estate was converted into an art gallery and exhibition centre.[12] By the 1930s, therefore, on the eve of the Second World War, only the Royal Hospital Chelsea remained.

# 1

# Pre-War Civil Defence Planning

*'The Bomber will always get through.'*[1]

The First World War resulted in over 10 million deaths and was widely believed to have been a war to end all wars.[2] However, not everybody accepted the terms of the 1919 Treaty of Versailles, and in 1922 a demobilised German soldier called Adolf Hitler railed against his country's defeat, 'It cannot be that two million Germans should have fallen in vain [...] No, we do not pardon, we demand – vengeance!'[3] With Hitler and the Nazi Party's subsequent rise to power, war clouds were once again forming over Europe and as calls for rearmament grew louder, attention in Britain turned to preparations on the Home Front.

Several towns and cities, particularly London, had faced aerial bombing in the First World War.[4] The Royal Hospital Chelsea sustained damage and casualties during a raid in 1918 when a 1,000kg bomb dropped by a Staaken 'Giant' bomber destroyed the North-East Wing, killing Captain of Invalids Ernest Ludlow MC and his family.[5] This was the largest bomb dropped on London during the First World War.[6]

Conventional thinking in the interwar years strongly favoured the view that the 'bomber would always get through' as articulated by Stanley Baldwin in a debate in the House of Commons on 10 November 1932, 'I think it is well also for the man in the street to realize that there is no power on earth that can protect him from being bombed, whatever people may tell him. The bomber will always get through.'[7]

This widely held view led to a debate around how best to protect the civilian population from the anticipated aerial Armageddon. From 1923, Air Raid Precautions (ARP) in Britain were the responsibility of the Committee of Imperial Defence, an advisory body founded by the government in 1904.[8] Initially, the 'committee worked on the development of wartime measures, such as Auxiliary Fire brigades, barrage balloons and inner-city trenches'.[9] However, cost considerations were a major factor in determining the level of pre-war Civil Defence expenditure, particularly given the crippling impact of the Great Depression following the Wall Street Crash of 1929.

In the mid-1930s, central government sought to include local government in the Civil Defence debate and the Home Office published a circular in 1935 'inviting suggestions from local authorities for their wartime measures'.[10] It is from this point that evacuation strategies can be traced as an integral part of defence planning on the Home Front. The debate moved from a focus on protecting civilians *in situ* to instead considering the merits of moving vulnerable groups from areas of potential danger to places of relative safety.

In 1938, a government committee set up under the chairmanship of Sir John Anderson to consider Civil Defence options reported its findings.[11] Detailed consideration was given to events surrounding the Japanese invasion of Chinese Manchuria and attacks against civilian targets in the Spanish Civil War. The well-publicised bombing of the city of Guernica was well known among both military and civilian society. The Anderson Report presented a compelling argument in favour of evacuation:

> Apart from the danger to life and limb, there are obviously strong objections on humanitarian grounds to the retention, in areas which are likely to be the object of deliberate attack of persons whose presence is not absolutely essential. It is impossible fully to envisage the horrors of intensive air attack by the forces of a major European power on a densely populated city; but events in Spain and China have at least given some indication of what might befall. No one would willingly expose children, the aged or infirm, or anyone whose presence could be dispensed with to the nervous strain entailed.[12]

The Anderson Report divided the country into three zones – evacuation, neutral and reception – with the intention that local authorities in evacuation zones would liaise with those in reception areas to facilitate and co-ordinate the movement of vulnerable groups to a place of comparative safety. Leadership at the national level was to come from the Home Office, with Anderson identifying 'the Home Secretary responsible for giving general directions regarding schemes for the evacuation of the civilian population'.[13] At the detailed operational level, the task of administering the evacuation proposals was delegated to the Ministry of Health. However, it quickly became apparent that evacuation planning would be fraught with difficulties. At the outset of the scheme there was little agreement as to which areas of the country should fall into each zone:

> Over 200 local authorities in England and Wales graded as reception asked to be ranked as neutral, and another sixty wanted to be scheduled for evacuation. It is significant of the temper of the country at that time that no authority zoned as evacuable disputed the Ministry of Health's decision, and no authority asked to be a reception area.[14]

Although it was envisaged that evacuation would be voluntary, the report nevertheless established officially designated 'priority groups' eligible for publicly funded support. These were identified, in the sometimes inelegant language of the day, as including:

1. Schoolchildren, removed as school units under the charge of their teachers.
2. Younger children, accompanied by their mothers or by some other responsible person.
3. Expectant mothers.
4. Adult blind persons and cripples where removal was feasible.[15]

Local authorities would co-ordinate their plans to best meet the specific requirements of each of these priority groups, with problems that were identified in advance by the Anderson Committee to be solved through local co-operation, co-ordinated at a national level.

It was recognised at the outset that the scale of potential evacuation envisaged was inevitably going to create significant logistical challenges which would need to be overcome. Nevertheless, government departments would rise to the challenges encountered and so it was expected that, for example, the Ministry of Transport would ensure 'transport facilities can be provided to meet the needs of any orderly scheme of evacuation'.[16]

Finding suitable accommodation for all the anticipated evacuees was, however, considered to be an altogether more difficult problem. It was felt that there was a 'definite limit on the extent to which billets can be found'.[17] Consequently, it was agreed that it would 'be necessary to give the authorities the power in time of war to requisition accommodation for the billeting of evacuees'.[18] The task of drawing up lists of suitable accommodation which could be requisitioned if necessary fell to the Office of Works.

Originally established in 1378, under the leadership of a Surveyor of the King's Works, the Office of Works was responsible for the construction and maintenance of royal castles and palaces. In 1682, it was the Office of Works, under the guidance of Christopher Wren, which had built the Royal Hospital Chelsea, and in the 1930s it still retained responsibility for the maintenance of the Hospital's buildings and grounds.

Although a quasi-independent entity within Whitehall, the Office of Works reported to the Home Secretary and as such was notionally under the control of the Home Office.[19] With extensive in-house expertise in property management, it was to play an important role in Civil Defence and as evacuation planning progressed, the role of the Office of Works was quickly formalised:

> At a meeting of the Imperial Defence Committee on the 15th April 1937, it was decided that secret surveys should be undertaken of buildings that could be utilised, and the information fed into a central requisitioning register. This was made the responsibility of the Office of Works.[20]

Officials subsequently toured the country compiling lists of properties which could be requisitioned should the need arise. Internal discussions were regularly held about which buildings could be used for meeting the various requirements the Office of Works had been asked to consider.

An important factor which significantly influenced evacuation planning was the widely held view about the likelihood of enemy bombers inevitably 'getting through'. It was anticipated that the unavoidable consequence of these attacks on heavily populated civilian centres, regardless of the prior evacuation of vulnerable groups, would undoubtedly result in considerable casualties among the remaining inhabitants of targeted areas. The Imperial Defence Committee estimated that should the United Kingdom face a sixty-day bombing campaign, this would most likely result in as many as 600,000 dead and 1.2 million wounded.[21] These considerations inevitably played a major part in the deliberations among officials at the Office of Works as they compiled the requisition register, and resulted in numerous buildings being identified as potential candidates for emergency casualty clearing hospitals for the anticipated flood of air-raid victims. This focus on air-raid casualties would have important implications for the Royal Hospital Chelsea.

Although in theory there was to be no distinction between the priority groups officially identified in the Anderson Report, in practice, this was not the case. The committee 'devoted special attention to the manner in which children in vulnerable areas should be dealt with'.[22] This was in part simply due to the scale of the potential numbers involved. A short working paper submitted to the committee, 'Evacuation of the Child Population of London – An Appreciation', suggested that 'up to a million children' would require evacuation from the capital alone.[23]

Schoolchildren, while collectively the largest of the priority groups, were also easy to identify and categorise, given that every schoolchild was individually registered at a particular school. School registers meant that, as a group, schoolchildren were relatively easy to deal with from an administrative perspective. So, it was perhaps inevitable that this priority group would attract a significant allocation of the available administrative and logistical resources devoted to evacuation planning.

The Anderson Report recognised that dealing with the other priority groups would be infinitely more complex. This was in part because unlike the evacuation of schoolchildren, which could be organised through the administrative unit of individual schools, these other groups 'have not this common focus, and the arrangements for the transport and accommodation of some of these groups will need special consideration'.[24]

In the case of the disabled, a further issue was also quickly identified in so far as in these pre-war, pre-National Health Service days there were no centralised records of the disabled. Nor indeed was there any definition as to who qualified as such. Despite attempts by the Anderson Report to clarify the issues around the expected treatment of the disabled, there was much confusion among local authorities as to what was expected of them. Eventually, the Ministry of Health issued a memorandum titled 'Government Evacuation Scheme', which tried to offer guidance in this area. Using the inelegant language of the day, the memorandum, under the heading 'Cripples', addresses the specific issues relating to the proposed evacuation of the disabled:

> 9. Different considerations apply in the case of cripples, since the degree of disablement of cripples varies greatly and there are no register or other records on which an estimate of the number of cripples in an evacuating area can be formed.
>
> 10. It appears, however, that facilities should be afforded for the evacuation of adult cripples who satisfy the two conditions of being capable on the one hand of locomotion without the aid of an invalid chair and on the other hand of being at a serious disadvantage owing to slowness of movement or limitation of powers of locomotion in seeking shelter in air-raids.
>
> 11. It will therefore be competent to local authorities to make arrangements for the evacuation of such cripples who notify them of their desire to be evacuated, and it is suggested that these arrangements should be linked with the arrangements for the evacuation of blind persons.
>
> 12. In order that an estimate can be formed of the numbers to be dealt with, it will be necessary for the local authorities of evacuating areas to make public their proposals and such facilities as they will be able to afford for cripples in this category, and to notify those who wish to take advantage of those facilities to register.[25]

In short, therefore, the disabled were identified as anybody who, because of frailty or infirmity, was likely to be at a serious disadvantage when seeking sanctuary in air-raid shelters during bombing alerts.

Despite these clarifications, further issues quickly emerged to create uncertainty as to how the disabled would be treated in practice. The Anderson Report had recommended that participation in government-funded evacuation schemes should be voluntary and many citizens subsequently chose to make their own arrangements. When war was declared in 1939, it was estimated that at least as many people evacuated under private arrangements as chose to use government-sponsored schemes.[26] In practice, many of those using the government schemes did so because they were unable to make their own arrangements, usually because they lacked the financial resources to do so.

As local authorities followed government advice and compiled registers of the disabled in their districts who wished to be considered for the government-sponsored evacuation schemes, it quickly became apparent that a significant number of those registering lived in Public Assistance Institutions.[27] In most cases, these institutions were workhouses, which had come under the control of local authorities as a result of the Local Government Act 1929. This realisation quickly created its own issues.

Unfortunately, although the official classification of workhouses had changed, the same cannot be said of attitudes and prejudices towards them. On the whole, Public Assistance Institutions were still the same organisations, housed in the same overcrowded and substandard buildings, staffed by the same unreconstructed individuals, as had been the case when they were part of the local welfare relief system administered under the much-maligned Poor Law legislation. Consequently, they tended to attract the same correspondingly unenlightened degree of stigma that had almost always been associated with the workhouse. Chronic overcrowding and institutionalised prejudice undoubtedly affected efforts to accommodate eligible inmates within the agreed evacuation planning protocols.

Officials responsible for the safety of blind and disabled inmates of Public Assistance Institutions in areas designated as evacuation zones tried diligently to put in place arrangements for the transfer of these inmates to corresponding facilities in the receiving areas. It soon became apparent, however, that due to chronic overcrowding and indifference among officialdom to the plight of workhouse inmates, there was simply not the appetite in the evacuation-receiving areas to offer accommodation for these potential evacuees. This sad situation is evidenced by a report from the Chief Officer of Public Assistance at the London County Council who, after making exhaustive enquiries, was forced to conclude 'that the results of the survey of accommodation make it clear that it will not be possible [...] to make arrangements for the evacuation of the aged and infirm inmates of [...] Public Assistance Institutions'.[28]

It is undoubtedly the case that most of the In-Pensioners of the Royal Hospital met the requirements for evacuation of the disabled laid out by the Ministry of Health, as their age and infirmities put them at 'serious disadvantage [...] in seeking shelter in air-raids'. Unfortunately, the challenges and prejudices which undermined attempts to accommodate the priority group described in official memorandum as 'cripples', and which in practice included the aged and infirm inmates of Public Assistance Institutions, created an unhelpful backdrop for the Royal Hospital's wartime preparations. The treatment of the inmates of Public Assistance Institutions would result in unfortunate consequences for the Royal Hospital as it prepared for war.

The evacuation plans envisaged in the Anderson Report required an unprecedented displacement of individuals and communities across Britain. Unfortunately, however, it soon became clear that the ad hoc organisational structure recommended by the report was unsuitable for the task in hand.

The Home Office increasingly struggled to provide effective leadership, with problems most obviously apparent in the capital, which the Anderson Committee anticipated 'presents special features'.[29] It was recognised at the outset that London was going to present its own unique challenges if for no other reason than the sheer scale of the potential numbers involved: between the 1890s and the outbreak of the Second World War, the population of the capital had grown from around 5.6 million to 8.7 million people.[30]

Quite apart from the daunting numbers of potential evacuees, the Anderson Report also cites the complexities associated with trying to co-ordinate on an ad hoc basis the planning activities of '28 Borough Councils'.[31] However, although the complex nature of local government administration in the capital undoubtedly represented a challenge, the real issue was a political one. A London County Council that was 'ruled by Herbert Morrison's Labour administration' had to work with 'a Conservative central government for which Morrison had only contempt'.³² In dealing with this political rivalry, the committee's approach to 'suggest [...] that as far as the evacuation problem is concerned an ad hoc organisation should be set up' was simply unrealistic.³³

As the scale of the organisational and logistical challenges became increasingly apparent and these competing political ideologies were unable to compromise, evacuation planning very quickly descended into a 'political squabble in Whitehall'.³⁴ The only common ground between the warring factions was a shared conviction as to the importance of establishing credible and workable evacuation provision for London's children. As such, the outcome of this political infighting eventually 'established the Education Officer's office as the most suitable government branch to oversee London's evacuation'.³⁵

Planning now focused even more closely on meeting the needs of London's schoolchildren with the result that the other priority groups became more marginalised. It was against this bureaucratically dysfunctional, institutionally indifferent and politically charged background that the Commissioners and Officers of the Royal Hospital set about preparing wartime plans for the protection and well-being of the aged and infirm In-Pensioners who were resident in Chelsea.

While Civil Defence preparations continued on the Home Front in Britain, tensions were building in Europe. In Germany, Hitler, having consolidated his position at home, now looked towards the near abroad as he sought to extend his Nazi Party's influence into the domestic politics of his neighbours. In March 1938, Austria was annexed in the *Anschluss* unification into a single 'Greater Germany' political union, before Hitler turned his attention to the German-speaking minority in neighbouring Czechoslovakia.

The Sudetenland bordering Germany in north-western Czechoslovakia, a heavily industrialised region hit particularly hard by the Great Depression, suffered endemic unemployment among its German-speaking population. By 1936, this minority accounted for over

60 per cent of the unemployed.[36] Growing discontent fuelled the rise of the Sudeten German Party (SdP) and in March 1938, shortly after the announcement of the *Anschluss*, party leader Konrad Henlein met with Hitler in Berlin. On his return, emboldened by Hitler's support, Henlein began making demands of the Czech government for greater autonomy for the Sudetenland, demands that were given greater force when the SdP won almost 90 per cent of the popular vote among the German-speaking minority in elections in May 1938. The Sudetenland Germans and the Czech government appeared to be on a collision course destined to end in a potentially violent separation.

2

# The Royal Hospital Prepares for War

*'... to evacuate nearly 600 useless mouths from London ...'*[1]

The first substantive preparations for war at the Royal Hospital Chelsea appeared in a confidential internal paper of 17 May 1938.[2] Presented at the Hospital's regular weekly board meeting, the paper summarised the conclusions of a meeting held at the Hospital the previous day with representatives of the Home Office and Office of Works responsible for evacuation planning. This meeting on 16 May was an opportunity for the parties present to discuss the merits of evacuating the Royal Hospital in the event of war and had been convened in light of the recommendations made in the recently published Anderson Report. Events unfolding on the Continent added a sense of urgency to the discussions.

The paper, presented by the Lieutenant Governor Major General Delano-Osborne, describes the meeting as a 'conference with the representatives of the ARP Department of the Home Office and H.M. Office of Works'. It had been called to discuss whether, on the outbreak of war, evacuation 'was the best solution with regard to the Royal Hospital', and outlines reasons why it would be desirable 'to evacuate the pensioners altogether from London on a Declaration of War'.

The first reason highlighted was the unsuitability of the Royal Hospital's 'buildings to be adapted to resist an attack', with the roof identified as 'easily penetrable by any type of projectile'. Furthermore, 'the floors of the main wards are so fragile from their age and lack of supporting cross walls, that, if the upper part of the building collapsed, the whole would go right to the bottom floor'. It was pointed out that 'even the vaulting of the crypts could not be counted on to support the debris falling from the roofs and walls of the chapel and Great Hall', the implication being that air-raid shelters located beneath the principal Hospital buildings would offer little protection should the buildings suffer a direct hit. On the other hand, 'the alternative solution of providing slit trenches outside' in the Hospital grounds would be of little use given that most In-Pensioners were either 'incapable of rapid movement or unable to stand the exposure involved' in sheltering outdoors, potentially during winter, in the event of air raids.[3]

This was, of course, the very reason this meeting was taking place, as most In-Pensioners were at 'serious disadvantage owing to slowness of movement or limitation of power of locomotion in seeking shelter in air-raids', and as such, met the Ministry of Health's definition of disability. Furthermore, the Anderson Report recommended evacuation from areas of danger of anybody 'whose presence is not absolutely essential'.[4]

Although this recommendation was based on humanitarian grounds, there were also logistical issues to be considered and it was thought 'advisable, on lines of general policy, to evacuate nearly 600 useless mouths from London thus relieving food problems, etc'.[5] The expectation was that in the event of London suffering air-raid attacks, debris from damaged buildings would make it difficult to supply and distribute food. It therefore made sense to evacuate those who did not need to be in the capital, including the 500 In-Pensioners at the Royal Hospital and their 100 support staff, collectively referred to as '600 useless mouths'.

The meeting also took broader considerations into account, however. It was recognised that once the Hospital had been evacuated, 'the vacated accommodation in the Infirmary would be of immediate utility for the military or civil authorities for use as a Hospital and, further, that the Wards themselves could be readily utilised for some other purpose connected with the emergency'.[6]

The Office of Works was conscious of the Committee of Imperial Defence estimates of the likely scale of air-raid casualties and the need to requisition buildings with the potential to be converted into casualty clearing hospitals. The Royal Hospital buildings afforded little protection to In-Pensioners in the event of air raids but once vacated, they provided a purpose-built infirmary and associated Long Wards, which could be used for treating air-raid casualties or providing temporary accommodation for displaced civilians.

Furthermore, a requisitioned Royal Hospital site did not have to be used in an entirely passive nature; it could also be utilised in a more overtly military manner. The Hospital is situated on the north bank of the River Thames, directly opposite what at the time was London's major source of electric power, Battersea Power Station. It is less than a mile downstream from London Underground's Lots Road Power Station, 'built solely for the purpose of powering underground railways'.[7] Located on the Embankment thoroughfare, it is adjacent to major crossing points over the river – Chelsea and Albert bridges. These were all strategically significant targets and consequently of prime interest to the Luftwaffe. The risk of collateral damage, given its geographic location was therefore very high, but once evacuated the Hospital's grounds offered useful potential for the deployment of defensive countermeasures such as barrage balloons, searchlights and even anti-aircraft guns. By all accounts, therefore, a compelling case was made for the complete evacuation of the Royal Hospital in the event of war, in part for the protection of the In-Pensioners, but also because a vacated and requisitioned site offered the Office of Works versatile and flexible possibilities for meeting its broader requisitioning objectives.

Finally, the paper addressed the possible implications on public morale of what could potentially be interpreted as an example of the army evacuating a military site on the outbreak of hostilities. It concluded, however:

> It was not considered by the officers of the Departments present that the moral factor of moving the Hospital would be of any importance because they considered that other Institutions of like nature were considering schemes for complete removal in the event of an emergency on humanitarian grounds.[8]

This was almost certainly a reference to the fact that at this early stage of implementation of the recommendations in the Anderson Report, it was envisaged that disabled residents of Public Assistance Institutions would also be evacuated. However, this meeting took place before it became apparent that there was simply not the appetite among the receiving areas to offer accommodation to workhouse evacuees; an issue which would become increasingly apparent over the ensuing weeks and months.

Nevertheless, as war clouds formed in early 1938, a comprehensive case was made by Officers of the Royal Hospital in consultation with government departments responsible for Civil Defence planning for the complete evacuation of In-Pensioners to an unidentified place of safety outside London in the event of war. The recommendations presented to the board were accepted and, having agreed on an evacuation strategy, the Commissioners of the Royal Hospital in a letter on 1 June 1938 sought authorisation from the War Office to sanction such a move. Officials from the Office of Works, meanwhile, consulted their register of requisition properties, seeking to identify potential candidates to meet the accommodation needs of the Royal Hospital once detailed requirements had been established.

In anticipation of the War Office endorsing the evacuation proposals, a short note dated 16 June was circulated within the Office of Works alerting staff to the probability that 'we are likely before very long to receive an official letter from the hospital authorities that they are in favour of evacuating the hospital in the event of an emergency'.[9]

In Czechoslovakia, on 19 May 1938, President Beneš ordered a partial military mobilisation in response to a build-up of German troops on the border. As tensions in Europe continued to rise, the Royal Hospital had wasted no time in digesting the contents of the Anderson Report and following its recommendations. Engaging in ad hoc consultation with the relevant government departments, Officers and Commissioners had acted quickly and proactively to determine an appropriate evacuation strategy for the Royal Hospital in the event of an emergency being declared. A response to the Commissioners' letter is noted in the Board Meeting Minutes of 7 July 1938, where the War Office is reported as:

> ... approving Commissioners proposals contained in R. Hospital letter [...] dated 1st June 1938 that in the event of an emergency the In-Pensioners of the Hospital should be evacuated to accommodation outside London + that the co-operation of the Office of Works and the Home Office is sought in the preparation of the requisite scheme.[10]

Having been granted the necessary approvals, attention turned to formulating an appropriate evacuation plan. For the Office of Works to identify a suitable property to meet the needs of the Royal Hospital a detailed schedule of what those specific requirements entailed was required, including how many In-Pensioners and staff were to be evacuated.

Evacuation of the Royal Hospital would only include In-Pensioners and those staff directly responsible for their care and well-being. The Pensions Secretariat, which oversaw the administration of army pensions, would not be included in the evacuation plans. These staff, although employed at the Royal Hospital, were not directly caring for the In-Pensioner community, with most living off-site and travelling into Chelsea daily to undertake clerical and administrative jobs. Some members of the Pensions Secretariat qualified for evacuation under the government's general evacuation scheme, but the Royal Hospital would not be involved in these cases.

Subsequently, at a board meeting held on 18 August 1938, draft letters were approved 'to be sent to the Home Office and Office of Works [...] in regard to the evacuation of the In-Pensioners and Staff in the event of an emergency'.[11] These letters explain the decision of the Commissioners, detailing the reasons as discussed at the 16 May conference. They confirm that 'in this decision the War Office has concurred and has authorised the Commissioners to seek the co-operation of your Department in the preparation of a scheme for the evacuation of the personnel concerned'.[12] The Hospital's requirements are duly outlined, namely, 'that arrangements will be made jointly by the Home Office and H.M. Office of Works to earmark in advance suitable alternative accommodation for the personnel concerned, and also arrange transport of the personnel and necessary stores to their new quarters if, and when, the time comes'.[13] A detailed schedule of requirements, giving numbers of In-Pensioners and staff to be included in the scheme, was enclosed.

This approach to evacuation planning diligently followed the Anderson recommendations of 'ad hoc organisation [...] set up with direct responsibility to the appropriate Department of State'.[14] The Home Office had overall responsibility for evacuation planning and liaised with relevant departments such as the Ministry of Transport and the Ministry of Health, while the Office of Works was responsible for finding suitable evacuation sites.

The conference held at the Royal Hospital on 16 May had prepared the ground and ensured that the letters sent by the Royal Hospital were anticipated. Furthermore, the War Office had endorsed the Commissioners' plans. It was reasonable to presume, therefore, that initial thoughts about potential options were already under consideration by the evacuation authorities, and thus, having duly delegated the organisational responsibilities to the relevant government departments, the Officers and Commissioners of the Hospital returned to the day-to-day management of the institution, while awaiting a response.

The schedule of requirements included with the letters sent to the Home Office and Office of Works is a remarkable document.[15] Extending to several pages and containing a wealth of detail, it is written in the style of a regimental movement order. It was in many respects exactly what was required in terms of outlining the specific evacuation needs of a unique institution providing succour and relief to old soldiers.

In light of the difficulties emerging in Whitehall, however, as civil servants struggled unsuccessfully to accommodate the evacuation requirements of Public Assistance Institutions, the militarily myopic tone of the Royal Hospital's submission was not universally appreciated by civilian authorities grappling with the realities of evacuation planning and implementation. The Royal Hospital's officers can of course be excused for their ignorance of the difficulties being faced by civil servants who were increasingly overwhelmed by the challenges they faced daily as they sought to balance a multitude of competing Civil Defence demands. Nevertheless, the seemingly tone-deaf nature of the Hospital's submission to the Home Office and the Office of Works was not entirely welcomed by those to whom it was addressed.

The document outlined the evacuation requirements of some 500 aged and infirm old soldiers who collectively, and for the most part individually, met the definition of 'disabled' as determined by the Ministry of Health. It also detailed the needs of the staff who would accompany this priority group of evacuees to their allocated place of safety in a designated reception area.

However, in typical military style, the list of evacuees is presented in a hierarchical descending order, with the most senior officer listed at the top of the first page. Consequently, the Governor, who at this point was General Sir Walter Braithwaite, is listed as the first evacuee, along with his 'dependents' – identified as his wife and their three domestic maids. Second on the list of evacuees is the Lieutenant Governor, Major General Huddleston, who had recently replaced Major General Delano-Osborne as the second-most senior officer at the Hospital. The recipients of this schedule would no doubt recall that it was the Lieutenant Governor who had represented the Royal Hospital at the evacuation conference held in May 1938, where it was agreed that evacuation was the most appropriate course of action for the Hospital in the event of an emergency. The Lieutenant Governor's dependants included his wife, one child and two maids. Next on the list was the Adjutant, his wife and one maid; followed by the Chaplain, his wife and their maid. Listed next are six Captains of Invalids, their wives, a total of nine children and each family's individual maid. The Organist, Sergeant Major, eight Hospital constables and fourteen Long Ward nurses complete the list of staff evacuees on page one of the evacuation schedule. Finally, represented by a single line at the foot of the page is an entry for '420 In-Pensioners, no dependents'.

The second page of the schedule focuses on the Hospital's infirmary and continues in a similar vein to the first. The Physician & Surgeon, as the most senior officer, is listed at the top of the page, with his dependents identified as his wife, two children and the family's maid. The Physician & Surgeon's deputy, his wife, three children and their maid come next, before the list continues with: one Matron, one Hospital Sergeant – with wife and child – four nursing sisters, two superannuated Long Ward nurses, one housekeeper, nineteen nurses, seventeen domestics, one ward-master and eight infirmary orderlies. The rank and file of some eighty predominantly bedbound In-Pensioner infirmary patients, who by any definition of disability would be at 'serious disadvantage in seeking shelter in air-raids', again feature as a single-line entry towards the bottom of the page.

Pages three and four cover the remainder of the staff who, it was assumed, should accompany the 500 In-Pensioners on their evacuation odyssey. This includes seventeen members of the Quartermaster's Department along with five wives, eight children and the quartermaster's live-in maid. Four cooks, three wives and three children make up the

Catering Department's contingent, and finally the administration team are represented by the staff clerk and his wife, three additional clerks, two typists, one of whom was a shorthand specialist, and finally an assistant office-keeper with his wife and two children.

Having detailed the particulars of the staff members and dependents who were to accompany the 500 In-Pensioners, the schedule goes into much detail as to the Hospital's real-estate requirements. The Governor, Lieutenant Governor and Adjutant would all need substantial individual offices in addition to their private living quarters. Also required would be guardrooms, storerooms, bath houses, kitchens, ablutions, lavatory facilities, waiting and medical reception rooms, a ward-master's office, Sister's night-duty room, medical store and dispensary, a linen store and additional stores for clothing, utensils, bedding, bread and groceries, meat, beer, vegetables, a scullery and a food preparation room. The In-Pensioners would need a recreation room with two additional billiard rooms, one for the non-commissioned pensioners and the other for the remainder. In addition, it was pointed out that the 'provision of a lift necessary if accommodation above first floor'. A further schedule listed the baggage weight allowance and requirements, anticipated as amounting to almost 80 tons in total. Transport requirements were obviously going to amount to a small convoy of vehicles.

Despite the presentational shortcomings of the evacuation schedule, it did nevertheless contain all the information required for organising the transfer of the Royal Hospital. The staff at the Office of Works focused on the substance rather than the style of the document, and a handwritten internal memo dated 20 August, two days after the letter was posted, outlines the issues which the department identified as needing to be addressed.[16]

Three principal points are highlighted: the first was the practical issue of simply identifying a suitable property which could be used to meet the requirements of what was, after all, a unique institution. Other organisations earmarked for evacuation were typically paired with a similar institution in a corresponding reception zone, such that schools in evacuation zones were introduced to a potential host school in a receiving zone and both parties were subsequently assisted by the relevant government departments in organising the practicalities of a move should the need arise. Similar situations pertained to maternity units, and it had been hoped that Public Assistance Institutions would follow the same model, if only these institutions had typically not been so chronically overcrowded to begin with.

In the case of the Royal Hospital Chelsea, however, there were simply no comparable institutions with which to pair off. Greenwich had closed decades earlier, and was in the wrong place anyway, whereas Kilmainham, Dublin, was obviously out of the question.

In addressing this issue, several properties that the Office of Works managed were highlighted as potential candidates for providing an evacuation home for the Royal Hospital. These included the royal family's former residence, Osborne House on the Isle of Wight, and the Office of Works' internal note further mentions that 'even Hampton Court [Palace] occurs to one' as a possible host venue. However, in each instance the terrifying estimates of expected air-raid casualties weighed on the decision-making process, and it is consequently assumed in the case of both these potential candidates 'that if they were at all habitable they would have to be used as hospitals'. This is indicative of the range of competing challenges the Office of Works was grappling with at this time as it sought to tackle the practicalities involved in putting evacuation planning into practice.

The second issue highlighted was the question of what to do if the Office of Works was unable to identify a suitable candidate within its existing portfolio of state-owned 'surplus buildings' which could potentially meet the evacuation needs of the Hospital.[17] In this instance, the note suggests that the alternatives would be for the Office of Works to either lease or purchase a suitable venue. However, this option was dismissed out of hand as it 'would be expensive and [the Office of Works] should have more urgent work on hand than hiring and adapting a building for this purpose'.

The justification for not pursuing this option demonstrates the relatively low priority the evacuation authorities accorded to the issue of moving '600 useless mouths' out of danger when considered alongside some of the other demands placed upon the Office of Works. Moving the Royal Hospital's resident In-Pensioners to a place of relative safety was simply not a high priority.

Having ruled out the options of either leasing or purchasing suitable accommodation, a third option is considered: the possibility of using the Office of Works' authority to requisition a building for use as an evacuation home for the Royal Hospital. This option is also dismissed, rather intriguingly on the grounds that 'it would be difficult to justify requisitioning for such a purpose'.[18] Once again, the difficulties the evacuation authorities were experiencing in trying to identify and accommodate disabled evacuees, and the realisation that many of these unfortunate individuals were living in Public Assistance Institutions, appeared to overshadow efforts to organise evacuation provision for the Royal Hospital.

This suspicion is reinforced when consideration is given to communications between the Ministry of Health and the London County Council as the 'squabble in Whitehall' identified earlier built in intensity. Throughout the summer of 1938 and indeed through most of 1939, a private battle raged between public institutions over the gulf between the recommendations in the Anderson Report for evacuating the disabled and the reality on the ground in terms of converting these recommendations into practical action.

Politics and prejudices undoubtedly played a part in the row, but there were also some practical logistical issues which needed to be overcome. Such were the difficulties experienced that the parties involved engaged in something of an unseemly game of institutional pass-the-parcel as the protagonists were all eager to offload responsibilities on to others. The increasingly dysfunctional organisation of the evacuation-planning framework and the seemingly intractable nature of the issues arising is summarised by an extract from a letter written by Sir George Gater CMG, DSO, Clerk to the London County Council, and addressed to the Permanent Secretary at the Ministry of Health, Sir George Chrystal KCB, which highlights advice from an official involved in evacuation planning for the disabled. In the advice, the official:

> ... pointed out the difficulties to be anticipated if, on the one hand, the cripple population of public assistance institutions is evacuated whilst the other inmates remain in London and, on the other hand, equal difficulties that are likely to arise if only the cripples living in their own home were moved away from London, whilst those cripples who happen to be inmates of public assistance institutions are left behind.[19]

This was a classic bureaucratic catch-22; in principle, it was agreed that the disabled as defined by the Ministry of Health were to be evacuated in the event of an emergency. In practice, however, many of those identified as meeting the Ministry of Health's definition were found to be living in Public Assistance Institutions and plans to evacuate these institutions en masse had all but been abandoned.

Evacuating only the disabled inmates of these institutions was seen as discriminating against their more able-bodied peers. However, not evacuating the disabled inmates of Public Assistance Institutions while nevertheless evacuating the disabled who did not live in these facilities was viewed as unfair on the 'workhouse' disabled. The inevitable outcome of this bureaucratic catch-22, therefore, was that although, in principle, anybody identified as disabled was eligible for publicly funded evacuation, in practice, no such individuals would be evacuated under government-sponsored schemes.

These were the issues that the Home Office had to grapple with as they sought to provide effective leadership for the squabbling government departments and competing factional interests involved in Civil Defence planning on the Home Front. This bureaucratic quagmire complicated matters in respect of evacuation plans for the In-Pensioners of the Royal Hospital.

Despite the unhelpful evacuation-planning background and the specific issues identified in internal notes, Office of Works officials nevertheless diligently sought to overcome the problems they faced. It was suggested that the War Office 'should convey and billet the pensioners out in some distant part', which could be achieved by providing In-Pensioners with a billeting allowance to be paid to residents in an evacuation-receiving area who were prepared to host a Royal Hospital evacuee. This was not an unreasonable suggestion, for, as the note goes on to claim, 'there are surely people who would gladly billet an aged Chelsea pensioner if properly paid'. Assuming all the In-Pensioners were to be billeted in broadly the same geographic location, their well-being could also continue to be overseen by Hospital staff billeted in the same area.

This note also, however, alludes to the political in-fighting taking place in the background, and officials are clearly conscious of the wider difficulties faced by the evacuation planners as it goes on to suggest that 'this would be a compromise between leaving the old men to the rough and tumble of civil evacuations and treating their evacuation as a matter of vital importance to the state'.[20] In other words, special provision was being suggested for aged and infirm old soldiers, but done in such a way that the Royal Hospital was not necessarily seen to be receiving special treatment. This is of course at a time when it was increasingly apparent that the disabled inmates of Public Assistance Institutions were being all but abandoned to whatever fate awaited them should the bomber, as widely anticipated, indeed 'get through'.

While these discussions took place between officials at the Office of Works during the long summer days of August 1938, the political situation in Europe continued to deteriorate. Despite frantic diplomatic efforts involving the British and French governments to achieve a compromise between Hitler and the Czech government, war looked increasingly likely. Throughout August, the German press was full of allegations of Czech atrocities committed against the Sudeten German minority, while the German Army continued to mass on the border. By the end of the month, some 750,000 Wehrmacht troops were involved in 'military manoeuvres' in southern Germany, bordering the Sudetenland and it was clear that Hitler could order their deployment into Czechoslovakian territory at any moment. Evacuation planning in Britain assumed a new urgency.

In early September, the Home Office responded to the letter received from the Royal Hospital on 18 August which, like the equivalent letter sent to the Office of Works, had included the highly detailed evacuation schedule. The Home Office, however, did not reply directly to the Royal Hospital as its role was to act in a broad oversight capacity, and as such, their response was addressed to the Office of Works in a letter dated 5 September 1938.[21]

It is immediately clear that the understaffed and overworked evacuation planners in the Home Office were unimpressed with the evacuation correspondence they had received from the Royal Hospital. Although the exhaustive detail provided was undoubtedly useful for the Office of Works in determining precise requirements for the Hospital, it was clearly not appreciated by the recipients in the Home Office. Neither was the military approach of listing Officers before ranks as, in this case, Royal Hospital staff consequently appeared to be placed before the In-Pensioners, who of course were to be the principal subject of any evacuation plans. Hence, the Home Office letter begins, 'We have received a long letter from the Lieutenant Governor of the Royal Hospital, Chelsea dated the 18th August asking that arrangements should be made for the evacuation of the staff and inmates of the Hospital in the event of emergency'. The letter subsequently continues in a manner which makes it perfectly clear just how unimpressed the Home Office evacuation planners were with the letter and schedule they had received and the extent to which, unlike the Office of Works, they had been influenced as much by the style of the submission rather than its substance, 'So far as general plans of evacuation are concerned these people would have to take their chances with others and certainly could not expect under a general scheme to get the comfortable quarters for which they ask in the schedules enclosed in their letter'.

It is abundantly clear from the Home Office letter that unlike the Office of Works officials, who were trying to ascertain whether a way could be found to treat the Royal Hospital as a special case, no such largesse would be forthcoming from the ARP Department at Horseferry House. However, something of an olive branch is hinted at within the final paragraph as the Home Office makes it clear that it is at least prepared to listen to alternative suggestions the Office of Works may wish to make, 'If, however, you are proposing to give them premises elsewhere, the situation is rather different and [the Home Office] should be grateful if [the Office of Works] would let [them] know how the matter stands'.

Nevertheless, such suggestions would need to be very convincing, for it is clear from the Home Office letter that the principal government department responsible for the oversight of evacuation planning was of the view that the Office of Works' time would best be spent on the myriad of other duties it was required to perform rather than expending valuable time and energy on 'these people'. What is not obvious from the Home Office letter, however, is who should convey the somewhat unwelcome news contained in this briefing to the relevant authorities at the Royal Hospital.

Meanwhile, in Germany, the Nazi Party convened for their 10th Party Congress held in Nuremberg between 5 and 12 September 1938, with the gathering ominously titled the 'Rally of Greater Germany'. The

*Anschluss* with Austria was celebrated to great fanfare, before Hitler used his now legendary speeches to rail against the government of neighbouring Czechoslovakia and their treatment of the Sudetenland German minority. Alarm bells were soon ringing throughout the capital cities of Europe, and in London the authorities responsible for Civil Defence planning subsequently held their own gathering, where at a 'Conference with Heads of Secondary Schools and Junior Technical Schools' held on 13 September, all the attendees agreed that in the event of war, 'children should be the first to leave London'.[22] Somebody clearly needed to speak to the Royal Hospital Chelsea, and as a matter of some urgency.

3

# The Munich Crisis

*'... we could provide you with spades [...] to dig trenches ...'*[1]

In August 1938, the Royal Hospital addressed letters to the Home Office and HM Office of Works in response to the 16 May evacuation-planning conference, outlining the needs of the institution in a meticulously prepared schedule of requirements. The Officers responsible for the care and well-being of over 500 old soldiers, however, also instigated several practical preparations, should evacuation become necessary.

In the Long Ward accommodation wings, In-Pensioners stored their personal possessions in wooden kit boxes outside their individual private berths, a feature of their accommodation which had not changed since the opening of the institution in 1692. But, with evacuation now being actively planned and the likelihood that the Royal Hospital would need to vacate Chelsea, potentially at short notice, it was clear to the Officers that in so far as the In-Pensioners 'keep their private belongings in oak kit boxes too bulky and heavy for transport', practical arrangements would need to be made in order for the In-Pensioners to take their personal possessions with them in the event of an evacuation order being issued.[2] Consequently, a letter was sent to the War Office explaining the position and asking for the 'immediate issue of five hundred sea kit bags to this Hospital [... to] be held in store for use in the event of the emergency contemplated in this correspondence occurring'.[3]

Matters in Europe threatened to come to a head in September 1938. Hitler's speech at the Nuremberg Rally denounced Czechoslovakia, created in 1918 on the collapse of the Habsburg monarchy, as a fraudulent state denying the right to self-determination of its German-speaking minority. This incendiary language inevitably had consequences and acts of violence between the disparate ethnic groups within Czechoslovakia's borders subsequently increased sharply.

In the hope of restoring calm, France attempted to mediate with the government of President Beneš, but was accused by Hitler of plotting to create an anti-German alliance with the Czechs. The British government had no choice but to intervene as peace in Europe appeared increasingly threatened.

On 15 September, Prime Minister Neville Chamberlain flew to Germany for a meeting with Hitler at his residence in Berchtesgaden, outside Munich, in the hope of easing tensions. In Chelsea, the Commissioners of the Royal Hospital felt sufficiently alarmed by the course of events to place the subject of evacuation onto the agenda for the next scheduled management board meeting to be held on 22 September. It seemed increasingly likely that the kitbags held in storage for the evacuation of the In-Pensioners would soon have to be issued.

Unfortunately, the Hospital had still not heard anything from either the Home Office or the Office of Works as to what arrangements had been put in place to be activated in the event of an emergency. The Assistant Secretary, Maurice Fitzgerald, was therefore charged with contacting the Office of Works to ascertain what preparations had been made and how quickly evacuation plans could be activated.

Fitzgerald was an intriguing choice to be given the task of making the necessary phone call. A Classics and History graduate of Trinity College Dublin, he was commissioned into the Royal Munster Fusiliers in 1914 and awarded the Military Cross while serving on the Western Front. Wounded in 1917, he was invalided out of the army and subsequently joined the War Office. Following a distinguished career as a senior civil servant, he was appointed Assistant Secretary of the Royal Hospital in December 1936, and as head of the Pensions Secretariat was responsible for the administration and payment of army pensions.[4]

His administration clerks were those employees at the Royal Hospital who had not been included in the evacuation schedules sent to the Home

Office and Office of Works. So, at first sight, it seems an odd choice to charge Fitzgerald with chasing up plans which did not directly involve his department. However, as the Assistant Secretary, Fitzgerald was responsible for preparing the agenda for the Hospital's weekly management board meetings and his name appears as an attendee in the minutes of virtually every board meeting held throughout the war. He was one of the few Pensions Secretariat employees with accommodation on site in Chelsea, where he lived with his wife Suzanne and their four children, sons Maurice and Paul and daughters Elizabeth and Denise.

The telephone conversation Fitzgerald had with the Office of Works on 17 September 1938 appears to have been a difficult one. So much so that Fitzgerald insisted that the information relayed to him by an official, Mr de Normann, was put into writing and sent to him, for it to be included in the papers submitted for the forthcoming board meeting.

De Normann's draft of his subsequent letter to Fitzgerald is held in the Office of Works archives where it is dated 17 September 1938 and marked 'Secret', such was the sensitivity attached to its contents.[5] The letter references the telephone conversation, and without explicitly mentioning that Fitzgerald was told that no provision had been made for the evacuation of the Royal Hospital, it is clear that he was made aware of this fact. De Normann proceeds to mention a conversation that he appears to have subsequently had with an official at the War Office in which he tries to involve this department in developing plans for the evacuation of the Royal Hospital, for he goes on to state:

> I have been in conversation with Mr. Boveniser, of the War Office, who tells me that certain training schools for boys, which are under the jurisdiction of the War Office, would become vacant in the event of war. I am wondering whether it would be possible for you to arrange with the War Office to accommodate your people in one of those schools. I have no information as to their whereabouts, but no doubt you will know more about them than I do.

This is a remarkably disingenuous response by the Office of Works to an enquiry from the Royal Hospital as to the state of evacuation arrangements for the 500 In-Pensioners, who it had been agreed as early as May 1938 should be evacuated from London in the event of war. Not only is the Office of Works informing the Hospital that no substantive plans have been made for this priority group by the key government departments responsible for evacuation planning, but the official goes on to suggest that given that the Royal Hospital was ultimately answerable to the War Office, then it was with the War Office that the responsibility for evacuating the In-Pensioners should rest. No matter that the War Office had rather more pressing matters to attend to.

Having failed dismally to arrange any form of accommodation for the evacuation of the Hospital, the official at the Office of Works is similarly disinclined to offer any assurances that suitable transport arrangements could be put in place, assuming the Hospital authorities were by some miracle able to procure the use of any surplus War Office properties at short notice, 'The arrangements for the evacuation would depend, to some extent, on the position of the alternative accommodation. The Ministry of Transport might be prepared to make special arrangements for you.'[6]

Almost as if to add insult to injury, the letter continues by helpfully suggesting, 'If a war should find you in Chelsea, we could supply you with spades, etc to dig trenches and you would have the services of our decontamination and rescue squads'. Thus, in September 1938, with winter approaching and war seemingly imminent, the only assistance extended to the Royal Hospital was an offer to provide spades to dig air-raid trenches. This was despite it having been agreed five months earlier that 'the solution of providing slit trenches outside' was impracticable due to the fact that the majority of In-Pensioners were 'incapable of rapid movement or unable to stand the exposure involved' – the very reasons they qualified as a 'priority group' and why evacuation had therefore been agreed as the 'best solution with regard to the Royal Hospital'.[7] The Hospital authorities may just as well have dug graves, for all the use such trenches were likely to be to the majority of In-Pensioners.

Finally, the letter from the official to Fitzgerald references the internal conversations held within the Office of Works about the possibility of billeting individual evacuated In-Pensioners with sympathetic members of the public, 'A possible alternative to evacuating the Hospital to other premises might be to billet the men out in some sheltered country town. I do not know if you would consider this.'[8]

The Office of Works letter was received at the Royal Hospital on 20 September and Fitzgerald did not wait until the scheduled board meeting to be held on 22 September before responding. His reply to Mr de Normann is scathing in its condemnation of the complete lack of any substantive preparations for evacuation undertaken by the key government departments responsible for making such arrangements:

Dear de Normann,
I received this morning your letter of the 17th September on the question of Evacuation. Forgive me if I say it does not help at all. When we submitted our official Evacuation Scheme to you and the Home Office on the 18th August we did so because we had been formally assured by the War Office that the Home Office and the Office of Works acting jointly were the competent Departments by whom the necessary arrangements would be made. Subsequently we were informed equally categorically by the Home Office that that responsibility rested with you. Now I see that the wheel has run full circle and you have gone back to the War Office and have put up, in consultation with them, some very nebulous proposals whereby the War Office and the Ministry of Transport [a newcomer to this discussion] 'might' be prepared to do something or other, whilst returning the onus of implementing the scheme to our shoulders though we are not equipped nor have we authority to undertake it.⁹

The obvious outrage and anger expressed by Fitzgerald in his letter is wholly justified. The Anderson Report, which clearly identified the aged and infirm as a priority group for evacuation, had been published in January 1938. The Royal Hospital had held a conference with the 'competent authorities' responsible for evacuation planning in May 1938, at which it was agreed by all parties that in the event of war, the In-Pensioners should be evacuated en masse. A detailed schedule covering the specific needs of the Hospital had been provided on 18 August to those responsible for, and with the legal authority to enact, the necessary arrangements. And yet, only now in mid-September, with war in Europe seemingly imminent, were the Hospital's management informed that no evacuation arrangements had been made for the In-Pensioners. Furthermore, the only practical expression of support from the authorities responsible for Civil Defence planning was an offer to provide the Royal Hospital with spades to dig improvised shelters against air-raid attacks, which pre-war planning anticipated would likely occur immediately upon a declaration of war.

Fitzgerald demands clarification from de Normann as to precisely what responsibility the Office of Works is prepared to shoulder when discharging its evacuation mandate with respect to the scheme submitted by the Royal Hospital:

> Will you, therefore, consider the scheme again and notify me categorically, for the information of my Commissioners, whether or not your Department is prepared to accept full responsibility for putting it into force. In the event of your being prepared to accept such responsibility I also want to know the period which you estimate must elapse between the occurrence of an emergency and the date when the evacuation could be completed.

Fitzgerald was not being unreasonable in demanding such clarification. For, as he goes on to state, the Hospital 'cannot work the scheme ourselves and we certainly cannot afford to remain longer in doubt as to the identity of the authority responsible for working it'.[10]

The Royal Hospital simply did not have the legal authority to implement the evacuation scheme in the way that government departments such as the Office of Works and the Home Office were so vested. The Commissioners and Officers were, however, responsible for the care and well-being of 500 aged and infirm old soldiers and they could not indefinitely remain in the state of uncertain limbo which had been the case throughout 1938 to date, due to no fault of their own. Fitzgerald ends his letter by trying to inject a sense of urgency into the evacuation-planning process, which had clearly been lacking hitherto among the government officials responsible for putting plans into action:

> We also want to know categorically whether you assume authority for supplying at an early current date all utensils, tools and stores necessary for trench digging, and for Fire, Decontamination and Rescue Squads, and we should also want to be informed who will be immediately available and responsible to us for this purpose.

We should require these tools and stores even in the event of evacuation, for use in the period which must intervene between the occurrence of the emergency and the date of evacuation.

Fitzgerald had neither the time nor the inclination to engage in diplomatic niceties with government bureaucrats, who although undoubtedly overworked and under pressure, seemed intent on passing evacuation responsibilities to others. In-Pensioners either needed to be evacuated forthwith or if evacuation was not going to happen, as now seemed the more likely case, arrangements needed to be made to protect them while they remained in Chelsea. With the situation in Europe deteriorating by the hour, something needed to happen, and sooner rather than later.

On 18 September, Benito Mussolini, the fascist leader of Italy, made his support for Hitler clear when in a speech in Trieste, he declared, 'If there are two camps, for and against Prague, let it be known that Italy has chosen its side.'[11] In response to Mussolini's intervention, Chamberlain on 22 September again boarded a plane for Germany, declaring to the assembled Press Corps, 'My objective is peace in Europe. I trust this trip is the way to that peace.'[12]

The Royal Hospital's management board, meeting the same day, also hoped for the best but nevertheless felt it necessary to plan for the worst. In attendance at this board meeting were the soon-to-be-appointed new Governor, General Sir Harry Knox KCB, DSO and his newly appointed Deputy Governor, Major General Huddleston.

The meeting was a sombre one and included an agenda item on 'A.R.P. Evacuation Scheme' under which it was noted as 'read to the Board, correspondence on the subject with H.M. Office of Works regarding the evacuation scheme in the event of emergency'.[13] Other than note the correspondence, there was little more the board could do until a reply was received to Fitzgerald's letter to the Office of Works.

It is also notable from the minutes of this meeting, however, that the Royal Hospital was not the only organisation in Chelsea alarmed by the deteriorating situation on the Continent. Note 11 records a number of requests for assistance from Chelsea Borough Council who, in the first instance, ask the Commissioners' permission to use Royal Avenue to 'store sand for sand bags'.[14] With the likelihood of imminent air raids, the council were encouraging residents and businesses to take steps to protect themselves and their properties, and a location was needed for contractors to deliver consignments of sand ordered by the council. The note goes on to record a further request for 'the use of Burton Court open spaces for an air-raid shelter and A.R.P. training huts' as the council grappled with its own Civil Defence plans.

Like all local authorities, Chelsea Borough Council was involved in Civil Defence planning from the mid-1930s. Until the summer of 1938, it had focused on organising evacuation strategies, while also stockpiling equipment for protection against gas attacks. However, on 28 July 1938, a strongly worded joint submission from 'representatives of the local Labour and Communist Parties' led to a rethink of Civil Defence planning. While commending the council for focusing on the risks from 'the most terrifying of all military engines, the bombing aeroplane', the submission nevertheless highlighted that 'since the outbreak of the war in Spain, it is clear that the order of importance as regards the type of projectile released from aeroplanes is: first, the high explosive bomb, next, the incendiary bomb, then the gas bomb'.[15]

Consequently, it was argued that the focus of the council's attention thus far on evacuation and gas attacks was misguided. In the opinion of these parties, 'nothing could be more pernicious than to lead the people to believe that the construction of a "refuge room" and the donning of a gas mask will give them any security'.[16] What was required was the provision of air-raid shelters for residents whose accommodation situation did not allow them to establish their own bomb shelter sanctuary.

The submission further argues that deep subterranean bombproof public shelters were needed. The council's ARP Committee replied to the submission at a full council meeting on 4 August. They argued that bombproof shelters could not be provided 'in view of the decision of the Government that the construction on any extensive scale of shelters which would be proof against direct hits by bombs is impracticable and prohibitive on account of cost'.[17]

The Home Office had, however, instructed local authorities to undertake surveys of properties in their boroughs whose basements could be adapted into shelters capable of providing 'protection against blast and splinters from high explosive bombs'.[18] Councils were also instructed to investigate the possibilities of providing 'trench shelters' on any suitable open spaces, and as such, the ARP Committee would 'in the near future be dealing with preparation of plans for digging trenches in open spaces in Chelsea, which plans could be put into execution immediately an emergency arises'.[19] As Neville Chamberlain headed for Germany on 22 September, such an emergency appeared imminent.

Despite concerns expressed about the potential long-term implications of allowing development of the Hospital's grounds by Chelsea Borough Council, given the urgency of the moment, the Commissioners put their reservations aside and granted permission to the council's requests. The practical outcome, therefore, of the board meeting of 22 September 1938, as war in Europe looked imminent, was that both the Royal Hospital and Chelsea Borough Council started digging air-raid trenches in the Hospital's grounds. Staff and able-bodied In-Pensioners dug air-raid trenches on the North Terrace, while council workmen excavated a series of trenches in the south-west corner of Burton Court. It is not clear who provided the spades.

Across Chelsea, residents prepared for war as best they could. Richard and Frances Faviell, renting a flat at No. 33 Cheyne Place, made use of the sand and sandbags provided by the council. Working with their neighbours, they created a communal air-raid shelter, building sandbag walls at either end of a garage archway more usually used by their landlord for parking his Rolls-Royce.[20]

In Czechoslovakia, on 23 September, a general mobilisation was ordered and over 1 million men joined the army, ready to defend the country from the threatened German invasion. The following day, Hitler issued the Godesberg Memorandum, demanding that Czechoslovakia cede control of the Sudetenland by midnight on 28 September or face invasion. Ironically, on the very day that Hitler issued this infamous memorandum and during a week in which frantic war preparations took place across Chelsea, the Royal Hospital hosted a visit by 800 German ex-servicemen, holding a joint parade with the British Legion in the South Grounds on the afternoon of 24 September.[21]

On 27 September, Chamberlain took to the radio, claiming, 'How horrible, fantastic, incredible it is that we should be digging trenches and trying on gas masks here because of a quarrel in a far-away country between people of whom we know nothing.'[22] Hours before Hitler's deadline expired, Mussolini persuaded the Führer to call one final conference with Britain and France at which Italy would also be present, and in response, Chamberlain agreed to fly one last time to Munich in a final desperate attempt to avert war.

As Chamberlain flew to Munich on 29 September, the Commissioners of the Royal Hospital gathered for their weekly board meeting, chaired by Governor Braithwaite, with Governor-elect Knox in attendance. The meeting was tense, with the mood not helped as it became clear that all was far from well with the evacuation plans.

Under 'Agenda Item Note 7 – Air Raid Precautions', the following appears: 'To read a letter from HM Office of Works on the subject of Evacuation.'[23] The enclosed letter, a reply to Fitzgerald's forthright missive of 20 September, made uncomfortable reading on the very day that Chamberlain and French Prime Minister Daladier headed to Munich to bargain with Hitler.[24] It begins with a reference to previous discussions concerning potential alternative uses proposed for the Hospital's buildings and grounds in the event of war being declared, stating that the Office of Works 'understand that, as a result of informal discussions with their officers, an allocation of refugee accommodation in the existing buildings has been agreed upon for use in the event of an immediate emergency'.[25] Such informal discussions had of course taken place at the conference in May 1938, but were predicated on the assumption that In-Pensioners had been evacuated. However, on this point the letter contained the following:

> With regard to the suggestion that the In-Pensioners should be evacuated to suitable quarters beyond the danger area, it is understood that the Home Office could not undertake to make any special provision for them as distinct from the general plans for the evacuation of the civil population.[26]

This reference to the observations the Office of Works had received from the Home Office concerning the Royal Hospital's evacuation schedule ignores the fact that officials could have pushed back if they felt it appropriate to do so. Instead, the Office of Works chose to adopt the same position as the Home Office in declining to arrange separate evacuation provision for the Royal Hospital. The letter goes on to state that while the Office of Works:

… are prepared to give any assistance they can they must point out that their responsibility, so far as the Hospital is concerned, is limited to the maintenance of the buildings. They do not feel able to accept responsibility for providing alternative accommodation nor indeed have they any suitable building for this purpose.[27]

This was another incredibly disingenuous observation by the Office of Works, for 'under emergency powers provided by Defence Regulation 51', Civil Defence services, on behalf of the government, had the authority to requisition any property deemed necessary for the war effort.[28] This authority had been endorsed by the Anderson Committee and the government had 'the power in time of war to requisition accommodation for the billeting of refugees'.[29]

This legal authority had been vested in the Office of Works since:

… at a meeting of the Imperial Defence Committee on the 15th April 1937, it was decided that secret surveys should be undertaken of buildings that could be utilised, and the information fed into a central requisitioning register. This was made the responsibility of the Office of Works.[30]

For the Office of Works to therefore claim in September 1938 that it had not identified any suitable property for the evacuation of In-Pensioners simply highlights its reluctance to push back against the Home Office position of no separate evacuation provision for the Royal Hospital. This position was in large part due to the toxic politics and complex logistics surrounding the issue of organising evacuation for the aged and infirm inmates of Public Assistance Institutions. The seemingly unavoidable consequence of institutional prejudice and official indifference towards former workhouses contributed to the Office of Works placing a low priority on finding evacuation accommodation for '600 useless mouths' at the Royal Hospital Chelsea.[31]

Finally, and no doubt to ensure that the Commissioners and Officers of the Royal Hospital were under no illusions that responsibility for the care and well-being of over 500 old soldiers and some 100 support staff was theirs, and theirs alone, the letter goes on to add, 'The Ministry of

Transport would in the event of war, allocate all transport facilities and it would be advisable for the Hospital authorities should they decide to evacuate the In-Pensioners to take steps to acquaint the Ministry with their proposals at an early date'.[32]

The consequences of delegating evacuation planning to disparate government departments were now laid bare. Despite the ad hoc outsourcing recommended by the Anderson Committee, it was seemingly the case that with respect to the Royal Hospital the political and logistical issues involved with evacuation planning for the aged and infirm simply meant that Civil Defence priorities lay elsewhere.

In response to this demoralising news from the Office of Works, the Hospital's board agreed that all further admissions to In-Pension should be suspended with immediate effect.[33] This would ensure that no further old soldiers would be placed in harm's way but did little to ease the plight of the In-Pensioners already resident in Chelsea. In this regard, a handwritten addendum to the board meeting minutes states, 'A proposal by the Governor that In-Pensioners should be given the option of proceeding on leave beyond the danger area for the period of the Emergency was approved.'[34]

In practical terms, however, this proposal was only of use to those In-Pensioners who had somewhere they could go outside of designated areas of danger. They would also need relatives or friends who could look after them, and assuming they were fit and able enough to travel, they would need to arrange suitable transport at short notice. Given that few, if any, In-Pensioners would meet these conditions, the air-raid trenches hastily dug in the North Grounds offered the only alternative for the overwhelming majority, who were compelled to stay in Chelsea.

Neither these proposals for individual evacuation nor the hastily constructed air-raid shelters would be of any practical use to those In-Pensioners in the Hospital infirmary, especially the bedbound. In essence, therefore, and as a result of the collective failure to properly prepare for the threat of war, the policy forced upon the Royal Hospital Chelsea in response to the Munich Crisis amounted to a case of little more than 'every man for himself'.

As the Royal Hospital contemplated its limited options at the board meeting on 29 September, discussions were under way in Munich as to what concessions would be acceptable to Hitler to avert war.

Eventually, after lengthy and difficult negotiations, a deal was reached and the Munich Agreement was signed between the four powers on 30 September, after which Czechoslovakia was informed that German troops would occupy the Sudetenland from 10 October 1938. The Czechs could either accept this fait accompli or choose to resist Nazi troops alone, without the support of either Britain or France.

Neville Chamberlain's return from Munich brandishing the agreement with its promise of 'peace for our times' averted an immediate slide into conflict and was met with widespread relief throughout Britain, which in the autumn of 1938 was wholly unprepared for war. Nowhere could this overwhelming sense of relief have been felt more keenly than at the Royal Hospital Chelsea. Nevertheless, the Munich Agreement also marked the end of appeasement, and preparations for war would now assume a greater urgency.[35]

The Commissioners of the Royal Hospital, faced with the obligation of discharging their responsibilities in respect of their duty of care to In-Pensioners, had experienced a rude awakening during the Munich Crisis. The ad hoc outsourcing of evacuation planning as recommended by the Anderson Report had been exposed as a dangerously naive and complacent fallacy. Moving forward, the Royal Hospital recognised that to whatever extent possible, it would need to take matters into its own hands.

4

# War Clouds Over Europe

*'... recalling all officers on leave ...'*[1]

In the weeks after Munich, the realisation of a new and sombre reality is evident in the deliberations of the Royal Hospital's management board. At a meeting on 20 October 1938, a letter received from the War Office was read:

> ... withholding approval to proposals of Commissioners [...] that in the event of an emergency, the In-Pensioners should be invited to proceed on leave [...] and proposing alternatively that In-Pensioners should be included in the general scheme for the evacuation of civilians, to be promulgated by the Home Office.[2]

A policy of every man for himself had now been officially outlawed, and, furthermore, it appears that the Royal Hospital would not receive any special treatment from those government departments responsible for organising evacuation. The War Office, like the Home Office, appeared reluctant to be seen endorsing any special treatment for aged and infirm In-Pensioners, given the difficulties of trying to secure evacuation accommodation for disabled inmates of Public Assistance Institutions. The bureaucratic catch-22, which ensured that neither the aged and infirm inmates of these institutions nor the aged and infirm among the wider civilian population would in practice be evacuated, meant it would be difficult to justify why old soldiers should be treated any differently.

October 1938 witnessed the change in leadership at the Royal Hospital, which was evident from the minutes of the board meetings held during September, as General Sir Harry Knox KCB, DSO formally succeeded General Sir Walter Braithwaite GCB.[3] The new Governor was fully conversant with the issues the Hospital faced, having attended all the key board meetings prior to confirmation of his appointment. The Lieutenant Governor's post had also witnessed a formal handover of responsibilities in June 1938, with Major General H.J. Huddleston replacing the incumbent Major General O.H. Delano-Osborne.[4]

The Munich Crisis had been a baptism of fire for the new management team, and although as a result there now appeared to be a new sense of realism, navigating a way through a myriad of overlapping challenges as the Royal Hospital prepared for war would be far from easy. Commissioners and Officers nevertheless persevered with evacuation preparations, and Dean, in his definitive history of the institution, notes, 'plans were approved by the War Office and other Government Departments for evacuating the whole establishment to a group of country houses near Ross-on-Wye'.[5]

It is clear from the available evidence that the plans for a complete evacuation referred to by Dean are in fact those which were agreed in principle in May 1938, but in practice they did not survive first contact with the realities on the ground. Plans for a complete evacuation had indeed been approved in May 1938, but this approval had, in effect, been withdrawn in September during the Munich Crisis.

However, Dean's reference to Ross-on-Wye is noteworthy. In the minutes of the board meeting at which the Commissioners were informed of the War Office's displeasure at the evacuation policy of every man for himself is a curious reference to this quiet little market town in Herefordshire. The following note appears under the heading of 'Air Raid Precautions':

To communicate to the Board an offer received from Mrs. W. Morland, Rudhall, Ross-on-Wye, Herefordshire to put at the disposal of the Commissioners accommodation for Fifty In-Pensioners at that address in the event of an emergency.[6]

It is not clear how this offer was communicated to the Commissioners, or indeed if it had been made unilaterally by the owners of Rudhall directly to the Hospital. There is, however, an intriguing paper trail of evidence in the Office of Works archives which suggests some unofficial conversations took place after the Royal Hospital's experiences during the Munich Crisis. In this archive is a collection of letters to the Office of Works from the War Office, pertaining to evacuation of the Royal Hospital undertaken later in the war.[7] Included within this tranche of correspondence is a letter from Assistant Secretary Maurice Fitzgerald to a Mr H.T. Fry in the War Office in which Fitzgerald claims, with reference to Rudhall, in 1938/39, 'that particular gamble you and I carried out between us, and the Ministry of Works were not consulted at any stage, or called to co-operate in any way'.[8]

Fry was a career civil servant who joined the War Office in 1916 attached to Section F3, the finance department responsible for service pensions.[9] He overlapped with Fitzgerald during the latter's time at the War Office and the professional association between the two men continued after Fitzgerald's appointment as Assistant Secretary and head of the Pensions Secretariat at the Royal Hospital.

The correspondence in the Office of Works archive suggests that Fitzgerald and Fry were given the name of a country house owner near Ross-on-Wye in Herefordshire, who could potentially help the Royal Hospital with evacuation planning. The two men subsequently worked together to facilitate an evacuation plan, which did not involve any of the government departments responsible for Civil Defence planning. The costs associated with this scheme were to be funded from commuted army pensions and hence were part of the War Office budget.

Other than Higher Clerical Officer Mr H.T. Fry, however, nobody in the War Office appears to have been made aware of these plans and they only received official sanction later in the war. Although the board minutes identify the owner of Rudhall as 'Mrs W. Morland', it is no coincidence that Mrs Morland was in fact the wife of a retired army officer, Major William Morland. This is an early example of many throughout the war, which illustrate that when the Royal Hospital needed help and support, it was invariably provided by members of the extended 'military family'. The agenda item in the minutes for the 20 October 1938 board meeting indicate that Fitzgerald, having been alerted to the possibility of Major Morland providing assistance to the Royal Hospital, passes this information on to the Commissioners by including this agenda item in the board papers, which Fitzgerald was responsible for preparing.

Whatever the means by which the Hospital had received the offer of evacuation accommodation in Herefordshire, Lieutenant Governor Huddleston was immediately despatched to Ross-on-Wye to investigate, reporting back at a board meeting on 17 November 1938.[10] The accommodation offered at Rudhall was considered suitable for patients in the Hospital's infirmary who were not confined to their beds and did not require close medical supervision, but could be cared for by appropriately qualified nursing staff without the need for the Physician & Surgeon to be in attendance.

However, the location of the property was too isolated for those infirmary patients requiring more specialised care. The Commissioners therefore approached the Ministry of Health to try to secure the use of dedicated hospital accommodation in the neighbourhood for the more vulnerable infirmary patients. The objective was to billet the least incapacitated of the infirmary patients at Rudhall, with the bedbound accommodated in local, dedicated hospital facilities.

The focus of activity for the Royal Hospital in this post-Munich period appears to have been aimed at following through on a strategy to at least evacuate the infirmary patients in the event of war, and on receipt of Major Morland's offer, Ross-on-Wye became the preferred destination. Herefordshire was beyond the anticipated effective operational range of Luftwaffe bombers, which was, for example, the determining factor in the government's relocation of strategically significant industries in which 'nominally the location of shadow factories depended on "distances from German bases [which] determined a boundary from Bristol in South West England to Falkirk in Scotland, excluding the eastern part of Britain"'.[11]

Using Rudhall, while simultaneously transferring the most vulnerable infirmary patients to hospitals in the local vicinity was therefore an attractive proposition. Unfortunately, a board meeting minute for 12 January 1939 notes that the Ministry of Health stated 'their inability to co-operate in the evacuation scheme to remove the Infirmary Patients to Hereford'.[12]

This rejection of the Hospital's plans by the Ministry of Health was a disappointing development. Fitzgerald's later admission that Rudhall represented a 'particular gamble' carried out under a cloak of secrecy meant the Ministry of Health were unaware of the Morlands' offer of the use of their country house.

By midsummer, terms were nevertheless agreed with Major Morland, and the following entry appears in the board minutes for 9 June 1939, 'To submit for execution by the Commissioners licence to occupy certain accommodation in Rudhall House, Ross on Wye, in the event of an emergency [...] Submitted and executed'.[13] The board meeting minutes at the National Archives do not include a copy of this agreement. However, a signed copy is held in the archives in Chelsea, which until recently were stored in cardboard boxes in an attic at the Royal Hospital.[14] This agreement makes for fascinating reading.

The document in the archives in Chelsea is an agreement between 'Major Walter Edward Thomson Morland' and 'The Commissioners of the Royal Hospital Chelsea', dated 12 June 1939. It provides for around fifty In-Pensioners and their support staff to use a substantial part of Rudhall if the Commissioners believe 'It is expedient that accommodation outside London should be provided for the inmates of the said Royal Hospital Chelsea in the event of a National Emergency'.[15] Clearly, therefore, this is an evacuation agreement in all but name. It provides for the sum of 'five shillings per week for each and every person' to be paid to Major Morland for the use of his home as an out-station of the Royal Hospital.

However, despite this document representing an evacuation agreement, there is no reference to Major Morland's house being requisitioned for this purpose. Neither is there any reference to the Home Office or the Ministry of Health being involved in the negotiations, despite these two government departments being the principal government agencies responsible for evacuation planning. The Office of Works is not mentioned either, despite its key role in evacuation planning and its long-standing responsibility for property-related matters at the Royal Hospital.[16] Neither is the War Office mentioned, the government department against whose budget the 5s per week, per person, will be charged. In short, this is a very unusual evacuation document which appears to simply represent a private, or indeed secret, arrangement between Major Morland and the Royal Hospital.

The only evidence in the Office of Works archives that references ongoing evacuation planning at the Royal Hospital is an internal note of a telephone conversation with an official, during which Fitzgerald confirms that the previous evacuation scheme submitted by the Royal Hospital in August 1938 'has now been abandoned', before proceeding to simply mention that going forward, 'it is only proposed to evacuate at as early a date as possible about 45 bed-ridden pensioners with 16 people to look after them'.[17] It is notably not mentioned in this telephone conversation, however, that plans were already well advanced, albeit with no obvious involvement from any of the authorities charged with evacuation planning. The secret agreement with Major Morland was signed eleven days after this phone conversation took place.

On resolution of the Munich Crisis, the suspension of admissions into the Royal Hospital was lifted on 6 October 1938.[18] Chamberlain's agreement with Hitler nevertheless marked the end of appeasement, and the Commissioners recognised that the buildings and grounds of the Royal Hospital would need to be adapted to face an anticipated aerial onslaught. Most In-Pensioners would be staying in Chelsea in the event of war.

The co-operation established during the Munich Crisis with Chelsea Borough Council was also developed further as the council worked on its own Civil Defence preparations. The trenches in Burton Court, excavated on the instructions of the Home Office, were made permanent when local authorities were advised to provide emergency air-raid shelter accommodation for 15 per cent of their borough's population. This was assumed to be the likely number who would find themselves caught out in the open during air raids.[19]

Chelsea Borough Council estimated that this guidance required the council to provide public shelter accommodation for approximately 9,000 people.[20] The government funded 60 per cent of the costs of local authority Civil Defence expenditure, while allowing councils to fund their 40 per cent share through additional borrowing, underwritten by an implicit central government guarantee. Emergency shelter accommodation would comprise basement shelters, supplemented by trench shelters in public open spaces.

For the Borough of Chelsea, which lacked any significant open spaces in the form of parks or public commons, the requirement for emergency trench shelters presented a particular problem. To address this issue, the council approached the owners of three significant areas of open space in the borough: the resident owners of Paultons Square, a garden square in the west of the borough; Cadogan Estates, owners of Cadogan Place Gardens in the north-east of the borough; and the Royal Hospital Chelsea, as owners of Burton Court in the south-east of the borough.

The intention was to seek permission from these owners for the council to excavate three super-shelters in these only significant open spaces in Chelsea. The shelters would be considerably larger than the recommended size for fifty to 100 people, which was the norm for most public shelters, designed to minimise concentrations of residents and hence limit potential casualties in the event of a shelter receiving a direct hit. Cadogan Place Gardens shelter was designed to accommodate 574 individuals, Paultons Square, 762; and the largest of all shelters in Chelsea, the Burton Court shelter complex, was designed for a remarkable 1,244 residents.[21] The council also allocated a separate budget to provide shelter-specific, designated Air-Raid Warden marshals for these three super-shelters; six each for Cadogan Place and Paulton Square, and twelve for Burton Court.

On 21 December 1938, the Commissioners agreed that the trenches dug during the Munich Crisis should be made permanent.[22] The council's super-shelter complex proposed for Burton Court was also approved.[23] This complex consisted of several separate shelters, each capable of accommodating at least 100 residents and managed by an individual warden. The agreement, signed in the summer of 1939, was drafted and executed under the guidance of the Home Office in their oversight capacity for Civil Defence planning, as is made clear in the preamble:

WHEREAS during the European Crisis in September One thousand nine hundred and thirty eight the Council excavated or partly excavated certain trenches in Burton Court Chelsea for sheltering the public against aerial bombardment AND WHEREAS His Majesty's Secretary of State has intimated to the Council that the said trenches should be completely covered in and given a permanent structure and the proposed method of doing so is to line the sides and floors of the said trenches with in situ reinforced concrete and roof them over with reinforced concrete.[24]

This Civil Defence construction project was a major undertaking which took many months to complete, whereupon the Burton Court shelter complex formed one of the three super-shelters in Chelsea, collectively capable of accommodating over 2,500 residents.[25] Throughout Chelsea, trenches were dug, shelters constructed and sandbags and barbed wire appeared around multiple sites as the borough prepared for the increasingly likely prospect of the country finding itself at war once again.

Artist and Chelsea resident Frances Faviell clung to the hope that war could still be averted but nevertheless joined a Volunteer Aid Detachment (VAD) to ensure she could make herself useful, should war come. Between first-aid sessions, she also trained as an operator in the Borough Council's central control room, located in a reinforced bunker beneath Chelsea Town Hall. Here, she met one of Maurice Fitzgerald's daughters, Denise, also mastering the intricacies of detailed, accurate and timely note taking, while memorising the precise location of streets throughout the borough to ensure that, if required, assistance could be despatched to the correct location in a timely manner.[26]

As war preparations continued in Britain during the early months of 1939, Hitler turned his attention to his eastern neighbour, Poland. East Prussia, with its capital Königsberg, was the historic and spiritual home of the Teutonic Knights and the coronation city for Prussian monarchs. In the 1919 Versailles Treaty, East Prussia and the Baltic port of Danzig were separated from Germany by a strip of land referred to as either the 'Danzig corridor' or the 'Polish corridor'. This now became the latest flash point for tensions in Europe as German-speaking inhabitants agitated for greater alignment with Hitler's Germany.

To counter its increasingly assertive neighbour, the Polish government on 31 March 1939 signed a security agreement with Britain and France in which both pledged to come to Poland's assistance should the need arise. Henceforth, the threat of force would be met with an equivalent response.

Throughout the summer of 1939, Royal Hospital board-meeting minutes document a steady stream of Civil Defence preparations, '20th April 1939 – Air Raid Precautions – trenching operations in Infirmary Court', which, given the historic nature of the site, go on to record, 'further human remains have been found in the course of trenching operations in Infirmary Court', including three male bodies, two female, the remains of a coffin and a seventeenth-century clay pipe.[27] Further air-raid trenching operations unearthed the skeletons of 'a man and a horse', along with 'a skull and some bones' believed to have been the remains of 'an unfortunate French prisoner' from the Napoleonic Wars.[28]

Despite these gruesome finds, air-raid shelters were prepared across the Hospital's estate. Preparations included reinforced shelters in the crypts below the chapel and the Great Hall, regardless of reservations about their ability to withstand the impact of falling debris from direct hits. In the Artificers Yard, beside the Soane Stable Yard, the Office of Works constructed a surface shelter for use by the wives and children of staff members who chose not to participate in the government's general evacuation scheme.

While preparations for protecting In-Pensioners and staff continued, co-operation with the Borough Council developed further: '25th May 1939 – To consider a request from Chelsea Borough Council for sanction to construct an Air Raid Warden Shelter in the Royal Avenue [...] Sanction provided.'[29] This warden's post, designated 'Post K' in the Civil Defence plans, would play an important role in organising support for the Royal Hospital during the Blitz.

More air-raid shelters were approved and constructed as work continued on the super-shelter complex in Burton Court: '9th June 1939 – To submit for execution by the Commissioners a Deed of Licence relating to the construction by the Chelsea Borough Council of trench shelters in Burton Court [...] Submitted and Executed.'[30]

Shelter developments became more elaborate with the super-shelters modified to include ramp access, rather than steps, to ensure rapid, easy access during air raids.[31] When the Home Office refused to fund modifications, the council chose to go ahead anyway and cover the increased costs themselves.

Construction delays, although inevitable, nevertheless resulted in a rebuke from the Commissioners, who on 6 June complained that the shelters in Burton Court should have been 'finished by 20th April and grassed over to provide football pitch above' to host fixtures for troops stationed in Chelsea Barracks.[32] The Guards were consequently forced to play their home matches in the South Grounds.

A report by the council's Civil Defence Committee on 12 July 1939 identified another issue for which the Hospital's Commissioners were approached for help. A review of air-raid precaution preparations reports:

> The stretches of Chelsea Embankment and Chelsea Bridge Road opposite the Royal Hospital frontage presents a special problem, as at any given moment there might be some hundreds of occupants of vehicles driving along there, for whom shelter must be provided. It is desirable to obtain the consent of the Royal Hospital Authorities to the erection of suitable surface shelters.[33]

The Royal Hospital consequently made land available in Ranelagh Gardens and the South Grounds near the entrance gates, in order to facilitate ease of access for motorists caught in the open during air raids: '3rd August 1939 – To report result of discussion with Borough Surveyor relative to proposal to construct an Air Raid shelter in the South Grounds adjoining the Embankment [...] The Board agreed.'[34] This particular shelter, located 'to the east of the Bull Ring [...] by the entrance to Royal Hospital grounds', was capable of accommodating up to 130 people.[35] Taken together with the Burton Court super-shelter complex and an additional sixty-five-person shelter located on Royal Avenue, the 66 acres of Royal Hospital grounds, representing around 10 per cent of the surface area of the borough, hosted in total a disproportionate 17 per cent of all publicly funded air-raid-shelter provision in Chelsea during the war.

However, running in parallel with these passive defensive measures, the Commissioners also had to address demands from the War Office for more overt military use of the Royal Hospital grounds. One of the reasons given at the May 1938 conference for the proposed wholesale evacuation of In-Pensioners was to utilise the Hospital's grounds for purposes connected with the defence of London. Consequently, in May 1939, the Royal Hospital received a request from the War Office 'that a strip of ground along the SW boundary of the South Grounds should be made available for hutting for 97th Anti-Aircraft Regt'.[36]

This request presented the Commissioners with a dilemma. The utilisation of the Hospital's grounds and buildings for alternative war uses had been predicated on the assumption that In-Pensioners would have been evacuated beforehand. With evacuation now unlikely for most In-Pensioners, the Hospital needed to consider the implications of situating overtly military functions within the confines of what was, in effect, an old people's home.

Would the Royal Hospital become a target if anti-aircraft units were based within the grounds? On the other hand, would it be in the line of fire anyway, given its geographic location and proximity to key infrastructure assets? If so, could more obviously offensive military countermeasures be justified?

The board minutes are frustratingly short on detail in terms of the discussion that took place around these issues, and in the case of this request from the War Office, the notes are merely annotated with: 'Read. Decided that approval be given on terms proposed in draft reply'.[37] The draft reply is not included within the archived minutes and hence the 'terms proposed' for what was undoubtedly a morally uncomfortable decision remain a mystery.

Chelsea Borough Council, working in partnership with the Royal Hospital and significant local businesses such as Cadogan Estates, continued their Civil Defence preparations throughout the early months of 1939. The borough was recognised as among the leading London councils in terms of its state of preparedness, and consequently, it was proposed to run a full-scale mock evacuation and air-raid defence drill to which other London boroughs were invited to send observers, while senior government officials including Sir John Anderson would also be present.[38]

The date set for this major Civil Defence exercise was 19 June 1939, and in a foreword to the detailed document outlining the plans for the day, the Chairman of the Civil Defence Committee of the Chelsea Borough Council, Alderman Lieutenant Colonel S. Boyle CBE, MC, DL, JP explained the rationale behind the exercise:

> The exercise is being held at the request of Mr. Harold Scott, the Regional Commissioner for Civil Defence (Metropolitan Area). It is an experiment rather than an exercise, its primary object being to test the effect of an air raid warning upon vehicular and pedestrian

traffic in a central borough, in which all sections of the community are represented.

As it is necessary, however, to call up for the occasion a large number of the volunteer personnel, it has been decided to seize the opportunity to exercise certain branches of the Civil Defence services, mainly to practice the system of report and communication between the Control Centre, the Warden's Posts and the Depot from which assistance would be sent.[39]

As part of the exercise, it was also decided to test the evacuation procedures of the borough to assess the extent to which the council could successfully discharge its obligations under the Anderson Report in evacuating priority groups. In this respect, however, the only priority group invited to take part in the exercise were 5,000 schoolchildren. Notable by their absence were the aged and infirm, including Chelsea Pensioners, confined to the grounds of the Royal Hospital for the duration of the exercise.

The exercise was deemed a tremendous success and received widespread coverage in the media. Civil Defence forces performed admirably on the day, and it was agreed that valuable lessons had been learnt. At 12 noon, as Chelsea came to a halt for a fifteen-minute mock air-raid attack, several volunteers, including Royal Hospital Road resident Frances Faviell, lay down on the pavement, playing the role of air-raid casualties as they were treated by Volunteer Aid Detachment medics.[40]

Newspapers the following day were full of pictures of Chelsea residents playing similar roles, including groups of smiling schoolchildren with luggage labels attached, carrying small suitcases as they were chaperoned to train stations to begin imaginary journeys to safety in the countryside. The Royal Hospital occasionally features as a small footnote: 'Pensioners at the Royal Hospital Chelsea went to the underground shelters in the grounds directly the warning sounded and remained there until the "All Clear" was heard.'[41] It would not be long before In-Pensioners would be spending considerably longer than fifteen minutes in air-raid shelters, which were now a regular feature of every corner of the Hospital's grounds.

The Royal Hospital spent the summer of 1939 balancing the competing demands of supporting broader Civil Defence preparations.

On 22 August, as the situation on the Continent deteriorated, Sir John Anderson mobilised Civil Defence forces, and the following day Germany stunned the world by announcing a non-aggression pact with Russia.

Signed in Moscow by the countries' foreign ministers, Vyacheslav Molotov and Joachim von Ribbentrop, the Molotov–Ribbentrop Pact of 23 August 1939 between Nazi Germany and the Soviet Union contained written guarantees of peace between the two powers. However, it also contained a secret protocol defining spheres of influence across Poland, Lithuania, Latvia, Estonia and Finland.

With war seemingly imminent, Britain warned Germany of its intention to stand by Poland in the event of hostilities. On 24 August, Parliament was recalled and passed the Emergency Powers (Defence) Bill, giving sweeping powers to the government. In Chelsea, the officers of the Royal Hospital felt it appropriate to begin a War Diary, and a standard issue Stationery Office lined notebook, 'Supplied for the Public Service by J.D. & Co', was duly acquired.

The War Diary survived the subsequent conflict and, like much of the original source material from this period, was until recently stored in a cardboard box in an attic at the Hospital.[42] As the Royal Hospital prepared to go to war, the first entries in its War Diary read:

23 August 1939 – The Lieutenant-Governor sent out telegrams recalling all officers on leave, in pursuance of instructions from the War Office. These telegrams were transmitted about 3pm.

24 August 1939 – The Governor returned to the Royal Hospital having received information from a Divisional Commander with whom he was staying that war was imminent.[43]

5

# The Outbreak of War

*'March out!'*[1]

With the signing of the Molotov–Ribbentrop Pact on 23 August, Europe once again stood on the brink of war and the momentum towards conflict seemed unstoppable. As German troops massed on the border, Poland contemplated mass mobilisation. In Chelsea, the telegrams sent out 'recalling all officers on leave' resulted in the return to the Royal Hospital of the Governor and most of the senior staff on 24 August.[2] At a board meeting called the same day, the following agenda item was submitted and approved: 'that in view of the Emergency, the admission [...] to In-Pension should be suspended until further notice.'[3]

During the Munich Crisis, as war had seemed likely, the Commissioners had tried to minimise the number of In-Pensioners resident within RHC by actively encouraging the voluntary dispersal of those fit enough to travel by allowing them additional allocations of leave entitlement but this had been overruled by the War Office. Now, as it became clear in the autumn of 1939 that Hitler was intent on moving against Poland and Britain and France would no longer stand idly by, the Commissioners tried instead to actively reduce the intake of new residents. The War Office may have prevented the dispersal of those In-Pensioners already resident in Chelsea to areas of safety beyond London, but the Royal Hospital was determined to ensure that no more old soldiers would be allowed to join the establishment as it prepared to go to war.

While the management board met, Captain of Invalids William Lockley motored to the Army Ordnance Depot in Wembley with a 'hired lorry and returned with a number of A.R.P. Stores'.[4] The adjutant, Major Frederick Inglis MC, rejoined his regiment, the Gordon Highlanders, handing his adjutant's responsibilities to Captain of Invalids Charles Dean.[5] The following day, the Royal Hospital practised blackout procedures as ARP wardens began to patrol the streets.[6] On Saturday, 26 August, Captain of Invalids Geoffrey May 'inspected the gas masks of his company, No.1 to ensure that they were all properly fitted'.[7]

As preparations for war accelerated, Faviell writes, 'By now we all knew that war was inevitable, and on the Sunday, the 27th streams of cars were already leaving London'.[8] As khaki-clad soldiers spilled from the Duke of York's Barracks, filling the streets of Chelsea, those residents able to evacuate on this hot, sunny day loaded families and possessions into cars and joined the exodus of traffic streaming out of London.

As their fellow Chelsea residents deserted the capital, In-Pensioners at the Royal Hospital attended Sunday Church Parade as usual. This Sunday, however, also witnessed the attendance of the Paymaster General and Chair of the Commissioners, Earl Winterton, who after the service, and knowing that most In-Pensioners would not be going anywhere, inspected the Hospital's air-raid shelters.[9] How effective they would prove to be in protecting In-Pensioners would soon be put to the test.

The following morning, a senior staff member was appointed officer in charge of each of the Hospital's major shelters with Assistant Secretary Maurice Fitzgerald responsible for the shelters in Light Horse Court, nearest to the administration offices. Captain Lockley was made responsible for the Infirmary Court shelters and Captain May, the shelters on the North Front. The quartermaster, Captain Jolliffe, would be sheltering in the beer cellar during air raids; the sergeant major would keep order in the Chapel Crypt; the chaplain and quartermaster sergeant would share responsibility for the cellar beneath the Lieutenant Governor's apartments; and finally, Maurice Fitzgerald's deputy, Office Keeper Mr Fry, would keep order in the shelter beneath Captain Bailey's quarters in the North-East Wing.[10] This shelter was also a short distance from the administration offices and would therefore, like the trenches in Light Horse Court, be used by staff working in the Pensions Secretariat. Each of the In-Pensioners was assigned to the shelter nearest their accommodation to minimise the time it would take from the air-raid sirens sounding to the old soldiers reaching their designated place of safety.

On 29 August, the Polish government ordered a military mobilisation, but then quickly withdrew the order in the increasingly forlorn hope that war could still be averted, even at this eleventh hour. Nevertheless, the following day, the Polish Navy sent its destroyer flotilla to Britain to join the Royal Navy, which was also mobilised the same day. At the Royal Hospital, In-Pensioners practised ARP drills, proceeding to their designated shelters and putting on gas masks.

On 31 August, the Minister of Health, Mr Walter Elliot announced over the radio that the evacuation of vulnerable civilians would begin the following morning. The announcement triggered a wave of emotional family gatherings as parents broke the news to bewildered children. On the Guinness Trust estate in the World's End district of Chelsea, 8-year-old Donald Wheal and his 6-year-old brother Keith, or Kit, as he was affectionately known, had for days been practising boarding a bus and quietly taking their places alongside their classmates. Now their parents sat them down and explained that in the morning they would be doing it for real. 'You'll be going with the school. The government's made all the arrangements. You'll be together with your friends. We'll come down to the country to see you. You can show us round. Show us the pigs and things.'[11] The youngsters were not convinced.

'I want Mum to come with us,' protested Kit as his father continued, 'We've just had an announcement from the government. It's tomorrow ... Now, you boys have to look after each other. You understand me?'[12]

On Friday, 1 September 1939, German tanks crossed the frontier into Poland. The Polish Army, which had again been ordered to mobilise on 30 August but was not yet fully deployed, was outnumbered and outgunned by a German Army trained intensively in a new form of blitzkrieg, or 'lightning war', in which ground and air forces worked in close co-operation to overwhelm a disorientated and confused opponent.

In London, the Home Office activated Operation Pied Piper, and 'nearly 300,000 school-children and their teachers left London' on specially chartered trains.[13] At train stations across the capital, volunteers from organisations such as the Women's Voluntary Service (WVS) were on hand to deal with every eventuality. In Chelsea, Frances Faviell helped to evacuate children to Charing Cross before returning to her home on Royal Hospital Road, where she found the poignancy of the sudden silence overwhelming.[14] At the Royal Hospital, as In-Pensioners watched the exodus of residents and schoolchildren from Chelsea, the Deputy Surgeon, Captain Bourne, departed, having received his call-up papers for mobilisation into the Royal Army Medical Corps.[15]

The announcement of the activation of the government's evacuation plans did not, in practice, contain any provision for the inclusion of the aged and infirm. The political squabble in Whitehall and the subsequent lack of any substantive preparations meant that the overwhelming majority would be left behind to take their chances in the anticipated aerial Armageddon expected to be unleashed within hours of war being declared. This included the In-Pensioners of the Royal Hospital. However, the Commissioners had organised what was, in effect, a secret plan to evacuate the least-incapacitated In-Pensioners from the Hospital's infirmary, and with tensions in Europe coming to a head, they did not wait for Britain to declare war before activating their own contingency plans. The War Diary entry for 2 September reads:

> A party consisting of 30 Infirmary patients, 15 disabled In-Pensioners from the Long Wards, 7 active In-Pensioners for fatigue duties, Sister Taylor, 5 Nurses, 1 Infirmary Orderly, 1 Cook and Mr Burke, Accounts Clerk were evacuated to Rudhall, a large Tudor house near Ross-on-Wye.[16]

It is not clear if the Commissioners had heeded the Office of Work's advice about alerting the Ministry of Transport to their plans, but the likelihood, given the sensitivities, is that the vehicles which arrived at the Hospital's gates early that Saturday morning had been hired privately, with no involvement from any of the government departments charged with evacuation planning. The War Diary entry continues:

> ... three char-a-bans and two lorries were provided and loading up occupied from 8 to 11.30am. The party, which was given a loud send-off by the Governor, Lt-Gov. and others, reached Rudhall about 5pm without any mishaps.[17]

The senior medical professional in charge of the party, Sister Edith Taylor, was a long-term employee of the Royal Hospital, joining the establishment in 1926. Born in Birkenhead in 1887, she was the sixth of nine children of Thomas Taylor, a shipwright, and his wife Mary. Trained as a nurse at the Hahnemann Hospital in Liverpool, Edith enrolled in the Territorial Army Nursing Service (TANS) in August 1914 and was posted to Basra via India in June 1915. She remained on active service in Mesopotamia throughout the First World War. Commended for her wartime service, Edith was 'Mentioned in Despatches to the Secretary of State for War' in 1918 and promoted to acting sister, before being demobilised on her return to Liverpool in 1920.[18] The In-Pensioners evacuated to Rudhall were thus in the care of a capable and reliable nursing sister, who prior to their evacuation had been responsible for their well-being in the Royal Hospital's infirmary and was therefore a respected, comforting and familiar presence.

The other senior member of the evacuation party was an intriguing appointment. Senior Clerical Officer Mr Albert Burke, a 36-year-old career civil servant reporting to Assistant Secretary Maurice Fitzgerald in the Pensions Secretariat, was born in Pimlico in 1903. The son of Walter Burke, a milk-delivery dairyman, a young Albert joined the Pensions Secretariat straight from school and had worked at the Royal Hospital for two decades. Burke had clearly been taken into the confidence of Fitzgerald and was aware of the exceptionally discreet nature of the Royal Hospital's arrangement with Major Morland of Rudhall, because prior to the evacuation party's departure from Chelsea, he was given clear instructions: 'Bedding kits and utensils were taken from Chelsea' and 'Mr A.F. Burke [...] applies to Chelsea for replacement of stores', thus ensuring that all provisions for the contingent at Rudhall were supplied from the Quartermaster's Department of the Royal Hospital. The instructions continue by stipulating that only 'stores which are required and cannot be despatched from Chelsea are purchased locally'.[19]

The out-station at Rudhall would not be recognised as a stand-alone establishment with its own separate financial accounts but would instead be funded from the same budget as the rest of the Royal Hospital. In organisational and accounting terms, it would not exist as a separate entity and, as such, would hopefully go unnoticed by those government departments responsible for financing the Hospital. Discretion was to be Mr Burke's modus operandi.

Meanwhile, for those In-Pensioners and staff who remained behind in London, the War Diary goes on to note, '10.45 a.m. Pay Parade as usual'.[20] As the Royal Hospital held its regular weekly Pay Parade on the morning of 2 September, the British and French governments met to consider their options for honouring their commitments to Poland. The following morning, Sunday, 3 September 1939, they issued a joint ultimatum demanding that by 11.00hrs, Hitler should provide an undertaking to withdraw his forces from Poland or the two allies would declare war on Germany.

In Chelsea, and across the United Kingdom, families, friends and neighbours gathered around radios to hear Prime Minister Neville Chamberlain announce in sombre tones at 11.15 a.m. that by the deadline set that morning for Hitler to respond, 'no such undertaking had been received' from Berlin, and as such, Britain was now once again at war with Germany. In the Royal Hospital, In-Pensioners and staff were at this moment attending Sunday church service and consequently missed Chamberlain's announcement. Nevertheless, it was soon clear that the long-anticipated war had begun, for at 11.30 a.m. air-raid sirens began to wail across the capital. The dire pre-war predictions of aerial Armageddon within moments of war being declared appeared to be on the verge of being realised.

At No. 33 Cheyne Place, Frances Faviell and her neighbours, huddled around a radio listening to Chamberlain's announcement, were unsure what they should do now that war had actually been declared. Momentarily frozen in a state of shock, they heard ARP wardens out on the street ordering residents into shelters. Unfortunately, Faviell's Rolls-Royce-driving landlord had dismantled the sandbag shelter built during the Munich Crisis, replacing it with a small shelter in the courtyard behind the flat. It was here they sought sanctuary from the expected aerial bombardment, with Faviell noting how the situation they suddenly found themselves in felt 'quite unreal to all of us – for the cloudless blue sky showed nothing untoward and the silence of that Sunday morning was only shattered by the orders of the wardens'.[21]

In the chapel of the Royal Hospital, staff and In-Pensioners were blissfully unaware that war had been declared until, 'as the Chaplain

## The Outbreak of War

was finishing reading the Epistle, Air Raid sirens sounded faintly in the distance';[22] so faintly, however, that the 66-year-old Governor, General Sir Harry Knox, did not at first appear to hear them, whereupon 'the Lieutenant-Governor leant over and informed the Governor, who immediately stood up in his pew and gave the order: "March Out!"'.[23]

There are some discrepancies in the Hospital's records as to what happened next. The War Diary records, 'The In-Pensioners filed out of Chapel as usual, got their gas masks from their bunks and went to their allotted shelters. There was no rushing or disorder.'[24] However, a first-hand account of the outbreak of war, written by Captain of Invalids Cecil Townsend and published some years later, recalls, 'all our people were in church' and as the air-raid siren sounded:

> ... they came out of the church, and I remember the Lieutenant-Governor running across the lawn in Figure Court to get home and change out of his uniform. The grass was sopping wet, he tripped over his sword and went sprawling on the wet grass and his wife had to come out with a towel and dry him down.[25]

Meanwhile, as the chaplain was conducting the Sunday service, a wedding reception was being held for Dawn Lockley, daughter of Captain of Invalids William Lockley, who earlier in the morning had married in the chapel. With the reception interrupted by the air-raid sirens, the guests now filed into the nearest shelters where, alongside Hospital staff and In-Pensioners, they nervously waited for the bombs to start falling.[26] The bride's mother, Mrs Lockley, was not at the reception as she was helping with the continued evacuation of schoolchildren, which was now in its third day, and the cumulative total had reached almost 600,000.

Elsewhere, at the entrance to Burton Court, leading off Royal Avenue, 'Sergeant Seaman reported that about 200 people used the A.R.P. trenches in Burton Court', as Chelsea residents caught out in the open hastily followed the air-raid wardens' barked instructions and hurried to use the shelters in the Hospital's grounds, which had been located close to the public entrances for just such an eventuality.[27]

It was soon realised that the aircraft which had triggered the alert was, in fact, a friendly plane and therefore bombs were not about to start falling on London so soon after war had been declared. As the first 'All Clear' of the war sounded, it is unlikely that anybody had any idea of how eagerly or with what relief its soothing tone would be welcomed amid the terror to come.

Despite the reportedly calm and orderly manner in which the War Diary describes the Hospital's response to this first air-raid alert, it is clear that not everything had worked as smoothly and satisfactorily as had been hoped. At 3 p.m., the Lieutenant Governor called an 'officers conference at his house [and] authorised some additional precautions, including the making of a small sandbagged shelter at the foot of the East Wing main staircase to accommodate a few badly disabled In-Pensioners' who were simply unable to reach their designated shelters in a timely manner.[28] It was already painfully clear that the old soldiers living at the Royal Hospital, who were there of course because they had been 'broken by age or war', were physically ill-equipped for coping with the rigours of another war – one in which the Hospital itself would be in the line of fire. As the opening day of the war drew to a close, and the In-Pensioners settled into their berths for the evening, the first night of London at war would highlight further the difficulties which must inevitably result from the failure to evacuate the Hospital.

The consequences of staying in Chelsea meant exposing the elderly and infirm old soldiers to a degree of danger and disruption to their lives which they would inevitably struggle to cope with, as evidenced by the War Diary entry for 4 September:

> 2.45am – Air Raid alarm given by the Royal Hospital hooter and other sirens. They were not heard by two deaf In-Pensioners who consequently remained in their bunks. I/P Howarth fell down in his bunk whilst dressing, bruised his head and made his nose bleed. He could not get up until assisted by the Sgt-Major, who had noticed his absence from the Chapel Crypt. Otherwise all reached their appointed places [...] the 'Raiders Passed' was sounded about 3.15am. It was a warm night and many of the In-Pensioners elected to sit out on the Colonnade and wait for daylight.[29]

These opening hours of war had exposed the folly of not evacuating the Royal Hospital and provided a taste of the disruption and breaks in the established routines that would become a feature of life at RHC, even without the danger and horrors that would accompany actual air-raid attacks. As the Royal Hospital continued to adjust to the new reality, at 12 noon on 4 September, another officers' meeting was chaired by the Lieutenant Governor in the Secretary's Office.[30]

This was also the final day of the evacuation of schoolchildren on which 22,340 stragglers left London, bringing the total to 607,635 over the first four days of September.[31] During the next few days, further officers' meetings were held as the Hospital continued its preparations for the anticipated massed air raids, which had so far failed to materialise in these opening days of war. The small, sandbagged shelter at the foot of the East Wing staircase that had been authorised earlier was completed, and additional sandbagged protection was provided at the guardhouses – at the entrances to the Hospital's grounds and the lower floor of the infirmary.

The Roman Catholic chaplain visited the Hospital on 6 September, just as another air-raid alert was signalled. He cut a fine figure, arriving 'on a bicycle, wearing a French steel helmet' as he distributed identity buttons to the Roman Catholic In-Pensioners, in order for their denominational status to be quickly recognised should the need arise at short notice.[32]

With air-raid alerts likely at any time of the day or night and In-Pensioners now on continual notice of being ordered to their shelters, 'the Governor gave instructions for tea to be issued in the event of air raids in the early morning. Later in the day the Quartermaster obtained 300 enamelled mugs from the Office of Works.'[33]

The partial evacuation undertaken on 2 September, prior to the declaration of war, is confirmed in the minutes of the next scheduled board meeting subsequently held on 7 September.[34] This same board meeting also considered a request which had 'been received from the War Office to suspend further awards of Commutation pending consideration of the question by the Army Council'.[35] The War Office had seemingly reached the same conclusion as the Hospital, or they were implicitly endorsing the decision made at the board meeting called by the Governor on his return to RHC on 24 August. Either way, no more In-Pensioners would be admitted into the Hospital until further notice to minimise the number of old soldiers placed at risk.

On the declaration of war, London was now officially designated as an 'evacuation zone' under the Anderson Report evacuation classification system. This would nevertheless have been of little consolation to the Commissioners and Officers, however, as they contemplated the situation facing the existing In-Pensioners. Major and Mrs Morland of Rudhall had originally offered accommodation for up to fifty In-Pensioners, but in the event, sixty-one In-Pensioners and staff made the journey to Herefordshire on the eve of the outbreak of the war. However, this was only a fraction of the establishment's total complement, despite it having been agreed as early as May 1938 by the War Office, Home Office, Office of Works and the Commissioners of the Royal Hospital that in the event of war being declared, it would be 'advisable' to evacuate the Hospital in its entirety.

Prior to this 10.30 a.m. scheduled board meeting taking place on 7 September, the Governor and other officers had waved the chaplain away as he left the Royal Hospital 'in his own car about 6.30am, accompanying three lorries filled with pictures and other treasures which are being removed to Montacute House, near Yeovil, Somerset. Packing and loading up had taken nearly three days.'[36]

Organising the evacuation of the Royal Hospital's works of art and other historical treasures to a place of relative safety had proven to be considerably more straightforward than had been the case for the Hospital's In-Pensioners. Montacute House was built around 1598 for Sir Edward Phelps, Speaker of the House of Commons from 1604 to 1611, and Chief Prosecutor during the trial of Guy Fawkes and his fellow conspirators in the Gunpowder Plot. It had been acquired by the National Trust in the early twentieth century, after the Phelps family fortune was gambled away by Sir Edward's descendant, William Phelps.

One of the first great houses bought by the National Trust, Montacute proved to be something of a white elephant, as most of its original art treasures and historical artefacts had been sold by the Phelps family as they tried to stave off bankruptcy. However, in 1938, as war in Europe once again seemed likely, Sir Eric Maclagan, Director of the Victoria & Albert Museum, identified Montacute as a suitable repository for storing the V&A's treasures in the event of hostilities. Consequently, the Office of Works was charged with requisitioning the property on behalf of the museum and terms were agreed on 28 September 1938, at a lease

## The Outbreak of War

of £450 per annum for the duration of the war.[37] It was subsequently agreed that the Royal Hospital's artwork and other artefacts would move to Montacute, alongside those of the V&A, and RHC's treasures would remain there for the duration of the war. Evacuating old masters was considerably easier than evacuating old soldiers.

The Hospital's War Diary notes that on 7 September, the first report was received from Mr Burke at Rudhall, 'where all were busily engaged in settling in'. Conscious of his instructions prior to his departure to Ross-on-Wye, he 'submitted a long list of requirements', which were duly forwarded to the Quartermaster's Department. It was further noted that 'Mrs Morland, wife of Major Morland the owner of Rudhall, has been appointed Commandant'.[38]

The following day in Chelsea, the chaplain returned to RHC having safely delivered the Hospital's art treasures to Montacute House, while a new Deputy Surgeon was appointed to replace Captain Bourne, who was now with his regiment in Folkestone 'before going abroad'.[39] The new Deputy Surgeon, Dr Trevor Howell, was a civilian doctor from Worthing, West Sussex, who had been called up on 7 September in the rank of Lieutenant in the Royal Army Medical Corps, whereupon he had been ordered to report for duty at the Royal Hospital.[40]

Dr Howell arrived in Chelsea just in time to treat the Hospital's first casualty of the war. In-Pensioner Hastings was returning to RHC 'after dark', and most likely after a Friday evening spent in a local pub, when he was knocked down by a car which failed to see him due to the blackout rules now in force. Hastings subsequently had to be referred to Millbank Hospital with a broken arm.[41]

On Saturday, 9 September as the first week of the war drew to a close with mercifully no air raids on London despite a number of false alarms, 'the War Cabinet issued instructions for plans to be based on a three year war, or longer'.[42] Unfortunately, as the Royal Hospital prepared to settle in for the long haul, two more 'In-Pensioners were knocked down outside the main gates after dark'.[43] It was only a week into the war and casualties were already mounting.

With In-Pensioners clearly struggling to adapt to the new realities, the Governor called the Hospital together in the Great Hall on 11 September for a Monday morning address, 'exhorting them to set an example of conduct and sobriety, reciting the words of the old song "I'm afraid to come home in the dark" as especially appropriate to current conditions'.[44] However, In-Pensioners needing to recalibrate their sobriety were not the only behavioural issues the Governor needed to address in only this second week of war. The following day, the Chief Air Raid Warden of Chelsea Borough Council visited RHC and 'asked for the gates of Burton Court to be kept locked day and night. They had first been thrown permanently open, and later had been closed at dusk, but both these arrangements were found unsatisfactory owing to the numbers of undesirable characters frequenting Burton Court.'[45]

Despite the increased numbers of In-Pensioners involved in road traffic accidents, and the unsavoury practices for which the air-raid shelters in Burton Court were being put to use, the first weeks of war were unexpectedly and disconcertingly quiet, with Frances Faviell noting 'a strange brooding spell hung over us all'.[46]

On 13 September, as German troops began a bombardment of Warsaw, having reached the Polish capital the previous day, the 'R.A.F balloon that had been moored in Burton Court since early in August, was moved from the East to the West side – on to the cricket ground. Its crew [took] over the cricket pavilion.'[47] With a barrage balloon floating above the cricket square, there was no doubt that the Royal Hospital Chelsea was now at war.

The balloon tethered above the cricket square in Burton Court was one of two barrage balloons eventually stationed at the Hospital, the other appearing in April 1940 and located in the South Grounds. These were part of a string of barrage balloons stretching across London, following the line of the River Thames, and were to prevent low-flying raiders diving to attack key infrastructure targets such as the bridges across the river.

The two balloons at the Royal Hospital were soon adopted by the few local residents who remained in Chelsea, the one in Burton Court nicknamed 'Blossom' and the one in the South Grounds, 'Flossie'.[48] With many of the houses around the Royal Hospital now empty, their residents having evacuated in late August or early September, and Ranelagh Gardens strangely silent with no children's voices to be heard playing in the grounds, there was still a residual hope that the Hospital's remaining residents might yet be evacuated.

With the situation in Poland deteriorating by the hour, the Hospital's War Diary for 14 September states, 'Chelsea Board met, Earl Winterton in the chair, and discussed the possibility of evacuation'.[49] However, the only reference to evacuation plans at the 14 September board meeting as disclosed in the minutes is the following: 'To read a letter from the London Necropolis Company Ltd, regarding burials in the event of deaths taking place at Ross on Wye, where a party of In-Pensioners were recently evacuated.'[50]

The London Necropolis Company owned the cemetery at Brookwood in Surrey, where a plot had been reserved some years earlier for the burial of In-Pensioners from the Royal Hospital, the burial ground in London having been filled. The costs of transporting bodies from Ross-on-Wye to Brookwood was obviously something the undertakers wished to discuss in good time, to avoid subsequent misunderstandings, as it was not something allowed for within their existing contract. This was clearly an issue which had been overlooked in the evacuation planning, and the entry in the board minutes is thus annotated, 'Enquire as to cost of burials in Ross on Wye and report'.[51]

While the board meeting on 14 September may have been lacking in terms of any discussions pertaining to further evacuation plans, the minutes nevertheless make interesting reading, for included among them is the following note: 'To read a Form of Requisition served on the Royal Hospital under the Defence Regulations, Part IV, Section 19, relating to the occupation of part of the South Grounds by 26th (L.E.E.) A.A. Bn. R.E.'[52]

Events were now moving beyond the control of the Commissioners. The wartime authorities responsible for evacuation planning had failed to execute an agreed pre-war strategy of evacuating in its entirety the establishment that constituted the Royal Hospital, and as a result, the institution remained home to over 400 invalid, infirm and vulnerable old soldiers. Despite this uncomfortable truth, the Royal Engineers nevertheless now occupied part of the grounds for the purposes of activating an air-raid defence station.

The searchlight subsequently installed in the South Grounds was part of the anti-aircraft defence plans for London, which, at this early stage of the war, consisted of a ring of anti-aircraft guns located predominantly in the outer boroughs of the capital, which it was hoped would prevent at least some bombers from getting through. Those that did successfully navigate their way past this anti-aircraft defensive belt would be met above central London by planes from RAF Fighter Command, which would be scrambled to meet them. Should bombing raids take place at night, searchlights situated throughout London would illuminate and track enemy planes for these RAF fighters to deal with.

At this early stage of the war, there were very few anti-aircraft guns positioned in built-up inner-city areas, as the risk from shells that failed to detonate, and consequently fell back to the ground, was considered to be at least as great as the risk from the enemy bombs. Despite the continuing presence of the majority of In-Pensioners, the Royal Hospital had now moved onto a war footing and was arguably at risk from hit-and-run raiders targeting anti-aircraft defence units. However, regardless of the threat from Luftwaffe hit-and-run tactics, the most immediate danger the Hospital's In-Pensioners faced in those early weeks of war was closer to home, as road-traffic accidents, particularly during the blackout, remained at an unacceptably high level despite the Governor's earlier address in the Great Hall. The Hospital's War Diary entry for 18 September notes the measures taken to lessen these risks, 'White armbands issued to In-Pensioners at the two guard houses for use after dark'. At least motorists would now have more chance of seeing the In-Pensioners crossing the streets after nightfall.

Meanwhile, in Poland, the situation became ever more desperate. After Britain and France declared war on Germany on 3 September, the Poles had 'counted on the French, with British assistance, to attack Germany's western border in order to draw off German divisions from the east as soon as the Wehrmacht marched'.[53] Germany's new blitzkrieg tactics had caught the Allies flat-footed and France and Britain were still mobilising their forces. With its air force largely destroyed and the Polish Army struggling to hold back the advancing tide of invading troops, the Polish government 'remained ignorant of the Molotov–Ribbentrop Pact, and so of the Russian threat to its army's rear'.[54] On 17 September, Russia invaded from the east, and the Poles were now forced into fighting on two fronts.

In Britain, on the Home Front, the danger of being knocked over in a road-traffic accident was a risk for Chelsea Pensioners in London which was not shared by those who had been discreetly evacuated to

Ross-on-Wye. However, the evacuees living quietly at Rudhall now faced a challenge of their own.

The National Registration Act 1939 had been passed by Parliament on 5 September with the aim of establishing a national register to be used for the purpose of issuing identity cards, and which from 1940 would also be used for the issue of ration books. Registration forms were distributed during the second half of September and 29 September was designated 'registration night', when households and institutions alike had to collate the personal details of everybody staying at that address overnight.

While these forms were being distributed, the Governor took it upon himself to visit Rudhall on 20 September, ostensibly for the purpose of an inspection, returning to the Royal Hospital the following day. He was accompanied on this visit by Assistant Secretary Maurice Fitzgerald, reporting manager for Chief Clerical Officer Albert Burke, the administrative and provisioning officer at Rudhall.[55]

The War Diary describes the visit in some detail and praises Major and Mrs Morland for having everything ready for the arrival of the In-Pensioners on the outbreak of war with, for example, rooms already fitted out as accommodation wards. The visit also confirmed the appointment of a local doctor, Dr Owen, to act as the approved senior medical officer for Rudhall and the authority to which Sister Taylor should turn if she needed professional medical help which could only be provided by a registered doctor. For example, when Sister Taylor needed a doctor's certificate confirming the cause of death for those In-Pensioners who would inevitably succumb to the passage of time, Dr Owen would be able to provide the necessary paperwork. Two local clergymen were also retained to provide for the spiritual needs of the In-Pensioners, including Prebendary P.C. Barber from Ross-on-Wye, who after the war would prove instrumental in ensuring the erection of a local memorial to those In-Pensioners who quietly passed their final days while at Rudhall during the war.

However, it would subsequently become clear that while the Governor was signing off on these local arrangements, Maurice Fitzgerald was having a quiet word with Albert Burke in relation to the requirements for completing the paperwork for the forthcoming registration night.

Back in Chelsea, while the Royal Engineers were busy utilising the grounds of the Royal Hospital for anti-aircraft defence preparations, the War Diary suggests that some elements of the Hospital's establishment continued to cling to the hope that a complete evacuation of the remaining In-Pensioners would take place. It appears that such a course of action remained a topic of conversation within the rank and file throughout these early weeks of the war.

The In-Pensioners had watched as numerous residents of Chelsea had left town by private transport and had witnessed schoolchildren being bussed to railway stations for onward evacuation by train. They knew from the publicity surrounding the Anderson Report that the elderly and infirm were included among the priority groups, and they had observed some of their fellow In-Pensioners from the infirmary being evacuated on the eve of war being declared. Naval kitbags had been stockpiled at the Hospital during the Munich Crisis, ready for distribution to In-Pensioners for the transportation of their personal effects, and it was not unreasonable, therefore, for them to assume that they would be next. The senior management of the Hospital, however, knew otherwise.

The War Diary entry for 21 September reports that evacuation plans were again on the agenda for the management board meeting, but notes, 'At the weekly meeting of the Chelsea Board, Earl Winterton reported that the Ministry of Health was adverse [sic] to the evacuation of the aged'.[56] Despite this assertion, the War Diary entry goes on to claim that 'In case it became necessary to evacuate the Royal Hospital, the Lieutenant-Governor was instructed to prepare a shadow scheme'.[57] Although a general discussion about evacuation may have taken place at this board meeting, there is nevertheless no evidence in the minutes to confirm that any formal discussions actually took place, or indeed that specific plans were approved.

This is one of the few occasions throughout the war when entries in the War Diary and minutes from the management board meetings do not readily corroborate each other, and this may arguably tell its own story about events and perceptions during these early weeks of war. The identity of the author of the War Diary is unknown and obviously, as such, the author's sources of information for these seemingly inaccurate entries, is unclear.[58]

It is possible that the Commissioners and Officers, faced perhaps with a degree of disquiet among the In-Pensioners, were keen to indicate that they were still actively trying to organise an evacuation, but had yet to successfully conclude the necessary arrangements, due to factors beyond their immediate control. To maintain morale, they may have felt that a modest degree of misinformation was warranted to reassure the residents of the Hospital that, despite the evacuation of a significant proportion of the rest of the population of Chelsea, the In-Pensioners had not been abandoned. Everything possible was being done to ensure their well-being at what was clearly a tense and uncertain time and the idea that meaningful evacuation discussions were indeed continuing was therefore an impression that was not discouraged. It is possible that what is being recorded in the War Diary is reflective of some of the rumours and misinformation, deliberate or otherwise, that appear to have characterised life in the Hospital during these early weeks of war.

Two days later, another confused and contradictory War Diary entry indicates that the Officers of RHC had, in effect, all but given up on their attempts to evacuate the remaining In-Pensioners. Furthermore, any pretence to the contrary had also been abandoned, but this would not, or could not, be publicly admitted.

The Governor, having returned from Rudhall in time for the 21 September board meeting and aware of the rumours circulating around the Hospital, called an officers' meeting on 23 September: '10.15am. Meeting in the Governors Room at the Secretary's Office by the heads of departments regarding evacuation. The Governor laid down that such a course was not to be considered except as a last expedient, nor to be publicly discussed.'[59]

Despite seemingly being clear that the Hospital would not be evacuated, the War Diary goes on to state that 'proposals for the reorganisation of the In-Pensioners, if necessary into four companies were approved. The adjutant was instructed to prepare plans for advance parties if a number of houses were taken over.'[60] The officers of the Hospital were thus being told that evacuation was not going to happen for the remaining In-Pensioners and they were not to publicly suggest otherwise. They were, however, also instructed to make plans, and be seen to make plans, just in case the situation changed.

Captain Townsend, in his memoirs published in 1980, references this decision, relayed to the officers at their meeting with the Governor, and describes it thus:

Just before the war began, there was some talk of evacuating the In-Pensioners out into the country, but the Governor we had then said, 'No, the In-Pensioners will stay in the Royal Hospital as an example to the people of London, and if I'm ordered to evacuate them I'll march them down the King's Road in column of three's and I'll be in the last three'.[61]

To all intents, this was an admission of defeat. The refusal of the 'competent' government departments to organise and execute an evacuation plan for the Royal Hospital, despite it being widely agreed that such a plan was both desirable and necessary, meant that it was highly unlikely that the Governor would be ordered to march the In-Pensioners anywhere, and consequently the majority of the Hospital's residents would be staying in London for the duration of the war. The Governor knew this, as did the Commissioners and senior staff members, but officers and senior staff were nevertheless being told to plan for the best, and to be seen to do so, but at the same time, to assume the worst.

The In-Pensioners would be staying in Chelsea, and their officers would simply have to put on a brave face – by order of the Governor. While the officers of the Royal Hospital considered the implications of this sobering reality, the news from eastern Europe continued to cause increasing alarm.

# 6

# The Phoney War

*'... miles away from any Public House ...'*[1]

The first Wehrmacht units reached Warsaw a little over a week after the invasion of Poland had begun. Attacks on the Polish capital soon ensued and by 13 September, the city was surrounded and under siege, from which point conditions for its inhabitants and the defending troops deteriorated rapidly. In London, residents who remained in the city waited in fearful anticipation of the pre-war predictions of how this war would be different from the last, with the civilian population targeted by enemy bombers which, people had been warned relentlessly, would inevitably get through.

As the news from Poland grew ever more desperate, it also became increasingly apparent how this war would be different in other ways. People gathered round radios, absorbed by reports of the valiant resistance of the Poles against the overwhelming might of the Nazi invasion forces. Unlike in the First World War, news on the Home Front did not have to wait for correspondents' despatches from the front lines. Instead, listeners would wait with a mix of excitement and fear for updates from the daily BBC news bulletins.[2]

The news from the Front may have been more readily available and accessible to a greater number of people than in the First World War, but that did not make it any more palatable. Throughout the month, bulletins from Warsaw grew ever more desperate until eventually, the city succumbed to the inevitable and on 28 September, the Polish government surrendered the capital to the invading German Army.

In Britain, 29 September 1939 was national registration night. All households were required to fill out the previously distributed forms, giving the particulars of everyone staying at the address overnight, with the information required including name, date of birth and occupation – details which were needed for issuing national identity cards to everybody in the country. These cards, in turn, were to be used in the event of rationing, which was widely expected to become a notable feature of the war at some point, petrol rationing having already been introduced from 22 September.

Although most people understood the reasoning behind the need for a national registration scheme, it was not universally popular, especially among 'a lot of people with unorthodox relationships', as it was felt to be an unwelcome intrusion into people's private lives.[3] For the Royal Hospital Chelsea, registration night also presented a particularly delicate challenge, given its timing so soon after a group of In-Pensioners had been quietly spirited out of London.

The response of RHC to the requirement for completing registration details for the In-Pensioners is consequently quite instructive and suggests something of an ulterior motive behind the Governor's recent inspection visit to Rudhall on 20 September, accompanied by Albert Burke's superior, Assistant Secretary Maurice Fitzgerald.

In Chelsea, the 421 old soldiers remaining in residence at the Royal Hospital are all listed in alphabetical order in the Hospital's registration submission documentation.[4] Alongside their names and dates of birth, they are categorised as 'inmates' of the institution, while under the section marked 'Occupation', they are each clearly described as 'In-Pensioners (I/P)'. Thus, I/P Robert Lloyd, latterly of the 10th Hussars, I/P Michael Tiernan, who had served with the Connaught Rangers throughout the First World War, and 99-year-old I/P Henry Augustus Rattrey, a career soldier with the 24th Foot, were all clearly identified on their national identity cards, issued a few days later, as In-Pensioners of the Royal Hospital Chelsea. Similarly, members of staff living at the Hospital were also identified under their 'Occupation' heading as employees of the Royal Hospital.

However, such clear identification with the Royal Hospital and association with the military is not a feature of the details entered onto the registration forms for those In-Pensioners and staff evacuated to Ross-on-Wye. The only association with the army which appears on the submission from Rudhall is that the owner of the property is identified as 'Walter Morland', who is described as a 'retired major' under the section marked 'Occupation'.[5]

The nature of the activities undertaken at Rudhall at this time, which of course was the provision of accommodation for a group of elderly and infirm residents, is not explicitly described in the document. The senior medical professional in charge, Edith Taylor, is simply listed as a 'Hospital sister' and described as an 'Officer' of Rudhall, whereas In-Pensioners Henry Barry and James Forth are listed as being employed as 'Hospital orderlies' and described as 'servants' of the house.

Likewise, each of the old soldiers is described as an 'inmate' of Rudhall, and not even one is identified as an 'In-Pensioner' under the section marked 'Occupation'. Instead, they are all identified by whatever trade they had been involved in after leaving the army and before joining the Royal Hospital. For example, 81-year-old Robert Buet, who served with the King's Shropshire Light Infantry, is described as a retired engine fitter; John Child, latterly of the Cameron Highlanders, is listed as a retired postman; 82-year-old John Elliot, who served with the Royal Horse Artillery, became a draper's assistant in civilian life; Charles Foan was employed as a bricklayer after leaving the Royal Engineers; Edward Patterson, after serving with the Manchester Regiment, worked as a dock labourer; and John Robinson served as a butler, following his army service with the Gordon Highlanders. The only hint of any military association is in the case of Harry Watts, who was severely wounded while serving with the Grenadier Guards and is described as a 'retired paralysed ex-serviceman'. Meanwhile, the ever-discreet Albert Burke is simply described as a 'Civil Servant – Senior Clerical Officer' and is also listed as an 'officer' of the household rather than a 'servant' at Rudhall.

There is no mention of the Royal Hospital Chelsea in the 29 September 1939 National Identification Records for any of the staff or In-Pensioners evacuated to Rudhall. In these early weeks of the war, given the difficulties and sensitivities associated with the evacuation of the elderly and infirm, the Governor and the Assistant Secretary had ensured that the discretion exercised by Senior Clerical Officer

Albert Burke in relation to his charges at Rudhall would also extend to the details entered onto the national identity cards issued to those In-Pensioners evacuated from the Royal Hospital on the eve of the outbreak of the Second World War.

⁂

As the first month of the war ended, Hitler took the salute at a victory parade in Warsaw on 5 October. The last Polish troops surrendered the following day in Lublin, the largest Polish city to the east of the Vistula River. Fighting valiantly against superior German forces, the Poles had retreated towards the south-east of the country in the hope of establishing a defensive redoubt in countryside which favoured the defender, but they were thwarted when Russia invaded from the east on 17 September. Facing overwhelming odds and fighting on two fronts, the outcome was inevitable and as the last Polish forces lay down their weapons, the world waited for Hitler's next move.

Poland's surrender to the Nazis in October 1939 marked the beginning of a six-year reign of terror that would witness some of the worst atrocities ever committed on European soil. The collapse of organised resistance by Poland's armed forces also allowed Hitler to redeploy his army and air force from the now subdued Eastern Front to bolster his forces manning the Siegfried Line in the west. Throughout the course of the Polish campaign, the British and French had made virtually no attempt to divert German forces by attacking from the west, other than 'a small flurry of activity between 8 September and 1 October known as the "Saar Offensive"', which achieved nothing.[6]

Interwar French military doctrine was based around the principle of defence and deterrence and, as such, the French government had poured resources into constructing an impregnable fortified line along its border with Germany, known as the Maginot Line. Designed to contain Germany and dissuade her leaders from any thoughts of ever invading France again, it did not lend itself to offensive warfare in the way needed to draw Hitler's forces away from his campaign in Poland.

Meanwhile, Britain spent the early weeks and months of the war transporting the major elements of its army to the Continent in the form of the British Expeditionary Force (BEF), which would need time to deploy before it could be brought into action. Hitler's blitzkrieg campaign in the east had caught both allies unprepared and incapable of offering immediate and meaningful assistance to the Poles. Now, with Poland's surrender, October 1939 brought a heightened sense of danger on the Western Front.

⁂

On the Home Front, the shocking news from Poland had an unsettling effect on the population, with an air of gloom reflected on the faces of people in the streets. By early October, the initial adrenalin-inducing rush of activity in August and September as war was declared had now subsided to be replaced by a more reflective mood as people waited in a state of nervous anxiety for the threatened bombing attacks which had so far failed to materialise.

Conventional thinking in the pre-war years overwhelmingly assumed that 'the bomber will always get through'.[7] London was expected to be devastated within days, if not hours, of war being declared.[8] Pre-war Civil Defence preparations had identified the potentially significant role that evacuation strategies could play in the protection of vulnerable groups. However, the difficulties and politics around the practicalities of evacuation planning in relation to the elderly and infirm had resulted in an overwhelming focus on the needs of children. But so strong had been the conviction about the inevitability of bombers successfully evading any form of defensive counter-measures that this expectation had dominated pre-war thinking around the government's approach to evacuation planning, to the extent that 'the physical safety of mothers and children from all-out, intensive and prolonged air bombardment by day and night was the first and dominant concern'.[9]

The bombers from which the government evacuation scheme had been designed to offer protection were, however, nowhere to be seen during these early weeks of war, which in turn created its own problems as 'the scheme was not planned to operate in peaceful conditions'.[10] The absence of imminent mortal danger exposed the shortcomings in pre-war evacuation planning and highlighted, in particular, important social and emotional factors which had been ignored in the rush to put in place an organisationally robust plan:

Inevitably, the effect on the sensitive mechanism of the child's mind took second place. To be torn up from the roots of home life and to be sent away from the family circle, in most instances for the first time in the child's life, was a painful event. This was no social experiment; it was a surgical rent only to be contemplated as a last resort. The whole of the child's life, its hopes and fears, its dependence for affection and social development on the checks and balances of home life, and all the deep emotional ties that bound it to its parents, were suddenly disrupted. From the first day of September 1939 evacuation ceased to be a problem of administrative planning. It became instead a multitude of problems in human relationships.[11]

It is hardly surprising that as the threat of 'all-out, intensive and prolonged air bombardment by day and night' continued to prove elusive, support for the government's evacuation scheme began to rapidly melt away.

The official schemes organised by the Home Office had resulted in around 1.5 million evacuees, predominantly schoolchildren and their guardians, being evacuated from those areas deemed to be at risk of bombing on the outbreak of war.[12] It has also been estimated that at least a similar number of individuals were evacuated under private arrangements, such as those witnessed by the In-Pensioners in Chelsea as local residents had loaded their families and possessions into their cars and fled the capital in late August.[13]

Almost immediately after war had been declared, however, and in the absence of the predicted air offensive, homesick and disillusioned evacuees were soon trickling back to their homes. This included families of Royal Hospital staff who had participated in the general evacuation scheme, and an entry in the War Diary as early as 11 September 1939 reports, 'The family of QMS [Quartermaster Sergeant] Doley, who had been evacuated under the Government Billeting scheme to Addlestone, Surrey, returned to R.H. [Royal Hospital], having found conditions there insufferable'.[14]

Mrs Doley and her children were not the only evacuees to find their billeting situation unbearable. Donald Wheal and his younger brother, Kit, had struck lucky as they were about to be evacuated from their flat in the Guinness Trust Buildings in the World's End, Chelsea. Their parents had originally decided that their mother Phylliss would stay in London to care for their grandmother, but as the prospect of evacuation became a reality after Health Minister Mr Elliot's radio address on 31 August, intense discussions ensued between the adults, once the boys had been put to bed. The following morning, Donald and Kit discovered that Grandma Eliza had insisted she could look after herself and Phylliss must accompany the boys. Similar, heart-wrenching decisions were no doubt made during the evening of 31 August 1939 in families across the country in the areas designated as evacuation zones.

The following evening, Phylliss Wheal and her sons found themselves billeted with Mr and Mrs Pink in a village outside Woking, courtesy of the local branch of the Women's Voluntary Service. Unfortunately, it did not take long for Mrs Wheal to discover that 'Mr Pink had more than the billeting allowance in mind' when he took the evacuees in.[15] He made his move while the boys were at school, but was clearly no match for Phylliss, as Donald described when he and his brother returned to the house:

> 'We're leaving', my mother said to Mr Pink. 'You can tell Mrs Pink we don't feel welcome here. I shan't say any more than that'. 'You don't have to go', he said feebly, and looked at us. 'Just a bit of fun. A laugh.' My mother glared at him. 'We'll be out of here in a week. Before if possible,' she said in an icy voice. 'Any more laughs and we'll see if Mrs Pink shares your sense of humour.'[16]

Regardless of the specific trigger point for individual evacuees, as the days turned into weeks and weeks into months, with no sign of the expected aerial bombardment materialising, the emotional impact of the human dislocation wrought by evacuation began to take its toll. The policy of evacuation was increasingly seen as the answer to a threat which did not appear to exist. The trickle of evacuees abandoning their allotted billets and making their way back to their own homes soon turned into a flood, 'To the government's dismay, by Christmas 1939 it was estimated that over 90 per cent of evacuees had returned to their original homes'.[17]

The evaporation of support for the policy of evacuation created something of a dilemma for the Royal Hospital. The transfer of

In-Pensioners to Herefordshire had of course been organised independently by the Officers and Commissioners of RHC and was not part of the nationwide scheme of evacuation under the central control of the Home Office. Major and Mrs Morland's house, Rudhall Manor, near Ross-on-Wye, was considered by the Hospital's management board to be an 'out-station' of the main RHC site in Chelsea and was funded from the same War Office budget as the rest of the institution. The evacuated In-Pensioners and staff remained on the books of the establishment for the duration of the war and Mr Burke had been instructed to source all the provisions he required for Rudhall through RHC in Chelsea, only sourcing supplies locally when this was not possible.[18]

These were important distinguishing characteristics of the evacuation scheme instigated by the Royal Hospital on the outbreak of war and significant differentiators between the Hospital's approach to evacuation compared to wartime evacuation schemes in general. This approach to evacuation had of course been forced onto the Commissioners and Officers of the institution because of the specific problems facing the Royal Hospital; problems which were in part logistical, due to the unique nature of the institution, but in the main resulted from the toxic politics surrounding the issue of evacuating the aged and infirm.

The nature of the Hospital's evacuation provision in these early weeks and months of war nevertheless set it apart from the broader, government-sponsored evacuation scheme, and would go on to set the tone for the Hospital's evacuation strategies throughout the war. Most schemes involving children, for example, typically required parents to hand over the care and responsibility of their offspring to government-appointed evacuation officials, and not all children were accompanied by a parent as they left an evacuation zone and headed to a part of the country designated a reception area. Parents usually had little further direct involvement unless they chose to withdraw their children from the billeting arrangements.[19]

By contrast, the Officers and Commissioners of RHC, due to the nature of the evacuation plan forced upon them, remained in day-to-day control of their principal evacuation site for the duration of the war. The out-station was seen as an integral part of the wartime organisational structure of the establishment. This differentiating factor would now determine the Hospital's strategy as support for evacuation among the broader population collapsed.

In the early days of the war, the evacuated In-Pensioners, much like the early wartime evacuees in general, considered themselves to be the lucky ones as those who had been left behind braced for the anticipated Luftwaffe onslaught from the air. Major and Mrs Morland had generously turned over the larger part of their home for the benefit of the Royal Hospital, retaining the use of only a few upstairs rooms in one wing for themselves and their modest complement of domestic staff.[20]

Prior to the arrival of the three charabancs of RHC evacuees from London on the evening of 2 September, significant alterations had been made at Rudhall, particularly to the easily accessible ground floor, which had been converted into wards for the use of the In-Pensioners. Sister Taylor and her nursing staff were accommodated in rooms on the first floor above the In-Pensioners wards, and the extensive grounds were made available to the evacuees.

After supervising the unloading of the two trucks carrying the provisions initially supplied from the RHC Quartermaster's Stores, Mr Burke completed an inventory check before submitting a long list of additional requirements back to Chelsea. The administrative oversight with the London Necropolis Company regarding the issue of transporting deceased In-Pensioners to Brookwood, Surrey, was quickly dealt with and alternative arrangements were soon agreed with the ecclesiastical authorities of St Mary's Church, Ross-on-Wye, where a plot in the graveyard was set aside for the Royal Hospital. The spiritual needs of the In-Pensioners were accommodated through retaining the services of two local clergymen and the only drawback of an otherwise exceptional evacuation refuge for the elderly and infirm old soldiers was that country houses in Herefordshire were disappointingly located 'miles away from any Public House'.[21]

As the leaves began to fall in Ranelagh Gardens, Chelsea, and the In-Pensioners at Rudhall enjoyed the changing autumn colours of Major and Mrs Morland's extensive gardens, the Royal Hospital authorities faced some important decisions in respect of their evacuation strategy. The German Army's *Blitzkrieg* in the opening weeks of September had now been replaced by a *Sitzkrieg* – a 'Bore War', the 'Twilight War' or, as it is most often referred to, a 'Phoney War' – as the German Army manning the Siegfried Line peered out of their defensive positions at the French and British armies facing them.

Other than occasional clashes between opposing reconnaissance patrols, very little shooting took place as the armies settled in to the monotonous routines of sentry duties, weapons checks and resupplies. Overhead, the RAF and Luftwaffe tested each other's response times as they patrolled the front-line airspace, but the only bombing runs conducted by Bomber Command in these early months of the war were to drop leaflets on the German forces now massing in the west. This helped to break the tedium but failed to win hearts and minds among German soldiers still basking in the warm afterglow of their crushing victory in Poland.

The clashes which did take place in these early months of war were between the Royal Navy and the Kriegsmarine, where honours were evenly split, with the Germans losing the pocket battleship *Admiral Graf Spee*, scuttled at the Battle of the River Plate, while two Royal Navy capital ships of First World War vintage, the aircraft carrier HMS *Courageous* and battleship *HMS Royal Oak*, launched in 1916, were both lost in encounters with U-boats.

In Chelsea, Civil Defence practice continued against the background accompaniment of Hitler's speeches justifying the need for *Lebensraum* – growing room – for the German people. In the First Aid Post (FAP) where Frances Faviell practised her medical skills, Hitler's exhortations 'had become a joke amongst us all – at the FAP, if we were crowded in the bandaging practices, we would ask each other for a little *Lebensraum*'.[22]

In mid-November, the recently appointed new adjutant, Captain Charles Dean visited the Royal Hospital's contingent in Rudhall and reported back that 'the In-Pensioners there appeared happy and contented and only two of them expressed a wish to return' to Chelsea.[23] However, only a few weeks later, dissatisfaction with the dislocation caused by evacuation had extended to the In-Pensioner evacuees in Herefordshire, and on 1 December 'a draft of seven In-Pensioners proceeded to Rudhall by motor coach to replace four others who returned by the same coach later in the day, and to fill three vacancies caused by death'.[24]

With the Phoney War slowly taking root, the economics of the Royal Hospital now came under threat. The institution had in part been modelled on the aptly named Hôtel des Invalides in Paris, and the economics of managing a retirement home for old soldiers were not dissimilar to those of a hotel, in the sense that the organisation operated a financial model which exhibited a high fixed-cost element. From a cost perspective, it was largely irrelevant as to whether the Royal Hospital had a full complement of around 500 In-Pensioners in residence or only half that number – the costs of running the establishment did not vary proportionately and these operating costs had to be covered.

The single most important source of income for the institution at this time was the army pension income forfeited by Chelsea Pensioners when they gave up or 'commuted' their out-pensions in return for a berth at the Hospital and the promise of three hot meals a day as they became In-Pensioners. The monies saved by the War Office from no longer paying these pensions were instead paid to the Royal Hospital's account and used to offset the running costs of the institution. This financial operating model now posed a serious risk to the Hospital.

The first act of the Governor on his return to RHC on 24 August as war looked imminent, at a board meeting called the same day, was to suspend 'the admission of Out-Pensioners to In-Pension [...] until further notice'.[25] This suspension of 'further awards of Commutation' was endorsed by the War Office on 7 September 1939.[26] It is the nature of the institution, however, that In-Pensioners eventually succumb to the inevitable, and in the early to mid-twentieth century, the Record of Deaths archive suggests a natural attrition rate of approximately 10–12 per cent of the In-Pensioner complement each year.[27] Consequently, with admissions to In-Pension suspended, the Royal Hospital's income stream began a gradual, but inevitable, decline.

The commitment to lease Rudhall as an evacuation out-station necessitated the funding of rental obligations to Major and Mrs Morland. However, due to the way in which the Hospital's evacuation scheme had been organised, completely independently of the official government evacuation schemes, these obligations were funded from the Hospital's existing resources without the benefit of any additional government-funded billeting allowances. This meant the Hospital's finances were quickly coming under significant strain. In these early months of the war, the Royal Hospital authorities were in effect running two cost centres, funded off a single and declining revenue stream.

With disillusionment towards the strategy of evacuation growing among the evacuated In-Pensioners, the Commissioners and Officers needed to act. The response of the Hospital to this unsustainable financial strain is indicated in a board meeting minute of 21 December, which reports, 'To read a War Office letter on the subject of sanction of commutation during the present war'.[28] This letter was a response from the War Office agreeing to a proposal from the Commissioners to recommence admissions into the Royal Hospital, but only from applicants living either in London or in other designated evacuation areas. No Out-Pensioners living outside of these danger areas would be approved for In-Pension.

This decision to recommence selected admissions into the Hospital is confirmed in a War Diary entry from the end of December, 'Vacancies for In-Pensioner are being filled as they occur, but only from old soldiers who are living in London or other evacuation areas'.[29] This eased the immediate funding crisis facing the Royal Hospital and also allowed the Commissioners to maintain the out-station at Rudhall while waiting to see how the war developed. This enlightened decision also meant that In-Pensioners could be offered a choice, with those wishing to remain in Chelsea able to do so, while evacuation accommodation was made available at Rudhall for those who preferred to leave London.

Throughout the remainder of the war, the Hospital's archives record a steady two-way transfer of In-Pensioners back and forth between Chelsea and Rudhall. Demand for places in Chelsea had also accelerated after the outbreak of war, as it had always been the case that for many old soldiers prior to securing a berth at Chelsea, the workhouse or Public Assistance Institution was where they often found themselves in their twilight years. The failure of the competent authorities to secure evacuation provision for these institutions during the build-up to war meant that on 1 September, many 'old people and other poor persons were turned out of public assistance institutions' and were essentially left to fend for themselves, with or without the assistance of whatever family support they may have had.[30]

These wholesale evictions included many old soldiers, and the reopening of the Royal Hospital's admission procedures would at least allow some of those living in London, or other evacuation areas, to secure a berth in Chelsea, and with the additional option of a potential transfer to Rudhall. Despite the disillusionment with evacuation policies which characterised the response of much of the population during this early war period often referred to as the Phoney War, the Commissioners of the Royal Hospital, despite the financial pressures, refused to follow the general trend of widespread abandonment of evacuation provision and instead took a more pragmatic and considered view. This was undoubtedly to the benefit of all concerned.

The Royal Hospital's early experience of wartime evacuation was not without further issues. At a management board meeting on 1 February 1940, it was reported that the experienced nursing Sister Edith Taylor, a popular and familiar face for the evacuated In-Pensioners in Rudhall, had been recalled to Chelsea for alleged 'misbehaviour'.[31] Although Sister Taylor was the senior Royal Hospital medical professional at Rudhall, the out-station was under the overall command of Mrs Morland, who had been appointed Commandant shortly after the arrival of the RHC evacuees.

With evacuation in general now viewed as more of an optional undertaking, and the discretion exercised thus far by the Royal Hospital in its occupation of Rudhall therefore less important, it is unlikely that Sister Taylor's alleged misdemeanour could in any way have been viewed as jeopardising the Royal Hospital's evacuation strategy. Whatever the nature of Edith Taylor's behaviour, prompting her recall to Chelsea, the transfer was most likely sanctioned by the Rudhall Commandant.

On her arrival in Chelsea, Edith immediately handed in her resignation. This was not accepted and she was instead invited to a meeting with the Governor, where although it was suggested that her behaviour at Rudhall had been incompatible with her position as senior nursing head of the Royal Hospital's evacuation out-station, she was nevertheless persuaded to withdraw her letter of resignation.[32] It was noted how highly the Hospital regarded her fourteen years of exemplary service at RHC and she was promptly reinstated at her previous grade of senior nursing sister. However, whatever the nature of her undisclosed 'misbehaviour', Sister Taylor's recall from the safety of evacuation at Rudhall would have poignant consequences later in the war.

In summary, during the so-called Phoney War of 1939–40, the disillusionment with evacuation policies experienced by much of the general population was also shared by the inhabitants of the Royal Hospital.

However, rather than abandoning evacuation plans, as was the case with many of the Home Office-sponsored schemes, the Officers and Commissioners responsible for the well-being of the Hospital and its residents chose instead to pursue a pragmatic strategy towards evacuation, which ensured a degree of flexibility was maintained as the war developed. This would subsequently prove to be an admirably far-sighted decision.

As winter gave way to spring, and despite the introduction of widespread rationing in early 1940, the war still seemed a strangely abstract affair for many people on the Home Front. Twenty-two-year-old June Spencer, presented as a debutante at Court in 1938, was still considering the extent to which she should participate, despite witnessing that 'all around her, people were signing up for the forces or volunteering as auxiliaries and for A.R.P. duties'.[33] She was part of a generation where it was increasingly acceptable, albeit still difficult, for young women to consider life beyond the confines of the home, and June had entered her occupation in the 1939 register as 'dress designer' rather than 'unpaid domestic duties', as was the case for most daughters still living at home with their parents.[34]

Compulsory conscription for women aged 20–30 was not introduced until late in 1941, and for now, June was uncertain about what to do, 'she knew she would have to do something for the war effort, but how could she combine it with her career as a designer, just as she was beginning to find success? Both Fortnum & Mason and Peter Jones had now given her orders.'[35]

However, in the early hours of 9 April 1940, German forces crossed the Danish border. Participation in the war would soon no longer be optional.

# 7

# Dunkirk and the Threat of Invasion

*'Wars are not won by evacuations ...'*[1]

The German invasion of Denmark, sometimes called the Six-Hour War, began at 04.15hrs on 9 April 1940. The Citadel in Copenhagen, headquarters of the Danish Army, was captured at 05.18hrs and the government capitulated at 08.34hrs. Communication difficulties resulted in some units fighting on, but by mid-morning Denmark was under the control of the Nazis. On the same day, Germany also attacked Norway, the Kriegsmarine landing troops at several locations. As the Norwegians resisted the German invasion, the Royal Navy was ordered to intercept the German fleet. Sea battles took place along the contested Norwegian coastline and on 28 April, British and Allied troops landed at Narvik to bolster the resistance of the Norwegian ground forces.

In Chelsea, on 20 April, with the Phoney War now clearly over, the Royal Hospital prepared the way for a second barrage balloon to be stationed in the Hospital grounds as 'An R.A.F. detachment arrived and prepared a balloon site between the Chillianwallah [sic] Memorial and Entrance Gates. They have taken over one of the wooden huts completed shortly before the war for the 3rd London Scottish Anti-Aircraft Battalion.'[2] 'Blossom', floating over the cricket square in Burton Court since the outbreak of war, was now joined by 'Flossie', tethered above the football pitch in the South Grounds. Troops from Chelsea Barracks began using the Hospital's grounds for 'exercise, morning and afternoon in the Lime Tree Avenue and Ranelagh Gardens, and on the temporary football pitch in the South Grounds'.³

The Luftwaffe quickly gained control of the airspace over Norway, and co-ordinated operations with the army steadily forced back the Norwegians and British. In London, Parliament was rapidly losing patience with Prime Minister Neville Chamberlain's war strategy and in a debate on 8 May, thirty-three Conservative MPs voted against the government after former minister Leo Amery, an ally of Winston Churchill and opponent of appeasement, gave a powerful speech denouncing Chamberlain, ending by quoting the words of Oliver Cromwell, 'You have sat too long here for any good you have been doing. Depart, I say, and let us have done with you. In the name of God, go!'⁴

Two days later, on the morning of 10 May, Germany invaded Belgium, the Netherlands and Luxembourg. The three neutral countries had refused to allow the BEF to prepare defensive positions on their territory, but as German forces stormed across the border, General Viscount Gort VC ordered British troops into Belgium to meet the threat.

In London, Westminster was preoccupied with the question of who should replace Chamberlain now that he had so clearly lost the confidence of the House. The War Cabinet met no fewer than three times during the day until eventually it was confirmed that Winston Churchill would take over, and King George VI consequently invited him to form a government.⁵

While German troops rampaged through the Low Countries, in Chelsea there was a preoccupied disbelief at events unfolding in Westminster. As the latest blitzkrieg swept all before it, shocked conversations along the King's Road could focus on only one thing, as everybody agreed 'the unprecedented overthrow of a leader by his own party was shattering to the British idea of loyalty'.⁶ There was, nevertheless, an acceptance that a change of leadership was long overdue as patience finally ran out with Chamberlain's policy of inaction. It was very late in the day to be reshuffling the Cabinet though, given the present and immediate danger Hitler posed to the very idea of western civilisation.

Moving into Belgium, the BEF pushed forward against an ever-increasing stream of evacuees heading in the opposite direction. The

Germans mounted an audacious outflanking drive through the supposedly impassable Ardennes with 7th Panzer, led by the charismatic General Erwin Rommel, forcing a crossing of the River Meuse on 13 May.

In London, newly installed Prime Minister Winston Churchill gave his first address to the House of Commons, asserting 'I have nothing to offer but blood, toil, tears, and sweat', before outlining a more assertive strategy for conducting the war, coupled with a clearly articulated objective:

> You ask what our policy is? I will say: It is to wage war by sea, land and air with all our might and with all the strength that God can give us [...] You ask what is our aim? I'll answer in one word: It is victory.[7]

In Chelsea, as in much of the rest of the country, there had for some time been a sense that more needed to be done to confront the Nazi threat, and Churchill's address was favourably received as it offered 'welcome relief to a long period of unbearable suspense'.[8]

In this latest blitzkrieg campaign, German forces used airborne troops to seize major objectives and throw the defending forces off balance. Paratroopers and glider-borne assault units overwhelmed unprepared defenders, causing confusion and panic.

The startlingly effective impact of this new and previously untested form of warfare was not lost on defence planners in London, and at the Royal Hospital 'The O.C. [Officer Commanding] of the local searchlight section R.E. [Royal Engineers], stated that the detachment in the South Grounds had been provided with a lorry, and given instructions to attack parachutists within a radius of two miles of their light'.[9]

The seriousness with which this new threat was being addressed was confirmed the following day when, in a meeting between representatives of Chelsea Barracks and the Royal Hospital:

> The O.C. Guards Depot, met the Lieutenant-Governor and after discussions, agreed to furnish a patrol, if and when necessary, for Ranelagh Gardens. He would also endeavour to make concerted arrangements with the searchlight unit and had already made plans for guarding the four bridges nearest the barracks.[10]

As London began drawing up plans to face this latest airborne threat, parachutists were the least of General Lord Gort's problems. Having bypassed the Maginot Line, German armoured formations raced for the coast, threatening to encircle Allied forces. The Netherlands capitulated on 17 May after Rotterdam was levelled by the Luftwaffe, while on the 24th, Boulogne fell and the port of Calais was surrounded. General Gort had no choice but to fall back to the coast.

Planning for a possible evacuation, Operation Dynamo, had begun as early as 20 May. As news of the scale of the catastrophe unfolding on the Continent began to seep back to Britain, at a board meeting in Chelsea on 23 May, it was decided 'that, in view of the military situation abroad, the ceremonial parade arranged for Founder's Day, 29 May 1940, should be abandoned'.[11]

Founder's Day is the most important ceremonial occasion in the Royal Hospital's calendar, held to celebrate its founder Charles II's birthday. It has been held every year since the foundation of the Hospital and includes an inspection of massed ranks of In-Pensioners by either a senior military figure or a member of the royal family. In May 1940, serious question marks hung over how many more Founder's Days the Royal Hospital would celebrate.

As the Royal Navy organised an armada of civilian craft to assist in the evacuation of troops from the beaches of Dunkirk, a fleet of little boats was already heading for Britain. Carrying 'refugees [...] arriving in every kind of vessel, trawlers, small fishing smacks, and every available craft', they brought with them terrible stories of atrocities inflicted on fleeing and defenceless civilians.[12]

With dozens of large houses in the borough standing empty after the exodus of residents in August and September 1939, Chelsea had already become home to Czech, German and Austrian refugees, and now it prepared to host those fleeing from the Low Countries. Multilingual Frances Faviell travelled to Dover to meet some of these poor wretches as they arrived, frightened, traumatised and destitute. From the coast, they travelled to Chelsea, where St Mark's College, off the King's Road, was used as a reception centre before the refugees were temporarily housed in Cheyne Hospital, the children's hospital on the Embankment that had been evacuated the previous year.

In response to a local appeal, Chelsea residents donated clothes, furniture and kitchen equipment, arranged on long tables in the dining room of Crosby Hall, a pre-war university hall of residence for visiting overseas students. Here, Faviell met Elizabeth Fitzgerald, sister of Denise, with whom she had trained in the Borough Control Room, and daughter of Maurice, Assistant Secretary of the Royal Hospital. After they had finished helping distribute the donated items, Elizabeth and Frances, together with the youngest Fitzgerald son, Paul, helped scrub clean and prepare some of the evacuated houses requisitioned for the use of the refugees. The Fitzgerald children invited Frances back to the Royal Hospital to meet their parents, where she discovered that Suzanne Fitzgerald was also involved in volunteering, helping French-speaking families as she was part-Belgian and the Fitzgeralds were bilingual.

On 29 May 1940, a subdued and low-key Founder's Day parade took place at the Royal Hospital. On the same day, off the beaches of Dunkirk, Luftwaffe Ju87 dive bombers exacted a terrible toll on the assembled evacuation fleet. The destroyer HMS *Grenade* was sunk, while HMS *Jaguar* and HMS *Verity* were badly damaged; the passenger ferry SS *Fenella* was hit and sunk while embarking troops at the pier in the harbour; and the Thames paddle steamer HMS *Crested Eagle*, requisitioned by the Admiralty in 1939, caught fire after a direct hit, going down with dreadful loss of life. Two rail company ferries, SS *Lorina* and SS *Normannia*, were also lost. However, despite the carnage, over 47,000 troops were rescued during the day.

The following day, in the minutes to the management board meeting, Note 7 states, 'The usual parade was held on 29 May 1940 at 11am. No guests, nor members of the general public, were present and there were no musical honours. The In-Pensioners were inspected by General Sir Charles Harington, GCB, GBE, DSO'.[13] Note 8 goes on to add, with more than a hint of defiance, that it was 'decided that steps should be taken to surrender the old German howitzer, a trophy of the war of 1914/18 at present in the South Grounds, to the State so that its scrap content may be utilised for arms production'.[14]

The Dunkirk evacuation changed the dynamics of the war on the Home Front.[15] The threat of bombing was now replaced by the more immediate threat of a likely invasion from across the English Channel.[16] In London a new wave of evacuees left the capital, although after the experiences of 1939 the numbers involved this time were much lower, with estimates of approximately 300,000, predominantly children and their guardians.[17]

However, evacuating to the relative safety of the countryside seemed somewhat pointless now that invasion appeared the more likely threat. Overseas evacuation offered the only realistic hope of salvation for those who could afford the cost of passage. Among those parents who could cover the costs, not all were able to accompany their offspring, resulting in a surge in demand for young women who could act as guardians and escorts for children on their voyages overseas, mainly to the United States or Canada.

In Chelsea, June Spencer saw an opportunity to do something for the war effort and 'called in at the Sloane Square office of Universal Aunts, a quirky company providing private carers and escorts for unaccompanied children'.[18] Nothing came of the interview, though, leaving June to reconsider her options now that participation in the war on the Home Front no longer seemed a matter of choice for anybody.

It was not only parents and children who were looking towards North America for potential salvation. With the realisation that invasion appeared imminent, there was something of an unseemly scramble for safety among those for whom overseas evacuation was a practical option. In the week that Operation Dynamo got under way, the noted photographer Cecil Beaton had, rather fortuitously, been offered a lucrative contract in New York and as his 'own private courage was badly bruised' by the news from the Continent, he agonised as to whether it would be sensible to 'go to America'.[19] He sought the advice of his friend Lord 'Bobbety' Cranborne who suggested he should go because 'the news is howwid [sic]', and was unlikely to improve.[20]

Thus, in late May 1940, Beaton embarked aboard the luxury transatlantic liner SS *Samaria* for the perilous, albeit mercifully uneventful, North Atlantic crossing.[21] On 4 June 1940, Churchill addressed Parliament, reporting on the success of Operation Dynamo in rescuing the bulk of the army, but was quick to point out, 'We must be very careful not to assign to this deliverance the attributes of a victory. Wars are not won by evacuations.'[22] On 14 June, Paris fell to the Nazis.

The friend to whom Cecil Beaton turned for advice, Lord Robert Cranborne, had recently joined the newly appointed Winston Churchill's

War Cabinet as Paymaster General. Among many other duties, his new office made him *ex officio* Chairman of the Board of Commissioners of the Royal Hospital and as such, he chaired a lengthy board meeting on 20 June 1940.[23] At this meeting, a decision was taken on the 'Formation of Two Units of Local Defence Volunteers at the Royal Hospital'.[24]

Discussions had taken place intermittently in the government about establishing some form of 'Home Guard' since the outbreak of war but had gathered momentum as the BEF faced collapse in Belgium. On 14 May 1940, the Secretary of State for War, Anthony Eden, announced the formation of a force of Local Defence Volunteers (LDV) and it was met with such enthusiasm that the following week, 250,000 recruits tried to sign up. In Chelsea, on 28 May, the Royal Hospital's War Diary records, 'The inaugural meeting of the Chelsea Local Defence Volunteers was held at 7pm in the Gun Shed in the South Grounds. The Mayor of Chelsea (a woman) and General Gough addressed about 200 volunteers, and steps were taken to form a company of two platoons.'[25]

The 'woman' was Lady Clare Hartnell, who served two terms of office as Mayor of Chelsea between 1939 and 1941, and she addressed the meeting alongside General Gough, the recently appointed Commanding Officer of the newly formed Chelsea Local Defence Volunteers. The creation of two independent sections of Local Defence Volunteers formed from Royal Hospital staff as separate units within the local Chelsea LDV force is noteworthy and reflected the new realities surrounding the possibilities for evacuation.

Since first opening its doors in 1692 as a home for In-Pensioners 'broken by age or war', the Royal Hospital had also been responsible for the payment of army pensions to Out-Pensioners. These pensions were administered by a secretariat based at RHC, which in 1940 numbered some fifty clerks and administrative staff.[26] The average age of the pension's secretariat was, of its nature, considerably younger than the average age of the In-Pensioner community, and it was this distinction which determined the formation of two Home Guard sections.

As the minutes go on to state, 'It was necessary to have two distinct sections in view of the possibility of the separation of the In-Pension Establishment from the staff of the Secretary's Office on evacuation.'[27] This clear differentiation in the treatment of the two distinct communities within RHC, based on their relative evacuation prospects, is more obviously apparent in the Hospital's War Diary entry for 15 July 1940, which states, 'The Secretary's Detachment, L.D.V. (Local Defence Volunteers) [...] under the Asst. Secretary [...] has been kept as an independent unit in case the Office should be evacuated'.[28] Significantly, there did not appear to be any plans for evacuating the In-Pensioner community now that the immediate threat was invasion rather than bombing.

One unit, 'twenty-three strong', was placed under the command of Captain of Invalids William Lockley and was 'responsible for the protection of the In-Pensioner Establishment and recruited from the staff of that Establishment'.[29] The other unit, 'sixteen strong', was placed under the command of Assistant Secretary to the Hospital, Mr Maurice Fitzgerald and was 'for the protection of the Secretary's Office and recruited from the Staff thereof'.[30]

The practical realities created by the threat of invasion now determined who could realistically hope to be evacuated and who would most likely be left behind. This was true of the inhabitants of the Royal Hospital as much as it was true for the population in general. In this sense, the Hospital's wartime experiences reflect the broader historiography of the period in suggesting that realistic evacuation options in the summer of 1940 were now no longer open to all.

Official evacuation strategies as articulated in the Anderson Report had, of course, included provision for the aged and infirm. This was in marked contrast to several other countries where, for example, in Russia, the 'most notably absent from evacuation categories were the elderly'.[31] Nevertheless, the actual outcomes of evacuation provision still meant the old and infirm in Britain were just as likely to be left behind and by 1940, this was even more the case.

The harrowing stories from the Continent of refugees clogging the roads as they tried to flee from the advancing Nazi army meant the Royal Hospital was never realistically going to contemplate a mass evacuation of elderly In-Pensioners in response to a German invasion. It should, however, be noted that the Hospital was not about to abandon the In-Pensioners to their fate. Provision was made for their continuing protection, and this was the role assigned to Captain Lockley and his detachment of Royal Hospital's Local Defence Volunteers. They would stay behind in Chelsea with the In-Pensioners, while Assistant Secretary

Maurice Fitzgerald's LDV unit would provide protection to the pensions secretariat, should a decision be made to evacuate the administration staff.

The evacuation of the BEF from Dunkirk and the subsequent capitulation of the French resulted in a reassessment of the threats on the Home Front and the consequent adaptation of evacuation strategies for non-combatants. The realities of the moment meant that evacuation provision now clearly favoured some groups over others, and this was as applicable to the Royal Hospital as to the population in general.

With evacuation options now all but exhausted, attention on the Home Front turned to defence and protection. At the Royal Hospital, Air Raid Precaution (ARP) drills increased in frequency throughout the summer of 1940 and the War Diary notes further preparations for the potential effects of bombing, 'A 5000 gallon water tank has been installed just inside the Chapel Entrance, on the west side of the gravel road'.[32] At the same board meeting which authorised the creation of two Home Guard units, the economic and logistical impact of the military debacle on the Continent was also discussed.[33]

A packed agenda included detailed consideration of correspondence received from multiple long-time suppliers to the Hospital seeking to renegotiate supply contracts. For example, a letter from United Dairies: 'beg to inform [...] that owing to Government having increased the price of milk [...] our price to your Hospital [...] will be increased.'[34] This was the first substantive indication of the increasing supply difficulties the Hospital would henceforth face as it sought to meet the basic needs of In-Pensioners now that the Phoney War had morphed into something altogether more serious. Increasing logistical difficulties would also have a bearing on the further evolution of the Hospital's evacuation strategies.

June Spencer's rejection by the Universal Aunts of Sloane Square was quickly followed by depressing news highlighting the terrible personal cost of the military debacle in Belgium. Although Operation Dynamo had, in Churchill's words, represented a 'miracle of deliverance' in rescuing some 335,000 troops of the BEF, 68,000 men did not come home. This included June's family friend Piers Edgcumbe, a 2nd lieutenant in the Royal Armoured Corps, who was killed during the retreat to Dunkirk.[35]

Shortly after attending Edgcumbe's memorial service at the Parish Church of Essendon, near her parent's home in Hertfordshire, June joined the London Auxiliary Ambulance Service (LAAS). A few days later, she found herself starting her first shift at Ambulance Station 22 (AS22), located in Danvers Street, Chelsea, after which she moved into a rented room in Lindsey House, a sprawling mansion on Cheyne Walk, near Battersea Bridge, a short distance from AS22. After the capitulation of the French on 25 June, the war no longer felt so distant.

With the battle for France over, the battle for Britain was soon to begin. On 16 July 1940, Hitler issued 'Führer Directive (No. 16)' on 'Preparations for a landing operation against England'. Operation Sea Lion, as the invasion plans were codenamed, depended crucially upon the success of the Luftwaffe. The objectives Reichsmarschall Göring's fighter and bomber pilots were given included 'prevent all air attacks', 'engage approaching naval vessels [...] destroy coastal defences [...] break the initial resistance of the enemy land forces and annihilate reserves behind the front'.[36] In short, the Luftwaffe needed to gain air superiority over Britain.

In Chelsea, the War Diary notes the Royal Hospital's preparations for this next stage of the war:

> The Secretary's Detachment of the L.D.V. furnished a guard of three men, armed with Ross Rifles for the Main Guardhouse. This detachment [...] has been trained by the Office Keeper [Fry] and one of the Messengers [Boustead]. Practice has been carried out at a miniature range at the War Office; and 10 rounds per man at 200 yards on a N.R.A. [National Rifle Association] range at Bisley. The standard of shooting has been unexpectedly good. At night the guard are to sleep in the Guardhouse fully dressed; the Hospital Constable, who is unarmed, acting as a sentry.[37]

The Ross rifles issued to the Royal Hospital as the Battle of Britain entered its preliminary stages were Canadian Army rifles, held in storage having been found to be wholly unreliable in the heat of battle during the First World War. They did, however, have the advantage of using the same .303 ammunition as the standard-issue Lee–Enfield rifles that were in use with the British Army at this time.

In late July and early August, the Luftwaffe concentrated on the English Channel, attacking shipping and coastal defences before shifting its attention to RAF airfields in southern England. The dogged resistance of Fighter Command's squadrons of Spitfires and Hurricanes took its toll on the men and machines of the Nazi air formations, and Göring consequently turned increasingly towards trying to break the will of the British to keep fighting. As Germany's air strategy evolved, towns and cities across the UK, especially London, began to witness an increase in air-raid alerts.

This evolving battle is recorded in the Royal Hospital's War Diary from mid-August:

15 Aug: Air Raid Alarm, 7.20–7.40pm. No firing heard.
16 Aug: Air Raid Alarms, 12.30–13.10; 17.10–18.10. No firing heard (Wimbledon and Maldon raided).
18 Aug: Air Raid Alarms, 13.05–14.10, and 17.40–18.15.
23 Aug: Air Raid Alarm, 3.30–3.55. Distant explosions faintly heard.[38]

The battle crept ever closer to Chelsea as the Luftwaffe targeted RAF stations around the outskirts of London. Inevitably, however, given the imprecise nature of airborne navigation, particularly at night, these incursions eventually 'led to the unintended dropping of bombs on London' when, 'on the night of the 24th some ten German bombers, which had lost their way *en route* to targets at Rochester and Thameshaven dropped their loads in central London'.[39] The Royal Hospital's War Diary records this first bombing in the capital:

24 Aug: Air Raid Alarms, 8.25–9.15; 15.45–16.45; and 23.30–1.25. During the last half an hour of the third alarm a red glow was seen in the sky to the north-east (a big fire in The City).[40]

Bomber Command immediately responded, and the following night, eighty British bombers attacked Berlin. As the Nazi capital was raided, the War Diary records a quiet night in London, '25 Aug: Air Raid Alarm, 22.30–23.25'.[41]

Soon enough, as tit-for-tat raids escalated, the air defence units deployed in the grounds of the Royal Hospital were brought into action.

During the afternoon of 26 August, an air-raid alarm sent staff and In-Pensioners to their respective shelters between 15.35hrs and 16.10hrs before the All-Clear sounded without incident. Overnight, however, and into the early morning of 27 August, during a raid between 21.30hrs and 3.40hrs, the searchlight in the South Grounds operated in support of anti-aircraft guns on Clapham Common, one of the few anti-aircraft batteries situated in a built-up area of London at this early stage of the Blitz. Another large anti-aircraft battery was located to the west in the open spaces of Richmond Park:

> 26 Aug: Air Raid Alarm, 21.30–3.40; Several single planes passed over Chelsea. One was picked up by the searchlight in the South Grounds, and then by about six other lights. Three salvos of two rounds each were fired at it – apparently by the AA battery on Clapham Common. Other AA gunfire flashes were observed to the west – possibly from the battery in Richmond Park. Tea was served out at 01.00 hours. (Addendum: This was the first time the Clapham Common battery fired, and the German airplane is believed to have been brought down).[42]

The war had come to Chelsea and soon the Royal Hospital would be on the receiving end of the Luftwaffe's attentions.

# 8

# The Battle of Britain

*'Aeroplanes could be seen ... twisting and turning ...'*[1]

The Battle of Britain raged throughout the late summer of 1940 as the Royal Air Force and the Luftwaffe fought for air superiority over southern England and the English Channel.[2] During a battle of attrition, the Luftwaffe were unable to break the fighting strength or spirit of the RAF, and through late August and early September, attention steadily transferred to the terror bombing of London.[3]

For the Royal Hospital Chelsea, the London Blitz would reveal the full extent of the consequences of failing to implement pre-war plans to evacuate the institution in its entirety prior to the outbreak of hostilities. What would also become clear, however, would be the resilience, stoicism and bravery of retired British Army veterans who had already risked their lives in the service of crown and country, and who once more now found themselves in the line of fire, despite their advancing years.

The early rumblings of the approaching storm culminated on the night of 26–27 August, with the air defence station in the Hospital's grounds being brought into action as the searchlight located in the South Grounds helped bring down an enemy raider. Two days later, however, it was the Hospital's turn to be on the receiving end of a Luftwaffe raid, when during the night of 28–29 August:

A whistling noise was heard at 00.15, just as an aeroplane passed overhead at a great height, followed by a dull thud. Captain May, who was sitting on a garden seat by No.3 trench, reported that some earth was thrown around him. A normally shaped crater was found in Burton Court about 15 feet across and 5 feet deep, a few yards north of the tennis courts.[4]

This first bombing of the Hospital's grounds is also referred to in an account of the war published privately in 1980 by Captain of Invalids Cecil Townsend, who gives a slightly different and, in some respects, more significant account of the event:

I think the first incident in Chelsea, was one night we heard a German plane flying round in circles above the Hospital obviously looking for the search-light site which had been placed in the South Grounds. Then down came the bomb and it landed in Burton Court.[5]

The implication from Captain Townsend's account of this first bombing attack on Chelsea is that the Royal Hospital was deliberately targeted because of the presence of the searchlight. This clearly raises questions as to the appropriateness of locating overtly military units within the confines of what was, in effect, an old people's home. Searchlights were legitimate targets and the presence of one in the South Grounds could be expected to result in collateral damage to be inflicted on the institution and its inhabitants.

Its location was, of course, the result of the requisition demand from the War Office served on the Royal Hospital on the outbreak of war in September 1939.[6] The confidential pre-war report of May 1938 gave as a justification for the proposed wholesale evacuation of the Royal Hospital the reason that it was to utilise the grounds for just such eventualities.[7] If Captain Townsend's account is taken at face value, the consequences of this earlier failure to evacuate were now laid bare. The Hospital grounds had become a target even though the institution remained home to over 400 aged and infirm non-combatants.

Legitimate or not, the targeting of the Royal Hospital was, by some accounts, a matter of much debate among the In-Pensioners. Frances Faviell, in her outstanding memoir of life in Chelsea during the Blitz, recounts, 'Bomb after bomb – some unexploded, some delayed action – were dropped on the buildings and grounds. The Pensioners insisted that Hitler knew that the place was under the administration of the War Office, and that it was bombed with intention.'[8]

Although this first bomb to target Chelsea may indeed have been specifically aimed at the Royal Hospital – and the Hospital's buildings and grounds were to be bombed repeatedly during the Blitz – it is difficult to believe it was deliberately singled out as a target. A more likely explanation of the amount of attention it received is its geographical location on the north bank of the River Thames, opposite Battersea Power Station and a little downstream from the Lots Road Power Station.[9] It was also adjacent to major crossing points of the river, such as the Chelsea, Albert and Battersea bridges. It was the presence of such key infrastructure assets in the neighbourhood which offers the most likely explanation of why the Borough of Chelsea 'was one of the most heavily bombed boroughs in London, only Holborn and Shoreditch receiving a heavier tonnage of bombs per acre'.[10] A clue as to why the Royal Hospital seemed singled out for attention by the Luftwaffe, and was to be bombed incessantly during the Blitz lies in its name – the Royal Hospital Chelsea was bombed simply because it was located in Chelsea.

Whatever the details around how the Hospital came to find itself the subject of this first bombing raid on Chelsea, the resulting crater nevertheless attracted the attention of curious residents of the borough. The following morning, a crowd of onlookers gathered at the gates of Burton Court where In-Pensioners, under the direction of the Governor's wife, Lady Knox, immediately capitalised on the situation as 'members of the public were admitted to view the crater on payment of a contribution to the Chelsea Spitfire Fund, and by 11am over £4 had been collected'.[11]

This lucrative initiative was brought to an abrupt halt with the arrival of the Borough Surveyor, who promptly 'found another crater about two feet in diameter and three feet deep, apparently caused by a [...] time bomb, on the edge of the football ground [...] Evidently, the two bombs had been released together.'[12] The area was immediately cleared, with a 100m cordon established, while the windows in the North Front of the Hospital were opened in order to protect them should the unexploded bomb (UXB) detonate before bomb disposal teams could render it safe.

Despite the excitement generated by this first incident in Chelsea, the most significant threat faced by the elderly, infirm and, in many cases, physically disabled In-Pensioners during the early weeks of the Blitz was the practical difficulty involved in constantly having to get to their shelters every time the air-raid sirens sounded. On 30 August, there were three alarms between late morning and early evening, each lasting over an hour, followed by a fourth alarm overnight between 21.10hrs and 03.50hrs the following morning, during which 'several single machines passed overhead' without incident. This pattern continued on 31 August with six separate air-raid alarms from early morning, lasting throughout the day until the All-Clear at 23.59hrs.[13]

This relentless endurance test continued over the following days and nights with three alarms on each of 1 and 2 September respectively, and the physical impact of this near-constant disruption soon began to take its toll on the health of frail, aged bodies. In-Pensioners struggled to reach their designated shelters in a timely manner before having to endure cramped and unhygienic conditions while waiting for the All-Clear to sound.

On 4 September, the War Diary notes, 'Long Ward Sisters report an unusually high number of colds for the time of year – attributable to stuffy shelters'.[14] Despite no more bombs having actually fallen since the two which landed in Burton Court on 29 August, it was clear that the In-Pensioners simply could not stand much more of this unremitting interruption in their lives and routines without a serious collapse in their physical well-being. Consequently, on 3 September, 'The Governor made it voluntary for In-Pensioners and other residents to go to their shelters when the sirens sound between 11am and 5pm', unless an enemy aircraft was seen approaching by an officer detailed as a lookout, who, in such an eventuality, would 'sound the alarm bells, whereupon everyone will go to their shelters'.[15] The following day, these hours were extended to between 8 a.m. and 7 p.m. as pre-war concerns about the impact of air-raid alerts were confirmed.

It had been anticipated that this 'priority group' would face difficulties in reaching shelters in a timely manner and would struggle to cope with the spartan conditions once inside. These fears were now being realised among an In-Pensioner community who were physically ill-equipped to deal with the remorseless demands of multiple alerts. However, as the Royal Hospital adapted its air-raid guidance to accommodate this evolving situation on the ground, the Luftwaffe was preparing to step up the pressure.

On 3 September, Göring, meeting with his senior officers at a conference in The Hague, ordered an all-out offensive against London involving mass day- and night-time bomber raids. The opening day for this new phase in the air war against Britain was set for 7 September, a date subsequently referred to as the opening day of the Blitz. London would be bombed for fifty-seven consecutive nights.

On the afternoon of Saturday, 7 September 1940, Reichsmarschall Göring stood on the cliffs at Cap Blanc-Nez, near Calais, and watched as 'an air armada of about a thousand aircraft of *Luftflotte 2* – over 300 bombers escorted by 648 fighters – set out for London'.[16] The escorts were to draw away any attacking squadrons of RAF fighters, leaving the bombers free to press home their attack on the capital. London would consequently rely on the anti-aircraft batteries under the command of Lieutenant General Sir Frederick Pile for its defence.

Originally a gunner in the Royal Artillery, Pile served with the newly formed Royal Tank Corps before being appointed to command Britain's anti-aircraft defences in 1937. Before the outbreak of the war, it had been agreed that Pile would have 2,232 heavy anti-aircraft (AA) guns and 1,860 light AA guns under his command. However, delays in pre-war rearmament production meant only 695 heavy and 253 light AA guns were available for deployment in September 1939, which was nevertheless a significant improvement on the 126 heavy guns available at the time of the Munich Crisis in 1938.[17]

The failed campaigns in Norway and Belgium also came at the cost of significant losses in materiel, including a number of precious AA guns, and hence, as Göring's air armada headed across the Channel, 'there were only 264 guns on the spot to defend London'.[18] Most of these were located in the outskirts rather than deployed in built-up areas to reduce the risk from defective shells falling back to the ground, causing damage to property and casualties among civilians. On this opening day of the Blitz, the nearest anti-aircraft batteries to the Royal Hospital in the Inner Artillery Zone (IAZ) were four 4.5in guns located on Clapham Common, which had brought down the raider caught in the beam of the searchlight in the South Grounds on 26–27 August; a similar heavy AA battery to the north in St James' Park; and a light AA detachment in Battersea Park.

As the Luftwaffe crossed the Channel, RAF Fighter Command scrambled to meet the approaching threat. However, controllers on the ground were expecting another attack on the inner-sector stations and the route to London was consequently undefended when, in mid-afternoon, air-raid sirens warned of the imminent danger. The Royal Hospital's War Diary records the alarm sounding at 16.55hrs and In-Pensioners made their way to the shelters as raiders were seen approaching from the south.

The first wave of bombers headed to the docks in the East End, where 'the cannonade to the east was the heaviest yet heard'.[19] There followed a break as these first bombers turned for home and 'during a lull, the men were dismissed to their wards, but almost immediately the heavy firing was resumed'. A second wave now flew over central London to carry on the attack on the blazing warehouses, factories and offices in the Docklands. Houses crammed into every available space between the wharves and warehouses were also hit and soon the whole area was a blazing inferno.

The War Diary notes, 'About six o'clock great clouds of smoke were seen rising, in the east, to a height of about 6,000 feet. As night came on the glow of a great fire illuminated the sky, and made it easy to see the Hospital buildings.'[20] Across Chelsea, residents left their shelters to witness the 'red-orange glow in the sky' as the East End burned.

Theodora Fitzgibbon, sheltering in the Eight Bells pub on Chelsea Embankment with two drinking companions, emerged to see the sky 'the colour of a blood orange, a seething, flaming mass'.[21] Whereas June Spencer describes, 'The sky was bright scarlet and remained so all night. The windows of the houses were brilliant sparks of reflected light.'[22] In France, Reichsmarschall Göring 'telephoned his wife, telling her triumphantly, "London is in flames!"'.[23]

The raid was far from over, and the blaze in the East End provided a beacon to more bombers heading for London after nightfall. Attacks now widened out across the city, including the West End, as the Hospital's War Diary records:

> Alarm: 20.30 to 04.55. Great enemy activity all night. About 23.00 six or more bombs fell in the Chelsea Barracks area [...] tea was issued as usual at 01.00 hrs [...] later a really big bomb was dropped on the western bay of Battersea Power Station. There was a big blaze as high as the building, but it soon died down. The electric lights in the shelters became dim after about five minutes, and eventually went out for a few minutes. During this time the emergency lighting was brought into use. About 02.00 hrs a Guards officer arrived from Chelsea Barracks to report that one of the bombs dropped earlier in the evening had been found there. As it might be a time bomb they proposed clearing one barrack block. After surveying the Burton Court shelter he returned and reported ample room for his men there.[24]

Finally, the sound of the last bombers faded into the distance in the early hours of 8 September, and 'towards dawn the pungent smell of burning wood was faintly perceptible' as In-Pensioners emerged from their shelters.[25] Daylight on this Sunday morning meant 'the glow was diminished' from the fires still blazing in the East End.[26] The All-Clear sounded a little before 5 a.m. and this first mass daylight raid had resulted in 300 civilian deaths and over 1,300 seriously injured, the overwhelming majority of whom were in the crowded shelters and tenements of the East End.

At the Royal Hospital, the only casualty of the night was I/P Delon, on duty as one of the Hospital's ARP orderlies, who 'fell down in the cellar below the Great Hall steps, hitting his head' and suffering concussion. He was taken to the Hospital's infirmary on a stretcher.[27]

Half an hour after the All-Clear sounded 'a dull explosion indicated that one of the bombs which had been dropped about six hours earlier had gone off'.[28] Delayed-action bombs and unexploded ordnance would be a constant feature of the Blitz, and with an all-out assault on London now under way, there would be no respite even as clean-up and rescue operations began.

The day after this first big raid, the War Diary notes, 'Alarm 12.30 to 13.20', followed by another big overnight raid, 'Alarm 20.00 to 05.35. Great enemy activity all night, machines passing from west to east, one after another with few breaks. No bombs dropped near the Royal Hospital.'[29]

Although the Royal Hospital escaped unscathed, bombs had fallen across Chelsea and the borough suffered its first major tragedy. Cadogan Shelter in Beaufort Street received a direct hit, resulting in many fatalities as the blast blew the sides of the public shelter in on its unfortunate occupants. Beaufort Street runs parallel to Danvers Street, and ambulances from AS22 were promptly on the scene. June Spencer was on duty at the station and describes the aftermath, 'Between 70 and 80 were killed but 35 were alive. Daphne Catt and Irene Briggs took them to hospital. At the office I made quite 80 cups of tea I should think during the night. There was no gas or water.'[30]

The following day, a mobile rescue squad assisted by popular local doctor Dr Richard Castillo was still retrieving bodies from the Cadogan Shelter when a hit-and-run raider appeared unexpectedly over Chelsea. It had been attacking anti-aircraft barrage balloons south of the river when it was itself pounced on by a patrolling RAF Spitfire, causing the panicked pilot to jettison his remaining bombs as he fled across Chelsea. The Hospital's War Diary relates the incident:

> Alarm: 17.10 – 18.25. At about 17.45 an enemy machine apparently tried to bomb a balloon to the south-west. The alarm bells were immediately rung, but before all the men had taken cover, three or four bombs were dropped to the north. One fell in the area of an empty house in St Leonard's Terrace opposite the Porters Lodge (at the entrance to Burton Court), and another in Smith Street near Woodfall Street, cutting the gas and water mains. The blast was felt in the Office of Works Yard. I/P Robinson, in rushing to gain his trench, fell over [...] in Infirmary Court, damaging his nose. He was taken to the nearest First Aid Room by the Long Ward Sister.[31]

Although the Royal Hospital was again unharmed in this latest raid, tragedy once more visited Chelsea as one of the jettisoned bombs hit the home of Dr Castillo as he was out working at the Cadogan Shelter incident. His wife, daughter and son, who were at home at the time, were presumed dead in the rubble of their destroyed house. Dr Castillo returned as local warden Jo Oakman, a doctor's daughter and acclaimed local painter, was joined by the Heavy Rescue squad searching desperately through the ruins, which had been reduced to ground level as the building collapsed into its basement.

There seemed little hope of finding anybody alive. As digging continued into the night, the Royal Hospital's War Diary records another overnight raid, 'Alarm: 20.35 to 05.45: Bombing was on a smaller scale than on the previous two nights. One bomb fell in the King's Road.'[32]

Despite the presence of patrolling RAF fighters, German bombers appeared to be operating with impunity, and the apparent lack of any effective defence against them was taking its toll on civilian morale. As the bombing intensified, the pre-war fears about the bombers inevitably getting through were seemingly being realised. But the question everybody was asking, as Faviell put it while venting her anger to her husband Richard, was 'Where are our anti-aircraft guns?'[33]

Lieutenant General Pile and Anti-Aircraft Command had not been sitting idly by since the first attack on 7 September.[34] Frantic orders had been despatched to every anti-aircraft unit in Britain to release any guns they could possibly spare – and more. In the days since these large-scale attacks on London had started, mobile anti-aircraft guns of all calibre had been streaming into the capital.

The morning after that first devastating raid, June Spencer shared tea with her ambulance crew colleagues and after attending a church service at Chelsea Old Church, headed back to her accommodation at Lindsey House, near Battersea Bridge. As she walked alongside the river, she noticed, 'There was a lovely sky and against it coming over the bridge, a line of great guns on carriers and lorries'.[35] In little more than forty-eight hours, Pile doubled the available anti-aircraft guns in London, and with ammunition stockpiled at the new batteries now stationed across the capital, they were ready for action.[36]

With the additional batteries in place, the order was given that on the night of 11 September all guns were to open up with everything they had. The objective – to throw as much at the enemy planes as possible.

At the Royal Hospital on the morning of 11 September, the Governor met with a representative of the Office of Works to discuss an increasingly pressing issue. The previous day, during more raids on Chelsea, In-Pensioners had again been slow in reaching their allotted shelters and it was obvious that they were simply unable to cope with the constant physical pressures being placed upon them. The War Diary thus notes:

> The Governor saw the Office of Works architect and arranged for bunks to be put up in the cellar shelters. The previous night the occupants of Nos. 1, 2, 9 and 10 Long Wards had been allowed to remain in their bunks for the first time, on condition that lights are kept switched off, doors and shutters of berths closed and no movement in the Wards. All the men, without exception, elected to remain in their bunks instead of going to the shelters.[37]

Despite the danger, In-Pensioners simply wanted a good night's sleep, and they could not get one while constantly interrupted by air-raid alerts. Also, by allowing some to stay in their berths and fitting bunks into the cellar shelters for the remainder, In-Pensioners were no longer forced to spend extended periods in the trenches that had been dug in the Hospital's grounds. A consequence of this move was that 'the Command Post was removed from the Beer Cellar to No. 3 Trench (East side of Chapel Entrance), North Terrace'.

While officers manned the command post on the North Terrace, In-Pensioners would now all shelter either on the ground floors or the cellars below the main Hospital buildings.[38] This was despite the pre-war fears expressed in the confidential report of May 1938 that the roofs were 'easily penetrable by any type of projectile' and 'the floors of the main wards are so fragile from their age and lack of supporting cross walls, that, if the upper part of the building collapsed, the whole would go right to the bottom floor'.[39] In short, the Hospital's buildings represented a likely death trap, should they receive a direct hit.

But In-Pensioners could no longer endure the constant scrambling between their wards and designated shelters during the seemingly endless air-raid alerts. It was now over four weeks since the first sustained alerts had begun in mid-August, and they desperately needed some respite.

While the new sheltering arrangements were being implemented, a raid reported in the afternoon was the first to face the improved London defences, 'Alarm 15.20–16.40: After about half an hour, heavy AA fire was observed to the East, South East, South and South West, and some distant machine gunning heard. Aeroplanes could be seen at a great height, twisting and turning, apparently an enemy formation being broken up.'[40] The additional gun batteries had clearly given the Luftwaffe something to think about.

The main event, however, was saved for the evening raids when the guns, as ordered, opened up with everything they had, accompanied with the sound of cheering from air-raid shelters across the capital. Frances Faviell notes with undisguised excitement that as the big guns pounded away at the raiders overhead, 'The noise was appalling – but the effect on [...] morale [...] was miraculous! "Now they're getting it! They'll shoot 'em down now!" [...] Joy greeted the angry bark of the guns.'[41]

At the Royal Hospital, as In-Pensioners observed 'Lights Out' for what they hoped would be their first decent night's sleep in weeks, the War Diary records the raid:

Alarm: 20.35–5.35: Enemy machines kept passing over almost continuously all night, but practically no bombing was heard in the Chelsea area. For the first time our AA guns opened up a regular barrage; many batteries previously concealed were in action. There were occasional lulls, during one of which cocoa was issued.[42]

As London's fightback started, In-Pensioners settled into their warm bunks with a mug of steaming hot cocoa and drifted to sleep to the background accompaniment of the terrific barrage, laid on courtesy of Anti-Aircraft Command.

The following morning brought a new optimism to London as the sound of the previous night's barrage 'had a great tonic effect on the morale of the population'.[43] Frances Faviell, out shopping, met Suzanne Fitzgerald and the two women compared notes on each other's tin helmets, which everybody was obliged to carry now that air raids were a constant threat. Suzanne had followed the lead of the Royal Hospital's

Roman Catholic chaplain in sporting an elegant French helmet, which in her case had belonged to her brother in the 1914–18 war.

Grim reminders of the present war were not far away, however. Digging was still ongoing at the ruins of the Castillo family home, destroyed by the jettisoned bomb from the hit-and-run raider on 9 September. The bodies of Dr Castillo's wife and young son, also called Richard after his father, had been recovered but after three days of tunnelling, the Heavy Rescue teams had still found no trace of his daughter, Mildred. The Hospital's War Diary for the evening of 12 September reports, 'Alarm: 21.10–5.45: Some bombs dropped in Chelsea during the night, but activity was less than on previous nights'.[44]

On the morning of 13 September, four days after the bomb had collapsed the Castillo house into its basement, members of the Heavy Rescue team heard a faint cry of 'Mama!' among the debris. Miraculously, although buried up to her neck in the rubble of her home, 12-year-old Mildred Castillo was alive and conscious. For four days and four nights she had somehow survived in the darkness and devastation around her, and as word now spread that she had been located, alive but buried, Chelsea held its breath.

It would take seven and a half hours of digging and shoring up with blocks of wood as a tunnel 30ft long was dug to reach the little girl, but eventually she was brought out alive, to be reunited with her father. Such courage and fortitude would be needed by many in the months ahead, but Mildred Castillo's story made a deep impression throughout the Borough of Chelsea, encouraging its residents to never give up – there was always hope, however desperate the situation.

During the evening of 13 September, the Luftwaffe returned to Chelsea, visiting a new terror on the embattled residents through the indiscriminate use of incendiary bombs. These weapons were 35cm-long magnesium-alloy tubes filled with an incendiary compound called thermite. On contact, an igniter needle was driven into a percussion cap, igniting the thermite and, in turn, the magnesium casing, producing a heat source capable of melting steel. They were dropped in wire baskets, referred to as 'bread' or 'grad' baskets, which would burst open after falling clear of the bomber, spreading their lethal cargo over a wide area.

The wooden roof spaces, internal walls of the Long Wards' berths and oak floors and staircases throughout the Royal Hospital meant the threat of fire was an ever-present danger and incendiary bombs had been anticipated. Hand-operated stirrup pumps were located throughout the Hospital grounds, with ladder and crawler boards placed on roofs to facilitate easy access in the event of incendiary bombs becoming lodged among tiles or guttering. Staff and able-bodied In-Pensioners formed fire-watch teams, patrolling the Hospital's buildings and grounds.

This night would represent the first serious test of the Royal Hospital's fire-control precautions. The War Diary describes the raid:

> Alarm: 21.00–05.30: About 20.15 [sic] a number of incendiary bombs were dropped over the Royal Hospital and adjoining parts of Pimlico. Two or three fell in Burton Court, 3 on the North and 2 on the South Terrace, 1 in the West Road, 3 or 4 in Light Horse Court, 2 or 3 in the Burial Ground, 2 in the In-Pensioners gardens. Two that hit the extension to the rear of the Secretary's Office were extinguished without much damage, by the Assistant Secretary, Officer Keeper and Clerks.[45]

Assistant Secretary Maurice Fitzgerald and his deputy, Mr Fry, on duty in their designated shelters in Light Horse Court and the North-East Wing, witnessed the incendiary bombs falling and immediately moved to extinguish those which hit the Hospital. One, however, hit the south-facing roof of the buildings, out of sight of their shelters, and consequently was not immediately noticed:

> Another bomb which lodged in the [...] Secretary's house, facing south, was not noticed for upwards of half an hour and some water damage was done to the house and No. 20 Ward in putting this fire out. The A.F.S. [Auxiliary Fire Service] was called by telephone and sent some trailer pumps, but it was not required.[46]

Having successfully tackled the fires in the Hospital, the War Diary goes on to note, 'A fire in the attic of Burton Court Mansions was noticed and reported to the Town Hall (Control Room). Fires also occurred at the Duke of York's HQ and in the Pimlico Road.'

This was the first significant incendiary attack on Chelsea, aimed at overwhelming the Auxiliary Fire Service (AFS) and as such, it presented a major test of the Royal Hospital's staff and their fire-control procedures. The Hospital's disciplined and efficient performance during the raid was noted at the subsequent weekly board meeting:

> In the course of the bombing raid on London on the night of Sept 13th 1940, upwards of 18 incendiary bombs fell on the Royal Hospital, of which two started fires at the Secretary's office and one at the Assistant Secretary's quarters. The fires were successfully extinguished.[47]

It was estimated that around 250 incendiary bombs were dropped on the Hans Town District, starting several fires, including one at a club at No. 51 Lower Sloane Street necessitating the evacuation of '13 ladies [...] who were accommodated in the Board Room for some hours at the request of the Borough authorities'.[48]

The following day, the Luftwaffe returned to dropping high-explosive bombs, albeit from a greater altitude than previously, given the scale of the anti-aircraft fire they now faced. The War Diary identifies Battersea Power Station as the primary target of this attack, 'Alarm: 15.50–17.10: In this afternoon's raid several large bombs were dropped around Battersea Power station, and for some hours afterwards a large volume of white smoke was observed coming from the middle of the roof.'[49]

Inevitably, the surrounding area suffered collateral damage, including the Royal Hospital and adjoining streets, 'a house at the southern corner of Royal Avenue was hit, and three other bombs fell in Burton Court, of which two were time bombs'.[50] These resulted in the evacuation of Hospital staff and their families from their accommodation in the lodges by the entrance gates to Burton Court. The public super-shelter constructed by the council during the Munich Crisis and extended during 1939 also had to be evacuated:

> Both Park-Keepers had to remove: their families being lodged in the Board Room and fed from the Great Kitchen. The public shelters in Burton Court have been temporarily closed, but the RAF balloon crew was carrying on. This attack developed quickly before all the pensioners had got under cover.[51]

Since the heavy anti-aircraft barrage of 11 September, the Luftwaffe had met only scattered RAF fighter resistance, in part due to adverse weather hampering interceptions. Reichsmarschall Göring optimistically assumed that the unremitting pressure was finally beginning to tell on exhausted RAF pilots, particularly No. 11 Group, covering the south-east. Consequently, another large-scale attack on London was ordered for Sunday, 15 September; but this time, the weather favoured the defenders, and the RAF was ready. Spitfires and Hurricanes of No. 12 Group, based in East Anglia, were able to join the battle alongside No. 11 Group, sweeping into action in a mass counterattack dubbed the Big Wing.

The psychological impact on German pilots of the RAF fielding such overwhelming reinforcements after months of sustained pressure was devastating, and Luftwaffe losses outnumbered the RAF's by three to one. The scale of the RAF's response was matched by the ferocity of its pilots, and none more so than in one of the most celebrated incidents of the Battle of Britain, played out in the skies to the north-east of the Royal Hospital.

Around midday, Flight Sergeant Ray Holmes, flying his Hawker Hurricane on patrol over London, intercepted a Dornier Do 17 bomber, which promptly tried to escape in the direction of Victoria Station. Firing at the German raider, Holmes closed on the bomber, but having been in action earlier in his patrol, he soon exhausted his remaining ammunition. Pressing home his attack, he rammed his Hurricane through the rear fuselage of the Dornier, the impact breaking off its tailplane, forcing both the Luftwaffe crew and Holmes to bail out of their stricken aircraft. In Chelsea, the Royal Hospital's War Diary records the incident:

> Alarm: 11.50 to 12.55: Machine gun fire was heard faintly, and an aircraft seen to fall to the north. Two parachutists were seen falling, one to the north-east, another to the east, over Victoria. A few minutes later two others were seen falling beyond the Battersea gas holder.[52]

The overwhelming success of the RAF meant 15 September would be immortalised as Battle of Britain Day, and as Hitler cancelled Operation Sea Lion, there would be no invasion of Britain in 1940. Henceforth, the

Luftwaffe was charged with breaking the fighting spirit of the British through sustained terror bombing, while the Kriegsmarine would starve the country into submission, using its surface raiders and submarines to enforce a naval blockade. The Royal Hospital Chelsea would need to adapt once more to face these latest threats.

9

# The Blitz

*'... worthy of the highest traditions of the army.'*[1]

Following its failure to gain air superiority and Hitler's subsequent postponement of Operation Sea Lion, the Luftwaffe redoubled its efforts to break the will of the British people.[2] Towns and cities throughout the United Kingdom faced an onslaught from German bombers, with London singled out for a sustained campaign of terror. The Blitz would test the resolve of even the most resilient of residents.

Chelsea, one of the smallest boroughs at 660 acres, would suffer a greater tonnage of bombs per acre than almost any other London borough. The 66 acres of the Royal Hospital, containing some of Chelsea's most revered and iconic buildings and representing home for over 400 Chelsea Pensioners, would not be spared in the onslaught. An institution which, as a home for old soldiers, has always been associated with warfare would find itself in the line of fire for a sustained period in a way hitherto unknown. The Blitz represented an existential threat to the Royal Hospital on many levels and ultimately its survival would owe much to the courage and resilience of its occupants – and more than a little luck.

Despite the prompt response in extinguishing incendiaries, the Royal Hospital was powerless in the face of high-explosive bombs. At a board meeting on 19 September, which praised the response to the incendiaries on 13 September, it was also reported that at 'about 11.25pm on the

night of 17th, a large calibre H/E bomb fell on [the] roadway inside
Chelsea Gate and blew up the water main situated there. There was no
casualty.'[3] The War Diary describes this bombing in some detail:

> Alarm: 20.10 to 05.55: An active night, though with long lulls. Several
> bombs appeared to fall in Chelsea. At 23.25 a large one, probably
> about 500lbs hit the West Road almost exactly opposite the stable
> entrance, but just leaving room for vehicles to pass in and out. The
> crater is oval in shape, 35 x 25 feet and 16 feet deep. Stones and debris
> were hurled as far as the South Terrace, but surprising few windows
> were broken. Panes were broken in the guardhouse, stable yard, Office
> of Works buildings, N.C.O's room and the West Wing – also in No. 1
> Ormonde Gate. The gas and water mains were broken, but turncocks
> (Gas and Water Officials) were summoned, and there were no serious
> leakages. In the morning a fire broke out but was soon extinguished.
> Water to the Great Kitchen and houses is cut off, but the hydrants are
> still available.[4]

Remarkably, the gas and water supplies to the Great Kitchen were
restored in little more than twenty-four hours.

The packed agenda at the 19 September board meeting also commended the behaviour of In-Pensioners in coping with the challenges they now faced as the Luftwaffe stepped up its bombing campaign. The pre-war Anderson Report had recommended the evacuation 'on humanitarian grounds [...] of the aged and infirm' away from areas at risk of 'intensive air attack' with its associated 'nervous strain' and 'danger to life and limb'.[5] However, pre-war politics and the logistical difficulties of accommodating such a unique institution meant that most of the residents of the Royal Hospital remained in London, where they now endured almost nightly bombing raids. A board meeting minute headed 'Behaviour of In-Pensioners and staff in Recent Air Raids' notes:

> Lord Croft, Under Secretary of State for War, commended in the
> warmest terms the steady conduct of the In-Pensioners during the
> recent air raids. He also paid tribute to the staff and In-Pensioners for
> the manner in which they dealt with a large number of incendiary
> bombs which fell on the Royal Hospital on Sept 13th and which were

successfully extinguished. He considered that the conduct of the aged pensioners had been worthy of the highest traditions of the army.[6]

The Royal Hospital undoubtedly demonstrated resilience under the pressure it faced as the Blitz intensified and, in many respects, this reflected the general mood of defiance reported in Mass Observation surveys of this time.[7] The so-called 'Blitz spirit' is more than merely a propaganda myth.[8]

Nevertheless, the Hospital's War Diary alludes to a rather more nuanced impact of the Blitz on the In-Pensioner community than the 'Keep Calm and Carry On' account suggested in the Hospital's board minutes. The day after this board meeting, an entry in the War Diary on 20 September 1940 notes that an 'In-Pensioner … fell from an upper landing window of the East Wing into Figure Court, fracturing his skull. An open verdict was returned at the Coroner's inquest.'[9]

There are several questions raised by this entry, including why the author of the War Diary felt compelled to include it at all.[10] There is no mention of this incident in subsequent board meeting minutes and were it not for the War Diary entry, it would have passed unnoticed and unremarked in official records of the institution. It is also the case that as the Blitz intensified and bomb casualties mounted, there were no coroner's inquests held to ascertain causes of death of Blitz victims. They had been suspended under Emergency Powers legislation and deaths during air raids were usually simply reported as 'Killed by Enemy Action'. In this particular case, the Chelsea Coroner's Office confirmed that no coroner's report exists for his death.[11] Furthermore, examination of the 'upper landing window of the East Wing' suggests that it would be very difficult to accidentally fall from this point, given how high the window ledge is from the floor. It is, of course, possible that he may have climbed onto the ledge to get a better view of an unfolding air raid and perhaps lost his footing.

The In-Pensioner who died was a First World War veteran who had served with the Connaught Rangers throughout the 'war to end all wars'. He originally enlisted into the 2nd Battalion, which disembarked in Boulogne with the BEF in August 1914.[12] The battalion was subsequently engaged in the Battle of Mons and the associated retreat, the Battle of the Marne, the Battle of the Aisne and the First Battle of Ypres.

By this time, the battalion was so depleted it was amalgamated with the 1st Battalion, which subsequently took part in the Battles of Neuve Chapelle, Aubers Ridge, Festubert and Loos in 1915 before being transferred to Mesopotamia. Here, it was engaged in gruelling attempts to relieve the besieged garrison in the town of Kut.

This First World War veteran became an Out-Pensioner in 1920, before commuting his pension in 1935 when he entered the Royal Hospital. Now, due to the pre-war failure to evacuate able-bodied In-Pensioners from the Royal Hospital, he once more found himself in the line of fire.[13] As air raids increased in frequency and intensity, the residents of the Royal Hospital were not only exposed to physical danger, but also to increased mental and psychological strain. It is impossible to say with any certainty what led to this I/P's death, and an 'open verdict' may well have been returned had a coroner's inquest been held. Clearly, the circumstantial evidence points to at least the possibility that the physical and mental strain the In-Pensioners were under during the Blitz was such that at least one may have chosen to take his own life.

As the physical and psychological pressures of the Blitz unfolded, the option of overseas evacuation continued to offer potential salvation, albeit only for a privileged few. Soon enough, even this increasingly divisive and controversial policy was all but abandoned as events on the ground intervened. On 18 September 1940, an evacuee ship carrying ninety children to safety in Canada, SS *City of Benares*, was torpedoed and sank with heavy loss of life, including seventy-seven child evacuees.[14] News of this tragedy quickly led to demand for overseas evacuation evaporating. Included among the victims was Chelsea artist and art teacher Sybil Gilliat-Smith, who, like June Spencer, had signed up as an Auxiliary Ambulance Driver but had subsequently resigned, when, unlike June, she was accepted as an escort for accompanying children to Canada. Spencer mentions the incident only briefly in her diary – there but by the grace of God ...[15]

Throughout September, the Hospital's War Diary records a constant stream of air-raid alerts and as a result, on 26 September, sleeping accommodation was prepared in the cellars for an additional '40 persons', although it is unclear if this entry refers to In-Pensioners or staff and their families.[16] The following day, 'two small bombs fall in the South Grounds without doing any damage'.[17] Across Chelsea Bridge Road, however, the soldiers of the Guards Division were less fortunate when 'a large bomb hit the canteen in Chelsea Barracks, causing 8 deaths and other casualties'.[18]

The anti-aircraft batteries nevertheless frustrated many attempted raids:

> A formation of eight bombers was seen approaching the Royal Hospital from the South East surrounded by puffs of anti-aircraft shells. In view of the scale and imminence of this attack, the In-Pensioners were sent down to the cellars, instead of the trenches [...] as they emerged from the Long Wards. Anti-aircraft fire split the formation; four bombers moving West and the remaining four returning on their tracks: no bombs were dropped.[19]

In early October, despite numerous air-raid alerts, the only sightings of planes were a couple of 'reconnaissance machines' spotted on 1 and 2 October, prompting an order that 'the spotting officer was only to ring the Royal Hospital alarm bells if an air attack in some force seems to be imminent and not if the hostile planes are few in number'.[20] This relative lull in air activity provided a welcome respite, during which essential repairs were carried out on damage caused in previous incidents.

The 500lb bomb which had hit the West Road on 17 September, severing the gas and water mains, had also severely damaged the sewer. This resulted in a blockage which could now be cleared when:

> ... during the day a pump was got into action by the London County Council to remove drainage from above the obstruction in the West Road sewer, caused by the large bomb some days ago. This obstruction had caused the area of the Sergeant-Majors and neighbouring apartments to become flooded with drainage. The smell is very oppressive.[21]

Repairs were also completed on the Embankment to the south of the Hospital grounds.

After a welcome respite, the bombers returned, initially with the intention of hitting specific targets. Recently reinforced anti-aircraft batteries in Battersea Park were singled out for attention when on 11 October the War Diary records, 'a stick of four bombs fell in or near

Battersea Park, and the blasts broke a number of windows facing the South Terrace, Nurses Home, Infirmary and a few in Infirmary Court'.[22] At lunchtime the following day, another hit-and-run raider followed up the attack as 'a single machine, apparently a fighter, passed overhead about 12.45 apparently coming from the direction of Dover Street, where bombs were dropped. It dropped a further two bombs across the river, apparently in Battersea Park'.[23]

The Luftwaffe returned in force on the night of 14–15 October when, during bombing which appeared more indiscriminate than the hit-and-run raids of the previous couple of days, 'Flossie', the barrage balloon in the South Grounds was hit:

> At 22.45 a bomb (about 200lbs) fell just east of the Chillianwala Obelisk, overturning and setting fire to the RAF winch lorry, and smashing the crews wooden hut. The balloon afterwards broke adrift. The crew was unhurt as they were occupying the public trenches on the Embankment, but their sentry had to be treated in the Infirmary for shock. About ten minutes later two time bombs fell to the west. One, which was not detected at the time, exploded at about 7am, making a large crater beside the yard in the South Grounds. The bomb which may have been about ¼ ton, torched the hut occupied by the RAF balloon crew as living quarters. Three of the airmen who were in the hut at the time had miraculous escapes. The smaller bomb broke over 100 windows on the South Front and in the two Wings [...] the smaller crater is about 15ft in diameter, the larger 30 feet.[24]

The following morning while the RAF crew attempted to retrieve 'Flossie', Royal Hospital staff assessed the damage from the overnight raid and made emergency repairs where possible, all the time interrupted by constant air-raid alerts. Chelsea residents, such as Frances Faviell, marvelled at the quiet efficiency with which the Hospital would get to work immediately after every raid, regardless of the risks and dangers from the subsequent alerts. Throughout Chelsea, the streets were strewn with the remains of houses that had been reduced to rubble, but by stark contrast, at the Royal Hospital, pavements were quickly swept clean, damaged roofs rapidly covered over, and salvageable bricks and tiles painstakingly collected for use in future restoration works.[25]

The confidential report of May 1938 had recommended evacuation as the 'best solution' for the Royal Hospital, in part because it was recognised that the seventeenth-century principal buildings of the institution were wholly unsuitable for withstanding air attack. As such, the Hospital faced a very real existential threat during the Blitz as it could quite literally disappear into a mountain of rubble at any moment. Despite this sobering reality and the acute personal danger faced by staff and In-Pensioners alike, there remained a grim determination to ensure that the institution would come through this darkest hour and rise again. To this end, as Faviell describes, running repairs are a constant feature of the archive records throughout the Blitz, in the expectation that the Hospital would ultimately survive. The Royal Hospital's archives record in detail the repair work undertaken during the war and the more extensive repairs planned for when the institution was no longer in the line of fire.

As darkness fell on 15 October 1940, the bombers returned once more to Chelsea. Flares were dropped to illuminate the evening's targets, with Battersea again singled out for attention. The district was home to London's largest power station and now hosted significant anti-aircraft batteries in Battersea Park:

> Alarm: 19.30 to 05.10: Very active night up to about 3am. About 19.45 a flare was dropped over the Royal Hospital, but no attack followed. Later a big fire was started across the river, downstream and lighting up Battersea Power Station. About 00.10 four bombs fell in that neighbourhood, others further off to the west and north.[26]

Although the flare recorded earlier had been dropped over the Royal Hospital, Battersea Power Station and the anti-aircraft batteries in Battersea Park were the principal targets. Inevitably, however, the inexact nature of Second World War night-time bombing meant collateral damage to surrounding areas was inevitable. The War Diary describes the events of the night as they unfolded:

> At 01.50hrs two or possibly three bombs fell near the Infirmary. One, computed to be 100kg hit the coping, scraped the brickwork, came through the wooden roof, and penetrated the ramp of the Infirmary

entrance in the West Wing. The other was not noticed until later. Colonel Nash (Physician & Surgeon) and Captain Lockley (Capt. of Invalids) who were first on the scene closed the two adjoining ground floor wards, removing the patients to the basement. On his arrival shortly afterwards the Lt-Gov held a conference, decided the bomb had not exploded and decided to evacuate the Infirmary. Every able-bodied man was pressed into service, police, fatigue-party, stokers and other Office of Works men, and some local A.R.P. Wardens who volunteered their assistance. The patients, about 40 in number, were led or wheeled over to Infirmary Court, 19 of the fittest being placed on mattresses (which were brought over from the Infirmary on trucks, wheelchairs, etc) on the floor in the Board Room. The 18 more feeble patients (all unable to walk) were placed in bunks in No. 2 Ward. The men displaced from their bunks lay on the floor in No. 1 and No. 2 Wards for the remainder of the night. All this was accomplished in two hours; everyone working with a will. During the first hour bombs were continuously being dropped in the neighbourhood and the barrage was heavy. There was a full moon, and that and the fire in Battersea lit up the roads, etc, thereby facilitating movement. About 4am Grice, the fireman reported a small crater in the road midway between the mortuary and Infirmary. An official from the Borough's Engineers Dept. decided this was also an unexploded bomb. About 06.15 the fireman found a third crater in the tennis courts.[27]

This was the heaviest and most serious raid the Royal Hospital had experienced thus far during the Blitz. An addendum to the War Diary notes, 'The Germans claim to have used 1,000 planes and to have dropped 1,000 tons of bombs on London. Two Land Mines (parachute mines) were dropped on Pimlico, one of which, with its parachute was clearly visible from the Royal Hospital as it fell.'[28]

At daybreak on 16 October, with the infirmary patients safely out of the building and temporarily billeted in the Board Room and Long Wards, 'quantities of medicines, foodstuffs, etc were retrieved from the infirmary by Captain Lockley and others'.[29] This salvage operation was accomplished despite the risks from the unexploded bombs.

In the afternoon, as air-raid alerts again sounded, 'a sergeant of a Bomb Disposal Section, Royal Engineers inspected the three bomb holes, and pronounced two of the bombs to be 100kg, and the third, on the tennis courts, of 250kg'.[30] The infirmary would be out of use until the Bomb Disposal teams were able to safely dispose of the three UXBs, while in the interim, infirmary patients would have to share Long Ward accommodation with able-bodied In-Pensioners.

This dangerous overcrowding, with infirmary patients sleeping in wholly unsuitable Long Ward berths while their regular occupants slept on the floor beside them created serious challenges for the nursing staff treating the bedbound patients. It also quite clearly presented the potential for a catastrophic loss of life should the Royal Hospital be hit again while these temporary arrangements were in place. The Hospital had been lucky that the bombs currently lying in and around the infirmary site had not exploded on impact; next time could be different.

As night fell on 16 October, air-raid alarms sounded at 19.05hrs. Mercifully, however, the night of 16–17 October was 'a pouring wet night, with very little enemy activity'. Nevertheless, despite this meteorological intervention, another suspected 100kg bomb hit the South Grounds. This latest bomb failed to explode and was discovered the following morning during the regular sweep of the grounds.

Delivery vehicles which had been diverted to using the gates in the South Grounds were switched back to using Chelsea Gate near the Soane Stable Yard despite the bomb crater from the earlier 500kg bomb still not having been filled in. Trucks and delivery vans had to drive around it as best they could.

At a board meeting on 17 October, Note 7 records the 'Evacuation of the Infirmary [...] as a precaution against the possibility of subsequent explosion' and records that infirmary patients were being temporarily housed in 'the Board Room and certain Long Wards'. These temporary measures could not be sustained for long, however, and the infirmary needed to be brought back into use as a matter of urgency. Consequently, Note 7 goes on to report a letter written by the Governor to General Sir Alan Brooke KCB, DSO, Commander-in-Chief Home Forces, explaining how the UXBs had necessitated 'the hurried evacuation of all our sick old men' and pointing out 'how difficult it is to carry on without our Infirmary'. The letter continues:

> I write to ask if you could put in a word which will assist Group 1 who are in charge of the disposal of the bombs, to expedite matters [...] there must, of course, be difficulties with regard to priority, and if you could assist, I would be more than grateful.[31]

The Royal Hospital worked closely with Civil Defence across Chelsea, and the Commissioners had thanked all who had helped evacuate the infirmary. For the Governor to try and secure special treatment for the Royal Hospital, despite acknowledging the sensitivities of trying to jump the queue with the Bomb Disposal teams, who at this time were facing a significant increase in incidents reported to them, is indicative of quite how vulnerable the Hospital felt while the infirmary was out of use and In-Pensioners were doubling up in Long Ward berths.

The inclement weather continued, reducing the number of air-raid alarms but also slowing the work of the Bomb Disposal teams. Nevertheless, and perhaps with some help from the Governor's letter, the War Diary reports that on 21 October, 'During the morning an Officer from a bomb disposal unit surveyed the three bomb holes near the Infirmary' and, after inspecting the hole in the South Grounds, determined it was caused by a 'dud' anti-aircraft shell.[32] The bombs which had straddled the infirmary were all discovered to be 250kg, and over the following several days were each defused without detonating.

After what had been a tense ten days, on 26 October, 'patients were removed back to the Infirmary from No. 2 Long Ward and the Board Room'.[33] This was the most serious incident the Hospital had faced thus far in the Blitz and could have caused serious damage and potentially catastrophic casualties among In-Pensioners and staff. The Royal Hospital had a lucky escape.

Not everybody in Chelsea had been as fortunate. As the death toll of air-raid casualties rose, so too did the number of bombed-out residents. Each morning, after a night spent in shelters, many sadly discovered they no longer had a home to return to and would instead report to the War Comforts department in the Town Hall. Here, they would receive emergency cash payments, a hot meal and warm clothes; often all they had left was what they were wearing. This short-term relief provided immediate succour until the displaced moved in with friends or family and started the laborious process of claiming longer-term support from central government funds to help rebuild shattered lives.

As the Blitz intensified, however, the council's War Comforts team was overwhelmed by the demands placed upon it. The mayor, Lady Clare Hartnell, consequently wrote to the Governor, seeking the Royal Hospital's support:

> Dear Sir Harry,
> It has been suggested to me that it might be possible for the Commissioners of the Royal Hospital to give us sorely needed help in the matter of accommodation for the Chelsea War Comforts Depot which, owing to the distress which has fallen on the Borough, is at the moment very difficult to arrange [...] I realise that it would entail great sacrifice [...] but if you could see your way to helping us we should be unboundedly grateful.[34]

Despite the Hospital's own problems, the Governor responded immediately, enclosing 'a formal letter giving the approval of the Commissioners to your War Comforts Depot being housed in our State Drawing Room'. The council's welfare team subsequently moved into the State Apartments to continue their relief work.[35] This public-spirited gesture, undertaken despite the Hospital's own pressures, was simply one example of a system of mutual support between the Royal Hospital and Chelsea Council. It would later memorably be described as Chelsea's very own version of 'Lend–Lease', the wartime supply-and-support arrangement agreed between Britain and the United States.[36]

As the weather improved, In-Pensioners moved back into the infirmary on the afternoon of Saturday, 26 October, during which the War Diary records air-raid alarms between 12.50 to 13.45; 13.50 to 14.15; 15.10 to 15.25 and 16.10 to 16.25hrs. As the patient transfers were completed, and despite the constant alerts, the Royal Engineers finished emptying explosives from the final bomb, when at 18.35hrs alarms again sounded, marking the return of the German bombers.

The first hours of this latest night raid passed without incident until, at fifteen minutes to midnight, with Battersea Power Station again the intended target, a pilot released a string of four bombs. Overshooting their target, the first bomb exploded in the Royal Hospital's grounds, narrowly missing the surface shelter constructed in 1939 for motorists caught in the open on the Embankment. The second detonated between the Chilianwalla Memorial and the South Terrace, causing the searchlight and barrage balloon crews to dive for cover. The third bomb hit the north end of the East Wing accommodation block, where it joins the Colonnade, while the fourth failed to explode as it landed on the tennis courts in Burton Court.[37]

Bomb number three in this string of four was the first high-explosive bomb to hit the Hospital's principal buildings. The confidential May 1938 pre-war planning report had recommended the complete evacuation of the Royal Hospital, in part because it was feared that if the Long Ward accommodation wings were to receive a direct hit 'the floors of the main wards are so fragile from their age and lack of supporting cross walls, that, if the upper part of the building collapsed, the whole would go right to the bottom floor'.[38]

Despite some previous near misses, the night of 26–27 October 1940 was the first time the main Hospital buildings had received a direct hit. Miraculously, the bomb exploded at the one point in the building which contained cross walls – in the stairwell at the north end of the Long Ward where it joins the colonnade. The War Diary describes the impact:

> [...] High Explosive bomb on the north-east staircase of the main building [...] in the darkness it was difficult to ascertain precisely what had happened and the full extent of the damage was not assessed until the following morning. The two dormer windows over the staircase facing east were blown to the ground, with part of the roof. The staircase was completely smashed [...] The ends of the Long Wards next to the staircase were also badly damaged, particularly on the first and second floors, facing east [...] The blast of the explosion travelled through the Organists Quarters, blowing some shutters onto the North Terrace. Windows were broken throughout the East Wing, and in the Officers houses on the north side of Light Horse Court, and on the south side of the Chapel. Glass was strewn on the adjoining roads and courts and dust lay thick in all the East Wing wards. The bomb was thought to have been of about 50 to 100kg.[39]

By any account, this first bomb to hit the Royal Hospital's main buildings was not a large one in comparison to others dropped during the Blitz. Nevertheless, the pre-war warnings of the likely impact of such a projectile hitting one of the principal buildings were largely borne out by this incident. The bomb passed through the roof and exploded inside the stairwell, causing the oak staircases and landings to collapse as predicted all the way to ground level.

It was incredibly fortunate that the bomb hit the stairwell and hence detonated just to the north of the cross-wall, which divided the stairs from the Long Wards. This was the only cross-wall in the building, and had the bomb landed to the south of this internal wall, it would have exploded in the Long Wards proper, causing much of the building to most likely collapse. Once again, the pre-war assessments of the likely impact of war on the Royal Hospital – and the consequent need to evacuate the In-Pensioners – had been vindicated by experience and, once again, the Royal Hospital had been incredibly lucky.

The Hospital's luck in this latest incident also extended to a remarkable lack of serious casualties. The War Diary states, 'the men lying on the floor, or in the bunks, of No. 9 and No. 10 Wards were unhurt, though shaken'.[40] However, the East Wing was also home to four severely disabled In-Pensioners who had proven incapable of reaching the main shelters during the first air-raid alerts in September 1939. Consequently, a sandbagged shelter had been built on the ground floor beneath the lower-level staircase at the base of the stairwell. As the air-raid alarm sounded, these men had duly taken their place in this small shelter and the bomb subsequently exploded above them, causing the staircase and landings to come crashing down onto them. Rescuers arriving on the scene dug through the debris to find the 'small sandbagged shelter under the stairs was left undamaged, and four pensioners in it were unhurt, though covered in, and blinded with, dust'.[41]

Given the damage sustained by the East Wing, In-Pensioners were 'instructed to use their air raid shelters in lieu of their bunks' and these now became their berths until repairs could be completed. Both Office of Works personnel and outside contractors helped with the clean-up operation, the War Diary noting:

Two lorries with H.M. Office of Works demolition gangs, arrived and barricaded off the damaged part of the building. They also effected an entry by ladders into the Organist's Quarters and No. 22 Ward and retrieved some personal effects [...] Mowlem's, a contracting firm began moving debris. The gardeners were employed in sweeping up glass in Figure Court, and Office of Works of all trades in boarding up the Long Ward windows of the East Wing.[42]

October had clearly been a bad month. Ministry of Home Security figures across the country counted 6,334 killed and 8,695 injured or admitted to hospital.[43] At the Royal Hospital, however, despite the challenges they faced, staff and In-Pensioners alike continued to display the stoicism and 'conduct [...] worthy of the highest traditions of the army', praised by Lord Croft. In doing so, they provided an inspirational example for their fellow Chelsea residents.

Frances Faviell records how her close friendship with the Fitzgerald family brought her comfort during the Blitz when, after terrible sleepless nights of bombing, she would head to their home in the Royal Hospital grounds to invariably be offered breakfast porridge and a hot mug of tea or coffee. Recounting the events of the nightly air raids, she marvelled at the compassion, dry humour and quiet efficiency of Maurice Fitzgerald and his fellow officers as they selflessly went about caring for the In-Pensioners in their charge, regardless of the horrors they faced. Their spirits seemed resolutely unbreakable.[44]

# 10

# A Winter of Bombs

*'... London can take it.'*[1]

'Alarm: 18.45 to 02.10hrs – At 19.00hrs there was a heavy explosion from a bomb in Shawfield Street.'[2] This is the only entry in the War Diary for an otherwise uneventful night at the Royal Hospital on 1 November 1940.

Along Royal Hospital Road, Frances Faviell put on her Volunteer Aid Detachment nursing uniform as she prepared to leave for the FAP in Tite Street to begin the nightshift. The inclement weather of mid-October had returned, but despite the overcast skies the anti-aircraft batteries were already in action against the first of the night's raiders. Suddenly, 'one tremendous thud shook the whole house [...] plaster fell from the ceiling', and as she ventured outside to investigate, Faviell notes, 'beyond the fact that the sky behind Cheyne Place seemed full of a haze which I took to be the first November fog, I could see nothing unusual'.[3]

Shortly afterwards, she was called to St Luke's Hospital because a neighbour had been rushed there after being taken seriously ill. With rain starting to fall, she decided to take a shortcut through Shawfield Street to the King's Road. Hurrying through the dark night, she describes what happened next, 'It seemed to me that the curious cloud of mist or fog which I had noticed behind the Royal Hospital Road was as thick as a blanket – so thick and dark that it was difficult to see'. Fumbling for her masked blackout torch, she tried to make sense of her surroundings:

It was so small a light that it revealed little, but I saw what the cloud was – it was dust, a great cloud of dust which was still rising in spite of the rain – rising from what appeared to be a great gap in Shawfield Street where a row of tall houses had stood.

Stumbling across a terrified woman whose clothes had been ripped off by the blast, Faviell realised they were 'standing on the edge of a vast crater – it loomed on every side seemingly never-ending – and the houses which had stood on that piece of ground had simply vanished!'[4]

Although the Royal Hospital had again got off lightly, November had started badly for the Borough of Chelsea. This was the biggest bomb to hit the borough so far during the Blitz and nine houses in Shawfield Street were destroyed, with another twenty so badly damaged they had to subsequently be demolished. Remarkably, despite the devastation, only twelve residents were killed, with six seriously injured and a further half a dozen treated at the FAP in Tite Street for light injuries.

Ominously for In-Pensioners, however, it was clear that this scale of devastation was visited upon houses built considerably later than the seventeenth-century Royal Hospital, with each consequently having load-bearing external walls and containing numerous internal cross-walls. It hardly bore thinking about what would happen if a similar-sized bomb scored a direct hit on either the East or West Wing Long Ward accommodation blocks. In-Pensioners had been lucky in October when a much smaller bomb had destroyed only the stairwell of the East Wing, but how much longer could the Hospital's luck continue?

The following day, rescue and recovery work continued in Shawfield Street, while a Bomb Disposal team worked on disarming the UXB which had hit the tennis courts in Burton Court the night the East Wing staircase was destroyed. Amid this clean-up activity, the Royal Hospital hosted a delegation of war correspondents. The visit was for propaganda purposes and is reported as such in the War Diary, 'A party of about 50 foreign and dominion journalists was conducted round the Royal Hospital, mainly to see bomb damage, at the insistence of the Ministry of Information'.[5] A board meeting on 7 November gives further details:

A party of 50 Foreign, Empire and British Journalists accompanied by representatives of the Ministry of Information, visited the Royal

Hospital on Saturday 2nd November 1940, to inspect and photograph damage resulting from recent raids. The party was received by the Lieutenant-Governor.[6]

Regardless of the failure to evacuate the Royal Hospital despite the recommendations in the Anderson Report, the government was quick to recognise the propaganda potential of publicising the experiences of old soldiers who once more found themselves in the line of fire. A letter from the Ministry of Information dated 4 November subsequently thanks the Royal Hospital for hosting the journalists, claiming, 'The resulting publicity in the Press and over the wireless was entirely due to your help', before adding, the Ministry 'very much hope that you will be spared any more bomb attacks, and that any future visit for which we may have to ask will be on a happier occasion'.[7]

The visit was part of a broader propaganda campaign conducted by the Ministry of Information aimed at swaying public opinion in the United States by depicting the impact of the war on non-combatants. The campaign included a short film denoting eighteen hours of the Blitz on London, in which ordinary Londoners commute home in the evening to face the horrors of the night, before calmly heading back to work the following morning. The film, *London Can Take It*, was widely distributed across the USA and a shortened version played in cinemas to a domestic audience in Britain, titled *Britain Can Take It*.

The heavy rain which had fallen on 1 November eased a little during the journalists' visit before returning on 3 and 4 November when London was subjected to torrential downpours. Although the wet weather reduced the number of air-raid alerts, it also created problems of its own as the War Diary notes, 'Owing to heavy rain for 36 hours, the walls of the concrete trenches were rendered too damp for occupation (except in one or two cases) and the pensioners were detailed to lie down on the ground floor of the Long Wards'.[8] Once again, the Hospital authorities were forced to make uncomfortable choices between having the In-Pensioners disperse into damp and unhygienic shelters or concentrating the old men into over-crowded wards in the main Hospital buildings and risking calamity should a ward receive a direct hit.

As warm autumn days gave way to a cold and wet start to winter, damp air-raid shelters became a constant source of trouble. The War Diary reports only partially successful efforts to improve the situation in the shelters, 'The work of widening the seats in the trenches was completed, so that they can be used as bunks. Only five trenches are occupied at present, the others having been condemned by the Physician & Surgeon on account of damp.'[9]

Early in the Blitz, Long Ward nursing staff had been reporting on the unusually high number of coughs and colds among In-Pensioners, which they attributed to long hours spent in overcrowded and stuffy shelters. Now the damp conditions caused by the early winter weather were taking a toll on the health of the frail and elderly residents. There is some evidence in the Hospital's Record of Deaths archives to support the observation that the extended time spent by In-Pensioners in shelters during the Blitz led to an increase in the winter death rate. In the six months from October 1940 to March 1941, forty-eight In-Pensioner deaths were recorded of which nine were attributed to pneumonia.[10] The corresponding data for the six months between October 1939 and March 1940 is twenty-four deaths, of which only three mention pneumonia.[11]

Unhealthy air-raid shelters were not the only difficulty faced by the In-Pensioners as the nights began to draw in. The effectiveness of the blackout regulations and their diligent enforcement by ever-vigilant ARP wardens again led to a spiralling casualty list from road traffic accidents. In-Pensioners who on 18 September had been allowed to switch to blue winter uniform earlier than usual, 'in order to prevent their Scarlet coats being soiled in the air-raid shelters', were invisible to motorists as they returned to the Royal Hospital after a night out.[12] On 19 October, 'In-Pensioner W. Stanley was knocked down and taken to St Luke's hospital suffering from minor injuries', while the following evening 'In-Pensioner M. Downs was knocked down by a bus and killed when crossing the Royal Hospital Road near Chelsea Gate after dark'.[13]

The casualty list continued to grow as the days got shorter, 'In-Pensioner Walker was knocked down by a car in the Royal Hospital Road about 6pm' on 3 November. Road traffic accidents were exacting a greater toll on In-Pensioner ranks than direct enemy action. A further hazard faced by the In-Pensioners came from friendly fire when, on the same day that I/P Walker was knocked down, another In-Pensioner was hit 'in the hand by a fragment of Anti-Aircraft shell'.[14]

The Royal Hospital's location meant that it was always destined to be a particularly dangerous place during the Blitz, given its proximity to key infrastructure assets, but the challenges faced by the In-Pensioners extended beyond those simply caused by enemy attempts to destroy these important targets in the neighbourhood. The central location of the Royal Hospital remained the main threat to its residents and on the night of 7–8 November, Chelsea Bridge was again targeted. The alarms rang at 18.55hrs, with the raid continuing until 3.15 the following morning. Flares were dropped to illuminate the surrounding area at 19.00hrs and again at 20.30hrs and bombing soon followed. As In-Pensioners and staff sheltered in the few serviceable air-raid shelters or on the ground floor of the Hospital's buildings, 'a stick of bombs fell to the south-east [...] straddling Chelsea Bridge' – which emerged unscathed from beneath huge columns of water thrown up by the detonations.[15]

The Luftwaffe returned the following evening when, on the night of 8–9 November, 'about 19.30hrs four flares were dropped along the river' as the bridges were again targeted. Despite the War Diary's assertion that 'no special activity followed', the Royal Hospital inevitably suffered collateral damage from being located so close to these perennial targets. One bomb, estimated at 50kg, exploded in Ranelagh Gardens, destroying a slit trench dug by the Guards and damaging part of the Hospital's boundary wall, while suspected bombs or anti-aircraft shells landed in the burial ground and 'close to the garden wall of Chelsea Embankment Gardens, opposite the Nurses House'.[16] (The disturbed ground near the nurses' quarters was, however, later found to be the result of subsidence caused by the constant explosions in the neighbourhood.)

Remarkably, despite the nightly bombing raids and the increasingly apparent inadequacies of its air-raid shelter provision, the Royal Hospital had somehow managed to avoid any direct casualties from air-raid attacks. However, this was not true of the wider Chelsea Borough and after a low-key Remembrance Day on 11 November, the War Diary for the following day contains a seemingly innocuous entry, which underplays the horror of another terrible night of the Blitz in Chelsea:

> Shortly before 22.00hrs a heavy bomb was dropped on Sloane Square Station. All the Hospital's telephones connected with the Sloane Exchange were put out of action. The night was unusually clear, with a very bright moon, and enemy activity was above normal.[17]

Frances Faviell was not on duty on this evening, but as the recent damp weather had resulted in the usual seasonal increase in coughs and colds among her fellow volunteer nurses, she had offered to go in to the FAP if needed. At 10.30 p.m. her phone rang, and she was asked to report for duty at the Royal Court Hotel in Sloane Square. Arriving a short time later, she describes the scene at the site of the Underground Station, 'Two great flaming jets guarded the pit which had once been the station. The bomb had severed the gas main [...] and the newly built station had just disappeared into the depth below.'[18]

Sloane Square Underground Station was modernised in the 1930s, with new escalators installed between the ticket hall and platforms. It received a direct hit just as a train was pulling out of the station. The rear carriage received the full force of the blast, with the remainder of the train blown along the tracks almost to the next station at South Kensington. Thirty-five passengers and staff were killed, with a further seventy-nine injured.

Raids on London reduced significantly during the second half of November as the Luftwaffe targeted other areas of the country. This lessening of activity is noted in the War Diary, where an entry on 21 November records, 'The past week has been unusually quiet, both by day and night, possibly owing to the enemy having transferred his attentions to the Midlands'.[19] The Royal Hospital took full advantage of the lull to complete further repairs and improve the state of the air-raid shelters.

Apart from the occasional sighting of a hostile machine, the respite lasted for around two weeks before attacks resumed on 29 November, with the bridges over the Thames and the anti-aircraft batteries in Battersea Park again targeted. The Royal Hospital once more suffered the inevitable collateral damage:

> At 19.15hrs a stick of four bombs fell, two in the Thames and two in Battersea Park, between the tennis courts and the river. Though the bombs were apparently only 50kg the blast broke a number of windows on the South Terrace, and in all three Courts. Up to midnight the enemy was more active than for two weeks past, and a number of bombs were heard falling in the distance.[20]

While the Luftwaffe recalibrated its terror-bombing campaign against British cities, the Kriegsmarine stepped up attacks against

Allied shipping. In early November, the heavy cruiser *Admiral Scheer* slipped undetected into the North Atlantic where on 5 November, it surprised Convoy HX84, inbound from Halifax, Nova Scotia. An overstretched Royal Navy could only provide the armed merchant liner HMS *Jervis Bay* as an escort to the thirty-seven merchant ships in the convoy. Hopelessly outgunned, she nevertheless engaged *Admiral Scheer*, sailing directly at the surface raider and bravely firing her pre-First World War guns, despite being out-ranged by the modern 11in main armament of her opponent. A sailor on one of the merchant ships described the engagement:

> Hardly had the *Jervis Bay* turned than she was hit and fire broke out. As the convoy split up and fled fanwise to the east and south, dropping smoke flares as they went, they watched this flaming torch still steaming against the adversary, still firing.[21]

The unequal contest lasted less than half an hour, but the brave sacrifice of the *Jervis Bay* bought vital time for the convoy to disperse and only five merchant ships were subsequently sunk.

However, commerce raiders were only one of a growing number of threats facing Britain's maritime supply lines. The capitulation of France made the length of her Atlantic coastline available to the Kriegsmarine, and U-boats were soon operating from submarine pens in Brest, Lorient and La Rochelle, wreaking havoc among poorly defended convoys.

As autumn gave way to winter, supply issues became an increasing feature of the Royal Hospital's management board meeting minutes, while food and rations begin to feature ever more prominently in personal diaries. On 27 September, June Spencer refers to walking 'down the King's Road to Sainsbury's to get my rations', while by early October, food has become such a preoccupation that when invited out to dinner, 'she listed exactly what she had been served'.[22] Although winter storms offered some cover to beleaguered convoys, the impact of the Atlantic War was becoming ever more acute.

During December 1940 the Royal Hospital's luck continued to hold. On 8 December, the Luftwaffe was again very active over Chelsea and the War Diary records:

Great activity from 18.00 to 03.30hrs. About 21.30 a stick of three bombs fell in the Tedworth Square area, the smoke drifting across the West Wing. Shortly afterwards, another stick of three bombs fell. The first, a time bomb or dud, fell on the North Terrace, penetrating the brick culvert that runs the whole length of the building. This was not found until daylight the following morning. The two other bombs fell to the South-West; one has not been located, while the other hit the Victoria Hospital, penetrating to the basement where it failed to explode. Almost simultaneously with this stick a number of incendiaries were dropped, at the bottom of Ranelagh Gardens, along the line of the path; also on the Embankment and in Battersea Park. They burnt out harmlessly in about five minutes.[23]

Victoria Children's Hospital was the site of the FAP where Frances Faviell was stationed. She was at home on the night of 8 December, but as she reported for duty early the following morning, she was met at the entrance by the sister in charge and told to take her shoes off so as not to risk waking up an overnight visitor. Thinking that a child casualty had been brought into the FAP, Faviell was instead introduced to the unexploded bomb referred to in the Royal Hospital's War Diary entry. Knowing that on the arrival of the Bomb Disposal teams the FAP would be evacuated until the UXB was made safe, the volunteer nurses bravely took turns to make one trip each into the surgery in order to remove all the medical equipment and medicines before the arrival of the Bomb Squad.[24]

Meanwhile, at the Royal Hospital:

A bomb disposal officer, Capt. Robson and the Deputy Borough Engineer, inspected the hole in the North Terrace and concluded it to have been made by a 250kg bomb. This necessitated clearing No. 21 Ward; building a sandbag wall across the corner of the Great Kitchen by the larder door; closing the Beer Cellar and No. 1 Trench; and removing four In-Pensioners liable to heart attacks from the beer cellar shelter.[25]

With these precautions in place, the Bomb Disposal team got to work on disarming the weapon and rendering it safe. It took until 14 December for them to complete their work, during which there were thankfully no further air raids recorded.[26]

With Christmas approaching, there appeared to be a lessening in the pace of German air activity, although this period of relative calm was nevertheless punctuated with occasional Luftwaffe raids. On 21 December, an unusually large bomb exploded in Ebury Bridge Road, breaking windows throughout the Royal Hospital, especially in Light Horse Court.

An 'unexplained incident' on 23 December, requiring the evacuation of the nurses' quarters due to ground disturbance and partial subsidence, was eventually attributed to the earlier bomb in Ebury Bridge Road. During these investigations, previously undiscovered brick archways were uncovered beneath the surface of the Hospital's grounds. Unfortunately, there was no time to investigate these newly unearthed archaeological curiosities.

On Christmas Eve, multilingual Suzanne Fitzgerald, in her capacity as translator and mentor for the Belgian refugees in Chelsea, hosted a reception at the Royal Hospital. Invitations extended to all the borough's refugees who wished to attend, whereupon they shared refreshments and sang carols around a beautiful Christmas tree overlooking the river, in 'a lovely ceremony in a lovely room'. It was a poignant and nostalgic occasion as 'almost all the refugees were remembering other Christmases in their own countries'.[27] This selfless act of kindness and generosity was a particularly poignant occasion for Maurice and Suzanne Fitzgerald, as they celebrated Christmas without their eldest son. Named Maurice after his father, he had been commissioned in July 1940 before being posted to North Africa to join his regiment, the Sherwood Foresters.

For In-Pensioners and staff of the Royal Hospital, the Christmas church service was held in the chapel as usual on 25 December.[28]

With Christmas celebrations over and a new year soon to be ushered in, London suffered one of the most destructive raids of the Blitz. The great fire raid of 29 December was not the largest witnessed by London, for 'on at least five earlier occasions more incendiaries had been dropped'.[29] What made this raid particularly devastating was its timing. It was the first Sunday after Christmas, and the streets of London were empty. Offices, warehouses, Livery Company halls and even churches in the city were all locked and deserted as fire-watching crews celebrated the festive season at home with their families.

The vulnerability of the city was further increased by an unusually low tide, which severely constrained the abilities of fireboats to manoeuvre to tackle the blazes. Fire hoses were too short to reach the water and the resulting conflagration was the nearest London came to the firestorms which would later consume the great city of Dresden and much of the port city of Hamburg. With nearly 1,500 individual fires merging into two great blazing infernos, the City of London around the Bank of England and the winding streets of Paternoster, near St Paul's Cathedral, were razed to the ground.

As Livery Company halls and the heart of the capital's literary trade were engulfed in flames, the War Diary records the scene, 'Great enemy activity after dark, a large fire was caused in the City, lighting up the buildings around the Royal Hospital in a red reflected glow'.[30]

Nowhere in London was spared the basket loads of incendiaries dropped during the raid, including Chelsea and the Royal Hospital. The War Diary goes on to note, 'about 19.00hrs a single incendiary fell in Light Horse Court, on the grass opposite the Deputy Surgeon's quarters and was put out by the Home Guard'.[31] The well-drilled defenders of the Royal Hospital tackled this latest raid with the same well-ordered, quietly calm and efficient discipline displayed during previous incendiary attacks. On this night, more than any other during the Blitz, the pre-war failure to evacuate the institution may have had a silver lining. Unlike much of central London, Christopher Wren's home for old soldiers was not abandoned, empty and locked, as its residents, 'broken by age or war', continued to hold their ground.

As 1940 ended, the War Diary records, 'There have been 73 In-Pensioners on furlough over Xmas, a record number. The total number of In-Pensioners is also higher than it has been for many years, though still below the official establishment.'[32] This is an intriguing entry and one which is not easy to interpret. The Hospital was still running two cost centres: the main site in Chelsea and the outstation at Rudhall, which was still not accounted for separately and officially, therefore, did not exist, but was still home to around fifty In-Pensioners. Consequently, with more berths theoretically available

– the 558 in Chelsea and the fifty at Rudhall – it is not surprising that the total number of In-Pensioners was higher than it had been for many years.

The 'establishment of In-Pensioner [...] number of 558' for Chelsea does, however, have to be treated with some caution as a number of wards, particularly in the damaged East Wing were closed by December 1940.[33] Nevertheless, the Hospital was also still allowing Out-Pensioners to join the establishment provided they were already living in a 'risk area' rather than an evacuation-receiving area. This continued recruitment to In-Pension was particularly helpful to those old soldiers who had been forced to leave Public Assistance Institutions on the outbreak of hostilities.

Annual leave conditions had also been relaxed, allowing In-Pensioners with friends or family able to support them the opportunity to spend extended time away from Chelsea without having to revert to their out-pensions, thus forfeiting their berth at the Hospital. This may explain the significant number on furlough over Christmas. Despite the difficulties of interpretation, it is clear from this War Diary entry that despite the challenges the Royal Hospital faced during the Blitz, and indeed the war in general, it nevertheless continued to deliver its core mission of providing care and support for old soldiers during their twilight years.

The first management board meeting of 1941, held on 2 January, included the now familiar mountain of correspondence with the Hospital's suppliers. Every three months, typically in March, June and September and around the Christmas/New Year break, the Royal Hospital would review its supply contracts, noting performance against contract terms and making any adjustments deemed necessary. The archive files for these meetings contain copies of contracts and correspondence with suppliers.

Before the war, the files are quite modest in size and meetings follow a routine rhythm with few adjustments made each quarter. Where changes were made, they were typically due to fluctuating numbers on the roll-call of In-Pensioners, requiring an adjustment to quantities ordered. Occasionally, a change of supplier was required due to performance shortfalls, albeit warning letters were usually sufficient to help a supplier get back on track. During the war, however, these file notes expanded exponentially, driven by rationing, government price controls, supply shortages, delivery problems, bombed-out premises and a host of other factors which combined to produce a myriad of issues. These were challenges the Commissioners needed to continually overcome simply to ensure the three hot meals a day implicit in their duty of care towards In-Pensioners.

The pre-war Anderson Report had anticipated logistical difficulties caused by bombing raids and hence the need to evacuate 'useless mouths'. Throughout London, the Blitz created enormous practical problems for businesses forced into financial survival mode. In Chelsea, the borough's largest landlord, Cadogan Estates, would after each raid 'send its surveyor, Arthur Steward, to examine the damage and decide whether or not to carry out repairs' to the estate's commercial properties.[34] Cadogan soon found itself supporting a growing number of tenants who were falling into arrears during the Blitz, and despite the support provided an increasing number, having lost their livelihoods, simply 'decided that they couldn't continue to rent from the Estate any longer. It was quite usual for them to come by the Estate office and simply leave the keys of their property'.[35]

At the January 1941 management board meeting, a letter from a long-time wholesale supplier is typical of the correspondence received by the Royal Hospital during the Blitz:

> Dear Sir,
> We acknowledge receipt of your letter of the 13th instant respecting accounts and cannot understand how it is that our advices of alterations have not reached you. According to our books [...] we advised you of the alteration in the price of Rice [...] the prices of Sugar were altered by the Government [...] we advised you of the following [increases in price], Peaches [...] Pines [...] Custard Powder [...] Vermicelli [...] Salmon [...] Oatmeal [...] Herrings [...] We trust therefore that you will be able to pass the accounts as rendered.
> We may say that we very much regret the unusual delays in rendering accounts but owing to our offices having been destroyed, we have

been working under chaotic conditions for some time past and we must ask you to make allowances accordingly.
Yours faithfully
George T. Cox & Sons[36]

The forbearance required in dealing with the difficulties experienced by regular contractors was not the only supply issue the Royal Hospital had to deal with. The black market also created particular problems, and sometimes with tragic consequences, as evidenced by a poignant entry in the War Diary for 3 January 1941, 'Four of five patients in one of the Infirmary Wards have died, one on the 31st December and three on the 3rd January. They were all taken ill after Xmas, and it is thought that they must have consumed something brought in from outside.'[37] As with the death of the In-Pensioner who fell from an upper-floor window in the early days of the Blitz, there is no record of these deaths recorded in the board meeting minutes. Were it not for this entry in the War Diary, it would again be the case that a tragic incident would be allowed to pass unremarked and unrecorded. Throughout the Blitz, In-Pensioners faced not only the threat from air raids, but also the privations wrought on London from the terror-bombing campaign of the winter of 1940–41.

During January and February, there was a marked fall in the number of air raids, reflected in a reduced number of entries in the War Diary. The greatest threat to the Hospital's residents was from the exceptionally cold weather that marked the start of the new year, and on 11 January, 'Electric heating and lighting was installed in the six trenches on the North Front. Each unit consists of a radiator, fan and transformer.'[38]

The few German planes which were seen over Chelsea in these early months of 1941 sought out the usual objectives. Faviell records, 'The two power stations, Battersea and Lots Road, were the real targets, and the hit-and-run raids proved this – for the planes came astonishingly low and near to them.'[39] The bridges over the Thames were the other perennial target and one such raid is recorded as In-Pensioners left chapel after the Sunday service on 16 February:

Shortly after the Sunday morning service, an enemy aeroplane flew over the Royal Hospital, below the balloon barrage, low enough for the markings to be visible with the naked eye. It returned a minute or two later, straddled the Albert Bridge Road with a stick of bombs, and is said to have been shot down near Shoreham, Sussex.[40]

Despite the attentions of these hit-and-run raiders, the Royal Hospital took advantage of the reduction in mass bombing raids to again undertake repairs to the damaged buildings and grounds. The East Wing received some much-needed attention and the large bomb crater outside the Soane Stable Yard was finally dealt with:

> The Fatigue Party resumed possession of No. 17 Ward. A temporary wooden staircase has been made to connect the landings immediately above the passage communicating with the Colonnade. The crater in the West Road has been filled in, and the pavement made good. The shrubbery is now being replanted.[41]

Throughout London, life was slowly returning to some semblance of normality, and as the days grew longer with the arrival of spring, people started socialising more, swapping stories over coffee, or even dinner if the ration allowance could be stretched far enough. In Chelsea, Richard and Frances Faviell had grown close to the Fitzgeralds and had become regular visitors to the Royal Hospital. Maurice Fitzgerald would indulge Frances' artistic interest by showing her around the chapel and other interesting areas of the buildings and grounds, while Suzanne was always on hand with coffee and conversation in the family kitchen.

Their visits also extended to invitations for dinner, but despite the fall in the number of air raids, an evening meal was always at risk of interruption, as on one occasion when Richard found himself lending a hand with the fire-watching team shortly after the main course. Incendiaries had been falling throughout the neighbourhood but as the raid grew uncomfortably localised, gas masks and Suzanne's French tin helmet had to be donned as Maurice and Richard helped to deal with the unwelcome interruption, while the dessert waited on their return.[42] The War Diary describes just such an incendiary raid in early March:

> About 20.00hrs, after an early alert and great enemy activity, fifty to sixty incendiaries were dropped in the Royal Hospital grounds

– probably from two breadbaskets. The area affected was from the King's Road to the river, and from the middle of Ranelagh Gardens to Tite Street. There were six hits on buildings: (1) punctured the roof and fell on the floor of No. 17 Ward, where it was extinguished by two of the Fatigue Party who were just on the point of leaving the ward. (2) dropped down the shaft at the southern angle of the Octogon [*sic*] Porch. (3) lodged in the gutter over the cornice near the middle of the West Wing, facing Figure Court. (4) fell on the roof of the Stable Yard lodge nearest the Chelsea Gate. (5) stuck in the gutter over the Quartermaster's stores, facing Infirmary Court. The Superintendent of Works tackled it by going through the Physician & Surgeons quarters and removing a small sash window facing the gutter. (6) fell inside the bedding store. All the bombs, and many others burning in the open, were put out by different squads covering various areas. The damage was negligible.[43]

The well-disciplined fire-watch teams had again gone about the task of saving the Royal Hospital from an attack which had the potential to cause catastrophic damage to the fabric of the institution. Dealing with such incidents increasingly seemed routine for the residents of Chelsea, despite their potentially terrifying consequences, and air raids now simply interrupted dinner, with the result that dessert was taken a little later than originally planned.

On 19 March, the Docklands were raided, but as with the incendiary attacks, it seemed 'London Can Take It' was an increasingly pertinent epitaph for a terror-bombing campaign that appeared to be losing its potency. Even the high-explosive bombing raids were having noticeably less impact, for as the War Diary records:

> From 20.00hrs to after midnight, a continuous procession of hostile machines passed overhead without any intermission. The barrage was as heavy as any yet heard. The raid was on the Docks, and no bombs were dropped within earshot of the Royal Hospital, nor were any distant fires observed, as last September.[44]

At a board meeting the following day, it was again time to review the Hospital's supply contracts as the folio of correspondence continued to grow. No fish was available from the Hospital's regular fishmonger; brewers could only supply weak beer; coffee was only available in sufficient quantities for those In-Pensioners in the infirmary; and even Harrods was completely out of jam.[45] Increasingly, it would seem that the problems of securing essential supplies for the residents of the institution would henceforth be the major preoccupation facing the Commissioners and Officers of the Royal Hospital now that the Blitz appeared to have passed its most intense point.

The Blitz, however, was far from over.

In 1918, the North-East Wing of the Royal Hospital was severely damaged in a bombing raid which killed a Captain of Invalids and members of his family. (RHC Archives)

Air-raid trenches were dug on the North Terrace during the Munich Crisis in the autumn of 1938. Air-raid trenches for Chelsea residents were also excavated in Burton Court by Chelsea Borough Council. (RHC Archives)

2/6

This Deed is made the twelfth day of June One thousand nine hundred and thirty nine

BETWEEN WALTER EDWARD THOMSON MORLAND of Rudhall Ross on Wye in the County of Hereford a Major in His Majesty's Army (Retired) (hereinafter called "Major Morland") of the one part and THE COMMISSIONERS OF THE ROYAL HOSPITAL CHELSEA (hereinafter called "the Commissioners") of the other part

WHEREAS Major Morland is the owner of the freehold property known as Rudhall Ross on Wye in the County of Hereford

AND WHEREAS it is expedient that accommodation outside London should be provided for the inmates of the said Royal Hospital Chelsea in the event of a National Emergency

AND WHEREAS Major Morland has agreed to permit the Commissioners to occupy certain rooms in his house Rudhall aforesaid upon the conditions terms and stipulations hereinafter mentioned in the event of such National Emergency as aforesaid

NOW THIS DEED WITNESSETH as follows :

1. IN pursuance of the said agreement Major Morland hereby GRANTS unto the Commissioners while such state of National Emergency as aforesaid shall exist LICENCE and LIBERTY to enter upon and occupy the following portions of the said premises Rudhall aforesaid namely such part of the stables as shall be mutually agreed and the several rooms mentioned in the Schedule hereto and delineated on the attached plan and thereon coloured pink TOGETHER with a right of access to the same along the staircase and corridor and by the external doors mentioned in the said Schedule PAYING therefor a nominal sum of FIVE SHILLINGS per week and proportionately for periods less than a week for each and every person who with the authority of the Commissioners shall live in and occupy the said rooms such sum to accrue from day to day but to be payable on the first Monday of every month during such occupation and on the last day of such occupation

2. THE Commissioners hereby COVENANT with Major Morland as follows :

(a) To pay the reserved sum on the days and in manner aforesaid

(b) After any state of National Emergency shall have ceased to

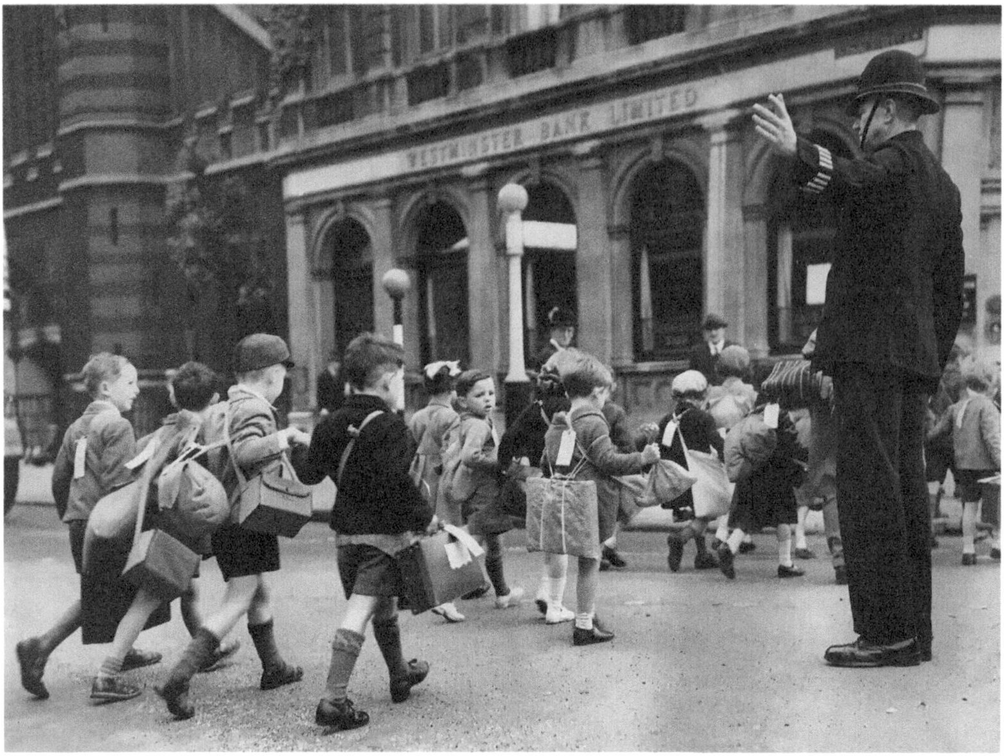

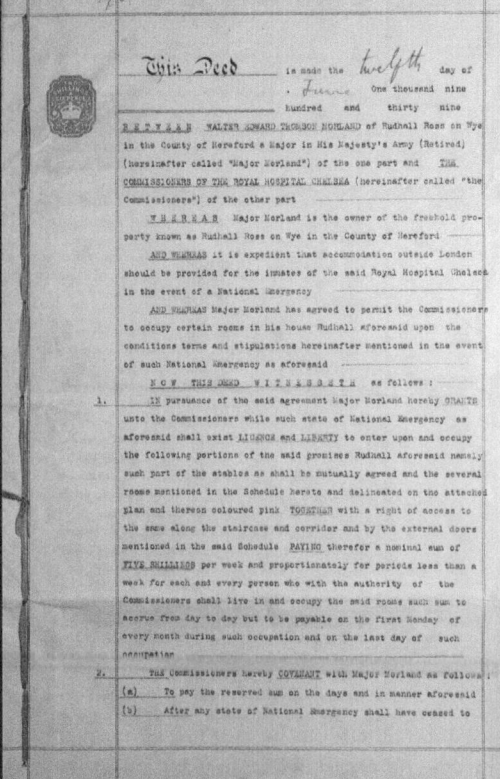

In June 1939, the Borough of Chelsea staged a practice Air Raid Precaution exercise to test the effectiveness of local Civil Defence forces. The exercise included a practice evacuation of local schoolchildren. (Associated Press / Alamy Stock Photo)

The Commissioners of the Royal Hospital signed a private agreement in the summer of 1939 for the evacuation of fifty In-Pensioners to the safety of the countryside in the event of an emergency. Government departments responsible for evacuation planning were not made aware of this arrangement until 1941. (RHC Archives)

The Munich Crisis of 1938 marked the end of the policy of appeasement. The Commissioners subsequently worked closely with Chelsea Borough Council to construct air-raid shelters throughout the Royal Hospital grounds for the use of In-Pensioners and Chelsea residents. (RHC Archives)

Kenneth Dean, son of Captain Charles Dean, in his gas mask and tin helmet. As the Royal Hospital prepared for war, In-Pensioners, staff and their families were issued with gas masks to be carried at all times. (RHC Archives)

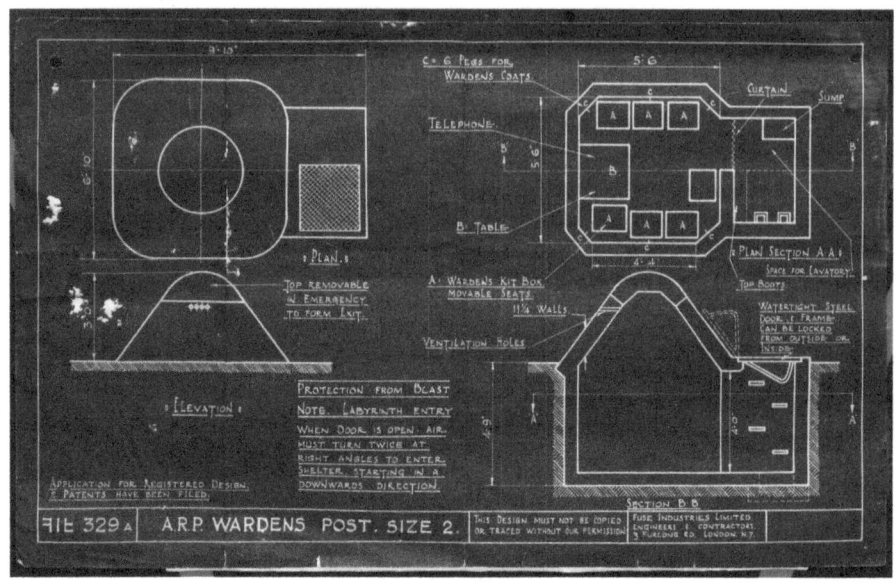

An Air Raid Warden's post, Post K, was established at the southern end of Royal Avenue. It comprised a sunken FUSE Industries control room, as in these plans, with a wooden hut above at ground level. Post K would go on to play a significant part in the Royal Hospital's war. (RHC Archives)

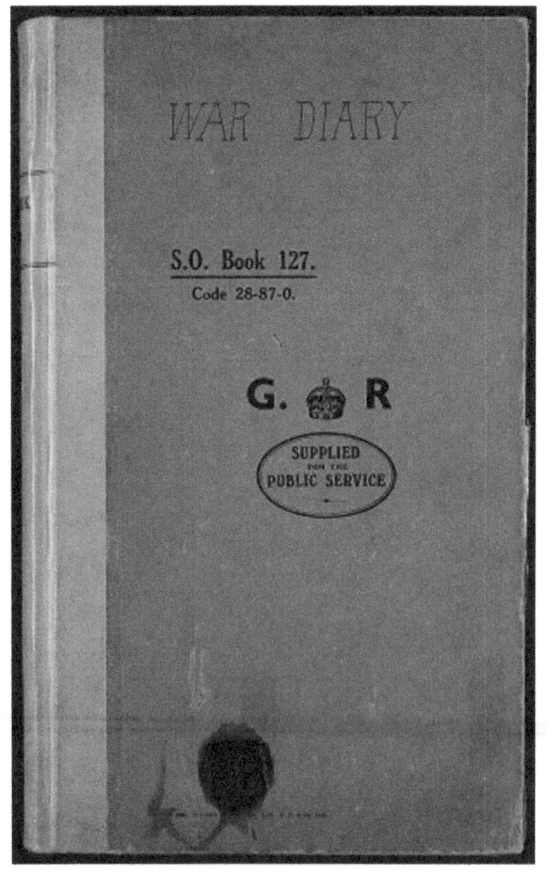

In August 1939, with war imminent, officers of the Royal Hospital started an unofficial War Diary. It contains a detailed day by day, hour by hour, and at times, minute by minute account of the Royal Hospital's war. After the war it was stored for decades in an attic at the Hospital. (RHC Archives)

On 2 September 1939, on the eve of war, fifty In-Pensioners were spirited out of London to the relative safety of Ross-on-Wye, Herefordshire. The Rudhall out-station would remain in operation throughout the war. (RHC Archives)

The discreet nature of the evacuation out-station at Rudhall required the provisioning officer, Senior Clerical Officer Albert Burke, to source all supplies from the Quartermaster's Stores in Chelsea and only buy locally as a last resort. (RHC Archives)

Evacuated In-Pensioners initially considered themselves the lucky ones. However, as the war settled into an uneasy calm, or Phoney War, the isolated location of Rudhall began to take its toll and by Christmas 1939, some of those evacuated had returned to Chelsea. (RHC Archives)

Throughout the Luftwaffe's bombing campaign against London, power stations and bridges were perennial targets. This image shows a bomber's-eye view of Battersea Power Station and the bridges over the Thames, including a temporary bridge built by the Royal Engineers. The Royal Hospital is visible in the background. (Historic England)

As the frequency of air-raid alerts increased and the Blitz intensified, In-Pensioners were constantly heading to their designated shelters, either beneath the Royal Hospital buildings or in trench shelters in the grounds. (RHC Archives)

On 17–18 September 1940, a large bomb severed the gas and water mains running under West Road, near the entrance to the Soane Stable Yard, putting the Great Kitchen out of service. This picture shows Canon Hogg and Captain Lockley inspecting emergency repairs. (RHC Archives)

After the first mass bombing raid on 7 September 1940, London endured fifty-seven consecutive nights of raids. In-Pensioners spent many hours in the Royal Hospital's air-raid shelters. (RHC Archives)

During a raid on 15–16 October 1940, three bombs straddled the Infirmary, one skidding off the roof and down the wall as seen in the photo above right. Miraculously, all three failed to explode. Over forty bedbound In-Pensioners had to be evacuated from the Infirmary as the raid continued overhead. (RHC Archives)

With In-Pensioners spending extended periods in the shelters, tea and cocoa rations were served at regular intervals during the longer air raids. (RHC Archives)

During the night of 26–27 October 1940, a bomb destroyed the East Wing stairwell. Four disabled In-Pensioners sheltering in a refuge at the base of the stairs survived as debris collapsed onto their sandbagged sanctuary. (RHC Archives)

With the onset of winter, trench shelters became unusable and deaths from pneumonia increased markedly. In-Pensioners living on the ground floor of the accommodation wings were allowed to remain in their berths, while bunks were installed in the cellars for the remainder. (RHC Archives)

Supply difficulties increased during the course of the war, with suppliers' premises bombed out and food increasingly scarce. Ration allowances were reduced and it became increasingly difficult for the Royal Hospital to provide for the In-Pensioners in its care. (RHC Archives)

Pre-war image of the infirmary showing the building before the destruction of the East Wing, which was hit by parachute mines on the night of 16–17 April 1941. (RHC Archives)

The parachute mines which destroyed the East Wing of the infirmary also caused extensive damage to the rest of the building. Bedridden survivors had to be carried from the blazing ruins at the height of the raid. (RHC Archives)

Chelsea Old Church, another iconic local landmark, was also destroyed in the raid on the night of 16–17 April 1941. The church was rebuilt after the war. (Associated Press / Alamy Stock Photo)

Reporter Wynford Vaughan-Thomas produced an early BBC outside broadcast as he interviewed survivors of the Infirmary bombing. The interviews helped raise awareness of the plight of the Royal Hospital and its Chelsea Pensioners. (RHC Archives)

An RAF reconnaissance Spitfire flew over Chelsea on a training flight on 18 June 1941. This picture shows the damage in and around the Royal Hospital. The barrage balloon flying above Burton Court is also clearly visible. (Historic England)

Anthony de Rothschild, wartime head of the banking dynasty, offered the use of his country home, Ascott House, as a replacement infirmary. Eighty disabled In-Pensioners were subsequently transferred, while Rothschild and his wife moved into an apartment above the stables. (RHC Archives)

Moraston House near Ross-on-Wye, owned by Guy's Hospital, was leased to the Royal Hospital after the infirmary bombing. It subsequently accommodated sixty In-Pensioners evacuated from Chelsea. (RHC Archives)

The Royal Hospital established a network of evacuation out-stations after the bombing of the infirmary in 1941. A system of unit rotation ensured In-Pensioners divided their time between the Royal Hospital in Chelsea and the relative safety of one of the out-stations. (RHC Archives)

With the evacuation of In-Pensioners after the infirmary bombing, much of the Royal Hospital was left deserted and abandoned. The infirmary ruins were demolished to provide hardcore for aerodrome construction. Railings were removed, with the salvaged metal used for war production. (RHC Archives)

In January 1945, the North-East Wing was destroyed by a V2 missile, causing further casualties among the remaining In-Pensioners and staff. More evacuations followed and the In-Pensioner population at Chelsea fell to a low point of only fifty. (RHC Archives)

By the end of the war much of the Royal Hospital was either destroyed or left derelict and abandoned. The number of resident In-Pensioners and staff had fallen to only a fraction of the pre-war total. (RHC Archives)

With much of the Royal Hospital site destroyed, derelict and abandoned, plans were considered for erecting prefabricated houses in Burton Court and Ranelagh Gardens. (IWM Collections)

As the Second World War ended, the Royal Hospital required significant rebuilding work before In-Pensioners could return. In-Pensioners returned from the out-stations as soon as accommodation was available. (RHC Archives)

A memorial erected in December 1946 in the graveyard of St Mary's Church, Ross-on-Wye, Herefordshire, commemorates Captain of Invalids William Lockley and twenty-two In-Pensioners who died while evacuated to Rudhall from the Royal Hospital Chelsea during the Second World War. (Author)

## 11

# The Bombing of the Royal Hospital's Infirmary

*'... ambulances urgently required ...'*[1]

Wednesday, 16 April 1941 was a beautiful spring day in Chelsea. It had been several weeks since any air raids had taken place, with Incident Reports recording numerous consecutive days of 'No Bombing throughout London Civil Defence'.[2] The nearest incidents to Chelsea had been a series of bombing raids on the London, Midland & Scottish (LMS) rail marshalling yards on the North End Road in Fulham, some four weeks earlier, on the night of 18–19 March.[3]

Chelsea residents, like their fellow Londoners across the capital, were beginning to think the worst was behind them and London had survived everything the Luftwaffe could throw at it. Therefore, the psychological impact of the raid on the night of 16–17 April would be even more pronounced. The scale, ferocity and duration of the attack itself was also unlike anything Chelsea had experienced up to this point in the Blitz, and such was the impact of this raid across London that in its aftermath, it would be known simply as 'The Wednesday'.

In the London Borough of Chelsea, the use by the Luftwaffe of several parachute mines during the raid would result in this attack inflicting particularly severe damage to the borough's buildings, and notably high casualties among its residents. These weapons were naval mines originally designed for use at sea, where they were deployed in major shipping channels or at the entrance to harbours with the intention of sinking passing Allied shipping. Early in the war in November 1939, one of the Royal Navy's latest warships, the cruiser HMS *Belfast* was struck by such a mine while exiting the Firth of Forth. The blast broke her keel and caused extensive damage which required a two-year refit before the ship could return to active service.

The parachute mines dropped over Chelsea were 2m-long cylindrical metal tubes, each containing 1,000kg of explosive charge, and were detonated either on contact with a target, in which case a twenty-five-second timer was activated, or by acoustic shockwaves usually caused by a ship sailing in close proximity, which triggered the mine to explode immediately. They had been used earlier in the Blitz, particularly in attacks on the London Docklands, but now they were to be used in some numbers against targets in the West End of London.

On the night of 16–17 April eyewitness accounts from Chelsea residents testify that the parachute mines were invariably dropped in pairs, although the bomb damage reports for the impacts of these 1,000kg monsters are confused and inconsistent, with some incidents treated as a single event, whereas other reports describe the separate impacts of each of the two bombs. However, the fact that these bombs were dropped in pairs over Chelsea is important when trying to piece together the sequence of events during the night and to assess the utterly devastating effect these weapons had at their point of impact.

The physical damage they caused, and the scale of casualties inflicted, were colossal compared to the other weapons used during the raid. Remarkable eyewitness accounts describe how, on reaching street level, one mine would hit either the ground or a building, thus triggering the twenty-five-second timer mechanism. The acoustic shockwave from the resulting explosion would immediately detonate the other mine. In effect, 2,000kg of high explosives were simultaneously detonated, laying waste to the surrounding area.

Both the Royal Hospital Chelsea and Chelsea Old Church, two of the borough's most iconic buildings, would suffer the appalling attention of these monstrous weapons during the raid. However, they were not the intended targets.

The same eyewitness accounts which describe the impact of the mines also provide information about the final seconds before impact, giving direction of travel and also suggesting a gentle rate of descent. The contemporaneous records from the eyewitnesses and the subsequent bomb-damage reports clearly indicate that the intended targets for the mines were almost certainly the key infrastructure assets in the neighbourhood, which again included the riverside power stations at Battersea and Lots Road, and the road and rail bridges crossing the Thames.

Bridges along this stretch of the river included the rail link into Victoria Station and the road bridges of Chelsea, Albert and Battersea Bridges.[4] The Royal Engineers had also built a wooden bridge across the Thames downstream from Albert Bridge, at the junction of Royal Hospital Road and Chelsea Embankment, linking Battersea Park on the South Bank to the Embankment on the north bank of the river.[5] This bridge was for military transport only and offered alternatives to the two permanent bridges, should these be damaged by air attack. It also provided resupply routes for the multitude of anti-aircraft guns now stationed in Battersea Park, as barges bringing ammunition along the Thames could be unloaded on both banks of the river with the ordnance quickly distributed among the gun batteries.

It was inevitable that the concentration of such important infrastructure along this short stretch of the river would attract the special attention of the Luftwaffe bombers, and it is equally unsurprising that they should employ the most devastating weapons in their armoury in attempting to eliminate these targets. However, given that at this stage of the Blitz German bombers were forced by the anti-aircraft barrage to drop their bombloads from anything up to 20,000ft, these were far from precision weapons. It was always likely that they would be dropped either too early or too late, thereby causing them to miss their intended target.

Nevertheless, had the Luftwaffe succeeded in hitting Battersea or Lots Road Power Stations, with what was effectively 2,000kg of high-explosive charge, they may finally have managed to put them out of action. Bombs which had successfully hit the power stations earlier in the Blitz had been too small to achieve anything other than superficial damage. The buildings were, after all, built of a standard to be able to contain a boiler explosion in the event of an industrial accident. They would need to be hit by something significant to cause any serious damage. The bridges, meanwhile, were some of the key central London crossing points for the Thames, and putting them out of commission would have caused considerable disruption to both civilian and military road and river transport.

Using a combination of archive sources, including the Royal Hospital's archives, bomb damage reports, ARP warden reports and first-hand eyewitness accounts, it is possible to piece together the events of this most significant night in Chelsea's wartime story, and in the history of the Royal Hospital. It can be seen how the various incidents throughout the night relate to each other and how the results of one bombing event impacted on the outcomes of subsequent incidents. Analysing the raid from the perspective of different sources also helps to explain some apparent inconsistencies in the account of the raid as described in the Royal Hospital archives.

Lights-Out at RHC on the evening of 16 April 1941 was at 20.00hrs and In-Pensioners and staff settled down in the hope and expectation of another quiet and uneventful night ahead. Along Royal Hospital Road at No. 33 Cheyne Place, Richard and Frances Faviell joined their neighbour Kathleen Marshman in welcoming home from honeymoon Kathleen's daughter Anne and her new husband, a Canadian soldier who had been billeted with them, Cecil Stainton of the Royal Canadian Army Service Corps. The young couple had arrived back in Chelsea happy and excited, and in the company of Cecil's army colleague, an American called Larry, toasts were drunk before the newly-weds disappeared upstairs to their flat.[6]

It being too late to cook, Richard and Frances instead walked to a local restaurant where, over supper, they talked with the owner, Madame Caletta, about the longer days, the quieter nights, the war in particular and life in general, before leaving after dark to walk the short distance home.[7]

Over in Cheyne Walk, June Spencer had a welcome night off from the recent tedium of her Auxiliary Ambulance Station (AAS) duties and headed up to the West End for dinner with an old friend, Sydney Cuthbert, whom she had not seen since before the war when they had skied together in Austria in 1937.[8]

It came as an unpleasant surprise, therefore, and something of a shock to everybody, when a little after 9 p.m. the wail of air-raid sirens was again heard across London.[9]

In-Pensioners who had recently returned to sleeping in their berths once more made their way to their places in their allotted air-raid shelters. The wives and children of staff living on site headed either to their family basement shelters or to the large above-ground shelter built by the Office of Works in the Artificers Yard beside the Soane Stable Yard, a short distance from the East Wing of the infirmary.[10] Members of staff and a number of able-bodied In-Pensioners took up their Fire Warden positions, while the nurses on duty in the wards of the infirmary checked on their respective bedbound patients.

Maurice Fitzgerald's daughter Denise made her way to Chelsea Town Hall to take her place in the Borough Control Room in the basement bunker.[11] Meanwhile, along Royal Hospital Road, Richard and Frances Faviell settled down in their studio lounge on the upper-ground floor of their apartment in Cheyne Place to wait and see how serious this raid would turn out to be.

In the West End, June Spencer and Sydney Cuthbert finished their dinner in the ARP wine cellar of the Barcelona restaurant in Beak Street, Soho, before moving on to the 400 Club in Leicester Square, intending to dance the night away.[12] Across London, ARP wardens once again settled into the methodical routine of checking the whereabouts of their air-raid shelter residents, reporting and logging incidents, and preparing to call for assistance should it be required.

The anti-aircraft batteries in Battersea Park were brought into action almost as soon as the sirens sounded. The earliest entries in the Chelsea ARP Incident Reports, however, simply record activity witnessed in neighbouring boroughs. At 21.28hrs, flares were recorded falling in districts south of the Thames, followed six minutes later by flares descending over the Lots Road Power Station to the west. At 21.40hrs, flares were again reported to the south, and five minutes later, more were seen floating down over Victoria.

Several eyewitness accounts for this early stage of the raid report on the difference in the appearance of the flares used when compared to previous raids. Faviell noted that 'huge flares – different to any which we had seen – were being dropped'.[13]

Part-time fire-watcher and War Reserve Policeman, Mr Cremonesi, a grocer living at No. 26 Old Church Street, joined the fire-watching party based at Chelsea Old Church to watch the novel display of flares, commenting, 'They were the biggest we had ever seen [...] like enormous chandeliers hanging over the river'.[14]

By this stage of the Blitz, the pattern of raids was well rehearsed, and the purpose of the flares was to illuminate the target areas for the following waves of aircraft carrying high-explosive bombs, which were soon falling across a wide area. Explosions were reported south of the river, while Lots Road, with its power station built specifically to supply the Underground Tube Network, was also attracting the attention of the bombers. The Chelsea Incident Report log noted explosions and fires in Victoria as the railway station and sidings were targeted.

At 22.35hrs, the Hans Town wardens reported seeing a large fire developing between their warden's post and Victoria Station. The noise was both deafening and continuous with several reports noting how the drone of aircraft engines above was constant and unremitting. This reflected the remarkable number of machines deployed by the Luftwaffe on this raid, estimated variously as between 450 and 700 planes, with many making multiple sorties as bombers in the first waves returned to their bases in occupied France, rearmed and were sent back to visit more death and destruction onto the streets of London.[15]

No incidents were reported in Chelsea during the first two hours of the raid. Frightened residents nevertheless had to cope with the noise, light and smoke filling the night from the attacks on neighbouring boroughs.

At the Royal Hospital, the chaplain, accompanied by Sister Christabel May, the senior nursing sister on duty, conducted his evening tour of the infirmary wards between 10 and 11 p.m.[16] Finding all but one of the more than fifty bedbound In-Pensioners sleeping soundly despite the raid, they stopped to talk with the ward sisters and nurses on duty. In Ward No. 7 in the East Wing, Sister Edith Taylor had settled her In-Pensioners for the night before the sirens had sounded and all were now blissfully unaware of the air raid unfolding above them.[17]

Sister Elizabeth Nicholson's patients were likewise asleep, and so she had taken her place in the little shelter she had made for herself beneath the East Wing staircase where, on this night, due to the intensity of the air raid, she found herself joined by Sister Edith McMullan.[18] Captain Townsend had tried on multiple occasions to get Sister Nicholson to go to one of the shelters once she had settled her In-Pensioners, but like the other nurses, she considered it her duty to stay with her charges in case she was needed – after all, she insisted, her little space beneath the stairs was probably as safe as anywhere.

At No. 33 Cheyne Place, Richard and Frances were becoming increasingly alarmed at the ferocity of the bombing and decided it would be sensible for them to move to their lower-ground floor, where they had taken to sleeping in the dining room during heavy raids. Frances phoned Kathleen, Anne and Cecil and begged them to move down from their top-floor flat to join them in the relative safety of the lower floor, but the young newly-weds in particular were reluctant to move, "'have a heart" laughed Cecil, "it's still our honeymoon – we've got two more days'".[19]

Denise Fitzgerald and her fellow Controllers in the Borough Control Room logged the first incident in Chelsea at 23.29hrs, when a report was filed of a flare seen hitting the ground near the Royal Hospital.[20] Given the time taken to phone through reports, incidents were typically recorded around 10–15 minutes after they occurred.

The flare had most likely been hit by anti-aircraft fire, and at around 11.15 it had crashed into the ground in front of Chelsea Gate, spilling its blazing contents and setting fire to the surrounding area, including the trees at the corner of Burton Court. The extraordinary size of the flares used in this raid meant the stirrup pumps and buckets of sand strategically placed around the Hospital would be insufficient to deal with the blaze and consequently the ARP wardens at Post K on Royal Avenue requested the AFS send an engine.

Frances Faviell witnessed the blaze erupt in Burton Court, and soon after she heard the fire engine from Station 6W, a few doors along Royal Hospital Road at No. 22 Cheyne Place, revving its engine. Auxiliary Firemen George Goldsmith, Alfred Haylen and Victor Wratten prepared to set off on the short drive to Burton Court for their first call-out of what was likely to be a long night. They would not get very far.

The AFS engine started out along Royal Hospital Road and as it did so, the first pair of parachute mines to hit the Borough of Chelsea during this terrible night floated gently down towards the ground. The Bomb Damage Reports indicate that the first mine landed in the area behind Cheyne Place, Caversham Street and the stretch of Tite Street to the north of the Royal Hospital Road, the impact activating the twenty-five-second fuse.[21] The second mine floated gently down into

Royal Hospital Road and was directly in front of Nos 27–33 Cheyne Place when the first mine exploded. The shockwave from the explosion immediately detonated the second mine. The crew of the fire engine, caught out in the open as the second mine exploded above them, didn't stand a chance and were killed instantly.

It was almost 11.20, and in the lower-ground floor of No. 33 Cheyne Place, Richard and Frances settled down to read as they tried to take their minds off the raid, but first, Richard thought he should check on the blackout curtains in the studio above to ensure they were secure.[22] He had barely stepped out of the door when the parachute mines exploded. The row of houses and flats along a 90ft frontage of Cheyne Place were caught directly between the two blasts as 2,000kg of high-explosives detonated. They simply disappeared in a cloud of dust, masonry, steel, glass and smoke as the buildings collapsed in on themselves.

Frances described what happened as she lay on her bed:

> There was a strange quiet – a dead hush, and prickles of terror went up my spine as a rustling, crackling, endless sound as of ripping, tearing paper began. I did not know what it was, and I screamed to Richard, '*Come down, come down!*' Before I could hear whether he was coming down the stairs, things began to drop – great masses fell – great crashes sounded all around me [...] I buried my face in the eiderdown of the bed as the rain of debris went on falling for what seemed ages ... ages.[23]

The huge double explosion when the mines detonated shook the ground as if an earthquake had hit Chelsea, and a few hundred yards along the street, the clock in the Quartermaster's Office of the Royal Hospital stopped at precisely 23.18hrs.[24] During the clean-up operations in the days after the raid, this clock would lead to some confusion at the Hospital as to the timings of events during the course of the night.

In the rubble of her wrecked home, Frances, with some difficulty, shook her head free of heavy, choking dust and as she did so, she felt the warm embrace of an arm around her neck. 'I thought that Richard had entered in the darkness and was holding me, but when very, very cautiously, I raised my hand to it, I found it was a woman's bare arm with two rings on the third finger and it stopped short in a sticky mess.'[25]

## The Bombing of the Royal Hospital's Infirmary

All the occupants in the flat above had been killed, and the dismembered arm lying across Frances' back was Anne's, the newly married bride, who had died instantly, along with her husband and mother. Richard, however, had miraculously survived, sheltered by the doorway at the bottom of the stairs, and he now called out to Frances, before lighting matches to give her some light as she slowly inched her way through the debris until he was able to grab her and pull her clear of the tangled, twisted wreckage.

They could smell gas as they scrambled over a mountain of broken glass, until finally they were standing in the Royal Hospital Road where, shaken and dazed, they surveyed the scene around them.

Both sides of the street were wrecked, and they knew people were trapped in basement shelters:

> The whole street was piled several feet high with glass and rubble. In the sky the light from fires was brilliant, it looked like Blake's picture of Hell [...] Fires blazed on every side, great masses of brickwork and masonry kept falling and falling, crashing into the already huge mounds, and the smell was like Guy Fawkes night.[26]

While Frances and Richard had been extricating themselves from the remains of their home, a bomb estimated in the subsequent Bomb Damage Report to be '250kg or larger', hit the nearby Elms Garage at No. 70 Royal Hospital Road, where the premises backed onto Paradise Walk.[27] It had exploded shortly after the parachute mines detonated, causing a crater 35ft across and 8ft deep. The garage and the adjoining properties were occupied by the Canadian Army as billets for service personnel and several soldiers were now trapped in the buildings as the garage caught fire. The trapped soldiers included Cecil and Anne's friend Larry, who would be pinned all night beneath the ruins of the house where he was billeted.

At the junction of Royal Hospital Road and Tite Street, a badly injured warden tried desperately to phone through a report. He was bleeding profusely but rebuffed Frances' attempts to help him, '"God, what a night!" he gasped', as he shouted to them to go to the Tite Street FAP.[28]

When the warden managed to get through with his report about the first parachute mine incident in Chelsea, it was relayed to the Borough Control Room and logged in the Incident Report at 23.32hrs:

District Warden, Hans Town reports cloud of black smoke near Royal Hospital Infirmary. Hit, Caversham Street – Tite Street. South part Tite Street badly damaged. Casualties trapped. Tommy Wallis says major incident.

This was followed at 23.40hrs with, 'Deputy District Warden, Hans Town reports casualties trapped, 25 Cheyne Place. Incident Officer on job.'[29] Rescue teams, ambulances and fire engines were immediately dispatched to the scene. The desperate situation unfolding on the Royal Hospital Road, however, was about to get dramatically worse.

Following shouted instructions from the ARP warden to go to the FAP, Richard and Frances turned into Tite Street in order to make their way to the FAP situated in the basement of the Victoria Children's Hospital, but as they did so, they 'saw two parachutes floating down in the direction of the river'.[30] The warden screamed at them to lie down and they threw themselves onto the glass-strewn road until 'after what seemed a lifetime there followed two long dull roars and then an appalling explosion'.[31] Picking themselves up, the couple rushed through the heavily sandbagged entrance and into the FAP. The scene inside 'was indescribable [...] Stretchers lay all over the floor awaiting ambulances and casualties were everywhere, humped on benches, huddled on chairs, lying on the floor'.[32] It was too much for Frances and she was suddenly overwhelmed by the enormity of what was happening:

> My legs gave way, and I sat down on a bench [...] Waves of terror came over me – each resounding crash of the bombs which were raining down sent fresh waves of awful sickening fear over me [...] I wanted the ground to open and swallow me up – to hide me from this fearful terror from the skies – it was a disgusting, degrading, nauseating feeling [...] I was literally petrified with terror.[33]

The floor of the FAP was strewn with stretchers as no ambulances were available to move the more seriously injured to hospital. More casualties were brought in, including Canadians from the Elms Garage bombing, with cuts and wounds from flying glass, while others had burns. Richard and Frances now heard from a warden who came in that the parachutes they had seen earlier had landed on the infirmary of the Royal Hospital and over forty In-Pensioners and nurses were trapped. Turning to Richard, the stretcher bearers implored him, 'Could you come and help us – we're overwhelmed.'[34]

The two parachute mines which hit the Royal Hospital descended on either side of the East Wing of Sir John Soane's infirmary building. The Bomb Damage Report treats the bombing of the infirmary as a single event, as does the Hospital's War Diary, and it is not clear which of the mines landed first. One floated down into the courtyard, where it dragged against the wall of the East Wing immediately outside Ward No. 7. The second mine drifted down to the east of the building, floating gently into the space between the East Wing and the back of the workshops running along the west side of the Artificers Yard.[35]

The 'two long dull roars' heard by Frances Faviell before the explosion are probably the result of one bomb being pulled along the wall of the infirmary, while the other dragged along the ground between the East Wing and the Artificers Yard. It is irrelevant as to which mine exploded first, as the shockwave immediately detonated the other bomb, and hence the single 'appalling explosion' reported by Faviell.

Shortly before the first mine floated into the infirmary courtyard, Sister May left the Duty Office and was walking across the Colonnade fronting onto the courtyard, running between the East and West wings of the building.[36] At this moment, Infirmary Orderly Marrable, stationed on fire duty in the Colonnade, 'saw the parachute and thinking it was a Boche bailing out, ran into the Infirmary Courtyard to tackle him'.[37] Seconds later, the two mines exploded, and the Royal Hospital's War Diary describes the moment of detonation:

> There was an extremely heavy explosion, without previous warning, evidently from a land mine. Clouds of dust filled the air, debris fell within a 300 foot radius of the Infirmary. The East Wing [...] was completely demolished, a large crater occupying the site. The remainder of the Infirmary was badly damaged, the roof being removed. So also was the Artificers yard [...] windows were broken all over the Royal Hospital.[38]

Ward Orderly Marrable had a miraculous escape as he was thrown back into the Colonnade by the force of the blast, suffering only cuts and bruises. Sister May, however, was less fortunate, as she was hurled along the Colonnade and flung against the brick wall at the end of the passage, breaking her legs, while her face and eyes were injured by falling masonry.

The East Wing of the infirmary, caught between the twin detonations, like the row of flats and houses in Cheyne Place, simply imploded into a tangled mass of dust and rubble. Ward No. 7 took the full force of the explosion from the mine which had landed in the courtyard, killing Edith Taylor and her bedbound In-Pensioner patients.[39] The shipwright's daughter from Birkenhead, who had devoted her life to looking after sick, injured and infirm old soldiers, and who had served with distinction in two world wars, died alongside those whom she had cared for over so many years.

The mine which exploded between the East Wing and the Artificers Yard created a huge crater into which the twisted mass of debris from the collapsing infirmary building simply cascaded, along with remnants of the Artificers Workshops on the other side of the gaping abyss.

Reports of the bombing of the Royal Hospital were rapidly relayed to the Borough Control Room, with the seriousness of the incident immediately evident: 'Post K reports several ambulances required Royal Hospital. Gate nearest end of Tite Street best approach. Many Casualties. Queer object with wires attached at junction of Redesdale Street.'[40]

The instruction to use the entrance near the southern end of Tite Street was recognition of the devastation and chaos on the Royal Hospital Road, where any approach from the west was impossible. Likewise, the failure of the AFS Station 6W engine to reach Chelsea Gate meant this entrance was also impassable due to the blaze caused by the flare which had fallen earlier. Meanwhile, the main entrance to the infirmary, facing onto Royal Hospital Road, could only be approached with difficulty via a stretch of Ormonde Gate Road. The 'queer object' reported in Redesdale Street was the first indication that Chelsea was under attack from parachute mines, as this appeared to be the remnants of part of the mine which had detonated behind Cheyne Place.

Five minutes later, at 23.50hrs, rescue operations became even more difficult when reports came in of the gas Richard and Frances had smelt earlier during their escape from their wrecked home. 'Deputy District

Warden Hans Town reports escape of gas opposite 25 Cheyne Place. He says he can't send Express Report – damage too widespread.'[41]

However, despite the danger, rescuers were beginning to arrive at the scenes of devastation. In the Royal Hospital, helpers rushed from all directions towards the site of the infirmary blast, including the off-duty reserve RAF crew from the barrage balloon tethered in the South Grounds, who leapt from their air-raid shelter and raced to help.[42]

The first rescuers to reach the infirmary were shocked to realise the East Wing had simply disappeared, replaced by the gaping crater. In the centre of the Artificers Yard, the wives and children's surface shelter was buried beneath debris from both the East Wing of the infirmary and the workshops running across the length of the yard backing onto the infirmary. Mercifully, the air-raid shelter itself was still intact, protected to some extent because it was located in a small hollow in the ground, and the workshops had taken the main force of the blast. The occupants, although badly shaken, were otherwise unharmed.[43]

One of the first to reach the scene of the explosion was 17-year-old Francis Doley, son of the Quartermaster Sergeant.[44] Francis had originally been evacuated from London on the outbreak of war along with his mother as part of the government's general evacuation scheme, but they had returned after only a few days due to the 'insufferable' billeting arrangements they had found.[45] Now he rushed forward to help one of the Hospital's resident firemen, Alfred Grice, who, caught out in the open, had been thrown to the ground by the force of the blast, breaking his pelvis and fracturing his arm. Despite being in much pain, Grice instructed the young Doley on how to open the fire hydrants and bring standpipes into operation as fires had broken out throughout the wrecked buildings.

Other Hospital staff to reach the scene included Captain of Invalids William Lockley, who immediately clambered down into the crater, where he tore into the ruins of the infirmary with his bare hands in a desperate search for survivors or any signs of life. His efforts were hampered by fumes and escaping gas, which was made all the worse for Lockley who had been invalided out of the army because of having been gassed in the First World War, and his damaged lungs and weak heart had been a source of constant trouble for him since. Despite his frailties and with a complete disregard for his own safety, he now tried desperately to reach those areas of the collapsed and ruined building, where, in spite of the carnage from the wrecked wards, he knew survivors could be sheltering, such as in the improvised shelter under the stairs used by Sisters Nicholson and McMullan.

The explosion of the mine in the courtyard created pandemonium throughout the infirmary building. Debris was hurled across the courtyard as the East Wing imploded and slammed into the West Wing, ripping the roof off, breaking windows and causing ceilings to collapse onto the nurses and In-Pensioners below. The ward occupied by patients under the care of Nurse Adela Howard 'received the full force of the blast of the explosion. The windows were blown in and [Howard] was flung across a bed next to another in which an In-Pensioner was killed outright.'[46]

In the adjoining ward, 27-year-old Nurse Hannah Deasy, who had been at the Royal Hospital for less than a year, was also buried in debris and broken glass, as the windows of her ward were also blown in by the explosion. Picking herself up, Deasy was checking on her In-Pensioners when, hearing cries for assistance from Howard's ward, she rushed next-door to discover a fire had broken out among the ward furniture. Helping Howard back to her feet, the two nurses quickly grabbed the stirrup pumps and set about extinguishing the blaze before it could take hold. Meanwhile, sheltering in the FAP located in the basement beneath the West Wing, the Physician & Surgeon's wife, Mrs Rachel Nash, felt the force of the blast as the parachute mines detonated and, recognising the proximity of the explosion, she realised that casualties would be inevitable. She 'immediately began clearing up the plaster and debris dislodged by the explosion' and prepared to receive patients.[47] She was soon joined by her husband, who had left the East Wing wards only moments before the mines had exploded.

Rescuers were now converging on these scenes of Armageddon, with the first report from the Heavy Rescue Squad received in the Borough Control Room at 23.55hrs, with what was now becoming an increasingly desperate plea, 'Daley, No. 1 of 20 Squad, reports ambulances urgently required'.[48] Three minutes later, the Deputy District Warden, having spoken to the local ARP wardens, who as the raid was getting under way had diligently checked on all their local residents to see who and how many were in which air-raid shelters, reported to Control, '23.58hrs: Deputy District Warden Hans Town, reports 25, 29, 31, 33, 35 Cheyne Place badly damaged. Approximately 70 trapped. Ambulances and Rescue (Squads) required.'[49]

Taken together with the estimates of over forty In-Pensioners and nurses in the bombed infirmary, and the Canadians still unaccounted for from the Elms Garage bombing, there were now well over 100 shocked and injured casualties trapped beneath collapsed and burning buildings along this short stretch of the Royal Hospital Road.

At the Royal Hospital itself, twenty-five Grenadier Guardsmen and their officer left their air-raid shelter beneath Chelsea Barracks. Rushing across Chelsea Bridge Road, they headed for the infirmary on the far side of the site.[50] Here, they assisted the officers and staff of RHC in fighting the growing number of fires taking hold in the wrecked infirmary building. Royal Hospital Sergeant, Frederick Harrison, in charge of the Hospital's Fatigue Party, quickly organised the operation of the stirrup pumps and standpipes. They were soon proving unequal to the task as the rescuers were increasingly losing the battle against the spread of the flames. Evacuation of the trapped In-Pensioners and nurses was an imperative.

Borough Control logged another report at 00.20hrs, relayed from the ARP wardens in attendance at the Hospital, 'Royal Hospital Infirmary reported 40 trapped casualties. No ambulances arrived. One Rescue Squad (Demolition) only arrived.'[51]

It was now well over half an hour since the infirmary had been hit and still no ambulances had managed to navigate their way through the blocked streets and reach the Hospital. With 6W, the nearest AFS, destroyed, no fire engines had managed to get through either and the single Heavy Rescue Squad which had arrived on site was struggling to free victims still trapped in the building, the situation rapidly becoming critical.

The fires in the ruined infirmary now merged into a single conflagration, which soon 'reached quite big proportions', with the improvised fire-fighting teams in danger of losing control of the blaze.[52] In a desperate bid to keep on top of the situation, the Hospital's Grounds Superintendent, Mr James Beezley, 'displayed great initiative in coupling up long lengths of hose from a distant stand pipe' in order to bring more water to tackle the now raging inferno.[53]

The focus of the rescue teams was on getting as many of the trapped In-Pensioners and nurses out of the building as quickly as possible. On more than one occasion, however, when they tried to move the injured Sister May from the Colonnade, she waved them away and insisted that they get the In-Pensioners out first.[54] Nurse Deasy, having successfully evacuated her own patients and helped move those of Nurse Howard, moved further into the wrecked West Wing where, 'finding the doors of a third damaged Ward blocked by fallen masonry, she entered it by climbing through a window opening, and set about moving debris from patients there'.[55]

Lines of rescuers had been formed by Sergeant Harrison and his Fatigue Party, and as In-Pensioners were dug free from their wards they were placed onto stretchers and passed gently, but as quickly as possible, along the lines of rescuers and across the mountains of debris before being carried away from the blazing ruins. All were in a state of shock with some also physically injured, such as 81-year-old In-Pensioner Robert Lloyd, who suffered broken ribs and a fractured fibula.[56] In-Pensioner Herbert Watts carefully wrapped his spectacles in his handkerchief to protect them from harm as his stretcher was manhandled along the line of rescuers, but inevitably the jolting actions as he was passed along proved too much for his 79-year-old hands and they were shaken from his grip to be lost among the mounds of debris.[57] In the absence of ambulances to take the casualties to hospital, the injured were taken to the FAP manned by the Physician & Surgeon's wife, Mrs Nash, 'most of whom she bandaged herself'.[58]

At 00.40hrs, a Situation Report filed at Borough Control again logged, 'Royal Hospital requests ambulances to take away old people. One man 101 years. All shock cases.'[59] The centenarian referred to in this report is In-Pensioner Henry Augustus Rattrey. Born in Dublin in 1841, the son of a soldier in the Royal Artillery, Rattrey enlisted as a drummer boy at the age of 11 with the 5th Dragoon Guards, rising to the position of bandmaster before transferring to the 24th Foot in 1869, where he served as a Sergeant Bandmaster. Three times married and the father of ten children, Rattrey was nevertheless subsequently 'unencumbered by spouse' when he entered the Royal Hospital in May 1938. He was, by all accounts, popular with his fellow In-Pensioners and RHC staff alike and during the Ministry of Information's propaganda visit in November had become something of a celebrity among the visiting press corps, subsequently featuring in newspaper reports which highlighted his cheerful demeanour despite the danger he now faced.[60]

Regardless of his advanced years, Rattrey was only in the infirmary for a slight indisposition, but was caught in the explosion as the parachute mines detonated. This latest situation report nevertheless implies that he had somehow survived the blast and subsequent collapse of the East Wing, before being pulled shocked and injured from among the debris. He now urgently needed hospital attention, and hence this latest desperate call for ambulances. Sadly, I/P Rattrey would not survive his ordeal and his name would join the others recorded as 'Killed by Enemy Action' on this most terrible of nights.

It was now almost an hour since the infirmary had been hit and still no ambulances had managed to get through to the Royal Hospital. Several towed trailer pumps did manage to successfully negotiate their way through the ruins surrounding the infirmary site, entering as instructed through the Tite Street gate.[61] Fire hoses could now be brought into play and the rescuers eventually began to make progress against the flames burning throughout the ruined building.

Casualties were still being carried from the ruins and with no ambulances available to transport them to air-raid casualty clearing hospitals and limited space in the FAP, which was itself in danger from the encroaching flames, they were lined up along the West Road in the open as the raid continued overhead with no easing in its intensity. The anti-aircraft batteries in Battersea Park continued pounding away at the raiders, with the deafening roar of the guns interspersed with the crashing of exploding bombs all played out against the unremitting drone of the enemy planes over Chelsea.

Finally, the first ambulances made it through to the Hospital and the more seriously injured were hastily loaded aboard. Not all would survive the journey to the casualty clearing hospitals.

By around 1 a.m., the rescuers slowly began to bring the fire in the infirmary under control. In-Pensioners were still being carried from the ruins and some were now moved from West Road and carried the short distance to the Vestibule, between the Great Hall and the chapel, so they were at least no longer out in the open.[62] It was clear that more ambulances were still urgently needed and the officer in charge of the Guardsmen now contacted Borough Control directly, with his report logged at 00.56hrs, 'Officer from Chelsea Barracks requests more ambulances for Royal Hospital'.[63]

However, the emergency services were stretched to breaking point dealing with the multitude of incidents along this stretch of Royal Hospital Road and simply did not have enough of any type of emergency-response equipment. There were simply not enough ambulances to deal with the demands placed upon the service. The mutual assistance protocol in which neighbouring boroughs would send emergency services to the help of adjacent boroughs was also inoperative, given that in this raid, everywhere was being hit equally hard.

At 01.20hrs, the Deputy District Warden for Hans Town filed an updated Incident Report, which was duly logged in the Borough Control Room:

> District Deputy Warden Hans Town reports: Royal Hospital Infirmary reputed 40 trapped. Cheyne Place, 25. Nos. 29, 31, 33, 35 badly damaged and collapsed. Caversham Street backs of houses (wrecked). One dead in 17. Evans, Incident Officer.

Although the emergency services, assisted by a myriad of volunteer rescuers, were beginning to make some progress, they still faced desperate conditions as they tried to deal with the situation in the multitude of incidents along this short stretch of the Royal Hospital Road. Unfortunately, this dreadful night was about to get even more desperate.

## 12

# The Bombing of Chelsea Old Church

*'Old Church hit [...] debris extends to the King's Road.'*[1]

The first indication at Borough Control that another serious incident had occurred was when the phone line to Auxiliary Ambulance Station 22 suddenly went quiet. Station AS22 'was tucked away in the yard behind No. 18 Danvers Street', located at its southern end where it meets Cheyne Walk, a short distance to the west of Chelsea Old Church.[2] The yard backed onto houses in Old Church Street and was in many ways typical of Auxiliary Ambulance Stations.

It had been 'requisitioned from its proprietors, Thomas Alfred Blanch, motor engineers, and Woodall & Napier, dairy farmers', with the site 'consisting of two double-height brick built sheds, one of which was used to house the vehicles and the other the crews. It had a petrol pump and an office. Although the main drawback was the glass roof.'[3] In the building used for accommodation, 'a wooden structure built into a corner and equipped with a desk and a phone' served as the station's operations room, where, 'on the wall outside there was a pinboard where maps of the local streets and order sheets were posted'.[4]

AS22 was the nearest ambulance station to Royal Hospital Road and was where June Spencer was based when on duty, rather than as, on this night, dancing in the 400 Club in Leicester Square, where news was slowly filtering through that Chelsea was having a difficult night. All the ambulances at AS22 were out attending to the incidents at Cheyne

Place, the Elms Garage and the infirmary bombing at the Royal Hospital. However, the station manager, Margaret Bridges, remained in Danvers Street in the small wooden operations room. From here, she was constantly on the phone as she relayed information about the whereabouts of her station's ambulances to operators such as Denise Fitzgerald in Borough Control in the basement bunker beneath Chelsea Town Hall.

Margaret also received back from Borough Control instructions as to which incidents needed ambulances in attendance. These she would relay to ARP wardens and police officers, who were continually coming and going into the station, passing on reports and receiving new instructions from Margaret, which they would take out to the ambulances in order for them to be redeployed around the local area as required. Except, of course, on this night, there were simply not enough ambulances to respond to the instructions coming into the station control room.

Now Borough Control had lost contact with AS22, as Margaret was no longer picking up the phone and it simply rang and rang. Alarmed, the controllers telephoned Warden Post D in the nearby Paultons Square and the call is logged in the incident report at 01.25hrs, 'Rang D to confirm Danvers Street ambulance station mishap. Told to get off line for Express Report.'[5] The filing of an Express Report resulted in the automatic mobilisation of a Rescue Party, Stretcher Party and Ambulances to an incident. Something terrible had clearly happened.

About five minutes before the phone line to AS22 fell silent the team of six fire-watchers stationed at Chelsea Old Church were heading back to the church in the direction of Danvers Street, having been patrolling along Cheyne Walk. As they walked, Henry Frankland, Yvonne Green, Michael Hodge, a 17-year-old schoolboy home for the school holidays, Sidney Sims, Frederick Winter and Arthur Mallett noted how the ground was littered with fragments of spent rounds from the heavy anti-aircraft barrage, as the batteries in Battersea Park had now been continuously in action for well over four hours. One of the group, Mallett, stopped to pick up a discarded shell-casing nose cap, thinking to himself, 'This is made of phosphorous bronze, expensive stuff to chuck about like this'.[6]

As he was examining the fragment of spent ammunition, a parachute mine, unseen by the fire-watchers, floated gently down into Old Church Street. It landed close to Petyt Place, the impact activating the twenty-five-second fuse. At this moment, Mallett heard a soft thud behind him, 'like a fifty-six pound coal sack falling on soft ground'.[7] Looking casually round, he was alarmed to see 'a big thing about seven feet long and as big as you could get your arms round', as the second parachute mine in this latest pair to descend on Chelsea hit the ground.[8]

Shouting a warning to the others, he started to run along Cheyne Walk towards Chelsea Old Church as the other fire-watchers raced ahead of him. On reaching the corner, Frankland, Green, Hodge, Sims and Winter turned swiftly into Old Church Street, as they sought shelter from the unexploded parachute mine behind them on Cheyne Walk. Mallett, racing to catch up, was moving too quickly to make the corner and instead dived behind a fire-alarm post on the corner of the street.

The five fire-watchers who had turned into Old Church Street did so just as the mine which had landed there a few moments earlier exploded in front of them. They were all killed instantly, while the blast from the explosion immediately detonated the second mine, just as Mallett was diving for the ground.[9] He was the latest to have a miraculous escape on this most terrible of nights, as he was sheltered from the blast by the low wall around the churchyard.

Petyt Place and Chelsea Old Church were caught between the two blasts, like Cheyne Walk and the Royal Hospital's infirmary earlier, and now imploded into a mass of tangled debris. The Bomb Damage Report, which again describes this impact as a single incident, details the extent of the damage to the church:

> Mine fell on that part of church which abuts on to Old Church Street. Church was demolished except for the old walls which vary in thickness from 18" to 30" but the upper parts of wall have been blasted. Damage is severe and extends as far as Beaufort Street – 20 yards away.[10]

The report also outlines the extent of the damage to neighbouring properties, which was extensive, with the impact described in four separate sections:

> A – Church – 50ft frontage – 4 Houses and Shops in Old Church Street – 65, 66 and 69 Cheyne Walk – 30ft frontage; B – 68, 69, 71 Cheyne Walk – 4, 6 Danvers Street – Petyt School – 4 houses Petyt

Place; C – Carlyle Mansions; D – 8 houses Danvers Street – Crosby Hall – 4 houses Beaufort Street; Glass Damage severe.[11]

As the explosions ripped through the buildings, the gas mains were ruptured, adding to the horror and chaos of the scene with Chelsea Old Church now 'nothing but an immense heap of timber and stone, flames licking through it; a large vaulted tomb with a stone urn on top rose up undamaged in the front'.[12]

Nearby, 'the New Café Lombard and all the large and small houses at that end of Old Church Street had been flung together in a giant mountain of shale like destruction, all lit by the fire and the gas main'.[13] Somewhere in among this devastation, the telephone at AS22 on Danvers Street was now ringing, unanswered.

The destruction of Chelsea Old Church was a profound loss to the borough and its residents. Numerous eyewitness accounts record the utter disbelief of those arriving at the scene of the parachute mines and expecting to see the reassuring presence of the solid tower of the church. The Post Warden at Cook's Town rushed over with the District Warden and as they approached along Cheyne Walk, it suddenly 'came to them both: *"The Old Church has gone!"* There was a jagged stump of brickwork and projecting timbers silhouetted where the eye had expected the massive square tower.'[14]

After racing back to his post, the Express Report filed by the warden was short and to the point, 'Post Don. Express Report. Chelsea Old Church. Trapped casualties. Fire. Time of reference 01.25hrs. Message Ends.'[15] Part-time warden A.R. Maxwell-Hyslop, who was on duty having returned from the country earlier in the evening, recorded his thoughts on reaching the scene of devastation:

> I could suddenly see a great pile, a great mountain of rubble, and behind it the bright flames of a burning gas main, and I realised that the church must have been hit. That was the most awful shock because people who live in Chelsea often talk about living in a village, and sometimes it's thought to be an affectation, but that night I don't think any of us felt that. The church always had been in Chelsea very much the heart of the village, and it was like seeing something that one loved killed in front of one's eyes.[16]

A dazed and disorientated Arthur Mallett, staggering to his feet with his trousers torn and legs soaked in blood, struggled to comprehend the enormity of what had happened, 'I couldn't see anything – it looked just like a mountain of rubble. "Blimey", I thought, "that lot's gone".'[17] Then, as he remembered his fellow fire-watchers, he tried searching desperately for them:

> I started shouting out all their names, I called them all out, what I knew, the nicknames I called 'em by, I didn't get any answers. Eventually I started to climb over all this rubble, it must have been twenty – maybe fifteen, twenty feet high. Anyhow, I climbed over it.[18]

Arthur was now met by his sister Alice, who was concerned for his safety and had gone to look for him. She also needed to tell him that their house had likewise been damaged by the blast from the parachute mines, 'The roof's gone and the windows are out'.[19] Having found him alive, but injured and badly shaken, Alice took Arthur home and put him to bed.

At 01.30hrs, Borough Control was in no doubt that they now had another major incident to deal with as a report was received confirming the earlier news from the Express Report, and indicating the extent of the damage sustained, 'Post B confirms Old Church hit, and debris extends to the King's Road'.[20] Five minutes later, the confusion and chaos into which the Civil Defence wardens were thrown by this latest parachute mine incident was evident, 'Post D; re damage to Danvers Street. Reports everybody on their heads over Chelsea Old Church incident.'[21]

At the Royal Hospital, rescue teams were still trying to reach those trapped in the infirmary bombing. It was now two hours since the parachute mines had detonated, and shocked and injured In-Pensioners were still being carried from the ruins. Those needing immediate medical attention were taken to the FAP in the basement, where the Physician & Surgeon, Colonel Nash, and his wife Rachel were now being assisted by the two ward nurses, Hannah Deasy and Adela Howard.[22]

At 01.45hrs, Daley, the head of the Heavy Rescue crew in attendance, once again asked the Borough Control Room for further assistance to be sent.[23] Although ambulances were by now getting through to the Royal Hospital, there were still not enough to deal with all the stretcher cases needing to be moved. The Hospital's War Diary details that over the course of the air raid, some thirty-six stretchers, three for staff members and thirty-three carrying injured In-Pensioners, were despatched to various casualty clearing hospitals.[24]

The staff members needing stretchers, Sister May, Fireman Grice and Ward Orderly Marrable, and one of the In-Pensioners were all considered to be serious cases. Three In-Pensioners subsequently died from their injuries.[25] At a board meeting held the day after the raid, following visits having been made to the hospitals to which the casualties were evacuated, the number of walking wounded In-Pensioners loaded aboard ambulances is also noted. Consequently, the board-meeting minutes note that forty-seven In-Pensioners were rescued and despatched to hospital.[26]

Eventually about a dozen ambulances were involved in the rescue operation at the infirmary during the night.[27] It is unclear whether those In-Pensioners who were rescued but subsequently died could have been saved had ambulances arrived earlier. The Auxiliary Ambulance Service was simply overwhelmed with the number and scale of incidents they were facing, with their task made even more difficult after Danvers Street was put out of action.

Nevertheless, despite operating under conditions of extreme stress, the volunteers of the AAS went about their work as quickly and calmly as they could, with their efforts at the Royal Hospital during this raid witnessed by none other than Admiral Sir Edward Evans KCB, DSO, London Regional Commissioner for Civil Defence.

Admiral Evans was known universally as 'Evans of the Broke' in recognition of his actions during a celebrated First World War naval engagement, when as captain of the destroyer HMS *Broke*, he led a successful attack against a superior German destroyer flotilla. Now, still leading by example, Evans was quickly on site at the Royal Hospital soon after the infirmary was bombed and watched as Sister May's stretcher was lifted gently into a waiting ambulance, 'I saw the poor nurse being helped into an ambulance and was told that she would immediately have to have both her legs amputated when she was taken to St Luke's Hospital'.[28]

Evans would also have cause to remember one of the ambulance crew orderlies he witnessed helping the Royal Hospital casualties, 'a young woman called Weir [...] a very stout-hearted lass'.[29]

Twenty-seven-year-old Margaret Weir lived with her parents John and Elizabeth Weir at No. 154 Ebury Street, a short distance from Victoria Station. Having been in one of the first ambulances to reach the Royal Hospital, she was inspiring those around her as she helped In-Pensioners into the vehicles, all the time out in the open and under fire from the raiders overhead. However, unknown to the young AAS volunteer, the large fire reported early in the raid at 22.35hrs by the Hans Town wardens developing between their warden's post and Victoria Station had acted as a beacon to subsequent waves of bombers. Shortly after midnight, while the first ambulances were converging on the Royal Hospital, Bomb Damage Reports record a series of explosions in Ebury Street at 00.35hrs involving parachute mines and 50kg high-explosive bombs.[30] The blasts severed the gas mains, adding more fuel to the already raging inferno, and resulted in serious casualties among the residents. It was not until she came off her shift that Margaret Weir would discover her own family were among the fatalities.

Meanwhile, at the 400 Club, when news reached June Spencer about the bombing of the Old Church, she immediately thought of her ambulance crew colleagues in Danvers Street. It didn't matter that she was off-duty; she knew she had to get back to Chelsea and insisted on leaving straight away.

At 2 a.m., as June and her companion Sydney Cuthbert were leaving The 400 Club, the Royal Hospital's War Diary notes the completion of the stretcher parties' efforts at the infirmary as the final casualties were loaded into ambulances. The entry highlighted the difficulties the rescuers had faced in what had been a harrowing task, 'Owing to the amount of debris obstructing the various roads and pavements this was a lengthy business, not completed until about 2am'.[31]

At 02.00hrs, Post K filed another report with Borough Control which simply noted, 'Blankets required for dead'.[32] Royal Hospital personnel were still working alongside the Heavy Rescue Squad, tunnelling into the ruins of the infirmary, but it had been some time since anybody had been pulled out alive. The bodies of the dead, 'mostly unrecognisable', were covered as best as possible while efforts continued to trace any remaining survivors. There seemed little chance of finding anyone else alive in the burnt-out ruins of the infirmary, but rescue crews refused to give up hope.

After the chaplain's evening tour of the infirmary wards between 10 and 11 p.m., Ward Sisters Nicholson and McMullan were known to have entered the little shelter under the stairs, which Sister Nicholson always used during air raids, rather than abandoning her patients for the relative safety of the main Hospital shelters. In October, four disabled In-Pensioners had been dug out of a similar shelter in the East Wing after the direct hit which had caused the stairwell to collapse onto their little sanctuary, and of course, everybody in Chelsea remembered the miraculous survival of 12-year-old Mildred Castillo after the bombing of her family home. Although the little sanctuary in the infirmary was buried under tons of debris, if rescuers could only reach it, there was still a chance that the two nurses might somehow have survived the building's collapse.

In both previous incidents, however, the ruins under which the hapless survivors had been buried were not subsequently ravaged by fire. But during this raid, the loss of the AFS Station 6W and the fire engine and crew caught out in the open as they raced to tackle the blaze outside Chelsea Gate led to inevitable delays in getting fire crews to the infirmary incident. Further difficulties experienced by fire crews trying to reach the Royal Hospital through the devastated surrounding streets resulted in the fires in the infirmary reaching 'quite big proportions' and for a while threatening to get out of control. It would represent yet another miraculous escape, therefore, if the two nurses were to be found alive in the infirmary ruins. Nevertheless, the ARP services in Chelsea were proud of the fact that they never gave up until everybody known to be present at the time of an 'incident' was accounted for, one way or another, and hence the rescue crews kept digging as the air raid continued relentlessly overhead.

In the West End, June Spencer and Sydney Cuthbert tried hailing a taxi for the journey back to Chelsea – remarkably, taxis continued to ply their trade even during air raids. Tonight, however, was different and there were no taxis on the roads. Undeterred, June and Sydney started walking, despite June 'wearing a long pink and black tulle dress!'[33] With bombs falling and fires raging all around, they were constantly ducking into doorways and throwing themselves onto the pavement. In Cadogan Square, however, they were able to flag down a passing vehicle which took them to the King's Road.

It was now around 2.15 in the morning and the next phase of the attack on Chelsea had begun, with waves of bombers dropping incendiary bombs to try to set fire to those damaged buildings not already alight, and consequently, June and Sydney witnessed 'Incendiary bombs all down the King's Road'.[34]

The first reports of this next phase of the raid reached Borough Control at 02.17hrs as 'Post B rang saying IBs falling Chelsea Park Gardens to King's Road', followed minutes later by reports of incendiaries falling over the devastated area along the Royal Hospital Road, '02.20hrs. Post K reports IBs falling over bombed area'.[35]

The incendiary bombs were dropped in baskets – grad baskets – which opened after falling clear of the bomber and spread their lethal load across the ground below. At the Royal Hospital, the last In-Pensioners had barely been loaded into ambulances when the War Diary reports, 'About 2.30am, a Grad basket spread over the Tite Street area. Incendiaries fell in Burton Court (1), South Terrace (2), South Grounds (1) and the Laundry.'[36]

Nurses Deasy and Howard, having been released from duty in the FAP in the basement of the West Wing, were at this moment returning to their accommodation in Gordon House, a short distance from the infirmary beyond the Hospital's laundry building. Here they could sit out the rest of the raid in the relative safety of their designated air-raid shelter.

The incendiary bomb which hit the laundry penetrated the roof space and started a fire just as the two nurses were making their way past the building.[37] Once again, they grabbed buckets of sand and water along with a stirrup pump and quickly dealt with the resulting blaze before it could take hold.[38]

By this stage of the night, reactions elsewhere in the immediate neighbourhood were no longer as fast as those of the two Royal Hospital nurses. Ten minutes after Post K reported the falling incendiaries to Borough Control, another report was logged, 'Post K reports fire at southern end of Paradise Walk'.[39] Unfortunately, the by now seriously overstretched fire services were simply unable to respond, and the report continues, 'Auxiliary Fire Service know, but report that hoses have run out'.[40]

The loss of the Station 6W fire engine as the raid was getting under way and the multitude of incidents since meant there were no longer any emergency fire crews available to respond to this latest incident.

No sooner had this call been logged than Borough Control received a report about a bomb which had fallen on or near Chelsea Bridge Road, bringing a tree down in Ranelagh Gardens and reportedly blocking the road. This latest incident was also in Post K's area and the warden's post was consequently asked to send an incident officer to check and confirm these latest reports.

The Post K wardens were at this moment, however, trying to substitute for the lack of fire crews at the Paradise Walk blaze and therefore replied that 'they cannot confirm if there is a crater near Chelsea Bridge as they are at the fire at Paradise Walk, which is reaching considerable proportions'.[41] Chelsea's overstretched Civil Defence forces were starting to buckle under the constant stream of incidents they were having to deal with as the raid continued overhead, never easing in its intensity.

June and Sydney, meanwhile, had finally managed to reach AS22, where on entering the yard behind No. 18 Danvers Street, they saw that 'the ambulance station was quite flat'.[42] The couple immediately started searching through the wreckage, looking for survivors beneath the shattered remains of the glass roof, which had collapsed into the ruins of the building, and soon June noted:

> One huge sheet of glass from the garage roof moved in the brilliant moonlight. Sydney pulled at it and from underneath rose a very tall policeman with a long beard, very drunk. He said he had no legs. To assure him he was standing on them, I pulled up his trousers. To his relief, he danced down the street holding Sydney's hand.[43]

Mercifully, the inebriated War Reserve Policeman, artist Stanley Grimm, was not the only survivor, for Margaret Bridges, although dazed and shaken, had also escaped harm. The crews stationed at AS22, meanwhile, had all been called out to the site of the infirmary bombing at the time the ambulance station was hit and consequently had not been caught in the blast.

While June helped Margaret back to her feet among the devastation of AS22, a short distance away rescue squads elsewhere on Danvers Street and in the immediate vicinity of Chelsea Old Church were 'tunnelling into the debris to see if they could find anyone'.[44] As the desperate rescue work continued, suddenly, 'somebody called out "There's another one coming!'", and everybody threw themselves into the rubble, desperately trying to 'make [themselves] as small as possible in the debris' before this next parachute mine detonated.[45]

This time, however, the parachute falling onto Chelsea Embankment was not carrying more death and destruction but was instead a young German airman who had been forced to bail out of his stricken bomber after it was hit by anti-aircraft fire from the batteries which had been pounding away all night. As he picked himself up and released his parachute harness, the airman was quickly surrounded by a curious and angry crowd of rescue workers and onlookers. The young German was quickly relieved of his revolver and manhandled roughly until two War Reserve Policemen arrived on the scene and marched him off to the King's Road Police Station.[46] Here, he was thrown into the cells just as the next wave of bombers arrived, once again dropping high-explosive bombs to explode among the fires caused by the recently dropped wave of incendiaries; one bomb narrowly missed the police station.

Three huge explosions occurred in quick succession, to the north and roughly parallel to the King's Road, as this next attack unfolded. The Bomb Damage Incident Reports record the first explosion hitting Cranmer Court, 'a block of modern flats, between Sloane Avenue, Elystan Street and Whiteheads Grove' at 02.48hrs, to be followed seconds later by simultaneous explosions at the 'Catholic Apostolic Church, Elystan Street' and 'Nos 49–50–51 Chelsea Square' as more parachute mines and high-explosive bombs hit the Borough of Chelsea.[47]

The devastation caused by these latest incidents was colossal, with the church 'two-thirds demolished' and only the buttressing 'prevented total collapse of all walls'. Whereas, across the road in Cranmer Court, 'workmen's dwellings' caught between the explosion of the first parachute mine and the blast which demolished the church were 'considerably damaged'.[48] Casualties were recorded as seven killed, twenty-eight severely injured and a further seventeen lightly injured.

Meanwhile, the explosion in Chelsea Square resulted in the deaths of another four Auxiliary Firemen, caught out in the open as they fought blazes caused by the earlier incendiary bombs. Firemen Charles Moore, Frederick Scate, Mervyn Taylor and Reginald Wakeman were all 'killed in the roadway opposite Nos 49–51 Chelsea Square'.[49] The already depleted fire service could ill afford these latest casualties.

There is no mention in the Royal Hospital's War Diary of these huge explosions to the north of the King's Road, for the Hospital itself did not escape unscathed during this latest wave of bombers and the attention of the residents was thus focused nearer to home. The War Diary records:

> About 3am there was another violent explosion, again presumably from a land mine, this time in the roadway opposite Burton Court Mansions, north of Turks Row. About 150 feet of boundary wall and railings were broken down opposite where the mine fell. The Secretary's Office and Officer's Quarters in Light Horse Court suffered much damage, doors and windows being blown up.[50]

Almost immediately after this latest huge blast shook the ground around the Royal Hospital, reports were relayed to Borough Control, '02.46 hrs, Post K reports High Explosive [bomb] near. Post full of dust.'[51]

There is much confusion in the Bomb Damage Report for this particular incident, with a detailed discussion as to whether this was another parachute mine or a conventional high-explosive bomb. It resulted in another devastating explosion in Chelsea as it landed in the roadway of Franklyn Row, between the mansion block on the corner with Turks Row and the boundary wall at the north-east corner of Burton Court. The resulting crater was later measured as 12ft in diameter and 6ft deep with the blast causing significant damage and throwing dust and debris over a wide area.[52]

The immediate impact of this latest incident was to cause chaos and confusion for the already overstretched Civil Defence forces. The newly unfolding situation at the Royal Hospital was made worse for Borough Control as the operators, such as Denise Fitzgerald in the bunker beneath Chelsea Town Hall, were now also being overwhelmed by the sheer volume of incidents being reported from across Chelsea. At 02.47hrs, a minute after this latest report from the Royal Hospital, more incendiaries were reported falling to the west. Two minutes later, at 02.49hrs, the Deputy Warden for Cheyne Walk 'reports about 11 casualties Chelsea Old Church, and that he has been blasted out of his office'. Fires were now reported at 03.00hrs by Post B, while minutes later, reports were received of another 'incident in Chelsea Square. Post E have one Warden dead and one with a broken leg.'[53]

While Denise Fitzgerald and her fellow controllers struggled to deal with this deluge of reports now flooding into Borough Control, a heart-stopping message was relayed from the ARP wardens dealing with the latest Royal Hospital incident, '03.10 hrs Deputy Warden Hans Town reports direct hit on Burton Court. Trapped casualties.'[54] This was the bomb that had originally been reported at 02.46hrs as having fallen near Post K, filling the warden's post with dust and showering it with debris. In the resulting confusion, it was unclear as to what had actually happened.

Initial reports as to precisely where the bomb had landed were confused, with fears that it had detonated inside the perimeter railings of Burton Court and therefore directly above the air-raid shelter complex first excavated in 1938. As this super-shelter was made permanent during the frantic preparations for war in 1939, it had also been extended and now covered a large area beneath what was one of the few open spaces in the borough. This was by some margin the largest air-raid shelter in Chelsea, but it was not a very deep one, and the concrete roof was located only a couple of feet below the surface of the football pitch above.

Although there are no records as to how many of Chelsea's residents were using this shelter on the night of 16–17 April 1941, given the duration and ferocity of the raid, it is likely that it was crowded by this stage of the night. If this shelter had received a direct hit from the latest bomb to fall in the vicinity of the Royal Hospital grounds, the resulting death toll and injuries would undoubtedly have eclipsed any other incident in the borough. This death toll would have been made infinitely worse by the fact that Civil Defence forces in Chelsea were now at breaking point, given the multitude of incidents they were trying to deal with.

The proximity of the blast, while creating much confusion among the Civil Defence wardens, also seems to have resulted in near panic in the Burton Court shelter complex itself, until the shelter wardens were able to restore calm. The council later recorded receiving grateful letters from members of the public 'in respect of the work of the Civil Defence Services at Burton Court'.[55]

Mercifully, the bomb fell a few metres outside the Burton Court railings, rather than in the Royal Hospital grounds. To a degree, this latest incident suggests that the Royal Hospital's luck experienced thus far in the Blitz had, at least in part, continued to hold, notwithstanding the carnage at the infirmary.

Meanwhile, despite the obvious danger to those caught out in the open, as evidenced by the growing casualty list of Civil Defence personnel, digging continued at the sites of the now numerous incidents across Chelsea. These included rescue work at the Royal Hospital infirmary, where staff members were also dousing the still-smouldering ruins.

At the scene of the Chelsea Old Church tragedy, Dr Castillo again performed selflessly heroic duty when, with complete disregard for his own safety, he crawled into a bombed house to administer morphine to 16-year-old Emma Chandler, who was trapped beneath the debris of her ruined home. He stayed with the young girl for some hours, talking calmly with her while the Heavy Rescue team worked delicately in the ruins, attempting to extract her without bringing the whole building crashing down onto the trapped victim and her courageous guardian, and overhead the unremitting raid continued, as the next wave of bombers dropped further death and destruction on the hapless victims below.

At 04.15hrs, another large bomb crashed into the Royal Hospital Road causing the rescuers in the infirmary ruins to dive for cover as it blasted a crater 40ft in diameter and 15ft deep in the roadway opposite the Hospital's ruined dispensary.[56] The shockwave caused more damage to the fire-ravaged infirmary as 'the Lion and Unicorn on the Infirmary façade fell down into the Matron's Quarters'.[57]

By now, water mains had been severed throughout the borough, including in the Royal Hospital Road, in the east of the borough, and in Cale Street, near the junction with Sydney Street in the west.[58] At 04.20hrs, fires were reported in Chelsea Park Gardens, but with no crews available and mains water pressure low, the report goes on to add, 'Auxiliary Fire Service not there'.[59]

Two minutes later, however, a fire crew did manage to get through, but the extensive damage to the water mains now presented serious problems for the AFS. The explosions which had severed the mains caused a drop in pressure to the firemen's hoses, leaving properties across Chelsea including the Royal Hospital now dangerously exposed to further incendiary attacks. The broken water mains also presented additional dangers, as Deputy District Warden Hans Town now reported, 'flooding, rapidly increasing, on Embankment. Wardens warning people sheltering in basements'.[60] Despite the obvious dangers of being caught out in the open, ARP wardens had no choice other than to start evacuating terrified residents from basement shelters which were in danger of flooding from the deluge of water escaping from fractured mains.

Finally, mercifully, the sky in the east began to slowly brighten with the first hint of the approaching dawn and as it did so, the last German bombers turned for home. A debriefing and hearty breakfast would welcome the Luftwaffe crews back at their bases in occupied France, while in Chelsea the All-Clear eventually sounded at five minutes to five. The longest and most ferocious air raid of the Blitz so far was finally over and the Borough of Chelsea, like much of London, would never look the same again.

# 13

# Aftermath

*'... we have not the means for nursing chronic cases ...'*[1]

As the sun rose over the smoke-shrouded ruins on the morning after the raid, injured and bewildered survivors tried to take stock. The mood was sombre and melancholy, with 'a strange dead stillness everywhere after the night's appalling havoc, as if the very earth had received a shock and was as numb as its inhabitants from the night's savagery'.[2]

Tragedies continued to mount even as victims were released and carried from bombed-out ruins. Sixteen-year-old Emma Chandler was freed from the tomb of her home in Old Church Street after Herculean efforts by the Heavy Rescue squad and the constant attention and encouragement of Dr Castillo, only to die shortly after her release.

Among the injured Canadian servicemen, newly-weds Cecil and Anne's friend Larry had been 'trapped under heavy stuff for hours' and was 'pretty far gone' by the time he was eventually carried from the ruins of his billet at the Elms Garage site. He was laid gently on the pavement to await a stretcher party. Sadly, stretcher-bearers were not necessary, because shortly after his release 'he gave a sigh – just as if he were very tired after the long night, and was falling asleep', as he breathed his final breath. Richard Faviell visited the mortuary to identify Cecil's body, but the remains of Anne and her mother Kathleen had still not been found.[3]

At the Royal Hospital, 'hosepipes trailed all across the front entrances and courtyards' as firefighters continued to damp down the smouldering ruins.⁴ Throughout the day, 'a Rescue Squad was employed in retrieving bodies from the Infirmary crater', which were wrapped in the blankets provided by Borough Control and placed initially in the chapel before being moved to the Board Room.⁵ As with all previous incidents at the Hospital, the clean-up operation began almost immediately, 'pavements were swept clear of debris', while 'Chelsea Borough crews assisted in removing the broken window frames and glass'.⁶

A detailed search of the grounds uncovered 'a hole, apparently from a delayed action bomb in Ranelagh Gardens' and another bomb, estimated at between 100kg and 250kg, had uprooted a plane tree, which had crashed through the boundary railings near the Ebury Road entrance, falling across Chelsea Bridge Road which 'was blocked for about a week afterwards'.⁷ This was the incident which Post K had been unable to confirm when asked by Borough Control, as their ARP wardens were attending the fire in Paradise Walk. Despite there being little hope of finding Sisters Nicholson and McMullan alive, their bodies had still not been recovered and tunnelling continued towards the site of the little sanctuary where they were believed to be sheltering.

On the morning of Friday, 18 April, the Governor, accompanied by the Sergeant Major, visited St Luke's Hospital where most of the casualties had been taken.⁸ Sister May had been operated on immediately upon her arrival and 'the skill of the surgeons saved her legs, but she will never be fit to nurse again'.⁹ She was so severely injured that she would remain in hospital for almost twelve months.

During the day, telegrams were sent to the next of kin of those known to have been killed, while letters of thanks were posted to the Auxiliary Ambulance Service, the ARP warden's office in Chelsea Town Hall and London Fire Brigade HQ for their assistance during the raid, and to the officer commanding the Guards at Chelsea Barracks for their help in organising stretcher parties to rescue the bedbound In-Pensioners. A letter was also sent to the officer commanding 'C' Flight, 905 Squadron, RAF, praising the actions of the 'Corporal and crew from the Balloon Section in the South Grounds', who although off-duty and sheltering in an air-raid shelter, were nevertheless, 'on the spot immediately' to offer assistance.¹⁰

During the afternoon, the Lieutenant Governor, Physician & Surgeon, Deputy Surgeon, matron and adjutant visited the Victoria Children's Hospital in Tite Street, where the Chairman of the Governors 'offered the use of the first and second floors as an Infirmary'.[11] Throughout the day, the Lieutenant Governor 'was in constant communication by telephone with the Ministry of Health and the Director General of Medical Services regarding accommodation for the Infirmary'.[12]

The difficulties the Hospital had experienced in October, when the infirmary was out of action for eight days while three UXBs were dealt with, were still fresh in everybody's mind. Without an infirmary the Royal Hospital could simply not function, for it was central to delivering day-to-day medical care to all of the In-Pensioner community and end-of-life care to the majority of In-Pensioners before their 'Final Posting'. The chronic cases the Royal Hospital dealt with on a daily basis could not be treated without the specialised provision provided by the institution's infirmary.

Meanwhile, digging continued at the site of the bombing, where 'more bodies were found by the Rescue squads, mostly unrecognisable, bringing the total to nine', and another In-Pensioner, I/P Wogan, died of his injuries. Sisters Nicholson and McMullan had still not been found.

The forthcoming weekend, however, would mark something of a watershed moment for the Royal Hospital during the Blitz. On Saturday morning, at the regular Pay Parade, the Governor 'addressed In-Pensioners and residents thanking them for their behaviour in the recent "Blitz"'.[13] Despite the wartime news blackout, the bombing of the Royal Hospital's infirmary had been widely reported and 'in view of newspaper reports of the bombing, there were constant telephone enquiries all day long'.[14]

That evening, however, on the night of 19–20 April, London witnessed another major air raid, the duration and ferocity of which meant it too earned its own moniker, 'The Saturday' – 'on the night of 19/20 April, another very large raid targeted the East End and the docks [...] In just a few days, another 2,000 Londoners [...] died.'[15]

This raid is noted in the War Diary, albeit with the East End being the principal target of the attack, the Royal Hospital was spared further damage.[16] This was not the case in the rest of the borough, though. Despite the raid being focused on the East End, bombs nevertheless fell across other districts of London. In Chelsea, one of the major incidents recorded during 'The Saturday' occurred at St Luke's Hospital, which received a direct hit.

This was the casualty clearing hospital to which the majority of the shocked and injured survivors from the Royal Hospital's infirmary had been evacuated three nights earlier. Now they had to be rescued again, as patients from St Luke's, including In-Pensioners and Royal Hospital staff, were carried to safety at the height of the bombing. For many, including the badly injured Sister May, this experience had a profound impact:

> This Hospital was [...] severely damaged by bombs and the ward in which Sister May was lying was closely adjacent to the 'incident'. This experience, while helpless in bed, affected Sister May considerably. She was again evacuated at the height of the raid.[17]

This time ambulances drove rescued survivors beyond the city limits, such that the following morning, In-Pensioners Herbert Watts, George Rowley, Jack Rodgers and Robert Lloyd found themselves under the care of the British Red Cross Society in the County Council Emergency Hospital in Old Windsor, Berkshire.[18]

On the morning after the raid, Sunday Church Parade in Chelsea was held as usual in the chapel. However, it was anything but a usual Sunday morning at the Royal Hospital, for the War Diary goes on to note:

> After Church the Governor addressed an Officers' meeting, in view of the Adjutant having informed the Lieutenant-Governor the previous day, that all heads of departments considered evacuation of the Royal Hospital essential. The Governor stated that he did not intend to evacuate without direct orders from the Government.[19]

There had been a comparative lull in the bombing in the weeks leading up to 'The Wednesday' and Londoners had begun to hope that the worst was behind them. Consequently, 'the renewal of heavy bombing, though in theory expected, took people by surprise', with the result that 'several Mass Observers, for the first time since September, independently suggested an appreciable deterioration in morale'.[20]

With the bombing of the infirmary followed so quickly by the bombing of St Luke's Hospital, this mood of despondency was clearly shared by the residents of the Royal Hospital, and as In-Pensioners and staff voiced their concerns, the mood of the troops was relayed up the chain of command. It fell to the adjutant, Captain Dean, to inform the Lieutenant Governor of the growing disquiet in the ranks, who, in turn, passed the news on to the Governor.

General Sir Harry Knox was in a deeply unenviable position. Evacuation could only be undertaken if the Hospital had somewhere to evacuate to, and the pre-war experience of the institution had shown that for political and logistical reasons there was simply not the appetite among the authorities to accommodate the needs of the Royal Hospital. If the Governor was ordered to evacuate, then clearly the authorities issuing such an order would have the responsibility of clarifying exactly where the In-Pensioners should go on receiving the instruction to 'March Out!' However, in the absence of such an order, the Governor had no choice but to assume the In-Pensioners would remain in London, despite the clear and present danger they now faced.

The mood in the Hospital at this time, as evidenced by this entry in the War Diary, was reflective of the general mood of foreboding that hung over London in the wake of these two devastating raids. After the pause from mid-March to mid-April, the Luftwaffe had returned, and with an intensity and ferocity even greater than previously. The American journalist Vincent Sheean, on returning to London from the United States in mid-April, remarked:

> You won't find any of the high-spirited we-can-take-it stuff of last year [...] people stay at home, they go to the shelters, they are getting a little grim. All the novelty is gone. The epic period is over. Food has something to do with it, too – everyone is probably a little undernourished. Whatever it is, there's a big difference.[21]

During the weekend of 19–20 April 1941, the Royal Hospital came close to breaking point.

Despite the seemingly impossible position facing the Royal Hospital in April 1941, and the depth of the challenges it now faced, help was at hand. Once again, as on other occasions during the war when the Hospital had its back to the wall, the broader military family stepped in to offer assistance.

On the night of 16–17 April, within moments of the infirmary being hit by parachute mines, the Grenadier Guards stationed at Chelsea

## Aftermath

Barracks and the reserve RAF crew of the barrage balloon in the South Grounds, without waiting for orders, had rushed forward selflessly to assist Royal Hospital staff in rescuing trapped In-Pensioners. Now, as the Hospital struggled to deal with the aftermath of the tragedy, help was again forthcoming from across the extended military family.

The Princess Christian Home near Brookwood in Surrey, run by the Incorporated Soldiers', Sailors' & Airmen's Help Society, which opened in 1914 as a convalescence home for wounded servicemen, contacted the Royal Hospital and offered berths for half a dozen survivors from the infirmary bombing. And during the weekend, the retired Major Morland, owner of Rudhall, who, with his wife Dulcie, had given over the greater part of their home to accommodate evacuated In-Pensioners in September 1939, also contacted the Royal Hospital with suggestions of a neighbouring property where the owners were willing to extend an offer of assistance.

Following on from these telephone conversations, the War Diary reports that on Monday, 21 April, 'in the afternoon the Lieutenant-Governor left to inspect a house near Rudhall', while the following day, six In-Pensioners departed for the Princess Christian Home at Brookwood.[22]

As Lieutenant Governor Major General Morgan-Owen left Chelsea, rescuers still digging in the infirmary ruins finally reached the site of the little shelter beneath the stairs in which Sisters Nicholson and McMullan had sought shelter. This time, there would be no miraculous escapes, as the War Diary notes, 'The last body, that of Sister Nicholson, was removed during the afternoon by the Chelsea Salvage party.'[23]

Eight In-Pensioners and five nursing staff were killed on the night of the infirmary bombing, and a further three In-Pensioners died later from their wounds.[24] The youngest of the nurses to die was 43-year-old Olive Jones from Wales.[25] The oldest In-Pensioner, Henry Augustus Rattrey, would have been 101 in May 1941, had he survived. It had taken five days to dig through the smouldering rubble before all the bodies were retrieved.

The Notice of Death certificates for the staff casualties are held in the Royal Hospital's archives and each one is signed by the adjutant, Captain C.G.T. Dean, whose experiences during the war and, in particular, after the infirmary bombing may go some way towards explaining his apparent reluctance to dwell on the war years in his subsequent published history of the institution.[26] The death certificates signed by Dean were for colleagues whom he had typically worked alongside for over a decade and who had died in the most traumatic of circumstances. Rather poignantly, these were nurses who, as with the In-Pensioners who died alongside them, should by all accounts have been evacuated to safety on the outbreak of hostilities in September 1939. The one casualty who had originally been evacuated, Sister Edith Taylor, the senior medical officer in charge of the Rudhall contingent, had returned to Chelsea in early 1940, whereupon she had been persuaded by the Governor to continue serving at the Royal Hospital. Her decision to continue to serve had tragic consequences.

In the days immediately following the bombing, letters of condolence were sent to next of kin by senior Officers of the Hospital, written with compassion and in a manner which attempted to gently soften the blow for those left to mourn:

> The Ward which was bombed was visited by our Chaplain about half an hour before it was destroyed, and he found all the patients fast asleep, so we have the great consolation of knowing that they were entirely blissful of their sudden end.[27]

Meanwhile, as the Lieutenant Governor was visiting Ross-on-Wye, further offers of help were received by the Royal Hospital. Most significantly, the British Red Cross Society contacted the Governor and offered the lease of Ascott House, near Leighton Buzzard, to be used as a replacement infirmary. Ascott House was a Rothschild family property, which Anthony de Rothschild had placed at the disposal of the Red Cross in September 1940 'for the duration of the war, or two years, whichever was shorter' at a 'nominal rent of 4s. 0d. a year'.[28]

With the bombing of St Luke's Hospital only three days after that of the infirmary necessitating a further evacuation of injured survivors, the prospect of taking up the offer to use the Victoria Children's Hospital on Tite Street now seemed less appealing. Evacuating the infirmary patients to a safer location outside London was a considerably more attractive proposition.

While these offers of help were received by the Hospital, the Governor also proactively approached several army regiments to enquire

## Aftermath

as to their willingness and ability to host some of the more able-bodied In-Pensioners at their regimental depots. With this request, Sir Harry Knox was trying to create a breathing space for the Royal Hospital while more permanent solutions were sought to assuage the increasing clamour for the evacuation of the institution. A copy letter is held in the archives of the correspondence sent to a number of regimental headquarters depots from the Governor, dated 22 April 1941:

> Dear Sir,
> You will have seen in the papers that the Royal Hospital Chelsea has suffered some damage from enemy action. I am considering various measures for reducing the number of our In-Pensioners who are in residence in Chelsea. There is no intention of evacuating the Hospital but it would be a convenience and to the benefit of the Pensioners if some of them could have a change. In the margin of this letter are the names of the In-Pensioners now at Chelsea who belong to your Regiment. I write to ask if it would be possible for you to put up any of them at your Depot for a prolonged visit.[29]

The letter was sent to at least five regiments, and although there is no evidence in the archives of replies being received, later entries in the War Diary suggest that on receipt of official endorsement from the War Office, these army regiments did indeed step forward to help the Royal Hospital in this hour of need.

A number of well-meaning members of the public, more often than not with army connections, also wrote to the Hospital and offered accommodation, some of which was gratefully accepted. On 23 April, the War Diary notes, 'A draft of four In-Pensioners left for White Hill, Berkhamsted, where they are to be the guests of Mrs Foote, widow of Brigadier-General Foote [sic]'.[30]

Shortly after this draft departed, a convoy of cars carrying Officers and a motor coach with a 'representative party of eighteen In-Pensioners' left for Brookwood, Surrey, for the funeral service of the infirmary victims.[31] The same day, the Governor also opened 'preliminary negotiations for Ascott House and Cobrey Park, Herefordshire'. The objective of the negotiations instigated by the Governor were twofold: to establish a replacement infirmary at Ascott House with Cobrey Park intended for use as a more general out-station, along similar lines to that of the nearby Rudhall, leased by the Hospital in 1939.

Cobrey Park was a country house near Ross-on-Wye, the owner of which, Mr Pearson, had been introduced to RHC by Major Morland of Rudhall. On his recent visit to Ross-on-Wye, the Lieutenant Governor had visited Cobrey Park and determined that it could potentially accommodate up to sixty In-Pensioners, who were not bedbound infirmary patients, but were struggling to cope with the intensity and ferocity that characterised the Luftwaffe's renewed bombing campaign.

Although the Governor had insisted at his meeting with the Officers and department heads after the recent Sunday church service, that there would be no wholesale evacuation of RHC unless ordered by the government, it was clear from his subsequent actions that he nevertheless intended moving as many In-Pensioners as possible out of the danger area that London had once again become in the wake of the two recent devastating raids. This would be achieved by whatever means possible.

The decision taken during the Phoney War to keep Rudhall open as an out-station, despite the general disillusionment with the policy of evacuation at that time, now proved its worth, as Rudhall was to be used as a blueprint for a further development of the out-station model. The owner of Cobrey Park was prepared to sign a similar agreement with the Commissioners to that signed by Major Morland, and this property could therefore also be operated 'under the radar', and hence outside the usual requisition framework.

The agent acting for the owner, Mr Pearson, was at pains to point out that his client would require additional compensation for relinquishing his home, as 'he grows mushrooms on a fairly large scale and maintains that in leaving Cobrey Park he is sacrificing his income from that source'.[32] The higher lease payment that the Royal Hospital was being asked to pay was not the only potential drawback with Cobrey Park, however. It also transpired that the country estate was not connected to the mains water or local sewerage network, and its independent sanitary arrangements were a cause of some concern. Consequently, the Commissioners of RHC commissioned a local sanitary engineer to produce a report to determine whether the estate's existing sanitary arrangements would be able to cope with the arrival of sixty Chelsea Pensioners. The subsequent report concluded that 'the present arrangements are suitable for a country house with a very small staff, but to accommodate the proposed numbers would seriously overflow the existing sewerage cesspit'.[33] This sanitary engineer's report, while casting doubt on the sub-optimal scale of the mushroom farm's ability to accommodate the needs of sixty In-Pensioners, would also set in train a sequence of events that would uncover the Royal Hospital's plans to expand its previously unreported out-station initiative.

In the days immediately after the bombing of the infirmary and the subsequent evacuation of survivors from St Luke's Hospital, the Royal Hospital received much correspondence from the various casualty clearing hospitals to which staff members and In-Pensioners had been admitted. These letters confirmed the admittance particulars of patients, and where applicable, described their injuries. They include some touching and compassionate details, such as a request from In-Pensioner Herbert Watts, who had lost his spectacles, which he had carefully wrapped in his handkerchief while being carried from the ruins on a stretcher, asking for their safe return should they be found among the debris.[34] In its reply, the Hospital promised, rather ambitiously, to make every effort to retrieve the glasses, 'if they can be traced amongst the debris at the Infirmary' ruins, but in the meantime, he could rest assured that 'two handkerchiefs will be sent by the Quartermaster direct to Watts'.[35]

However, within two weeks of the bombing, the Royal Hospital began to receive rather more formal correspondence about the casualties, and the tone became noticeably less compassionate. For example, a letter dated 28 April 1941 was received from the Commandant of Winkfield Place Convalescent Home in Windsor Forest, Berkshire, enquiring as to what future plans RHC had for I/Ps Rowley, Rodgers and Lloyd.[36] These In-Pensioners had been evacuated to Winkfield Place after also being bombed out of St Luke's, but as the Commandant points out:

> They are not really suitable cases as this is a Military Convalescent Home and though we are always prepared to take air-raid casualties, we have not the means for nursing chronic cases [...] our Medical Officer feels that we ought, if possible, find somewhere more suitable for such chronic cases, and has asked me to write and ask you whether you could advise us in the matter.[37]

In fairness, these were not unreasonable points to make. The night of 16–17 April had been the heaviest bombing raid of the war so far, and as evidenced by the following weekend's bombing, further heavy raids were correctly anticipated. Emergency hospitals needed to be emptied of walking wounded as quickly as possible to prepare for potential further waves of casualties.

The letter from Winkfield Place on 28 April was followed up with a letter the following day from the Head of the Ministry of Health Emergency Medical Service, 'I would be very glad to have from you any suggestions or instructions as to when you would be able to receive these men [Rodgers, Rowley and Lloyd] back, or if there is any other Institution to which your infirm pensioners have, or are, being transferred'.[38]

This put the Commissioners and Officers of RHC in an invidious position, for I/P Rodgers was 89 years old, I/P Lloyd was 81 and I/P Rowley was 75.[39] Quite apart from the injuries each had sustained during the bombing, all three men were chronically ill and bedbound. It had proven impossible to evacuate them before the war, in part due to the refusal of the Ministry of Health to allow the Royal Hospital to requisition suitable medical facilities in Hereford as part of a broader plan to evacuate the institution in its entirety to Herefordshire.[40] It was, however, now impossible for RHC to take the men back. The infirmary was a burnt-out ruin and it was impracticable for these men to be accommodated in the Long Wards. Nevertheless, similar letters were also received from other emergency hospitals to which In-Pensioners had been evacuated.

In the weeks immediately after the infirmary bombing, the Commissioners and Officers of the Royal Hospital were forced to grapple with the challenges of trying to discharge their duty of care to an increasingly despondent In-Pensioner community in Chelsea, while simultaneously attempting to organise suitable evacuation accommodation for the survivors of the infirmary bombing and all the time fearing what else may be in store for the institution and its remaining residents. The contents of some personal letters written during these dark weeks are further revealing as to the mood in the Hospital at this time. For example, Assistant Secretary Maurice Fitzgerald received a letter from the ex-chaplain of the Royal Hospital, Reverend H.T. Malaher, who had transferred to a new posting in Catterick, Yorkshire, shortly before the Blitz, enquiring as to the events of 16–17 April.[41] In his reply, Fitzgerald goes into much detail about the raid and describes 'a night of considerable tribulation'. Listing the casualties of the bombing, he reassures Malaher that he and his family were physically unharmed, having 'suffered merely in their morale in the catastrophe'.[42] He goes on to add rather ominously, 'one wonders however, when we will have the second half so to speak'.

The publicity surrounding the bombing of the Royal Hospital's infirmary was not confined to the extensive reporting recorded in the newspapers of the time. On 30 April, two weeks after the raid, the BBC visited the scene of the infirmary bombing to conduct on-site interviews with some of the survivors. This outside broadcast was recorded in the form of a 'gramophone recording for broadcast purposes'.[43] The reporter, Wynford Vaughan-Thomas, interviewed Colonel Nash, the Physician & Surgeon who, alongside his wife Rachel, had manned the FAP in the basement of the West Wing until they were forced to abandon it due to the encroaching flames. Also interviewed were 27-year-old nurse Hannah Deasy, who had displayed such heroism on the night and would subsequently be gazetted in recognition of her bravery; Sergeant Harrison, who had organised the Fatigue Parties during the rescue operation; the Hospital's chaplain, the Reverend Hogg, who had visited the wards on his evening rounds shortly before the parachute mines struck; Ward Orderly Marrable, who had such a miraculous escape after rushing into the infirmary courtyard when he mistook the parachute for a German airman bailing out of his stricken plane; and finally, Colour Sergeant Jones and the Sergeant Major, who had visited evacuated In-Pensioners to St Luke's Hospital before they had been bombed out again during 'The Saturday' raid, the following weekend.[44]

This extensive publicity surrounding the infirmary bombing played an important role in shaping attitudes towards the plight of the In-Pensioners. This was the case among members of the public and officialdom alike. Opinions about how the elderly and infirm should be treated had moved on since the bureaucratic indifference witnessed during pre-war planning, and these more sympathetic attitudes, combined with the Ministry of Health's urgent need to free up beds in casualty clearing hospitals occupied by displaced In-Pensioners, would play to RHC's advantage in the weeks ahead.

The military Officers of the Royal Hospital had also learnt much since 1939, not only about the difficulties of dealing with government bureaucracies, but also the potential advantages of blitzkrieg – lightning war – tactics. Such an approach would now be employed by Assistant Secretary Maurice Fitzgerald and his ever-reliable ally at the War Office, Mr H.T. Fry, to conduct 'administration at high speed and short notice [...] to beguile the tedium of long Victorian twilights' as they forced the Governor's evacuation plans onto an unsuspecting and disorganised Whitehall Civil Service.[45]

Since the opening of the Royal Hospital in 1692, its funding arrangements were never particularly straightforward, and this remained the case during the Second World War, with a Treasury official commenting in 1941, 'The finances of Chelsea seem to be complicated and mysterious'.[46] In short, however, the provision of care and sustenance for the In-Pensioners was funded primarily through the surrender of out-pensions, which were 'commuted' on entry into the institution. These pensions were paid by the War Office, and so in a practical sense, the day-to-day operating expenditure of the Royal Hospital was funded by the army element of the War Office budget – army votes, in the parlance of the day.

The maintenance of the Royal Hospital's historic buildings and grounds, on the other hand, was the responsibility of the Office of Works, which since 1940, in recognition of its important role in the government's requisitioning programme, had been upgraded to a full ministry in its own right, and was no longer answerable to the Home Office. Royal Hospital capital expenditure and property-related costs were, therefore, the responsibility of the Ministry of Works and – in the parlance of the day – fell on the Ministry's votes.

It was this distinction that had allowed the Royal Hospital to surreptitiously operate Rudhall, unreported since 1939, as the out-station was funded entirely from the Hospital's operating budget. Rudhall had not required any significant capital expenditure to fit it out for the evacuated In-Pensioners, and consequently, the Office of Works had not been consulted.

The Hospital's operating budget was covered by a grant from the War Office, the level of which was determined by the number of In-Pensioners on the roll call each year. However, the number of such pensioners reported to the War Office as being on the register in the early years of the war made no mention of the fact that since 1939 the Commissioners had been running two separate locations – Chelsea and Ross-on-Wye. Hence, in April 1941, it remained the case that no government departments were aware of the existence of the Royal Hospital's Rudhall out-station.

Unlike Rudhall, however, the proposed additional out-stations, particularly Cobrey Park, were going to require some capital expenditure in order to upgrade the facilities and make them habitable for occupation by the Hospital – the mushroom farm's cesspit, in particular, was in need of some serious attention. This differentiation would quite quickly result in the exposure of the plans for establishing these new out-stations, which at this point in time, did not appear to have been sanctioned by, or indeed communicated to, either the War Office or the Ministry of Works.

The exposure of these plans would, in turn, reveal the existence of the Hospital's current out-station at Rudhall and would lead to Fitzgerald having another uncomfortable telephone conversation with officials at the Ministry of Works. The exposure of the Royal Hospital's evacuation plans would also require the employment of administrative blitzkrieg techniques by the Hospital's officers in order to force the issue.

In recognition of its new status, the Ministry of Works in 1940 moved into newly acquired offices at Lambeth Bridge House, an office block on the south bank of the Thames, on Albert Embankment adjacent to Lambeth Palace. These newly completed offices, although architecturally uninspiring, had the wartime advantage of being constructed in concrete around a steel frame and boasted a purpose-built reinforced concrete air-raid shelter in the basement. However, despite occupying one of the most bomb-resistant buildings in the capital, the Ministry had still seen fit to exercise their legal powers under Emergency Regulations legislation to requisition buildings outside of the danger zone of London for use by a significant number of officials from the Ministry. This included the officials at the Ministry of Works with responsibility for the Royal Hospital buildings and grounds, who on the outbreak of hostilities had evacuated themselves to the requisitioned Palace Hotel, a genteel establishment on the seafront at Rhyl on the coast of North Wales. The Ministry also operated several regional offices, officials from which had drawn up the original requisition registers on instructions from the Committee of Imperial Defence in 1937.

One of the many responsibilities of Maurice Fitzgerald in his capacity as Assistant Secretary was to liaise with those officials at the Ministry of Works whose briefs included responsibility for the Royal Hospital. In 1941, Fitzgerald probably knew that the people he should be dealing with in his interactions with the Ministry were those officials now safely ensconced in the Palace Hotel in North Wales. Nevertheless, on realising that the proposed new evacuation sites would require some capital expenditure and would incur other property-related costs to prepare them for the arrival of evacuated In-Pensioners, Fitzgerald did not contact Rhyl, but instead spoke to a Ministry of Works official at Lambeth Bridge House.[47]

Mr W.D. Marshall of the Lands & Accommodation Division of the Ministry of Works was very sympathetic when contacted by Mr Fitzgerald. He too had survived London's 'night of considerable tribulation' and could only imagine how traumatic it must have been for the In-Pensioners, who must of course now be evacuated, given the total loss of the Hospital's infirmary. Mr Marshall consequently gave Fitzgerald the contact details of a Ministry official in Cambridge who would assess the proposed evacuation site at Ascott House and also furnished the Assistant Secretary with a contact name at the Ministry's Birmingham office, who would arrange for a sanitary engineer to visit Cobrey Park. Hopefully, all could be arranged in short order and the In-Pensioners evacuated forthwith.

The first that Mr A. Miller of the Headquarters Section of the Ministry of Works knew about the proposed evacuation plans of the Royal Hospital was when he received a report dated 7 May 1941 about a sub-optimal cesspit at Cobrey Park, a modest country estate and mushroom farm in Herefordshire.[48] The report had been sent by a sanitary engineer, Mr W. Barnett, appointed by the Ministry's regional office in Birmingham. It would appear that the report was sent automatically to Mr Miller because, despite having been evacuated to the Palace Hotel in Rhyl, North Wales, he retained responsibility for the Ministry's dealings with the Royal Hospital in Chelsea. On receipt of the report, Mr Miller

*Aftermath*

made strenuous efforts to try and contact Maurice Fitzgerald, but with little initial success.

⁂

In Chelsea, on 4 May, the War Diary records, 'Captain Lockley, who has been ill since his exertions on 16 April, was removed to Westminster Hospital'.[49] Captain of Invalids William Lockley, as the Officer in Charge of the air-raid shelter in Infirmary Court, had been one of the first on the scene after the East Wing of the infirmary was struck by the parachute mines on the night of 16–17 April. Upon reaching the site of the bombing, and with complete disregard for his own safety, he had clambered down into the crater in a desperate search for any survivors among the In-Pensioners and staff caught in the blast. This was despite the 52-year-old Lockley being in less than robust health himself.

Enlisted into the ranks of the King's Own Royal Regiment (Lancaster) in 1911, Lockley had served on the Western Front during the First World War, where he received a field commission in 1917. After being gassed during the war, he was invalided out of the army in 1921 and joined the staff of the Royal Hospital on 5 May the same year. He had subsequently served as a captain of invalids for exactly twenty years.

On 26 April, Captain Townsend had been recalled from leave, 'in view of Captain Lockley being unfit from lung trouble incurred on the night of the 16th from fumes and dust'.[50] Now Lockley's condition had deteriorated further, and he had to be admitted to Westminster Hospital. His health would never recover from the effects of the night of the infirmary bombing. The following day, the Governor submitted recommendations for gallantry awards for seven members of staff, including Lockley, for their conduct and bravery on the night of the infirmary bombing.[51] Eventually, however, and despite extensive lobbying by the Governor, only the bravery of nurses Deasy and Howard would be officially acknowledged.[52]

A few days later, on the night of 10–11 May, there was a clear sky over London illuminated by a full moon. The bright evening coincided with another low tide on the Thames, creating ideal conditions for German raiders, and the Luftwaffe once more returned in force for what would prove to be London's worst raid of the Blitz.[53]

During a prolonged attack, which killed or seriously injured over 3,000 Londoners, the casualty list of familiar and famous landmarks continued to grow: the Law Courts of the Old Bailey, the Tower of London and the Royal Mint all suffered damage, while Westminster Hall was set alight, and the House of Commons gutted. Over 250,000 books were destroyed in the British Museum and Westminster Abbey suffered severe bomb damage. Every bridge across the Thames between Tower Bridge and Lambeth was impassable, while Beckton Gas Works blazed as over 700 gas mains were fractured.

The fires around the Elephant and Castle were the worst since the firestorm of 29 December, and water had to be transported through over 9 miles of hose from the Thames and Surrey Canal to fight the blaze, which was not brought under control until well after daybreak. The Royal Hospital was spared further bomb damage, but was again hit by incendiaries:

> Alarm about 23.00 – All Clear 06.00hrs. A heavy raid all night, though not in the immediate neighbourhood. About midnight a breadbasket opened over Burton Court, most of the incendiaries falling there. One fell near No. 2 trench and was put out by Captain Townsend [...] The Chaplain put out another near his house on the South Terrace [...] and the Home Guard one in the bushes opposite the Chapel and another in the Infirmary ruins. Later in the night, this flared up and one of the stokers brought a hose into action and played on the fire. About midnight two fires started in the King's Road [...] smoke drifted across the Royal Hospital and served to screen it from view. About 2am more incendiaries were dropped in the Pensioners Gardens and Ranelagh area. One fell in Light Horse Court opposite the Quartermaster's house and was put out by two of the War Office Detachment, Home Guard. There were no further incidents, but the last raiders did not pass overhead until it was getting light.[54]

Elsewhere in Chelsea, St Luke's Hospital received another direct hit, resulting in casualties among hospital staff and causing such extensive damage to the building that it was forced to close as it was simply

*Aftermath*

impossible for it to continue operating.⁵⁵ This was the hospital to which survivors of the infirmary bombing had originally been evacuated and where surgeons had saved Sister May's legs after the terrible injuries she suffered when thrown along the colonnade as the parachute mines exploded.

After the devastation of this latest raid, there was now no doubt that the infirmary patients could not return to London. The Governor consequently spoke to Mr Anthony de Rothschild, and it was subsequently agreed with the British Red Cross Society that thirty wounded soldiers currently convalescing at Ascott House would move to other Red Cross facilities, and the Royal Hospital would take over the Rothschild property for use as an infirmary for up to eighty In-Pensioners.⁵⁶

This decision was confirmed at a board meeting held on 22 May.⁵⁷ Fitzgerald, however, had still not contacted Mr Miller of the Ministry of Works, based in Rhyl, to discuss the proposed transfer of the lease obligations despite the Ministry having responsibility for property-related expenses of the Royal Hospital.

While this board meeting was taking place in Chelsea, Captain Howell RAMC, Deputy Surgeon of the Hospital, motored up to Ascott House to supervise preparations for the anticipated arrival of the first In-Pensioners, scheduled for the following Monday, 26 May. The Royal Hospital archives contain the petrol ration coupon issued to Dr Howell for this 'Visit to Ascott House to arrange for occupation as an Infirmary'; accompanying him in his 'Private Car M.G. 18 horse-power', the ration coupon records the name of a passenger, the ever-resourceful Mr Albert Burke, who had overseen the administration of the Royal Hospital's clandestine out-station at Rudhall since its opening in September 1939. He was now called upon to utilise the experience he had gained in this post to facilitate the Hospital's smooth takeover of the Red Cross Society's medical facility at Ascott House.⁵⁸

⁙

Captain Howell and Albert Burke were not the only advance party travelling on this late spring day in May 1941. On the Continent, Field Marshal Kesselring was also on the move on 22 May, when he transferred his headquarters from occupied France to the delightful academic and cultural centre of Poznań in Poland.[59] Hitler had determined to attack Russia as the latest step in his campaign of conquest and in preparation for Operation Barbarossa, Luftflotte 2 began moving aircraft and personnel to the east.

While the Wehrmacht and Luftwaffe undertook to establish combined operations on a new Eastern Front, the responsibility in the western theatre for the subjugation of Britain now passed to the Kriegsmarine. Although Londoners did not yet realise it, the raid of 10–11 May 1941 was to be the last mass air attack on the capital, and as Grand Admiral Raeder prepared to step up the tempo of offensive operations by the German Navy, the Luftwaffe's attacks on London were to be dramatically reduced; the London Blitz, to all intents, was effectively over.

14

# Out-Stations

*'... comfortably housed beyond the danger area ...'*[1]

In May 1941, as Field Marshal Kesselring established his new headquarters in Poland, Grand Admiral Raeder, Commander-in-Chief of the Kriegsmarine, welcomed the recent improvement in the weather following the storms in the early months of the year. On 21 May, British Intelligence reported sightings of the battleship *Bismarck* accompanied by the cruiser *Prinz Eugen* as they passed through the Kattegat and out into the North Sea, the latest surface raiders dispatched to prey on Allied convoys. The Royal Navy was ordered to intercept and sink the German warships before they could disrupt the vital supply lines across the North Atlantic, and there followed a six-day game of cat and mouse before *Bismarck*, disabled by a strike from Fleet Air Arm torpedo bombers, was sunk as she made for Saint-Nazaire. However, the sinking of the *Bismarck* was only the opening round in a renewal of the Battle of the Atlantic – Raeder was determined to bring Britain to her knees by starving the country into submission.

In Chelsea, the Officers of the Royal Hospital, unaware of the evolving priorities of the German High Command, continued their strenuous efforts to evacuate as many In-Pensioners as possible, and ensure they could be 'comfortably housed beyond the danger area'.[2] To this end, Maurice Fitzgerald decided that the time had come for him to finally respond to Mr Miller's attempts to contact him.

At a board meeting on 22 May, the Commissioners had approved the signing of agreements for the lease on Ascott House to be transferred from the British Red Cross Society to the Royal Hospital. The same day, the Hospital's Deputy Surgeon had travelled to Leighton Buzzard to assess the equipment needs for fitting out the mansion to receive up to eighty evacuated high-dependency In-Pensioners. Captain Howell had been accompanied on his visit by Senior Clerical Officer Albert Burke, who was to prepare a report on the anticipated operating costs of the out-station.

Although the Rothschild family had generously set a peppercorn rent of only 4s a year, the Royal Hospital would nevertheless also be liable for the annual running costs of the building, including property rates and utility bills, and the operating and insurance costs for state-of-the-art new boilers that had been installed before the outbreak of war. The annual charge for these basic, property-related fixed costs was estimated to be approximately £1,000 per annum, and as property charges at the Royal Hospital were the responsibility of the Ministry of Works, these costs would ordinarily be expected to be borne by Mr Miller's department. Mr Miller, however, had yet to be consulted, and hence Fitzgerald's decision to finally return his calls.

The conversation between Fitzgerald and Miller on the morning of Friday, 23 May 1941 is another telephone call, the notes of which the Ministry of Works felt compelled to retain in their archives. Furthermore, immediately after the call the two men wrote to each other, outlining their interpretations of the key points which each felt had been addressed during their conversation, their correspondence subsequently passing in the post. Later the same day, Fitzgerald also wrote to his erstwhile supporter and confidant, Mr H. Fry, enclosing a copy of his letter to Miller, while also disclosing in an attached covering letter his less than entirely transparent approach to dealing with Mr Miller's enquiries. Herbert Fry was now based in a War Office administration contingent, housed in the Victoria Hotel in Westminster, where he retained responsibility for the Royal Hospital's dealings with the War Ministry.

Fitzgerald opened his telephone conversation with Miller by highlighting the difficulties now facing the Royal Hospital and stressing the pressure being placed on the institution by the Ministry of Health:

From a telephone conversation with Fitzgerald, the Assistant-Secretary of the Royal Hospital Chelsea, this morning, it was gathered that in consequence of the damage done to the Infirmary of the Hospital, the inmates had had to be removed temporarily to other London hospitals. The Ministry of Health were pressing for these men to be removed as soon as possible.

Fitzgerald goes on to report the undertakings he claimed to have received from the Ministry of Works' London office that 'the Department could bear the […] costs of a new establishment' in lieu of the costs 'that it now bore in respect of the Chelsea Infirmary'. He also outlined the contents of the Ministry's report on Ascott House and the likely property-related cost of £1,000 per annum. Having covered the infirmary, the Assistant Secretary moves on to explain that 'a portion of the ordinary ward accommodation had also suffered at enemy hands. For the men so displaced, and for a few old men who could not stay in refuges, it was necessary to find accommodation in the country'. It does not appear from the notes, however, that Fitzgerald made any reference to specific numbers of In-Pensioners requiring evacuation accommodation.

He goes on to mention Cobrey Park and the unsatisfactory report received on this property from the sanitary engineers, before explaining that the Hospital had therefore decided against pursuing negotiations to take over this property and was instead looking at potential alternative accommodation, identified as Harewood House in Hereford. Fitzgerald was awaiting reports from the Ministry's Birmingham office on Harewood but does not explain the reasons why the Royal Hospital was so focused upon Herefordshire as a preferred evacuation location for the Long Ward In-Pensioners. It would appear that the Ministry of Works was still in the dark as to the existence of the Rudhall out-station.

Fitzgerald concluded the phone call by returning to the subject of Ascott House, again stressing the point that this was an 'urgent matter, as he was wishing to send an advance party to the house on Monday 27th [*sic*, 26th] May, and would arrange for the patients to be transferred as accommodation was made ready: he wanted the whole transfer concluded within three weeks'. Fitzgerald promised to send a letter to Mr Miller confirming an official request for assistance in evacuating several In-Pensioners, while insisting that 'total evacuation of the premises at Chelsea was not proposed at present'.[3]

Immediately upon concluding his call with Miller, Fitzgerald composed the letter he had promised to send, outlining in an official capacity the evacuation proposals of the Hospital. Although this correspondence reaffirms the content of the discussion the two men had in their phone conversation, it also contains some significant additional information which Miller does not appear to have been made aware of during the phone call. Notably, Fitzgerald's letter to the Ministry of Works Headquarters Section on Friday, 23 May 1941 appears to be the first occasion on which the department responsible for the property assets of the Royal Hospital is finally made aware of the out-station at Rudhall, which had been in operation since the outbreak of war in September 1939.[4]

Fitzgerald also confirms the termination of negotiations for Cobrey Park and the subsequent interest in Harewood House, before again stressing the urgency attached to the proposed transfer of Ascott House from the British Red Cross Society to the Royal Hospital:

> Our advance party, that is to say, the nursing staff, move in on Monday 26th, and our sick so soon after as I can collect them from the civil hospitals where they are at present being treated. I am under continuous pressure from the Ministry of Health to do this, hence the urgency in getting Ascott House running.

Despite property-related decisions at the Royal Hospital theoretically being the exclusive responsibility of the Ministry of Works, Fitzgerald was in effect presenting Miller with a fait accompli at this point. The lease transfer had been agreed by the Commissioners at a board meeting the previous day and Fitzgerald's letter was posted on a Friday and would be unlikely to arrive in Rhyl until sometime the following week, whereas the Royal Hospital would be moving in to Ascott House on the Monday morning. By the time Miller was in any position to challenge the terms of the property deal agreed between the Royal Hospital, the British Red Cross Society and Mr Anthony de Rothschild, it had already been signed and implementation was under way. Nevertheless, Fitzgerald helpfully suggests, 'It will be useful, I think, if I add some particulars to bring these various schemes into focus'. He goes on to reiterate the reasons for the move and gives an outline of the costs which the Ministry of Works budget should expect to fund, before adding somewhat cryptically, 'The scheme has, however, the approval of the War Office and the Treasury'.

Fitzgerald appears to be a little disingenuous in his choice of words when making this claim, for contemporaneous archive material suggests that the War Office and Treasury had at this stage simply been made aware of the Royal Hospital's predicament and had agreed in principle that 'a scheme' needed to be put in place in order to address the problems the institution now faced. Specific proposals, and indeed approvals, had not yet been agreed between the Hospital and either of these two major government departments. This becomes clear in the covering letter Fitzgerald sends to his ally at the War Office, Mr H. Fry, on the same day, in which he states:

Dear Fry,
I enclose herewith copy of a letter I have just written to Miller of the Ministry of Works, Rhyl, giving the latest picture of Ascott, Cobrey Park and all that, in their general perspective [...] You will see that Cobrey Park is out of the picture, and that Ascott House is booming. It only remains for you to hurry up acceptance of our staff proposals for the latter.[5]

Staff costs at the Royal Hospital were funded from the monies received from commuted out-pensions and were thus charged to the War Office budget. The implication from Fitzgerald's letter to Fry is that despite having agreed in principle that 'a scheme' to replace the Hospital's infirmary needed to be found, nothing had been agreed with the War Office, and by extension the Treasury, as to specific funding agreements for Ascott House.

Reinforcing the sense that the Assistant Secretary was now conducting his own version of institutionalised blitzkrieg in order to push forward the Hospital's evacuation plans are his concluding remarks to Fry, 'Don't let us play spillikins – this is administration at high speed and short notice.' Spillikins, a game played with small rods of wood or bone in which players try to remove one at a time without disturbing the others, is a telling analogy for Fitzgerald to use as he tried to manoeuvre the Ministry of Works, War Office and Treasury into accepting the Royal Hospital's latest evacuation plans – which the institution was already in the process of implementing, regardless of the potential fall-out of moving ahead without having secured the necessary prior agreements from the relevant funding departments. This was spillikins played at blitzkrieg speed.

Meanwhile, Fitzgerald's letter to Miller also clarified the scale of the Hospital's proposed evacuation plans for Long Ward In-Pensioners, and in doing so, exposed the existence of the Rudhall out-station as the reason for choosing Herefordshire as a preferred evacuation location:

> We need a further house for the reason that shelter and trench accommodation at the Royal Hospital leaves some 150 or more of our In-Pensioners exposed to blast and splinters during air raids. We, therefore, wish to evacuate as many of these men as possible, and it is for this purpose that we want to get a house in the Ross-on-Wye area. We have chosen the Ross-on-Wye area because, at the beginning of the war, we created a branch Infirmary at Rudhall for certain bedridden patients, and the nursing and administrative staff of that establishment could cope with the administration and sick of the detachment we now propose to evacuate there.[6]

Fitzgerald goes on to double down on his claim that these proposals have already been agreed by the relevant authorities, whose officials are quite tellingly still located in Blitz-torn London, 'The War Office and Treasury will approve any scheme which you recommend and, of course all the expenditure [...] is a proper charge for public votes'. Finally, he adds, 'There is no question of evacuating the Royal Hospital in its entirety. The policy is to retain at the Royal Hospital as many of the In-Pensioners as can be provided with shelter or trench to sleep in during Blitz nights [...] I hope this clears matters up [...] it only remains to impress on you the extreme urgency of the Ascott House scheme.'[7]

Fitzgerald was taking a calculated gamble in trying to force the Hospital's proposals through the bureaucratic quagmire and so avoid the issues which had bedevilled the pre-war evacuation plans of the institution. In suggesting that the evacuation plans and their associated costs had already been agreed by the relevant authorities from whom such agreements were required, Fitzgerald hoped to move the debate swiftly on to the practicalities of organising the evacuation of the In-Pensioners. However, in some respects, subsequent correspondence suggests that he appears to have been pushing at an open door with regard to those government departments and officials who were still based in the capital, and who had themselves been living with the reality of the Blitz. It therefore only remained to carry along the likes of Mr Miller and his colleagues, safely evacuated to Rhyl, at a speed which prevented them from mounting any serious opposition to the Hospital's plans.

In this regard, Miller's letter to Fitzgerald, also dated 23 May 1941, and which passed in the post, suggests the Royal Hospital was right to be nervous about attitudes in Rhyl to the proposed evacuations. Miller begins his letter to Fitzgerald by expressing his relief that he has finally been able to get hold of the Assistant Secretary after weeks of trying, 'I am very glad that we have been able to get in touch with you over this partial evacuation from Chelsea'. He then proceeds to inform Fitzgerald that 'Mr W.D. Marshall is in the Lands and Accommodation Division at Lambeth Bridge House and is not connected with Chelsea Hospital [sic] in any way', before pointedly noting that he did 'not think that he could have intended to give you any undertaking that we would, or would not, bear any particular charges in connection with your partial evacuation'.

As Miller points out, 'that is a point on which we shall have to give the decision here'.[8] However, this assertion of authority on behalf of the Headquarters Department of the Ministry of Works does of course miss the point – as far as the Commissioners were concerned, a decision had already been taken and the move to evacuate would commence immediately after the weekend, regardless of any thoughts Mr Miller and his colleagues in Rhyl may have.

The remainder of Miller's letter is a series of questions seeking points of clarification as to precisely what the evacuation of the infirmary patients would entail, couched in a somewhat condescending, tone deaf and excessively bureaucratic manner. He goes on to inform Fitzgerald that he has sent a telegram to the Ministry's Cambridge official, Mr Carlisle Hardy, authorising him to proceed with helping to fit out Ascott House ready for the In-Pensioners' arrival. Miller was of course playing catch-up as he was swept along by Fitzgerald's blitzkrieg.

Despite the pressure the Royal Hospital was under to remove In-Pensioners from civilian hospitals and the consequent efforts to put in place a durable long-term solution to the loss of the Hospital's infirmary, the senior staff of the institution nevertheless found time to offer assistance and guidance to those well-meaning members of the public who had stepped forward to help RHC in its hour of need. Shortly after the Governor had faced down the officer's request for a full evacuation after the Church Parade on 20 April, he had written to Mrs Foot of White Hill Farm, Berkhamsted, widow of Brigadier General Foot, accepting her offer to accommodate a number of In-Pensioners in her home to be cared for by her and her house staff. In a letter to Mrs Foot on 21 April, Governor Knox describes four In-Pensioners he intended sending to White Hill – Sampson, Cox, Hope and Ellaway – as all 'over eighty and I hope you will find them satisfactory guests' before adding, 'a thousand thanks for all you are doing'.[9]

Two days later, the War Diary records a draft of four In-Pensioners leaving for White Hill. Over the next several weeks, a regular series of letters were exchanged between the Royal Hospital and Mrs Foot as she and her staff settled the old soldiers into their new home and made them as comfortable and welcome as possible. Mrs Foot enlisted the services of her local doctor, Dr White, when one of the In-Pensioners, Cox, fell ill and had to be admitted to a local hospital.[10]

Now, on 24 May, after composing his letters to Miller and Fry the previous day, Maurice Fitzgerald also wrote to Mrs Foot. He was replying to an earlier letter about Cox and writes, 'We are glad to hear that Cox progresses: he was a great favourite here'. He also enclosed sprigs of oak leaves for Mrs Foot to present to her house guests so that the In-Pensioners could celebrate the forthcoming Founder's Day on 29 May.[11] Sprigs of oak are traditionally worn on Founder's Day to commemorate the escape from the pursuing Parliamentarian soldiers of Charles II by hiding in an oak tree after the Battle of Worcester in 1651.

Unusually, however, Mrs Foot did not immediately reply to Fitzgerald's letter, which caused a little consternation in Chelsea. The welfare of the In-Pensioners remained the legal responsibility of the

Commissioners, and to have seemingly lost contact with four of them was therefore a matter of some concern.

A few days later, on Monday, 26 May, the War Diary notes, 'Captain Howell, Deputy Surgeon, with the Matron and infirmary staff went to Ascott House, Wing near Leighton Buzzard. This house had been equipped by the British Red Cross Society as a convalescent hospital with 80 beds [...] the house is now being reequipped by His Majesty's Office of Works.'[12]

❖

Meanwhile, in the Atlantic, a battle group which included the aircraft carrier *Ark Royal*, whose aircraft had disabled the *Bismarck*, battleships *King George V* and *Rodney*, and the heavy cruiser *Dorsetshire* converged on the outnumbered and outgunned German raider. Out at sea, an unequal battle ensued throughout the night and into the next day before *Bismarck*, ablaze from bow to stern, slipped beneath the Atlantic waves at 10.36 a.m. on 27 May.

The surface raider had been hoping to reach the safety of the port of Saint-Nazaire in occupied France, which would have offered shelter and protection from the attention of the Royal Navy and Royal Air Force as it was a heavily defended naval base. Her fellow raider *Prinz Eugen*, unlike the *Bismarck*, succeeded in evading her pursuers, and on 1 June successfully reached the safety of occupied France as she entered the port of Brest.

This latest stage in the Battle of the Atlantic marked an important turning point, for 'these dramatic events of May 1941 marked the climax, and final defeat, of the German plans and efforts to win the Battle of the Atlantic with surface ships'.[13] However, the battle to defend Britain's Atlantic supply lifeline was far from over. Attention would now shift to the Kriegsmarine's increasingly formidable U-boat flotillas, which under the command of one of Germany's most capable strategists, Admiral Dönitz, had also taken advantage of the availability of bases on France's Atlantic coast.

The decision by the French government in 1940 to seek accommodation with Hitler through capitulation presented an unexpected advantage to Dönitz. In the early months of the war, U-boats had been lost en route to the Atlantic while traversing the North Sea and English Channel, both heavily patrolled by the Royal Navy. However, with the signing of the armistice with France in June 1940, Dönitz was able to move eight of his sixteen U-boat flotillas to French naval bases: two each to Brest, Lorient and Saint-Nazaire, with the other two based at Bordeaux and La Rochelle.

Despite regular maritime and airborne patrols by Britain, it was now impossible to prevent U-boats reaching the North Atlantic convoy routes in force. The use of French naval bases also allowed Dönitz to keep more U-boats at sea for longer, allowing for the deployment of a more focused operational strategy involving concerted attacks on convoys by several U-boats working together – the 'Wolfpack'.

The Kriegsmarine estimated 'that to defeat Britain their sinkings must average 700,000 tons a month', and to achieve this, Dönitz calculated that he needed 300 operational U-boats, compared to the fewer than 100 he had available in 1941.[14] Up until the summer of 1941, the monthly average of tonnage sunk was less than 200,000 tons, but with the effective ending of the surface-raider campaign, German naval construction focused on expanding the U-boat fleet, and as Dönitz's flotillas received bigger, faster and stronger vessels, the initiative in the Battle of the Atlantic would once more swing in favour of Germany. The Royal Hospital would soon feel the effects of this emerging shift in the fortunes of war.

❖

On 29 May 1941, another low-key Founder's Day was held at the Royal Hospital at which Field Marshal the Lord Milne was the Reviewing Officer, 'with the band of the Coldstream Guards in attendance. The ceremonial was as usual, but no invitations were issued to visitors. Captains Bailey and Goring were on leave, Captains Lockley and Townsend sick and Captains Dean and May were the only officers on parade.'

Regardless of the subdued nature of the parade, 'in his speech Lord Milne said that the parade was the smartest he had seen at the Royal Hospital'.[15] However, despite the best efforts of Fitzgerald, as the Royal Hospital paid its annual ceremonial homage to the memory of its founder Charles II, efforts to evacuate the more vulnerable residents to a place of safety before the expected resumption of hostilities by the Luftwaffe had still not resulted in any significant numbers of In-Pensioners having been moved. Ascott House was not yet ready for occupation and its funding arrangements had still to be agreed, and after the termination of negotiations to take over Cobrey Park, it now seemed that its proposed replacement, Harewood House, was also going to present insurmountable problems. The War Office were being slow in approving the temporary transfer of In-Pensioners to their regimental training depots, and the Ministry of Health was continuously pressing for the removal of Royal Hospital residents from casualty clearing hospital beds.

The sense of gloom pervading the Royal Hospital at this time was lifted somewhat when a letter from Mrs Foot was received a few days after the Founder's Day parade. To the relief of all concerned, contact had been restored with the Hospital's modest out-station detachment in Berkhamsted, and the 64-year-old Mrs Foot made clear the reasons for her recent 'radio-silence' in the opening remarks of her letter, as she alludes to the occasional occupational hazards associated with taking a hands-on approach to managing her estate. 'Unfortunately I have been laid up as a result of getting too close when gassing rabbits,' she explains.[16] However, despite being incapacitated by this unfortunate mishap, she was 'very much honoured to receive your request that I should distribute the sprigs of oak leaves to the Chelsea Pensioners' and goes on to add that due to her recent unfortunate misadventure, she had:

> ... asked Brigadier-General J.H. Bush, who lives in Berkhamsted, if he would very kindly give the oak sprigs to the men. He is over 80 himself [...] and had Ellaway, Hope and Samson up to tea with him. I am told they had a very happy time [...] They still seem very happy and it is delightful to have them here.[17]

Clearly, there were still beacons of hope among the gloom as the Royal Hospital pressed forward with its proposed evacuation plans during the early summer of 1941. Furthermore, while the Royal Hospital was digesting the welcome news from the White Hill Farm out-station, indications from the Treasury seemed to imply that this important department of state was prepared to adopt something of a wait-and-see approach to giving its blessing to the funding of the Hospital's more ambitious evacuation proposals, while still allowing preparations for the In-Pensioner transfers to continue.

On 3 June, Mr Miller of the Ministry of Works wrote a lengthy letter to the Treasury, explaining how his department had 'suddenly become aware of certain evacuation proposals of the Commissioners of the Royal Hospital, Chelsea' in a reference to the sanitary engineer's report, received unexpectedly in early May.[18] Having outlined the Hospital's other evacuation proposals, Miller tried to ascertain the extent to which the Treasury and War Office had, or had not, given their blessing. Despite Fitzgerald's assurances, he nevertheless notes, 'We were not clear how far the Treasury might have agreed to this partial dispersal on representations of the War Department', before asking whether the Treasury agreed that the proposed 'evacuation necessitated by enemy activity is a liability upon public funds'. Miller was clearly suspicious of Fitzgerald's blitzkrieg tactics and was consequently seeking clarity and reassurance from the Treasury before giving his own department's blessing to the Hospital's plans. For its part, however, the Treasury had more important matters to attend to and Miller would be made to wait before receiving a reply to his lengthy letter of enquiry.

Meanwhile, on 7 June, an entry in the Hospital's War Diary served to remind the residents why evacuation was once again deemed desirable as 'shortly after 2am an enemy plane passed over, dropping at least one bomb somewhere in the locality, [it] was enough to dislodge plaster. No alert was sounded.'[19] Staff and In-Pensioners alike remembered the pause in bombing during the autumn, when only the occasional reconnaissance aircraft was seen, before hostilities were resumed, with renewed intensity.

The Royal Hospital remained keen to take advantage of this latest apparent pause in Luftwaffe raids to move as many In-Pensioners as possible 'to be comfortably housed outside the danger area'. In early June, permission was finally received from the War Office for drafts of In-Pensioners to leave the Royal Hospital for extended stays at the initial training camps (ITCs) and regimental depots of their former regiments. This would at least buy the Hospital some time while the officers fought to put in place more permanent evacuation accommodation.

Consequently, at the end of successive weeks on 9, 15 and 20 June, 'parties of In-Pensioners went off to the I.T.C and training centres of their Regiments (usually at, or near the Depots), by arrangement with the War Office and Officers Commanding; in all a total of 56'.[20] Once again, the extended military family had come to the assistance of the Royal Hospital and In-Pensioners were widely dispersed across the country, with, for example, ten I/Ps being housed with the Royal Sussex Regiment in Chichester; eight with the Hampshires in Winchester; six with the Somerset Light Infantry at their depot in Taunton; five I/Ps of the South Wales Borderers were dispatched to Brecon; and four members of the Oxford & Bucks Light Infantry were housed in the regimental depot at Cowley Barracks in Oxford.[21] In many cases, the evacuated In-Pensioners quickly became local celebrities in their temporary new homes, with an article in *The Times* on 16 June 1941 describing the experiences of five In-Pensioners 'adopted by their Regiment', interviewed while sat in the Sergeants' Mess.[22]

In London, meanwhile, the management board meeting on 19 June again highlighted the problems suppliers were experiencing in meeting their obligations to the Royal Hospital as Admiral Dönitz's U-boats slowly stepped up their campaign against supply convoys in the North Atlantic.[23] The logistics of feeding In-Pensioners who remained in the capital were becoming increasingly difficult.

The meeting also discussed the equally stretched nature of the Hospital's finances, which were once again under pressure from the costs associated with discharging the institution's duty of care to the In-Pensioner residents. This was despite some welcome news from solicitors acting for the Treasury, who confirmed that the Royal Hospital was entitled to financial compensation for the significant bomb damage it suffered during the Blitz, as the 'buildings fall within the exception mentioned in Section 37 War Damage Act 1941'.[24]

The war, however, was about to take another decisive turn. Three days after this board meeting, on the morning of 22 June 1941, the German Army, supported by warplanes from Kesselring's Luftflotte 2, launched their attack on Russia. Operation Barbarossa had begun, and further mass air raids against London would consequently be suspended for the foreseeable future.

The following day, with the Royal Hospital still unaware that the Blitz was effectively over, the first In-Pensioners were moved to their new out-station accommodation, 'nine sick In-Pensioners were evacuated by motor ambulance coach to Ascott House. They had been preceded on the 20th by one Colour Sergeant and one Corporal to assist the Medical Officer in Command'.[25]

With the Hospital's infirmary now relocated to Ascott House, the medical contingent remaining in London was significantly reduced:

> The medical staff remaining at the Royal Hospital comprises, The Physician & Surgeon (who can be relieved in an emergency by the Medical Officer at Chelsea Barracks), Dispenser, a male orderly; and a Sister, Nurse and Domestic Servant who are getting their meals from the Great Kitchen and living in Gordon House.[26]

Chronic and end-of-life care for In-Pensioners would henceforth be provided in the Royal Hospital's relocated, out-station infirmary at Ascott House, courtesy of the generous lease terms offered by Anthony de Rothschild. The infirmary would remain in Wing, Buckinghamshire, until 1947. During July and August, as Hitler's latest blitzkrieg campaign overwhelmed the poorly prepared, badly equipped and incompetently led Russian Army and Air Force, the Royal Hospital continued with its transfers of bedbound chronic-care patients to the newly created out-station infirmary.

The next to move were the In-Pensioners being treated in civilian hospitals in Emergency Medical Service Sector 7, which included the Windsor area, and whose administrators had been particularly vocal in their demands to move their Royal Hospital patients, with the War Diary noting, '9 July – Twelve In-Pensioners were removed from Civil Hospitals in the Windsor area to Ascott House'.[27] This transfer was followed on 19 July when another 'six In-Pensioners went to Ascott House', who were followed by 'the last party of Infirmary patients, 12 in number, were removed from Civil Hospitals [...] to Ascott House' on 22 August.[28]

On 28 August, the management board meeting notes the completion of the transfer of In-Pensioners from civilian hospitals and gives an update on the distribution of Pensioners between Chelsea and the developing network of out-stations now operated by the Royal Hospital, 'RHC 299, Ascott House 48, Rudhall 47, Princess Christian Home 6, Mrs Foot (White Hill Farm) 5, Scots Guards Pirbright Depot 2, Furlough 59, civil hospitals 3; Total 469'.[29]

In the months since the bombing of the infirmary, the Commissioners and Officers of the Royal Hospital had succeeded in evacuating a third of the In-Pensioners. This compares to less than 10 per cent of the establishment who were originally evacuated on the outbreak of war in September 1939.

Despite these evacuations taking place, however, the question of who would pay the costs of these additional facilities had still not been settled and continued to preoccupy Mr Miller in the Palace Hotel, Rhyl. Having had no reply to his lengthy letter sent to Mr Herbert Gatliff in the Treasury in June, Miller followed up with a polite reminder on 15 July:

Dear Gatliff,
I should be very glad to know whether you have yet reached a decision as to the incidence of the costs that will be incurred through the taking over of a country house for certain of the in-pensioners of the Royal Hospital at Chelsea, suggestions as to which I put forward to you in my letter of the 3rd June last.[30]

Mr Gatliff in the Treasury did not appear to share Miller's sense of urgency and simply replied in a short note a few days later, 'We have consulted with the War Office on this, and as the finances of Chelsea seem to be complicated and mysterious it is taking them some time to make up their minds about it'.[31] Civil servants in London clearly had more important matters to deal with.

Funding arrangements were going to have to be agreed at some point and the Commissioners were no doubt aware that they were taking something of a risk, and probably exceeding their authority, in agreeing lease terms with Mr Anthony de Rothschild without having received the necessary prior approvals from the department responsible for Royal Hospital property matters, namely the Ministry of Works. The Commissioners did, however, have a fall-back financial position insofar as the Royal Hospital had some modest endowment funds which could be drawn on if necessary, should the Ministry of Works ultimately refuse to pay. Some of these funds were invested in properties which were rented out by the Hospital, with the rents generating a useful if modest degree of independent income.

Given the lack of agreement around the funding situation for Ascott House in these early summer months of 1941, the Commissioners sought to review the state of their lease agreements with their tenants and make sure rental receipts were up to date. In this regard, there is an interesting, albeit poignant entry in the management board meeting minutes for 28 August, where it is noted that the Royal Hospital instructs its lawyers to begin repossession proceedings against a tenant at No. 22 Embankment Gardens who had not paid his rent for two years. The tenant, Mr Sacha Roman, had last been heard from in Bucharest.[32]

At this stage of the war, as with the Royal Hospital's funding arrangements, some mystery still surrounded the activities of the Nazi Party towards Jews and other minorities in German-controlled territory. This was despite some uncomfortable and scarcely believable reports and rumours emanating from the Continent about the treatment of those deemed undesirable by the Nazi authorities and the alarming nature of the policies to which these unfortunate groups were now being subjected. Unfortunately, there was nothing complicated about the outcomes – Mr Sacha Roman did not survive the Holocaust.

Despite transfers of In-Pensioners to Ascott House, the Commissioners continued with their efforts to secure additional evacuation accommodation for some of the Long-Ward men. A further letter from Mr Miller at the Ministry of Works to the Treasury on 27 August confirms progress in this regard, 'Since writing my letter to you of the 3rd June, about certain proposals for the evacuation of the pensioners of the Royal Hospital, there have been two developments'.[33] The first development concerned some unexpected additional expenditure required at Ascott House 'to render the House suitable to the needs of the pensioners', but more significantly, Miller also notes:

> ... another property, Moraston House, near Ross on Wye, was considered by the Hospital Commissioners to be suitable for some of the pensioners surplus to the shelter provision at Chelsea, and we were asked to inspect it. It is intended for 60 pensioners and 12 staff.[34]

Moraston House was owned by Guy's Hospital, but leased to a tenant who was in the process of vacating the property. The Royal Hospital had consequently been offered the opportunity of taking on the lease for the use of Moraston as an evacuation out-station, to be administered from Rudhall by the ever-resourceful Mr Burke. Keen to take advantage of this situation, the Commissioners had instructed Fitzgerald to press ahead with negotiations, and he again utilised the services of the Ministry of Works' Birmingham office to assess the suitability of the property.

Meanwhile, Mr Miller in Rhyl, still struggling to contain Fitzgerald's administrative blitzkrieg, had buckled under pressure but was nevertheless clinging to the hope of finally getting some clear guidance from the Treasury as to the legitimacy of Fitzgerald's claims of funding approval. In his letter to Gatliff, he adds, 'In the absence of any instructions to the contrary, we have taken it as accepted by you that such evacuation of these surplus pensioners is agreed.'[35]

Since first becoming aware of the Royal Hospital's evacuation plans on 14 May, when he had unexpectedly received a sanitary engineer's report about a house in Herefordshire, Miller had been pressing the Treasury for confirmation that the proposals put forward by Fitzgerald had been costed and approved. Herbert Gatliff at the Treasury finally decided to offer him some reassurance, while also quite pointedly noting the more important matter of principle. On 1 September, he writes:

Dear Miller,
Thank you for your further letter of the 27th August, 1941, about the evacuation of the pensioners of the Royal Hospital. It is proving very difficult to disentangle the financial complications of this matter, but it is obvious that however the financial responsibility should be divided the actual job is right and has got to be done.[36]

Fitzgerald's blitzkrieg tactics had succeeded and the details around how the evacuation of In-Pensioners from Chelsea was to happen and how the costs were divided did not ultimately matter anymore; the old soldiers had been through enough and, by any measure, had done their duty. It was time they were evacuated, to be 'comfortably housed beyond the danger zone'. This point of principle had now been accepted and everything else was simply background noise.

While negotiations continued around the tenancy of Moraston House, the process of concentrating the infirmary patients at Ascott House was completed. This included those patients at Rudhall, who had been evacuated from the infirmary in Chelsea on the outbreak of war. The War Diary notes the completion of this reorganisation during September:

> Ten infirmary patients were removed from Rudhall to Ascott House on the 17th, and ten others on the 24th, with all the nursing staff except one nurse, who is remaining to act as Long Ward Sister. By these moves the infirmary patients and staff are concentrated at Ascott House.[37]

While these moves were under way, the Commissioners continued to address the deteriorating supply situation in London, with minutes from the management board meeting highlighting reports from suppliers who were unable to meet their obligations to the Hospital as a result of rationing constraints.[38] Such was the seriousness of the developing situation that discussion was held over to the following week's board meeting, at which it was agreed that some suppliers could move from the usual three-month contract lengths to contracts of one month duration only. This would at least secure some supplies for the Hospital, if only on a short-term basis.[39]

With the forty-eight In-Pensioners identified on the 28 August roll call accommodated at Ascott House, and a further twenty having subsequently transferred from Rudhall, almost seventy out of the eighty available high-dependency beds in the Royal Hospital's new out-station infirmary were occupied by September 1941.

The Commissioners now shifted their attention to the evacuation of the more vulnerable Long Ward inmates, and on 20 October, the War Diary notes, 'a draft of 21 In-Pensioners and a Long Ward Nurse went to Rudhall, where the establishment has been fixed at, one Colour Sergeant, two Sergeants, two Corporals and 40 In-Pensioners'.[40]

Meanwhile, in December, Fitzgerald's ally in the War Office, Mr H. Fry, was finally able to write to the Treasury confirming his department's agreement to fund the costs of the new network of out-stations. The funding agreement covered not only the existing one at Rudhall and the new infirmary at Ascott House, but also extended to additional out-station accommodation for those Long Ward In-Pensioners whom it was considered necessary to evacuate due to the inadequacies of the shelter provision at Chelsea:

The trench shelter system at Chelsea was designed for vertical accommodation only, and when air raids became a nightly affair, a proportion of the In-Pensioners had to sleep in the building itself. This was considered an unsatisfactory arrangement, in view of the target presented by the Hospital and the fact that it admittedly afforded no protection, and it was accordingly decided to reduce the number of inmates of the Hospital to the number which could be accommodated in the trenches, the surplus being evacuated. Accordingly, Chelsea sought a house preferably in the neighbourhood of Ross-on-Wye to accommodate some of the non-infirmary in-pensioners.[41]

Such had been the change in attitudes to the evacuation of In-Pensioners from Chelsea since the bombing of the infirmary on 16–17 April that the War Office was prepared to shoulder the costs in full, if necessary, regardless of whether the Ministry of Works were prepared to cover a proportion of the property related expenses in lieu of the costs they ordinarily funded at the Royal Hospital.

However, Fitzgerald's blitzkrieg tactics had also borne fruit, and a reply from the Treasury to Mr Miller at the Ministry of Works in January 1942, confirming the Treasury's blessing to the evacuation proposals, comments:

> … as to evacuation the War Office seem to have gone ahead on the assumption that they were going to pay, and you seem to have gone ahead on the same assumption. I don't think however that this has resulted in two jobs being done or still worse two houses being hired when one would have been enough; at least I hope not. Provided the arrangements actually made are satisfactory to all parties and the minimum necessary we don't much mind whether you or the War Office bear the cost.[42]

All that remained to be done was to agree terms with Guy's Hospital for the assignment of the lease of Moraston House to the Royal Hospital and the transfer of In-Pensioners from Chelsea could then commence.

⁕

While this latest agreement to evacuate more In-Pensioners from London was being finalised, the war was moving rapidly. The German Army supported by the Luftwaffe crushed Soviet forces and pursued Stalin's demoralised army deep into Russian territory. Leningrad was under siege, Crimea was threatened and Moscow itself could soon be occupied; only the arrival of 'General Winter' would slow the German advance.

As Stalin contemplated capitulation, the Japanese chose to move against the Western powers. In a surprise attack on the US Naval base in Pearl Harbor on 7 December, major elements of the United States Pacific fleet were destroyed, while on the same day, the Imperial Army landed forces on the Malayan Peninsula. Battle-hardened troops, transferred from fighting against the Chinese, began a rapid advance towards the symbolic heart of British military power in the Far East, the 'Impregnable Fortress' of Singapore.

For the Royal Hospital, these unfolding events would soon exacerbate the already acute supply and logistics problems and ultimately bring into question the very survival of the institution's historic Chelsea home.

## 15

# Dispersal and Demolition

*'... urgently required for construction of aerodromes ...'*[1]

The capitulation of France in July 1940 had created a 'Happy Time', *Die Glückliche Zeit*, for Germany's U-boat flotillas. Sailing from French naval bases, they wrought havoc on poorly defended convoys, until in September 1940, under the terms of the Lend–Lease agreement, the United States provided Britain with surplus destroyers from the US Navy Reserve and the U-boat threat steadily reduced. Between April and December 1941, 'submarine sinkings had been 328 ships of 1,576,000 tons, but only one-third of these had been sailing in convoy'.[2] At less than 180,000 tons a month, losses were significantly below the 700,000 tons believed necessary to bring Britain to her knees.

America's entry into the war in December 1941, however, coincided with the delivery of bigger and more powerful U-boats with greater range and endurance. A 'Second Happy Time', *Zweite Glückliche Zeit*, now ensued as U-boats sank unescorted and unarmed merchant ships silhouetted against the bright lights of America's east coast.

In the early months of 1942, Allied shipping losses rose dramatically, 'in February to nearly 500,000 tons, in March to over 500,000 tons, in May 600,000 tons and in June sinkings reached the ominous figure of 700,000 tons'.[3] Meanwhile, in the Far East, the fall of Singapore, the cornerstone of Britain's regional defence structure, destroyed the supply network throughout the region.

The Royal Hospital soon felt the effects of these dramatic and desperately serious developments. One of the first impacts of the deteriorating supply situation damaged the very fabric of the institution.

The Defence (General) Regulations Act 1939 allowed the government to requisition any property deemed necessary for the war effort and had been used to facilitate the removal of wrought-iron railings, which were melted down and used in armament and munitions production. However, buildings of historic significance had been exempted as the quantities of wrought iron collected thus far, combined with imported scrap iron, had satisfied the needs of the war industries. The rapid increase in shipping losses meant these exemptions no longer applied.

With over half the pre-war In-Pensioner population evacuated from Chelsea by December 1941 and much of the site deserted, a more direct contribution to the war effort was demanded. In January 1942, the War Diary notes, 'Railings removed in Royal Avenue', with a further entry in February, 'Railings removed from Burial Ground, East and North sides', followed soon after by the biggest single scrap-iron contribution from the Hospital in April, 'Railings removed from Burton Court'.[4]

An escalation in Dönitz's U-boat campaign, combined with the successful efforts of the Hospital authorities to evacuate vulnerable In-Pensioners from Chelsea resulted in ominous consequences for the physical integrity of the Royal Hospital, which in its own way would eventually prove to be every bit as serious as Göring's terror-bombing campaign during the recent Blitz on London.

In April, as the railings enclosing Burton Court were removed, an advance party of staff left for Ross-on-Wye to make Moraston House ready for the planned arrival of In-Pensioners, the lease agreement having recently been signed.

Supply issues continued to dominate management board meetings in Chelsea, with the Hospital's regular fruit and vegetable supplier suggesting moving to weekly pricing, given the increasingly uncertain supply situation. A supplier in Sloane Square highlighted government guidance advising businesses to restrict their operations to only supplying customers located within a mile distance from their premises or risk losing their petrol ration allowances.[5]

Despite these difficulties, the Commissioners were able to procure a welcome supply of rum, as noted in the War Diary for 28 March

1942, 'Issue of rum to mark the 250th anniversary'.[6] Question marks nevertheless hung over the likelihood of the Royal Hospital celebrating many more anniversaries in its historic London home. The transformation of attitudes towards evacuating the In-Pensioners combined with the provisioning and logistical difficulties of remaining in Chelsea had resulted in a significant reduction of the London roll call. These developments, although welcome on one level, would result in unforeseen consequences.

In the early months of 1942, Allied forces were on the defensive everywhere. Hitler renewed his Russian offensive, thrusting towards the symbolically significant city of Stalingrad, hoping to capture the oilfields bordering the Caspian Sea. In the Far East, the Japanese were all-conquering, pushing south towards Australia while advancing north through Burma to threaten India. In the North Atlantic, the U-boat menace continued to exert unrelenting pressure on Britain's supply lines. The Allies desperately needed to take the war to the enemy.

During these dark days of 1942, the means to do so were provided by the strategic bomber forces of the RAF and the USAAF. In March, the RAF's iconic Lancaster bomber flew its first operational sortie and increasing numbers of Boeing B-17 heavy bombers of the US 8th Air Force began arriving in Britain. These heavily armed Flying Fortresses, capable of long-distance daylight raids beyond the range of fighter escorts, enabled the Allies to mount a round-the-clock strategic bombing campaign against targets deep into occupied territory. However, unlike fighter planes capable of operating from improvised grass airfields, these four-engine 'heavies' required purpose-built concrete runways. In the summer of 1942, a major aerodrome construction programme was undertaken across south-east England, which soon resulted in the increasingly empty Royal Hospital being called upon to again play a part in the wider war effort.

For the inhabitants of some of the most heavily bombed districts of London, the rapid build-up of air power in Britain was disconcertingly accompanied by the sound of high explosives detonating once more among already devastated buildings and neighbourhoods. However, this did not signify the long-anticipated return of bombing raids on London by the Luftwaffe, but was instead the result of the work of demolition teams seeking to salvage and reuse material from bombed-out buildings.

The Royal Hospital was not exempted from their attentions, and on 14 May 1942, the Commissioners received a letter from F. Boultwood & Son, outlining proposals for the demolition of the infirmary ruins in order for the resulting rubble to be used in the construction of the much-needed additional aerodromes.[7] Referencing the urgent nature of the building programme was an accompanying note from the Ministry of Works, the government department charged with delivery of the new airfields as quickly as possible.[8]

It is not clear how much, if any, influence the Commissioners of the Royal Hospital had on the discussions around this decision. The ruins of Sir John Soane's infirmary, completed in 1816, were to be unceremoniously demolished by Boultwood & Son, with the resulting hardcore used in the construction of a wartime runway somewhere in south-east England. A board minute entry simply notes receipt of 'a proposal [...] transmitted by Superintendent of Works for removal of debris from the demolished buildings which is urgently required for construction of aerodromes around London'.[9] The minutes go on to record that 'permission for removal of debris should be granted provided that any part of the structure or fittings that may be required for future use of the Royal Hospital is retained intact'.[10]

This was a very important condition attached to the Commissioners' agreement in principle. The Blitz had highlighted the inability of the Royal Hospital to operate without a functioning infirmary and although heavily damaged in the raid on 16–17 April, much of the building was still standing. It could almost certainly offer an effective starting point for post-war reconstruction, and it was vital that as much as possible should be preserved in order to ensure that the evacuated In-Pensioners would eventually be able to return to their Chelsea home. Unfortunately, the evidence suggests that the immediate demands the country faced during these dark days of 1942 took precedence over any post-war considerations and much of Sir John Soane's infirmary was razed to the ground by F. Boultwood & Son's demolition squads.

Founder's Day on 29 May 1942 was marked by the attendance of a very important Reviewing Officer. King George VI, accompanied by the queen, inspected the assembled In-Pensioners. The War Diary notes, 'Beforehand, when enquiries were made from the King's private secretary whether he would wear oak leaves, the reply was that the Queen would, but not the King.'[11]

The Governor conducted the king along the lines of In-Pensioners, while Her Majesty the Queen was escorted by the Lieutenant Governor. The royal party subsequently visited 'the Chapel, Great Hall, Cookhouse, and No. 1 and No. 2 Long Wards', during which a number of staff members and In-Pensioners were presented to the royal couple.[12] The visit also included a tour of the infirmary ruins, where they met the Physician & Surgeon, matron and 'available medical personnel'.

It is very unlikely that anybody involved in this walkabout through the Royal Hospital's bomb site had any idea as to the fate that awaited the ruins. The Founder's Day visit ended with a reception in the Governor's House before the royal party departed via London Gate, with the East Road lined by cheering In-Pensioners.

A few days after Founder's Day, the evacuation and dispersal of In-Pensioners from the Royal Hospital accelerated once more. On 1 June, the adjutant, Captain Dean, accompanied by Captain of Invalids Geoffrey Bailey, drove to Moraston House taking two In-Pensioners with them. Reporting back to Chelsea that the 'house was ready except for certain pieces of furniture [...] a draft of 24 In-Pensioners went to Moraston' on 3 June, followed on 1 July by 'a draft of 13 In-Pensioners'.[13]

Before their departure, however, these latest evacuees ominously witnessed, 'the Royal Hospital struck by lightning [...] Brickwork of chimneystack over No. 8 ward damaged.'[14] As the exodus of In-Pensioners from their historic Chelsea home gathered pace during the summer of 1942, the subsequent destruction of this symbol of benevolence towards retired army veterans seemed almost preordained.

Shortly after this latest draft of In-Pensioners departed for Ross-on-Wye, demolition crews began arriving in Chelsea. The process which had started in January 1942 with the removal of railings from around the Hospital's estate accelerated during the summer as work began on tearing down an institution that embodied the very essence of the covenant between the nation and its old soldiers, 'broken by age or war'. The Ministry of Works' efforts to meet the airfield requirements of Bomber Command would ironically result in Allied bombers exacting a greater toll on the fabric of the Royal Hospital than the Luftwaffe, as demolition crews finished the job originally started during the Blitz.

As the evacuation of In-Pensioners continued, the news from the front lines remained grim. On the Eastern Front, the Germans renewed their offensive as soon as the ground was hard enough after the spring thaw, and on a battlefield which favoured the attacker, the Russian Army again collapsed for 'the southern steppe – the treeless, roadless, almost unwatered "sea of grass" which Cossack horsemen had made their own in their escape from tsarist autocracy – offered the army no line of obstacles on which to organise a defence'.[15]

In North Africa, the Afrika Korps swept eastwards towards Egypt, overwhelming British forces in the stronghold of Tobruk, which in 1941 had withstood an eight-month siege. This time, the defenders were outflanked by Rommel's fast-moving armoured vanguard and collapsed before they could mount an effective defence.

For Maurice and Suzanne Fitzgerald, the loss of Tobruk brought personal anguish in its wake, for among the captured British Army units was the 1st Battalion of the Sherwood Foresters, their eldest son's battalion. Fortuitously, however, Lieutenant Maurice Fitzgerald narrowly avoided becoming a prisoner of war, having been posted to a training course in Gaza, Palestine, shortly before the German advance. He was en route to rejoin his battalion when he was ordered to join the general retreat into Egypt.[16]

While Lieutenant Fitzgerald's battalion lay down their arms in North Africa, in Chelsea Assistant Secretary Fitzgerald attended a board meeting on 18 June at which supply issues again dominated the agenda. Curry powder and mixed spices were difficult to obtain, 'owing to the shortage of supplies due to the far eastern situation' and prices had risen accordingly.[17] The continuing supply difficulties led to a reduced ration allowance, and the Commissioners became increasingly concerned about the Hospital's ability to source the provisions necessary to meet their duty-of-care obligations.

It was felt the shortages were having an adverse effect on the health of those In-Pensioners who remained in Chelsea, and as a consequence, the Government's London District Catering Advisor visited the Royal Hospital to assess the health of the In-Pensioners and advise on whether an application should be made for an increase in ration allowance.

Whether the Hospital would be able to successfully source any recommended increase in rations was, of course, another matter.

The subsequent report was discussed at a weekly board meeting on 16 July, where it was fortuitously noted that there was actually no need for the Royal Hospital to apply for an increase in ration allowance as the catering advisor had conveniently concluded that 'personnel […] no doubt owing to age, remain more healthy on the slightly reduced ration as at present'.[18] The 'useless mouths' who remained in London evidently appeared to be thriving, despite the deteriorating supply situation.

Regardless of the suspicion that the authorities in London could be making a virtue out of necessity, the supply situation outside the capital appears to have been somewhat less acute than that faced in Chelsea. With a system of out-stations now in place, all with official sanction from the relevant government departments, the Royal Hospital determined an 'establishment strength' of sixty In-Pensioners and staff at Rudhall, seventy at Moraston House, and eighty patients and fifty nursing staff at Ascott House. Regular rotations of personnel between the front-line berths in Chelsea and the rest centres in the countryside were subsequently established, thus ensuring no In-Pensioners were continuously exposed to danger or to the provisioning difficulties faced in London.

The difficult supply background was eased enormously for the Royal Hospital by the fact that the out-stations now had official sanction from the relevant funding departments in Whitehall. Maurice Fitzgerald's administrative blitzkrieg as he sought to secure official approval for the growing network of out-stations meant that by the summer of 1942, Senior Clerical Officer Mr Albert Burke could henceforth be more open in his dealings with local suppliers. This improved freedom of action helped with efforts to tackle one of the more pressing local provisioning issues faced by the Royal Hospital, as it sought to supply its out-stations in Herefordshire.

Moraston House, like Rudhall, 'was miles away from any public house', and this unfortunate geographical shortcoming caused much disquiet among In-Pensioners rotated out of Chelsea. However, it was now possible for Mr Burke to do something about this unhappy predicament and consequently, 'arrangements were made for a brewery to every so often deliver a barrel of beer'.[19] This well-received provisioning initiative led to the establishment of a thriving social club at the out-station, in turn creating a legacy which continued after the war, for the club was 'so successful that later on it was thought it would be a good idea to start an In-Pensioners club in the Royal Hospital'; one that still thrives to this day.[20]

Despite the absence of any further mass air raids since the devastating night of 10–11 May 1941, the prevailing mood continued to believe this extended quiet period was merely a temporary pause and the war would eventually return to London. The Russians, forced back into Stalingrad, were now fighting with their backs to the River Volga and could capitulate at any moment; in North Africa, Rommel pursued the British 8th Army into Egypt, threatening the Suez Canal, the vital supply lifeline from what remained of British interests in the east. In the Pacific, the United States, notwithstanding the spectacular success at the Battle of Midway, remained under intense pressure. Consequently, this theatre of war necessarily commanded the focus of the American military in 1942.

Sooner or later, massed formations of Luftwaffe bombers were expected to once again be seen in the skies over London and so preparations for their return continued, despite the welcome respite. In August, the War Diary notes, 'Fire watching becomes obligatory for men between certain ages. After discussions between the Lieutenant-Governor, War Office and A.R.P. offices [...] arrangements were decided upon.'[21] Fire-watching rosters were subsequently organised, and their composition serves to highlight the changing nature of the occupants of the Royal Hospital.

By the summer of 1942, In-Pensioner numbers had fallen to little more than 200, from a pre-war level of around 500, with most of the live-in nursing staff also evacuated alongside the infirmary patients. On the other hand, the number of administrative staff in the War Office Pensions Secretariat had risen to over 100, from only fifty in December 1939.[22] An increasingly large daily workforce of Ministry of Works personnel was to be found in the area around the bombed infirmary, the Soane Stable Yard and the West Wing, where they supervised the likes of Boultwood & Sons in the demolition of the infirmary ruins and other properties in Chelsea destined for hardcore aerodrome foundation landfill.

In recognition that much of the wartime population of the Royal Hospital were now transient daytime residents or In-Pensioners rotated in from the out-stations, the War Diary entry reflects the fire-watch crew arrangements that necessarily had to be made, 'The Royal Hospital's A.R.P officer to be responsible for fire-guards accommodation and general supervision. A roster of ten Senior Fire-Guards was proposed, one to be on duty each night.'[23] The ten regular fire-guards included only four senior Royal Hospital personnel: Captain Loyd, the Hospital's ARP officer, Assistant Secretary Maurice Fitzgerald and his deputy, Office Keeper Richard Fry, and Colonel Martin, the Chief Clerk. The other regular fire-guards had to be recruited from 'various Ministry of Works employees and Secretary's Office clerks', who ordinarily did not live on site and for whom temporary accommodation would be provided during their shifts.[24]

Teams of fire wardens were responsible for patrolling the Royal Hospital grounds. The area around the administration buildings on the eastern side of the site was the responsibility of a team drawn from staff in the Pensions Secretariat. Light Horse Court was patrolled by wardens drawn from the 'War Office Platoon of the Royal Hospital Home Guard', with Figure Court the responsibility of the Royal Hospital staff platoon of the Home Guard. Meanwhile, the western side of the site around the 'West Road area' was the responsibility of 'Ministry of Works staff', and an observation post was established on the 'roof of the East Wing', manned by clerks from the 'War Office team, who are housed at night in No. 22 Ward'.

The composition of the fire watch teams clearly illustrates that by 1942, the Royal Hospital increasingly resembled simply another place of work into which office workers and maintenance personnel commuted daily, only staying overnight in order to fulfil their fire-watching roster responsibilities. The war had changed the composition and nature of the Royal Hospital community in a way that would have serious implications for the future of the institution.

Despite the increasingly transient nature of the Hospital's on-site community, a high level of alert and vigilance was maintained, regardless of the absence of enemy bombers, and preparations for the expected resumption of air raids continued in October:

> ... at the suggestion of Captain Townsend a trailer fire pump has been obtained through the Ministry of Works. The National Fire Service has provided an instructor to train all able-bodied men in its use. Other local fire precautions instituted by the N.F.S. are the provision of a concrete tank at the North end of Royal Avenue; the conversion of part of the site of the demolished Burton Court Mansions into a water tank; and the installation of fire mains up Chelsea Bridge Road and up Royal Hospital Road by the Burial Ground, thus enabling water to be pumped direct from the river.[25]

Lessons had been learnt from the experiences during the Blitz when fires had blazed out of control as fire-fighting teams had struggled with water availability. During the summer of 1942, as demolition crews reduced damaged buildings down to ground level, crushing brickwork to produce hardcore for the aerodrome-building programme, the exposed basements were used to accommodate concrete water tanks for fire crews to use when the Luftwaffe's bombers returned.

With Civil Defence preparations continuing as the Home Front braced for the anticipated resumption of hostilities, the Royal Hospital's War Diary records the operation of the rotation system for In-Pensioner occupancy in Chelsea.[26] Adopting this well-established military doctrine of rotating men, with time spent in the front line interspersed with rest and recreation in the rear areas, undoubtedly held a number of attractions for the Hospital authorities. The network of out-stations supported the maintenance of an ongoing presence in Chelsea, while ensuring that no In-Pensioners were to be constantly exposed to the dangers and difficulties of life in London.

The rotation system did, however, have the disadvantage of reducing the sense of association to Chelsea of an increasingly transient In-Pensioner population. Nevertheless, it was soon working well enough for the Hospital to close the smaller and less-efficient out-stations at White Hill Farm and the Princess Christian Home. Shortly after Moraston House reached its roll-call capacity, the Governor wrote to the Princess Christian Home and to Mrs Foot at White Hill, informing them of RHC's evolving evacuation strategy, 'now, however we have rest accommodation available at Ross-on-Wye, and I am calling in our various small detachments'.[27] The transfer of In-Pensioners from the more peripheral out-stations was completed during September, after which the Governor, on behalf of the Commissioners, once again wrote to the Princess Christian and Mrs Foot, expressing the gratitude of the institution for their assistance as they had stepped forward to offer help during the Royal Hospital's hour of need.

An extract from one of the letters gives an insight into quite how much difficulty the Royal Hospital faced in 1941 in the aftermath of the infirmary bombing:

> Your invitation was extended at a time when the Commissioners were seriously concerned how they would continue to fulfil their obligation to provide for the safety and well-being of the In-Pensioners in their charge, in view of the repeated and heavy bombing of the Chelsea district. It lightened their pre-occupation to know that some, at least of the older men, without dependents able to receive them, could as the result of your good offices, be so comfortably housed beyond the danger area.[28]

As In-Pensioners settled down to face the winter either in out-station accommodation or on rotation in the increasingly empty buildings of the Royal Hospital, the first heavy snowfalls of late 1942 appeared to mark the arrival of 'General Winter' and the subsequent end of another fighting season in Russia. General Paulus and his 6th Army reached the banks of the Volga, south of Stalingrad, on 12 November, completing the encirclement of the city.

In Chelsea, photographs taken of the Royal Hospital's damaged infirmary building show that a comprehensive clearance project was well under way and much of the ruined structure had already been demolished. The Royal Hospital's treatment at the hands of the demolition squads had potentially ominous consequences for the future of the institution. The destruction of much of the Hospital's on-site infirmary would inevitably complicate plans for any permanent return of In-Pensioners to Chelsea. The temporary loss of the infirmary in October 1940, while Bomb Squads dealt with the series of UXBs which had hit the building, highlighted the inability of the institution to function successfully without the means of providing acute care to the most vulnerable of the Hospital's residents. Evacuation of the Royal Hospital Chelsea came at a price.

In late 1942, however, the tide of war was starting to turn. In October, Rommel's Afrika Korps were defeated at the Battle of El Alamein, followed in November by the amphibious landings of Allied troops in Morocco and Algeria. Forced to fight on two fronts, the Afrika Korps were crushed in the ensuing pincer movement.

At the Royal Hospital, as it became increasingly apparent that victory would be achieved in the North African campaign, on Sunday, 15 November, 'to celebrate the winning of the Battle of Egypt, an old bell [...] was erected on the roof of the Chapel and rung before the Parade Service'.[29] Meanwhile, on the Eastern Front, despite the onset of winter, the Russian Army launched a surprise counter-attack on 19 November, as Operation Uranus forced the Germans onto the defensive and led to the encirclement of the 6th Army at Stalingrad. The tide of war in Europe had turned decisively.

With Christmas approaching, the Royal Hospital was again eager to encourage as many In-Pensioners as possible to accept furlough payments and leave Chelsea to spend the festive season with friends or relatives beyond the danger zone. Despite the recent successes on the battlefield, memories of the firebomb attacks on London in December 1941 persisted and any In-Pensioner who could leave London was encouraged to do so.

The impact of Dönitz's U-boat campaign was being felt more widely than simply in Chelsea. The most recent management board meetings to discuss supplier contracts had again highlighted supply difficulties, where it was noted the price of tea had risen substantially, while supplies of vegetables and coffee were difficult to obtain.[30]

Supply difficulties and price rises were also impacting the population in general and meant friends and relatives were either unwilling or unable to host an In-Pensioner, given the burden of having to feed them. The Commissioners therefore approached the War Office, with whom it was agreed that In-Pension allowances would be increased 'as a temporary measure', thereby allowing a more generous furlough payment to be made.[31] This additional payment helped to alleviate the burden on families and friends in meeting the spiralling costs of ever-reducing rations and enabled more In-Pensioners to leave London, although it was agreed that the increased payments would be reviewed after the war.

In January 1943, despite the difficulties and shortages on the Home Front, the mood among the Allies was one of quietly growing confidence. It was only a matter of time before Rommel would be forced out of North Africa; General Paulus and the 6th Army were being driven into an ever-decreasing defensive perimeter at Stalingrad; and the Japanese advance in the east had slowed as their supply lines became hopelessly overstretched. In Western Europe, the strategic bombing offensive grew in intensity as the new aerodromes constructed at speed across southern England enabled more heavy bomber squadrons to join the fray. The limiting factor on the RAF's operational capability was the appalling casualty rates among Bomber Command's crews, and training replacements as quickly as possible became a strategic imperative.

However, a poignant entry in the Royal Hospital's board meeting minutes highlights the human cost of this fast-track training initiative, when on 28 January 1943 it is noted, 'Reported – the death of ex-RHC clerical officer Mr Cyril Ring who joined the RAF on the 26 June 1941. He was killed on the 13 January 1943 aged 21 years and 11 months.'[32]

Cyril Ring lived with his parents in Finchley, north London, from where he commuted into the Royal Hospital each day to work in the Pensions Secretariat, responsible for the administration of army out-pensions. He was called up shortly after his 20th birthday and on joining the Royal Air Force was posted to Silloth in Cumbria with the 1st Officer Training Unit (1 OTU). Here he trained as a bomber pilot on the twin-engine trainer, the Lockheed Hudson light bomber until, tragically, in January 1943, having almost completed his training, his plane crashed near the runway and burst into flames during a night-flying exercise. Flight Sergeant Cyril Ring and his three crew members died at the scene and are buried in the Commonwealth War Graves Commission Cemetery in Silloth, near the perimeter of the old wartime base. His is one of sixty-one graves of aircrew at the cemetery, the majority killed in training accidents, with many being recovered from the water after their planes crashed in the Solway Firth. The accident rate was such that the locals nicknamed this stretch of water 'Hudson Bay'.

On 2 February 1943, the German 6th Army surrendered at Stalingrad. Henceforth, the Germans would be on the defensive on the Eastern Front, conducting an ever-more desperate, scorched-earth fighting retreat until the fall of Berlin in 1945 and the final capitulation of the

Nazi regime. During 1943, it would become increasingly evident that the final defeat of Germany was simply a matter of time, and as this expectation became more widely prevalent, it was remarkable how quickly thoughts soon turned to post-war reconstruction.

For the Royal Hospital Chelsea, however, the 'brave new world' envisaged by post-war planners for those returning from the battlefield would create its own problems, which in turn, presented a further existential threat to the future of the institution.

## 16

# Post-War Planning

*'... just another unwanted structure ...'*[1]

Despite the mood of quiet optimism in London which characterised the early months of 1943, the war was still far from over and the Royal Hospital's War Diary notes, '17 January – Alert: with several raiders overhead, Anti-Aircraft barrage the heaviest yet heard, and a great display of the new projectiles. Some 'delayed-action' bombs fell in Battersea Park.'[2]

The mention of 'new projectiles' is a reference to a recently installed anti-aircraft rocket system as the latest addition to the batteries in Battersea Park, and this appears to have been the target for this latest raid near the Royal Hospital. A few days later, the Luftwaffe returned with another hit-and-run 'Daylight raid – overcast sky. Guns around the Royal Hospital fired, but no bombs heard.'[3]

However, although these nuisance raids created unease and disruption, they were infinitely less destructive than the mass air raids of the Blitz during the winter of 1940–41, and by the summer of 1943, it was increasingly clear that the tide of war in Europe had turned. The German Army's defeat in the battle for the symbolically significant Soviet city of Stalingrad was a crushing blow to Hitler's ambitions in the east and forced his troops onto the defensive.[4] As the Wehrmacht conducted a scorched-earth fighting retreat across recently conquered territory, the

Red Army began the long march towards Berlin.[5] The Nazi regime would soon reap the poisoned fruit of the harvest it had sown.

In the Battle of the Atlantic, the first half of 1943 also marked a decisive turning point in the conflict. In November 1942, the Royal Navy had appointed a new Commander-in-Chief of the Western Approaches, Admiral Sir Max Horton, an outstanding submarine commander in the First World War, and in early 1943, the poacher-turned-gamekeeper introduced a new offensive tactic designed to take the battle to the U-boat Wolfpacks.

The close-support naval escorts which accompanied each convoy now also included carrier-escorts to provide air cover and reconnaissance. More significantly, however, Admiral Horton also deployed independent support groups of modern, fast destroyers and frigates which would 'come to the aid of convoy escorts and, after making contact with the U-boats, hunt them to the death'.[6] When convoys were attacked by multiple U-boats operating as a Wolfpack, they could now call on these support groups, who would race to their assistance and launch co-ordinated counter-attacks against the German submarines.

Although in February, sinkings had again reached over 600,000 tons and in early March two westbound convoys sailing close together suffered serious losses at the hands of an attacking force of thirty-eight U-boats, these attacks marked the zenith of the Kriegsmarine's Atlantic war. From March 1943 onwards, the tide turned, and as the Royal Navy's new tactics were deployed, U-boat losses began to rise dramatically, such that by May 1943, Dönitz reported to Hitler, 'We are facing the greatest crisis in submarine warfare, since the enemy, by means of new location devices [...] makes fighting impossible, and is causing us heavy losses'.[7]

At the Royal Hospital, the dramatic reduction in convoy losses soon began to have a noticeably positive impact on the Hospital's suppliers. The management board meeting on 18 March 1943 notes that supplies across most product areas were more readily available, although 'packaging must be returned or it will be charged for'.[8] Three months later, supplies in general were considerably easier to source, albeit with some notable exceptions, 'Rangoon rice has all gone [...]and only Brazilian or American is left'.[9] Supply difficulties were now increasingly localised, rather than more general in nature.

With the skies above London now quiet for weeks at a time, the Royal Hospital's War Diary contains noticeably fewer entries. It is recorded that the Reviewing Officer for Founder's Day 1943 was Field Marshal Lord Birdwood GCB.[10] And in July it is noted that the 'Commander-in-Chief Home Forces awarded a Certificate for Gallantry or Good Service to Sergeant F.H. Harrison, Royal Hospital Platoon, Home Guard'.[11]

This was, in fact, a belated recognition of the selfless and efficient efforts of Sergeant Harrison, who was in charge of the Fatigue Party on the night of the infirmary bombing in April 1941. The Governor had worked tirelessly to secure recognition for the bravery displayed by many of the staff at the Hospital on this most terrible of nights, but such was the deluge of recommendations at the height of the Blitz, the reviewing bodies simply felt unable to confirm many of them, regardless of how deserving each may have been. Persistent lobbying by the Governor, Sir Harry Knox, eventually resulted in Sergeant Harrison at least receiving some rather belated recognition for his efforts and bravery throughout the war on numerous occasions at the Hospital.

Knox was due to retire later in the year and was determined to achieve some recognition for his staff before he departed. He had lobbied hard on behalf of the Royal Hospital ever since the dreadful night of 'The Wednesday'.[12]

As the extended period of relative calm continued throughout the summer of 1943, it is remarkable how quickly thoughts across Britain soon turned towards post-war reconstruction. At the Royal Hospital, a series of internal reports and memorandums during the summer outlined in detail the work that needed to be done to restore the fabric of the Hospital's buildings to their pre-war state.[13] Work was prioritised on the basis that funding was likely to be quite limited in the anticipated world of post-war austerity.

At a board meeting held on 19 August – which also confirmed the date of the Governor's impending retirement as 27 October – a lengthy discussion took place around the subject of the post-war reconstruction of the Hospital. The debate focused on the Hospital's infirmary and the difficulties associated with trying to manage the Royal Hospital efficiently while the infirmary operated out of a geographically separate location. The infirmary was a key component in the provision of the Commissioners' duty-of-care obligations to the In-Pensioners, delivering day-to-day routine minor medical services to all the Hospital's residents, while also providing specialist acute, high-dependency end-of-life care to many In-Pensioners before they embarked on their Final Postings. The discussion at the board meeting concluded that it was of 'essential importance' that a new infirmary must be 'located within the precincts of the Royal Hospital'.[14] This meeting was not the final word on the subject of post-war reconstruction, and a series of papers and memos appeared throughout the summer months as discussion continued among the Officers and Commissioners about how best to plan for the anticipated brave new post-war world.

With success on the battlefield continuing through the summer of 1943, peace was eagerly anticipated, and it was hoped it would only be a matter of time before the guns fell silent once more across Europe. It was also expected that the eventual peace would be accompanied by a world in which the expectations of the population in general would be somewhat greater than those before the war, while the country's economic capacity to meet such heightened expectations would unfortunately be severely constrained given the financial costs of the conflict. At the Royal Hospital, one memo from this summer of debate stands out from the rest, for it contains an altogether more radical vision of a post-war Royal Hospital.

On 4 October 1943, the adjutant, Captain Dean, wrote a detailed note addressed to his fellow Officers, outlining a particular post-war vision for the institution. It is unclear if the contents of the note simply reflect the personal views of Captain Dean or if they are the result of a more general discussion among the Officers, and potentially, other residents of the Hospital. In his role as adjutant, Captain Dean acted as the conduit through which the views and opinions of fellow officers, and on occasion, the rank and file, were transmitted up the chain of command. It had fallen to Dean to inform the Lieutenant Governor of the mood of the Hospital in the immediate aftermath of the infirmary bombing and the overwhelming belief that evacuation of the In-Pensioners was henceforth a necessity. Now, in the autumn of 1943, with post-war reconstruction an increasingly significant preoccupation of the Hospital authorities, Dean circulated a memo, the contents of which were as explosive as anything thus far used by the Luftwaffe in its air campaign over Chelsea.

The memo begins by suggesting that the polluted air of London was an unhealthy environment within which to situate a retirement home for old soldiers, a view which was, of itself, hardly controversial. Frances Faviell described the numerous air-raid attacks on the Battersea and Lots Road Power Stations during the Blitz, and comments on how, after each raid, the two great temples to power would always emerge still standing, with their colossal chimneys continuing to pump smoke from the boilers in their cavernous turbine halls.[15]

However, what may have been a reassuring sight for Chelsea residents during the Blitz did not detract from the inconvenient truth that the smoke belching out of these great chimneys had a seriously detrimental impact on the health of those living in the immediate neighbourhood, not least of course the residents of the Royal Hospital. Dean proceeds to claim, 'It may be noted that since the opening of Ascott House and Moraston House there has been a great improvement in the mortality figures'.[16] However, despite this claim and its implicit assumption that life in the countryside had exerted a notably positive impact on the Royal Hospital's mortality data, there is nothing in the way of statistical analysis to support the contention. Furthermore, analysis of the relevant entries in the Hospital's Death Register is also inconclusive on this point.[17]

Entries for the war years include deaths that occurred not only in Chelsea, but also at Rudhall, Ascott House and Moraston House, and although the date of death is recorded in each case, there is very little additional information included. For example, for those In-Pensioners who died while at one of the out-stations, information is not provided as to how long they had been at the relevant location before death occurred. It is also the case that no account is taken of return movement between Chelsea and the out-stations – that is, those In-Pensioners who may have remained in Chelsea for a time but also spent rest and recuperation time outside London.

The War Diary, of course, also contains evidence of the system of rotation introduced by the Hospital as the out-station network was developed, after the bombing of the infirmary. Furthermore, no evidence is provided for differences in the underlying health of the various In-Pensioners who may have spent more time at the out-stations relative to the health of those who stayed behind in Chelsea more often.

Despite the fundamental shortcomings inherent in a lack of any form of rigorous statistical analysis, Dean's memo goes on to propose, based on these supposed observations, a radical suggestion as to what the post-war future of the Royal Hospital should entail, namely:

> Old soldiers are proverbial grouser's: but it would seem that much of the grumbling among the In-Pensioners is attributable to friction generated by the uncomfortable conditions in which they live. Indeed were their health, comfort and convenience the only considerations, it cannot be doubted that the Royal Hospital would be moved, either to the outskirts of London, or to some place such as Aldershot, where the In-Pensioners would be in touch with their old Regiments.[18]

The memo goes on to cite the example of the Royal Hospital Greenwich, the Royal Navy equivalent of the Royal Hospital Chelsea, which had closed and hence permanently 'evacuated' its In-Pensioners in 1869. On its closure, the Commissioners in Greenwich had been relieved of the financial burden of maintaining an institution with an In-Pensioner capacity that was ten times the size of Chelsea and which, for years, had suffered a serious shortfall of In-Pensioner numbers. Consequently, relieved of this burden and the financial costs associated with running a retirement home at significantly below its operating capacity, they were able to increase Royal Navy out-pensions from 5*d* per day to 9*d*, an uplift of some 80 per cent.[19] Many of the beneficiaries of these enhanced out-pensions chose to settle in coastal communities near to the home ports of the ships they had served in during their naval service and were able to keep in touch with their old shipmates.

Dean's memo was suggesting two potential alternatives for the Royal Hospital's future, one of which proposed the permanent relocation of the Royal Hospital Chelsea from London, to be replaced by one or more out-stations, such as the ones brought into operation during the war. The other suggestion was to follow the lead of Greenwich and close the Royal Hospital Chelsea completely, using any financial savings to enhance out-pensions, and thus enabling old soldiers to remain with friends or family without being a financial burden, in the same way that enhanced furlough payments had helped Chelsea In-Pensioners during the war.

However, the financial comparison with Greenwich is a dubious one. After the closure of Greenwich in 1869, the government under Prime Minister William Gladstone established a committee to investigate the institutional role and associated financial cost of the Royal Hospital Chelsea, and it reported its findings in 1871.[20] The committee concluded that the Hospital played an important role in supporting old soldiers, and any financial savings from the closure of Chelsea would be too insignificant to have any material effect on the average level of pension paid to the large body of Out-Pensioners. Unlike Greenwich, where the In-Pensioner capacity of around 5,000 berths was significant, relative to the number of Royal Navy Out-Pensioners, this was not the case with Chelsea. The Royal Hospital was to be considered as:

… an almshouse of the best description for the most infirm and helpless of a body of about 64,000 pensioners; and although it involves the separation of its inmates from their friends, it is certain that no increase in pension that could be given would compensate for the comforts both in lodging, food and medical attendance afforded by the Hospital to those who are, without friends and are incapacitated by infirmities from taking care of themselves.[21]

In short, the Royal Hospital Chelsea was institutionally large enough to make a statement in terms of representing the bond of covenant between the nation and those who had served in the army, while at the same time, the financial cost of maintaining the Hospital was insignificant enough to not really matter. The Commander-in-Chief of the Army in 1871, the Duke of Cambridge, put it more bluntly in describing the role of the Royal Hospital Chelsea, when he declared, 'Its main purpose was to save old soldiers from dying in the workhouse'.[22]

The suggestions in Dean's memo, therefore, to either reduce the Hospital to one or more small out-stations established near army garrison towns or to close the institution entirely would prima facie appear to hold little merit. However, the memo is indicative of the potential existential threats the Royal Hospital now faced as the country began to look beyond the war towards a future in which priorities could be somewhat different than in the past. Evacuation, which had seemed to offer salvation to the residents of the Royal Hospital as war clouds gathered in the late 1930s, now appeared to represent a very real threat to the continued existence of the institution in its historic but increasingly empty, abandoned and largely evacuated London home, as peace in Europe seemed tantalisingly close.

It is probably something of an understatement to suggest that this revolutionary proposal was not particularly well received by the Hospital authorities. The Lieutenant Governor, Major General Morgan-Owen, having clearly taken some time to collect his thoughts before responding, replied on 12 November 1943, 'Interpretation of statistics is not a useful field for amateur speculation. Interpretation of vital statistics in particular should be left to the medical authorities.'[23] The Lieutenant Governor goes on to address further points in Dean's memo, in particular focusing on the subject of evacuation. The nature in which the Royal Hospital Greenwich is cited in the memo and the effect its closure in 1869 subsequently had on the level of Royal Navy pensions is rightly dismissed for its irrelevance when considering the likely impact of a similar closure of Chelsea, while the broader impact of such a radical proposal is also considered:

> Evacuation of the In-Pensioners from Greenwich Hospital is not a precedent for the evacuation of Chelsea Hospital [...] If we did evacuate the Royal Hospital, the buildings would become a white elephant [...] The Royal Hospital would become just another unwanted structure and nothing in the world could prevent its demolition to clear one of the most valuable building sites in London for more profitable exploitation.[24]

It is clear from this reply that the Hospital authorities were not ready to embrace the type of full-scale permanent evacuation suggested in the memo written by the adjutant. This was not viewed as evacuation so much as abandonment of the Royal Hospital. Evacuation, in the sense proposed in Dean's memo, was not seen as a potential source of salvation for the Hospital and its residents but was instead viewed as threatening the very existence of the institution itself. Move the establishment out of its historic Chelsea home and the site would soon disappear. The institution itself, as 'an almshouse of the best description', dedicated to the comfort and care of old soldiers, 'broken by age or war', could swiftly follow into oblivion.

The timing of the adjutant's explosive memo was also a cause of much concern to the Commissioners of the Hospital. The Lieutenant Governor's reply was sent only a week after the retirement of the Governor, General Sir Harry Knox, and the Lieutenant Governor, Major General Morgan-Owen, who had been appointed in May 1940, would also soon be retiring after completing his fixed-term appointment of four years.

Fixed-term appointments for these two senior posts at the Royal Hospital had been introduced shortly before the outbreak of war. Prior to this move, there had been no limit on the length of tenure for either post. The Commissioners, however, now felt a sense of unease that such time-limited tenures resulted in the appointment of individuals who were given little time to get to know and understand the Royal Hospital and were instead destined to become a 'bird of passage', which was not necessarily to the long-term advantage of the institution.[25]

Such was the level of concern that the Commissioners wrote to Sir Herbert Creedy at the War Office, asking for an extension in the term of appointment from four years to seven years, particularly considering the uncertain post-war challenges the institution now faced. The issue had been raised with the previous Secretary of State for War, Leslie Hore-Belisha, in 1938 prior to Knox's appointment, but with no success. Sir Herbert Creedy was more sympathetic to the concerns of the Commissioners, and a compromise agreement of five years was eventually agreed for Knox's successor, General Sir Clive Liddell, who took up his appointment on 27 October 1943. The Commissioners of the Royal Hospital were increasingly conscious that the advent of peace was likely to bring its own unique challenges for the institution, and Dean's memo simply reinforced their level of concern as to what the future may hold.

As thoughts increasingly focused on the likelihood of current hostilities soon being brought to an end, reminders of the closing chapter of the First World War were apparent in the latest entries in the Hospital's War Diary, where it is noted in November 1943, 'an epidemic of influenza began towards the end of the month'.[26] In the closing months of the Great War, Spanish Flu had swept across the world, claiming the lives of millions weakened by the deprivations brought on by five years of conflict, and now history appeared to be on the cusp of repeating itself. In-Pensioners, no doubt weakened by wartime rationing despite the conveniently expedient views of government catering officials, were increasingly reporting sick, and the difficulties of running the Royal Hospital without an on-site infirmary were once again highlighted. On 25 December, as 'pork and Christmas Pudding' were served to celebrate Christmas Day, the War Diary notes, 'influenza still raging'.[27]

However, despite having to deal with the accelerating incidence of flu among the In-Pensioner ranks, the Commissioners also needed to attend to the quarterly supplier contract agreements, and as the provisioning situation with suppliers continued to improve, the Officers of the Hospital now found themselves facing disquiet in the ranks. An attempt to shift a coffee contract from a long-term wholesale supplier, George Cox & Son, to a cheaper competitor resulted in a backlash from the In-Pensioners, who were less than happy with the quality of the coffee provided by the alternative supplier. While the Hospital authorities had more than enough to deal with in tackling the influenza outbreak, they had no stomach for an In-Pensioner mutiny over the coffee ration and Cox & Son were quickly reappointed.[28]

Despite growing optimism that the war would soon be over, this was not yet the reality on the ground, and as fighting continued on many fronts, the management board meeting minutes in November contain some potentially troubling developments. At a meeting held on 18 November, the minutes note an agreement between the Commissioners and Chelsea Borough Council for the use of the Great Hall as a reception centre for evacuees from other districts in the event of 'crash raids'.

Following advice from central government of the potential for renewed bombing raids on London, the council's officers were preparing plans for potentially processing up to 300 displaced evacuees from neighbouring boroughs prior to billeting them in Chelsea. Although the Commissioners felt compelled to agree to this proposal, it was nevertheless considered an ominous development. One of the reasons given in the confidential 1938 report, which had recommended evacuation of the In-Pensioners en masse from the Royal Hospital in the event of war, was to utilise the buildings and grounds for other uses, if necessary – which included evacuee accommodation. Now, in late 1943, with the Hospital home to considerably fewer In-Pensioners with many having been transferred to the network of out-stations and the Commissioners increasingly alarmed as to what the post-war future may hold for the institution, outside bodies were beginning to encroach upon the Hospital's estate. In this regard, and almost by way of reassurance, Chelsea Council insisted that any 'aged and infirm' civilians who arrived at the Great Hall reception centre would not be housed in the Royal Hospital, but would be moved into billets 'with the persons with whom they arrived'.[29]

Regardless of the Commissioners' reservations about this somewhat unwelcome approach from the local council, the reason the government was urging local authorities to prepare evacuee reception centres at all was because it had become increasingly apparent in the closing weeks of 1943 that the war could soon return to the skies over London.

In many respects, it came as little surprise that in January 1944, the realities of the moment once more intruded upon any thoughts of post-war reconstruction with all its attendant visions of a brave new world. For months, the combined bomber forces of the RAF and USAAF had been pounding Berlin night and day, reducing Hitler's capital to smoking ruins. In July 1943 Operation Gomorrah, the bombing of the shipyards and U-boat pens in the port city of Hamburg, had created a firestorm which virtually destroyed the city, killing and injuring tens of thousands of civilians. An outraged Hitler, increasingly losing the trust and confidence of the German people, ordered revenge attacks by the Luftwaffe in retaliation for these humiliating failures of the Third Reich to protect the German population. These counter-attacks began with renewed bomber raids against London and southern England, to be followed soon after by newly developed secret weapons, the V1 doodlebugs and V2 ballistic missiles: the *Vergeltungswaffe*, 'vengeance weapons'.

The war returned to Chelsea on the same day that the Commissioners of the Royal Hospital discussed the latest proposals for the post-war future of the institution. At a management board meeting held on the morning of 21 January 1944, the suggestions put forward in Dean's memo were discussed, and there does not appear to have been any support from the Commissioners for such radical proposals. In relation to the suggestion to move the Royal Hospital out of Chelsea, the following somewhat disparaging reference by the Lieutenant Governor appears in the subsequent board meeting minute, 'The most drastic suggestion is that the Royal Hospital be moved to the suburbs, or a military centre like Aldershot [...] I am [...] averse to any suggestion of moving the Royal Hospital from its present site'.[30]

✣

Sometime after the Commissioners completed their deliberations and the *ex officio* members not resident at RHC had departed the Hospital's grounds, the Luftwaffe returned to Chelsea, 'Alert about 8.50pm. Several German aeroplanes heard passing from West to East. Heavy barrage.'[31] With German raiders once more overhead, the War Diary describes the unfolding attack, 'Alert about 4.50am: smaller raid than earlier in the night. A dud high explosive bomb or anti-aircraft shell fell in Radnor Walk.'[32]

The raid was not a heavy one compared to those of the Blitz of 1940–41 and over the next few days several unexploded bombs were unearthed, whereupon it was discovered the Luftwaffe was using a new type of projectile, albeit given the number of unexploded examples it was one whose use they had yet to perfect:

A dud 50kg bomb located [...] in the middle of Colonel Martin's (Chief Clerk) allotment, near the nurses home, was dug up by the bomb squad [...] a similar dud bomb was removed from a sewer in Radnor Walk. These two bombs were of a new type – half high explosive and half incendiary.[33]

What would become known as the mini-Blitz had started, and although less intense than the bombing of earlier in the war, it would be characterised by the use of a range of new weapons by the Luftwaffe; weapons it would take time for the defenders to learn how to counteract.

While the Royal Engineers were examining these latest German bombs, the Royal Hospital management board met once more to discuss the future of the institution. It was decided to write to the War Office again, expressing concern at the length of tenure of the senior staff, given the potential for dramatic changes to be incorporated into post-war planning at RHC, and asking for an extension of Lieutenant

Governor Morgan-Owen's term of office so that he might 'lead RHC representations on post-war rebuilding'.[34]

During his time at the Royal Hospital, and particularly during the summer of debate around the post-war future of the institution, Major General Morgan-Owen had seemingly become convinced that the Hospital now faced an existential threat every bit as serious as that created by the war thus far, and the Commissioners agreed that for the future sake of the institution it would be expedient to retain Morgan-Owen's services, if at all possible. This time, however, the War Office was less sympathetic, and subsequently turned down the Royal Hospital's request for an extension to Morgan-Owen's tenure of office.[35]

During February, Luftwaffe activity steadily increased, but with limited direct impact on the Royal Hospital despite the key infrastructure assets in the neighbourhood once more attracting the attention of the bombers, '18 February: Alert at 1am. Barrage exceptionally heavy. No bombs locally, but the glow of fires seen in several directions.'[36] This raid was followed a few days later by one much closer to the Hospital, and in which the new hybrid high-explosive incendiary bombs were deployed in great numbers:

> Alert at 10pm. A sharp, short raid with heavy barrage. Several hundred incendiaries (explosive type) fell between the rocket battery in Battersea Park and The Thames, and about a dozen on The Embankment and in Ranelagh Gardens, near the end of Lime Tree Avenue. These all fell at once – probably from one or two large canisters. Glow of fires in various directions; no bombs locally, but several heard falling.[37]

The Royal Hospital again escaped serious damage from this latest air raid, and its luck would continue to hold when on the night of 22–23 February another seemingly innocuous entry appears in the War Diary, 'a bomb hit some working class flats near Lots Road'.[38] The flats in question were the high-density accommodation blocks of the Guinness Trust estate in the World's End district of the King's Road, which were hit by a number of bombs which were again targeted at the nearby Lots Road Power Station. ARP Warden Jo Oakman, on duty that night, describes the raid:

> 22.07: Air raid sirens. Most awful barrage and a spectacular sight of flares and gun flashes.
>
> 22.34 – Four bombs fell all together on the World's End.
>
> 23.12 – All Clear. Got sent to Guinness Trust which had a heavy bomb on the third wing (block) [...] and gas main in King's Road was alight in crater full of water [...] it was a truly awful night. The Guinness was one awful heap of rubble and the other blocks were terribly blasted [...] There were queues at the First Aid Posts of injured.[39]

The Guinness Trust estate was home to Donald Wheal and his brother, Kit, who had originally been evacuated with their mother to Woking in 1939, but like many other evacuees, had returned to Chelsea within a few months. Their father worked as a stoker in the basement of the Whitelands apartment block, at the more salubrious end of the King's Road, responsible for keeping the central heating boilers fired up.

During the bombing of 1940–41, he would protect his family by sneaking them into the boiler house basement during air raids, but towards the end of the Blitz, a resident had seen them and complained. On the night of 22–23 February 1944, therefore, the family were sheltering at home in their somewhat less well-appointed tenement as the bombs hit the Guinness Trust estate. Donald describes the moment of impact:

> The first 2,000kg high explosive bomb screamed down and exploded in Upcerne Road, between us and Lots Road power station [...] the impact of the second bomb was so huge, so terrifying, so much closer [...] we waited [...] A second or two only, [...] *one more bomb in the stick will bring the whole block crashing down on us*, was running through my head in that second or two of suspense [...] It exploded. The wall behind my mother split a two-foot gap but held. The heavy window frame leapt into the room [...] plaster was ripped from the ceiling. I fought for air, trying to scoop the dust and soot from my mouth [...] The next explosion burst as a more familiar hollow crack and rumble [...] falling a hundred yards or more away.[40]

Between them, these four bombs taken as a single incident were the deadliest to hit Chelsea throughout the war. Over seventy residents were killed and more than 200 were trapped beneath collapsed and burning debris. Tony Smith of the Heavy Rescue Squad, a chimney sweep and veteran of the First World War, was later awarded the George Cross for his bravery during the night for 'again and again entering the teetering, burning ruins to bring out survivors'.[41]

Donald Wheal and his family, although badly shaken, managed to free themselves from the ruins of their home and set off walking along the Embankment. Their intention was to seek cover from the terror raining down from above by once again sheltering in the boiler room beneath the Whitelands flats, regardless of the views of the residents. Then, as Wheal relates, while they trudged forlornly along 'at some point on our journey the flares faded and the gun flashes ceased [...] outside the Royal Hospital [...] the All Clear sounded'.[42]

Meanwhile, at the Royal Hospital, after this most deadly of nights in Chelsea, the seemingly innocuous War Diary entry continues, 'The blast broke a few panes of glass in Infirmary Court'.[43]

Destructive and deadly as these raids were, the Luftwaffe was also suffering serious losses in both men and machines; losses which, at this stage of the war, the Germans were simply unable to sustain. It was also increasingly apparent that despite a cloak of secrecy surrounding the detail, the Allies were planning an invasion somewhere along Hitler's Atlantic Wall, and the Luftwaffe was thus called upon to disrupt these preparations. The baton for continuing the air campaign against London would have to pass to the vengeance weapons, as V1 launch sites were prepared in France and Germany.

Meanwhile, in Chelsea, the Reviewing Officer, Field Marshal Sir Cyril Deverell GCB, KCB, inspected the In-Pensioners on Founder's Day on 31 May, after which the Royal Hospital witnessed a quiet exodus of specialist members of staff as preparations for D-Day continued at pace.[44] On 4 May, the Physician & Surgeon, Major Napier, applied for a leave of absence for the period 5 June to 26 June;[45] on 25 May, the chaplain, Reverend Gatehouse, applied to leave on 5 June to 'take up a posting with Southern Command';[46] and on 30 May, a postcard was received from a Commissioner who was ordinarily resident in

Cirencester, informing his fellow board members that he would not be available for meetings until at least mid-June.[47]

The night of 5–6 June 1944 was one that Captain Townsend recalls vividly as 'hundreds of our bombers flew over the Royal Hospital on their way to France'. He went into Figure Court and 'flashed at the aeroplanes the V for Victory sign', to which 'one of the planes flashed the same signal down'.[48] Operation Overlord, the D-Day Landings heralding the liberation of France and Western Europe, had begun.

It was not long before the success of the landings in Normandy provoked the anticipated vengeance response, and on 12 June, V1 rockets were launched from Pas-de-Calais launch sites. This was with limited initial results due to technical failures and most missiles in these first waves failed to reach the English coast.

On the night of 15–16 June, however, the first successful mass attack took place with almost 150 missile launches, of which half reached London. The Royal Hospital's War Diary reports:

> 15 June Alert: 8.30pm until 9.20am on the 16th. A flying bomb passed over the Royal Hospital and was seen by several observers, whilst others were seen in the distance. This was the first occasion on which this type of bomb had been used locally, though some were reported elsewhere in England on the 13th.[49]

The only damage to the Hospital in this first attack was caused by friendly fire when 'about midnight an anti-aircraft projectile fell and exploded in the cloakroom of the out-office of the Governor's House, doing some structural damage'.[50]

Over the next several weeks, the Royal Hospital's War Diary records the airborne assault on London as V1s were fired indiscriminately at the capital. The distinctive sound of their rocket engines was soon familiar to the population below, who waited with bated breath for the motor to cut out, followed soon after by the explosion as the bomb fell to earth, '17 June, Alert: about 1am to 5.30am. Flying bombs again seen in the distance.'[51]

The following day was a Sunday and as church services were held across Chelsea, the In-Pensioners gathered for Church Parade:

All-Clear sounded at 10.50am, just in time for Church Parade, which otherwise would have been cancelled. During church a flying bomb came over, though no alert had been sounded, and it was met by heavy gunfire. Later heard that Vincent Square and Wellington Barracks Chapel had been bombed, the latter during church. This afternoon and evening bright, clear and sunny. No more gunfire at flying bombs, which can clearly be seen as rather small aeroplanes travelling on a straight course, fairly fast, at about 1,000 feet.[52]

While observers at the Royal Hospital familiarised themselves with aircraft recognition, rescue operations were under way in Vincent Square and Wellington Barracks. The casualty toll at the former was ten killed and sixty-two injured, but this paled into insignificance compared to the toll at Wellington Barracks.

At 11.20 a.m., the V1 hit the Guards Chapel in Birdcage Walk as a mixed military and civilian congregation had gathered for morning worship. The chapel received a direct hit as the rocket engine cut out and the bomb crashed through the roof of the building, exploding among the worshippers below. One hundred and twenty-one soldiers and civilians were killed and a further 141 were seriously injured. Dozens were trapped beneath the wreckage, and it was forty-eight hours before the last survivors were carried clear.

With Heavy Rescue teams working to free survivors from the remains of the Guards Chapel, the latest airborne assault on London continued, '19 June: excellent view of a flying bomb, the engine clearly visible with the naked eye'.[53] However, as news of the casualties at Wellington Barracks reached the Hospital, 'the Lieutenant-Governor held an Officers meeting at which it was decided to make it compulsory for In-Pensioners and staff to use their shelters at night'.[54]

As In-Pensioners once again returned to bedding down in their shelters for the night, Chelsea was not spared from the attentions of the V1s. On 3 July, the War Diary records, 'at 6am a flying bomb fell in Battersea Park, near the river, breaking many windows especially on the South Terrace', and as this early morning attack continued, it goes on to note:

About 7.30am a flying bomb hit Sloane Court East, breaking many more windows at the Royal Hospital, particularly in the Secretary's Office and on the North Front. Traffic on the Royal Hospital Road was temporarily diverted, as it was also from Lower Sloane Street. Twisted metal fragments of this bomb fell in the Burial Ground. Many American soldiers were killed.[55]

While Royal Hospital staff once more got to work on sweeping broken glass from pavements and roadways, and the police and ARP wardens set up roadblocks and diverted traffic, ambulance and rescue teams converged on a scene of utter carnage in Sloane Court East. Several residential buildings in Sloane Court were being used as billets for American troops and, shortly before the V1 appeared overhead, a column of trucks had arrived to transport the troops to their next posting. As the soldiers were climbing aboard the vehicles, the rocket's motor cut out and the bomb fell to the ground, detonating among the assembled soldiers. Seventy-four American military personnel and several civilians were killed in the blast.

Despite the growing casualty list from the first of Hitler's pilotless vengeance weapons, RAF pilots and Royal Artillery anti-aircraft gun crews were nevertheless beginning to get the measure of what they were up against, and counter-measures were rapidly improving. The Royal Air Force began to mount regular round-the-clock interceptor patrols along the south coast, using squadrons equipped with high-speed Spitfire, Tempest and Mosquito aircraft capable of matching and catching the speeding rockets. On interception, pilots would either shoot the V1 out of the sky or fly alongside, gliding a wingtip under the stabilising fin of the missile and flipping the V1 into an uncontrolled premature dive before they reached built-up urban areas.

Meanwhile, the Royal Artillery were using air-burst shells and were soon enjoying much greater success against a target which followed a reasonably predictable course and trajectory. The final elimination of the threat, however, ultimately required the neutralising of the launch sites in France, which in turn required the Allied armies to break out of their Normandy bridgehead. After heavy fighting throughout June and July as the Wehrmacht mounted a dogged defence, the breakthrough was finally achieved in August as German forces were encircled and annihilated in the Falaise Pocket, opening the way to Paris, while liberating the Pas-de-Calais and thereby overrunning the V1 launch sites. By early October, all launch sites within range of London had been captured.

On 9 September, as V1 attacks had all but ceased, 'sleeping in shelters made voluntary' is recorded in the War Diary.[56] As Allied armies raced across Europe, expectations that the war could be over by Christmas were soon growing, and at a management board meeting held on 28 September, plans were discussed to hold a victory dinner in the Great Hall, 'to celebrate the conclusion of hostilities with Germany'. The estimated cost of £300 was to be borne by the Army Prize and Legacy Fund, one of the Hospital's principal endowment funds.[57]

Attention also quickly turned, once more, to the prospects for peace, and thoughts again began to focus on post-war reconstruction and redevelopment. At a management board meeting held on 12 October, it was recognised that for the Royal Hospital, the evacuated infirmary patients presented a particular challenge, and in a memo submitted by the Lieutenant Governor, it was agreed that 'if accommodation can be found in an existing Hospital on the outskirts of London [this] would be the best solution to the problem'.[58]

However, this was to be the final contribution to the post-war redevelopment debate by the Lieutenant Governor. As blueprints for a brave new world were once again dusted down and placed before the relevant planning bodies, the Royal Hospital's board minutes record the retirement of the individual who had become recognised within the Hospital as synonymous with preserving the integrity of the institution and ensuring it would remain in its historic Chelsea home. At the 12 October 1944 board meeting, the minutes record the retirement of Lieutenant Governor Major General Llewellyn Isaac Gethin Morgan-Owen.[59]

A week after the retirement of Morgan-Owen, Major General Witts was confirmed as his replacement.[60] Also noted in these minutes is the receipt of a letter from Chelsea Borough Council, forwarded by the Ministry of Works, the contents of which cast an ominous shadow over the post-war future of the Royal Hospital.

The letter contained detailed proposals discussed between the local council and the Ministry of Works for the erection of mass-produced, prefabricated and factory-made houses to be built in Ranelagh Gardens and Burton Court.[61] These 'Homes for Heroes' were required to accommodate up to 6,000 soldiers returning from the war, 2,000 of whom were married and 'for whom accommodation would have to be provided on demobilisation'.[62] Chelsea Council were also expected 'by order of the Ministry of Health to make 75 per cent of such accommodation available for East End evacuees', as there were '23,000 families in the London area now living in shelters'.[63]

The wartime evacuation of In-Pensioners from Chelsea now had very serious implications for the future of the institution. The number of old soldiers resident in the Royal Hospital had fallen from around 500 immediately prior to the outbreak of war, to only around 200 by the autumn of 1944. Much of the Hospital lay empty and seemingly abandoned and the message from the Ministry of Works to the Commissioners could not be clearer – use it or lose it.

As the irresistible force of brave new world idealism met the immovable object of post-war austerity and fiscal constraint, the solution to Britain's housing shortage was to be the prefab home. With the pressing need to find sites for these architectural carbuncles, the future of the Royal Hospital once more hung in the balance. It was now of the utmost importance that the evacuated In-Pensioners and staff return to Chelsea as soon as practicable.

17

# Peace Returns to Chelsea

*'... short of 350 beds ...'*[1]

In late 1944, as Allied armies raced towards Berlin, the final defeat of the Nazi regime appeared imminent. The aerodromes that had been hastily constructed across south-east England using rubble from bomb-damaged buildings in London were in constant use as it was Germany that now faced the terror of aerial bombardment:

> Air raids were so frequent, with the British by night and the Americans by day, that Berliners felt that they spent more time in cellars and air-raid shelters than in their own beds.[2]

With the festive season approaching, German citizens had little to share other than gallows humour, 'Be practical: give a coffin'.[3] Hitler was facing almost certain defeat and reacted by stepping up his vengeance weapon campaign, including previously unimaginable ballistic missiles, the V2, *Vergeltungswaffe 2*.

Rumours that German scientists had developed an altogether more potent missile than the V1 doodlebugs were initially disregarded as unnecessarily alarmist. The government's Chief Scientific Advisor, Oxford Professor Frederick Lindemann, raised to the peerage in 1941 as Lord Cherwell, 'dismissed evidence that the Germans were developing a rocket capable of damaging London'.[4] He considered the reports a Nazi hoax designed to distract the Allies and divert military resources from completing the destruction of Germany's conventional forces. Furthermore, if the V2 did exist, there was nothing that could be done to defend against it and the threat would only be eliminated with the final defeat of Germany.

In September 1944, the first V2 missiles hit London, exploding without warning. In November, as V2 attacks increased and attempts to dismiss the resulting explosions as caused by gas leaks were widely dismissed as implausible nonsense, Churchill was forced to report to the House of Commons that Britain had indeed been under rocket attack 'for the last few weeks'.[5]

⁕

Lord Cherwell had been appointed Paymaster General on 31 December 1942 and became *ex officio* Chairman of the Board of Commissioners of the Royal Hospital. As 1944 drew to a close, the principal concern of the Commissioners remained the post-war future of the institution. At a board meeting on 7 December, a letter to the Ministry of Works was approved, setting out the Hospital's plans for reconstruction, with a particular focus on the requirements for a new infirmary in Chelsea.[6] Since receiving the joint letter from the Ministry of Works and Chelsea Borough Council about developing Ranelagh Gardens and Burton Court into council-managed estates of prefabricated houses, the Commissioners had been frantically working on plans to return In-Pensioners to the Royal Hospital. To do so, however, they recognised the critical importance of re-establishing an infirmary within the Hospital's grounds, and detailed discussions centred on the redevelopment of an existing overflow ward to be used as an interim measure until a permanent facility could be established.

Ward No. 18, on the north-east corner of the East Wing, had narrowly avoided destruction on 26 October 1940 when the adjoining stairwell was bombed. This ward, used for In-Pensioners requiring specialist nutritional support – so-called 'varied diet men', was managed by infirmary nursing staff rather than Long Ward sisters.[7] From October 1944, plans were developed to establish Ward No. 18 as a comprehensive care facility to treat a broader range of infirmary patients to be returned to Chelsea from Ascott House, where representatives of Anthony de Rothschild had recently made tentative enquiries for returning the property to the family on the cessation of hostilities.

Plans were given greater impetus when at a board meeting on 14 December, a letter from the council was noted, outlining further the proposals to develop prefab houses within the Royal Hospital's grounds. They requested a site visit to discuss this proposed post-war development.[8]

On 29 December 1944, news was received that 55-year-old Captain of Invalids William Lockley had passed away at the Cottage Hospital, Ross-on-Wye, near the Royal Hospital's out-station at Rudhall.[9] Lockley was praised for his conduct on the night of the infirmary bombing in 1941, but his exertions that night had taken a toll on his already frail health. 'Lockley was indefatigable on this occasion, despite his injuries in the 1914–19 war, and overstrained himself so badly that he never recovered.'[10] He had been evacuated to Rudhall to convalesce, but died three years after 'The Wednesday', another victim of that dreadful night.

Plans were arranged for him to be buried in the plot at St Mary's Church, Ross-on-Wye, that had been set aside in 1939 for In-Pensioners destined to embark on their Final Posting while evacuated in Herefordshire.[11] Lockley's funeral was held on the afternoon of 2 January 1945, attended by a party of fellow officers from the Royal Hospital, including the Lieutenant Governor Major General Witts, Assistant Secretary Maurice Fitzgerald and fellow resident of the North-East Wing Staff Married Quarters, Captain of Invalids Captain May. Other officers from the married quarters, who were unable to attend, included the Physician & Surgeon, Major Napier, convalescing after returning from duty in the D-Day Landings, and 63-year-old Captain of Invalids Geoffrey Bailey who, after joining the Royal Hospital in 1911, had narrowly survived the First World War when the North-East Wing Married Quarters were bombed in 1918.

The morning after Lockley's funeral, on 3 January 1945, as the Royal Hospital party travelled back to London, at 8.51 a.m. a V2 missile detonated as it hit the ground in Chelsea. The point of impact was the North Front of the Royal Hospital grounds, immediately adjacent to the Officers' Married Quarters in the North-East Wing. Board meeting minutes describe the aftermath, 'An enemy High-Explosive Rocket fell in the close vicinity of the Officers' quarters on the north side of Light Horse Court. The quarters were demolished and the north-east Wing and the Secretary's Office seriously damaged by the blast.'[12] The Hospital's War Diary gives a more detailed account of the incident:

> A 'V2' or Rocket Bomb fell on the North Front about fifteen feet from the Deputy Surgeon's house at 8.51am. It ripped the wall off all the houses in the Wing (except Captain Bailey's next to the East Road), destroyed most of the Deputy Surgeon's and the houses on either side of it, and brought down the two middle chimneystacks. Considerable damage was also done to the east side of that portion of the East Wing nearest the bombed buildings, as well as to the Main Guardhouse. There was also much damage to the roof timbers and wainscoted berths of the East Wing and in the Office Keeper's house and adjoining parts of the Secretary's Office. All the windows overlooking Light Horse Court were broken, as were most of those in Figure Court. The framework in the Chapel and Great Hall windows were badly damaged, and the Chapel doors broken.[13]

The explosion ripped through the building, killing several occupants including Captain Bailey, who had survived the 1918 bombing:

> The following were killed, probably instantaneously: Captain G. Bailey, Captain of Invalids since 1911. Mrs May, wife of Captain G.C. May, M.C.; Major W. Napier, Physician & Surgeon since 1941 and his younger daughter, Deirdre. Also In-Pensioner E. Gummer, late York and Lancaster Regiment, Assistant Chapel Orderly, who was killed whilst standing in the aisle near the Governor's Pew – probably by one of the dummy facing pipes (from the Chapel organ), several of which were dislodged and fell onto the floor of the Chapel. Gummer's head was cut open.[14]

Several residents and In-Pensioners were also injured, some seriously, including the Quartermaster, Major Gingell, who suffered 'multiple flesh wounds and shock'; Captain Dean's wife suffered a head wound and concussion, while his son Kenneth suffered deep cuts to his hand. Mrs Bailey received facial injuries from the blast that killed her husband,

and several In-Pensioners required hospital treatment. In Burton Court Mansions, opposite the Royal Hospital, twenty-one residents were injured, three seriously.

There were, however, some lucky escapes, including In-Pensioner Connolly, who was blown off the temporary bridge spanning the bombed stairwell in the East Wing, 'but escaped serious injury'. Richard May, Captain May's young son, had a miraculous escape as he 'was standing in the kitchen, almost directly opposite where the rocket fell. The wall of this room was demolished, the floor gave way and he fell through into the basement on top of a big pile of rubble.' Although he suffered a cracked pelvis, he was pulled alive from the ruins by rescuers, who were quickly on the scene. These included 'Ministry of Works workmen, Royal Army Pay Corps clerks employed in the Secretary's Office, some U.S.A. soldiers – also National Fire Service and A.R.P. wardens who were soon on the spot'.[15]

Post K in the Royal Avenue quickly phoned an incident report through to Borough Control, who sent an incident officer to liaise with the Lieutenant Governor, who had arrived back at the Royal Hospital from Lockley's funeral at around 10 a.m. Captain May, however, was travelling on a later train and was unaware of the death of his wife and the injuries suffered by his son. Captain Townsend was quickly despatched to meet him at the station and describes the encounter in his memoirs, 'He wanted to see his wife. Well. I'd seen her and I said to him, "No, you're not going to see your wife. You've got to remember her as you always knew her". So I took him down to a cellar and I stayed with him all night.'[16] The compassion displayed by Officers of the Royal Hospital was not only reserved for In-Pensioners.

The blast damaged the recently converted Ward No. 18, but it was still functioning and therefore, 'most of the casualties were taken first to No. 18 Ward, dressed by Sister Vaughan-Williams, and then evacuated to St Stephen's and other hospitals'.[17]

The physical damage to the Royal Hospital was extensive and severe, with the North-East wing practically destroyed by the explosion, while the East Wing suffered structural damage, rendering it unusable for In-Pensioner accommodation. Consequently, 'the Ministry of Works offered accommodation for the In-Pensioners of the East Wing in Sloane Gardens', from where most were subsequently put on furlough with friends and relatives and others were evacuated to the out-stations in Herefordshire.[18] This latest evacuation from the Hospital was supervised by 'a working party of 50 Corps of Military Police from Chelsea Barracks', while for the displaced staff members, 'the homeless families were billeted in various houses, both in and outside the Royal Hospital'.[19]

The recently activated plans to develop Ward No. 18 into a temporary infirmary for In-Pensioners returning from Ascott House were now rendered redundant by these latest events on the ground. The extent of the structural damage was such that repairs would take some considerable time to organise and complete. Plans for a sustained return to Chelsea were thus seriously disrupted and these latest evacuations led to In-Pensioner numbers falling to an all-time low – from the 200 shortly before the blast to only fifty in its immediate aftermath.

As war clouds had formed across Europe in the summer of 1939, evacuation had been seen as a source of potential salvation for the Royal Hospital until a combination of toxic politics and challenging logistics meant that, in practice, only fifty out of a complement of 500 were evacuated on the eve of war. In 1945, as peace seemed tantalisingly close, evacuation was increasingly threatening the very survival of the Royal Hospital, with Chelsea now home to only around fifty In-Pensioners out of an establishment strength of over 500. The sight of the distinctive Chelsea Pensioner in his iconic and easily recognised uniform, virtually unchanged from when the Royal Hospital first opened its doors in 1692, had all but disappeared from the streets of Chelsea.

As the end of the war in Europe drew near, serious question marks hung over whether the Royal Hospital would itself become a casualty of a conflict. The institution itself was in the line of fire in a way hitherto unknown.

This was to be the last incident in Chelsea during the Second World War. The V2 which hit the Royal Hospital detonated on the North Front, just to the south of Royal Hospital Road, opposite the tennis courts in Burton Court. These were the same tennis courts that had narrowly survived the first incident in Chelsea, when a bomb had exploded a few metres to their north shortly after midnight on 29 August 1940. Consequently, the first and the last bombing incidents in Chelsea during the Second World War both involved the Royal Hospital and occurred within 100m of each other. Much had happened during the intervening years between these two events and as peace returned to Chelsea, the Royal Hospital faced an uncertain future.

The site visit by Chelsea Borough Council, noted at the management board meeting of 14 December, finally took place on 31 January 1945. Its significance can hardly be overstated, and a detailed account of proceedings was discussed at a board meeting the following day.

The deputation from the council included 'the Mayor, Chairman of the Housing Committee, Town Clerk, and Borough Surveyor', who were 'received by the Governor, Lieutenant-Governor, and the Assistant-Secretary'.[20] The council delegation opened proceedings by explaining the background to their request to build prefab houses in the Hospital's grounds. They faced an 'urgent need for finding space for a substantial number of pre-fabricated houses' as a pre-war scheme of slum clearance and 're-settlement of 300 overcrowded families [...] had now increased to 500' because of bomb damage during the Blitz:

> In addition, accommodation had to be found for families evacuated from the borough owing to the total destruction of their homes who desire to return. Finally there would be 6,000 soldiers with claims to reside in Chelsea, of whom 2,000 were married, for whom accommodation would have to be provided on demobilisation.

As well as providing new homes for bombed-out Chelsea residents, the council was also required 'by order of the Ministry of Health [...] to make 75% of such accommodation available for East End evacuees [as] there were 23,000 families in the London area now living in shelters'.

The council's surveyor had consequently assessed several sites throughout Chelsea to facilitate the significant post-war building programme envisaged to meet these obligations. Plans were being drawn up for 'converting existing property in Cadogan Avenue, Onslow Dwelling Site, Tite Street, Elm Park Gardens and elsewhere', but the council would also have to consider buying private property on the open market and converting it for evacuee use. This would raise some serious economic and financial issues, for 'only medium priced property could economically be adapted for working-class occupation [whereas] property in Cadogan Square and similar well inhabited neighbourhoods could not be economically converted because of the expensive ground rents'. Similarly, the low rise, single-family dwelling nature of the pre-fabricated houses did not suit the higher density nature of housing in Chelsea generally, and therefore, 'It would also be un-economical from the accommodation aspect to set pre-fabricated houses, accommodating one family only, on the sites of houses which, on reconstruction, would contain three or four or more families, and would operate to postpone development of such sites as permanent'.[21]

The residential market economics of a relatively small and compact borough were compounded by a singular lack of significant public open spaces when compared to many other London districts. This combination of factors had therefore driven the council to approach the Royal Hospital once again for assistance, in the same spirit as the Lend–Lease relationship which had operated so successfully throughout the war.

This latest request from the Borough Council was, however, fundamentally different from previous co-operative initiatives. Despite the supposedly temporary nature of the proposed prefab houses, the scale of development envisaged would inevitably change, probably forever, the very essence of the architectural harmony of the Royal Hospital site.

However, as the site visit continued, it became apparent that it had not in fact been the council's idea to approach the Royal Hospital with another 'Lend–Lease' suggestion. The initiative had instead come from the Ministry of Works, the department charged with meeting the government's demands for large-scale post-war new housing:

> The Council had been asked by the Ministry of Health, at short notice, to produce an estimate of space available for temporary housing, and it was arising out of this that the Ministry of Works approached the Commissioners. Such procedure was not intended by the Council and would not have been adopted by them.[22]

With the council's position clear the Governor responded, pointing out that by January 1945 the Royal Hospital had suffered such extensive damage that it was only possible to provide berths for around 200 In-Pensioners from a theoretical establishment strength of around 550, and as such, 'while anxious to assist in every way, it was necessary to remember that the Royal Hospital itself was short of 350 beds'. The Governor went on to add, 'it was quite possible that delay in permanent construction would force the Commissioners to satisfy part at least of this requirement by putting up huts in the Grounds for their own In-Pensioners'. In determining that In-Pensioners should be returned as quickly as possible to Chelsea, the Commissioners were prepared to pursue any avenue required to ensure their return was expedited with all possible haste, including the erection of temporary wooden accommodation huts in Burton Court if necessary.

Having outlined the Hospital's plans for the open spaces of Burton Court, the Governor turned to the council's proposals for Ranelagh Gardens and explained:

> The choice of the zone abutting on Chelsea Bridge Road was not a very happy one for the reason that it was not quite clear that houses could be erected there without permanent injury to the trees. They would also interfere with access to and utilisation of the Ranelagh Gardens by the Royal Horticultural Society on the occasion of their summer show.[23]

These were not unreasonable objections. The erection of prefab houses would result in permanent damage to the gardens, rendering them useless in meeting the requirements of the RHS for their annual Chelsea Flower Show, which in turn would have serious ramifications for the Hospital's finances. The Flower Show was an important source of non-governmental income, enabling the Royal Hospital to provide a level of care to In-Pensioners which would not otherwise be possible. The Governor instead suggested that 'the central area of Royal Avenue could be utilised with less objection for temporary housing, and this alternative might be explored'. However, 'it was agreed on behalf of the Borough Council that the suggestion might be further considered, but prima facie, the space seemed too circumscribed for the purpose in view'.[24]

With the site visit concluded, it was clear that the council was not particularly enthusiastic about the development proposals. The plans under discussion had been suggested by the Ministry of Works and with the Commissioners reluctant to agree to them, it was decided that 'the Council did not propose to take any immediate action [...] they accepted the Commissioners' decision for the moment, but they desired to keep the door open for further negotiation in case they should be forced to reconsider their position in a year or eighteen months' time'.²⁵ In essence, therefore, the Royal Hospital and Chelsea Borough Council agreed on a stay of execution over a post-war redevelopment plan that neither party really supported.

The onus now lay with the Commissioners to return In-Pensioners as quickly as possible to Chelsea and render redundant any plans for alternative post-war redevelopment of their historic Chelsea home. The Royal Hospital was determined that the time bought through this stay of execution would not be wasted.

✥

As an understanding was reached in Chelsea, the war in Europe was entering its final phase. The Wehrmacht's last major counter-attack, the Ardennes Offensive, launched in December 1944, had ground to a halt by late January, as the Allies switched to the offensive. Subsequently, 'in the February drive to the Rhine, allied forces were to advance across a front of some 250 miles'.²⁶ Despite dogged resistance, the Germans were pushed back remorselessly, and by April, Captain David Fraser, an officer in the Grenadier Guards, 'spoke for millions of his comrades when he observed: "The sense that, with luck, one might be able to see the end became a dominant emotion"'.²⁷

On the Eastern Front, the Red Army crossed the Vistula, captured the Polish capital, Warsaw, and raced towards the German frontier. As Russian soldiers entered East Prussia, political officers erected signs aimed at arousing the worst instincts in often brutalised conscripts, '"Soldier, remember you are now entering the lair of the Fascist beast!"'.²⁸ With the drive on Berlin gathering pace, German civilians would pay a terrible price for the merciless excesses perpetrated by the Nazis during their conquests in the east.

With the war in Europe almost over, Churchill was fearful that the scale of Britain's sacrifice would quickly be forgotten and asked the Cabinet Office to provide figures for the scale of losses compared to her allies. The relative mortality statistics provided in response to the Prime Minister's question illustrated that 'by April 1945, one in 165 Englishmen had died [...] one in 385 Australians, one in 385 Canadians, one in 175 New Zealanders and one in 775 Americans'. By comparison, figures provided for the Home Front revealed a death toll of 'one in 130 Londoners'.²⁹

At a board meeting on 12 April, it was agreed 'that the admission of a limited number of applicants to In-Pension may now be approved, in view of the improved conditions in the London area'.³⁰ With the bombing of London over, the Commissioners were eager to rebuild In-Pensioner numbers as quickly as possible. On 20 April, the War Diary reports, 'the rebuilding of the wall of the main building at the north corner, facing east, has been completed and the scaffolding is being taken down'.³¹ Repairs of the structural damage caused by the V2 missile were completed in rapid time and with the East Wing again operational, the drive to return In-Pensioners to Chelsea accelerated.

⁂

Meanwhile, in Berlin, as the Third Reich entered its death throes, Hitler committed suicide on 30 April in his bunker beneath the Reich Chancellery, as Red Army troops stormed the Reichstag less than a kilometre to the north:

> In the centre of Berlin that night the flames in bombarded buildings cast strange shadows and a red glow on the otherwise dark streets. The soot and dust in the air made it almost unbreathable. From time to time there was the thunder of masonry collapsing. And to add to the terrifying effect, searchlight beams moved around above, searching a night sky in which the Luftwaffe had ceased to exist.³²

While Victory in Europe on 8 May 1945 was marked with dancing in the streets, at the Royal Hospital, there is no mention of VE Day in the War Diary. There is instead a summary of the wartime casualty list: twenty-one killed and thirty-three wounded, five seriously. Those killed included twelve In-Pensioners, seven staff members and two other residents.

The buildings and grounds had been struck by fourteen bombs, including the parachute mine incident at the infirmary and the V2 rocket on the North Front. A further ten bombs hit the Royal Hospital but failed to explode, while 117 incendiaries were recorded striking the buildings or grounds during the Blitz. Further damage was sustained from three anti-aircraft shells which hit the institution.[33]

The ten bombs which hit the Royal Hospital but failed to explode represent a failure rate of 40 per cent which compares to a more typical rate for UXBs of around 10 per cent of bombs dropped, underlining the extent to which the wartime survival of the Hospital can be attributed to good fortune. To put the human cost of the conflict into some form of context, Dean records, 'the deaths of twelve pensioners, seven members of the staff and two other residents. Excluding cases of shock, thirty-three other persons were injured, so that the casualties, exceeding 10 per cent of the numbers in residence, were comparable with those suffered by units on active service.'[34] The Royal Hospital paid a high price for the pre-war failure to evacuate the institution in its entirety, as recommended in the provisions of the Anderson Report.

With peace having returned to Europe, the threat the Royal Hospital now faced was of unsympathetic redevelopment by overzealous bureaucrats seeking to meet the demands of a brave new post-war world. At a board meeting on 31 May, it is recorded that the reviewing officer at Founder's Day on 29 May 1945 was General Sir Herbert Gough ECB, GCMG, KCVO. Also recorded is the appointment of a 'Special Commissioner' in the person of Major General Morgan-Owen, who was to take the lead in the Hospital's discussions with the relevant authorities as the Royal Hospital sought to seize the initiative in the discussions around the post-war future of the institution.[35]

As the Hospital focused on the post-war challenges it now faced, the final entry in the War Diary is another almost innocuous entry. Maurice Fitzgerald and an In-Pensioner visited the BBC to record a valedictory address for the World Service, 'BBC broadcast by the Assistant-Secretary and I/P Delpiano in French for the Overseas Programme'.[36] The content of the address is not recorded in this final War Diary entry.

At a board meeting on 7 June, 'The Governor informed the Commissioners of the proceedings of a meeting between him, the Lieutenant-Governor, the Assistant-Secretary and representatives of the Ministry of Works'.[37] At this meeting, the Ministry of Works was pushed to progress the rebuilding of the Royal Hospital as quickly as possible through the 'repair of bomb damage, provision of interim accommodation on the surrender of Ascott House and properties in Herefordshire, and progress with plans for rebuilding'. In taking the initiative, the Royal Hospital hoped to dissuade the Ministry from any further consideration of alternative uses for the buildings and grounds.

However, the representatives of the Ministry of Works were unmoved, particularly with respect to the pressing need to re-establish an infirmary within the precincts of the Hospital's estate in Chelsea. Consequently, a further board meeting was called to discuss the urgent rebuilding needs of the institution. Chaired by the Paymaster General Lord Cherwell, the agenda for this board meeting, held on 28 June 1945, is interesting from several perspectives.

New claims for out-pensions feature prominently, as had been the case for some weeks. The most significant reason for a new pension claim is recorded as 'disability', as wounded soldiers continued to be discharged from service.[38] The inevitable legacies of war would continue for years to come and led to increased staff numbers being employed in the Pensions Secretariat as demobilised soldiers returned to civilian life, many 'broken by war'. Claims for 'Commutation from Out-Pension to In-Pension', however, were recorded as 'None', such was the state of disrepair of the Hospital's buildings, and the number of In-Pensioners remained at the all-time low of only fifty.[39]

Despite the Hospital's best efforts, accommodation provision was still inadequate to allow for the return of In-Pensioners from the various out-stations, quite apart from the admission of new recruits to In-Pension. Note 8 records the most significant discussion at the meeting:

> Provision of temporary accommodation pending repairs to the Royal Hospital [...] General (Sir Ronald) Charles submitted that the Ministry of Works should be moved to hasten the provision of temporary accommodation nearer London for the Infirmary at Ascott House and the detachments at present maintained in Herefordshire. Such accommodation would, however, only be a temporary solution.[40]

The development of a network of out-stations during the war had successfully removed Chelsea Pensioners from the horrors of the London Blitz. This success did not necessarily mean they were universally popular, however, or that they offered an attractive peacetime option for the future of the Royal Hospital. Their most significant shortcoming was the remoteness of their locations and the sense of isolation this engendered. Despite the popularity of the newly established In-Pensioner social club in Herefordshire, aimed at addressing the disadvantages of being located many miles from the nearest public house, the board note continues:

> Residence in the country was unpopular with In-Pensioners, only illness or compulsion would persuade them to leave London, and what was really required was acceleration of the repair of damaged buildings in the Hospital itself so that In-Pensioners might be able to return as soon as possible.[41]

The extent of the required rebuilding work is again highlighted, with the Commissioners noting the need:

> ... to provide for existing numbers, including Infirmary, accommodation for 300 persons approximately would be required. The ideal, however, was that the Royal Hospital should return so soon as possible to its pre-war content of 500 In-Pensioners, and this would require provision for 450 persons in addition to those now resident at Chelsea.[42]

The report highlights the responsibilities of the Commissioners for the provision of succour to old soldiers, and the fact that such obligations represent the very essence of the bond of covenant on which the Hospital was founded. It also identifies the real source of the delay the Hospital was facing, 'It was felt that the Board's obligations to In-Pensioners, actual and potential, entitled them to press for some priority in this matter. Unfortunately they did not feel that they had been able to persuade the Ministry of Works.'[43]

At the conclusion of the 28 June board meeting, the Commissioners recognised the need to circumvent the opposition and intransigence of the Ministry of Works. Consequently, Lord Cherwell 'undertook to make representations on the Hospital's behalf to the responsible Minister', and favours would be called in as the Royal Hospital moved onto the diplomatic offensive.[44]

Events on the ground subsequently began to move more quickly, and at a board meeting on 12 July, Lord Cherwell's intervention appears to have produced results.[45] The Royal Hospital was offered the tenancy of the Royal Victoria Patriotic Building in Wandsworth, south-west London, as a temporary home for a relocated infirmary. This was closer to Chelsea than Ascott House and could suffice until a permanent replacement was built in the Hospital's grounds.[46]

Originally built as a home for orphaned daughters of Crimean War casualties, the Royal Victoria Patriotic Building had been used as a convalescence home for injured soldiers in the First World War and, more recently, as an internment camp for suspected enemy aliens in the Second World War. Meanwhile, the Pensions Secretariat establishment numbers continued to expand as the Royal Hospital processed an increasing number of applications from demobilised soldiers who were eligible to join the out-pension register. By 19 July, the numbers employed in Maurice Fitzgerald's department had expanded to 141 clerks and administrators; three times the pre-war total.[47]

With the unconditional surrender of Japan on 15 August, marking the cessation of hostilities in the Far East and with it the end of the Second World War, the Royal Hospital's return to Chelsea gathered momentum. In late autumn, the Borough Council's War Comforts depot vacated the State Apartments, which they had occupied since approaching the Royal Hospital for assistance in October 1940. As the Hospital accelerated its move back to Chelsea, bathing facilities which had been damaged during the Blitz were brought back into operation. This allowed the Hospital to relinquish the use of public baths which had been provided by the council as an alternative. Assistant Secretary Maurice Fitzgerald wrote a noteworthy letter of thanks to the Town Clerk:

> ... now that we are once again equipped with baths sufficient for our In-Pensioners and need therefore no longer avail ourselves of the facilities for using the municipal baths which you placed at our disposal, I should like to express, on my Commissioners' behalf, their cordial appreciation of the public spirit with which you came forward in our hour of need [...] local lease–lend [sic] between the Royal Hospital and your Council has operated actively during the war to our mutual advantage; it is a policy which we must keep alive, in spirit at least, during the Peace.[48]

The Town Clerk, Mr E.W.T. Nicholson, replied in similar vein, thanking Fitzgerald for his 'courteous letter', before adding:

> I am impressed by your appropriate reference to lease–lend between the Royal Hospital and the Council and like you, I hope that it will continue during the Peace. Co-operation between the Local Authority and the most famous Institution in the Borough is bound to result in benefit to everyone.[49]

In September, the out-station at Rudhall, opened in secret in September 1939, was closed and In-Pensioners returned to Chelsea. A letter from the Commissioners to Major and Mrs Morland thanked them for having stepped in and helped the Royal Hospital at such a difficult and sensitive time.[50]

In October, the Incorporated Soldiers', Sailors' & Airmen's Help Society, which had provided accommodation for In-Pensioners after the bombing of the infirmary, held their Annual Meeting at the Royal Hospital in the presence of Her Majesty Queen Mary. A guard of honour included two In-Pensioners from regiments of which Her Majesty was Colonel-in-Chief and one In-Pensioner who 'formed part of the guard of honour on the occasion of her Majesty's wedding' in 1893.[51]

On 8 November, 'a Board of Officers comprised of the adjutant, chaplain, Captain Loyd (Duty Officer), and the Quartermaster, assisted by an expert assessor from the Ministry of Works, [were] appointed to inspect and report on the condition of the Communion Plate, Pictures and Trophies recovered from Montecute House', as the Hospital's art and chapel treasures were returned in time for the annual Remembrance Day Service.[52]

It was proposed that a Victory Cocktail Party should take place in December 1945 to mark the end of the war. This was to be a considerably scaled down event compared to the lavish dinner proposed in 1944 as Allied armies raced towards the German border, with expectations that the war would be over by Christmas. Instead, it was suggested that 'residents, resident staff and those of the non-resident staff and any others who contributed by their efforts to the defence of the Royal Hospital during the war, should be entertained to a cocktail party in the

State Drawing Room on 12th December 1945'.[53] Both the number of invitees and the anticipated costs of the event were on a much-reduced scale when compared to the previous plans, as befitting the more austere outlook now that the war had finally ended:

> The total number concerned is of the order of 150–160. The cost of such a party, including cocktails, tea, beer, cigarettes and refreshments, is estimated at £100. Sanction is sought to charge expenditure to this amount against the Army Prize and Legacy Funds. The Dinner which it was proposed to hold in the Great Hall to celebrate the conclusion of hostilities with Germany, which was approved by Board Minute of 28th September 1944, at a cost of £300, will not now take place.[54]

In 1945 as the Second World War ended, so too did the wartime story of the Royal Hospital Chelsea. As a home for old soldiers, the Hospital has always been associated with warfare, but the war years represent a unique chapter in its history as the institution itself was in the line of fire for a sustained period in a way hitherto unknown.

During the conflict the Hospital and its residents were pushed almost to breaking point and challenged as never before, with the war representing an existential threat to the institution on many levels. Its survival is a wartime story of resilience, courage – and not a little luck.

As the war ended, an institution which first opened its doors in 1692 to provide succour to old soldiers who were broken by age or war continued to deliver on its original founding objective. Peace would bring its own challenges which the Commissioners, Officers, staff and In-Pensioners of the Royal Hospital would all need to meet to ensure the continued survival of a worthy and much-loved national institution.

Today, in the twenty-first century, after the nation has celebrated the coronation of King Charles III, the Royal Hospital, founded in the seventeenth century by Charles II, provides a sanctuary for the last of the old soldiers who fought in the Second World War. The echoes and scars of this unique chapter in the history of the institution are still faintly discernible if you know where to look.

Turning to the future, however, the Royal Hospital not only survives but also thrives, as it continues to deliver on its never-changing mission, representing the bond of covenant between the army and the nation, and providing succour to 'such Land Souldiers as are [...] old, lame or infirme'.

# Epilogue

Although the Second World War ended in 1945, it would be sometime before life returned to any sense of normality at the Royal Hospital Chelsea. The plans that had initially been agreed for the Hospital to move its infirmary to the Royal Victoria Patriotic Building in Wandsworth, although well advanced, ultimately came to nothing as the Ministry of Works unexpectedly withdrew the offer with little by way of explanation. Eventually, however, the Hospital was offered, and accepted, a lease on the Royal School for the Blind in Leatherhead, to the south of London.

In-Pensioners were subsequently transferred from Ascott House and Moraston House, with the final transfers taking place in December 1946. Throughout this period of uncertainty Anthony de Rothschild remained incredibly patient and supportive as he appreciated the efforts the Commissioners were making to organise alternative infirmary accommodation as quickly as possible and transfer Ascott House back to the Rothschild family.

Leatherhead would remain the Royal Hospital's infirmary until the 1970s when a new purpose-built, albeit architecturally uninspiring, infirmary was opened within the grounds of the Chelsea site. This twentieth-century utilitarian structure, while singularly unsympathetic to the rest of the Chelsea buildings, nevertheless served its purpose until it was replaced by the somewhat more elegant infirmary which now stands on the opposite side of the site to the one built by Sir John Soane.

The site of the demolished infirmary in the north-west corner of the Hospital's estate remained derelict until the opening of the National Army Museum by Queen Elizabeth II in 1971, which relocated to Chelsea from the Royal Military Academy Sandhurst. The destroyed North-East Wing, on the north side of Light Horse Court, was rebuilt in the late 1960s with its external appearance identical to the original. The East Wing Long Ward accommodation stairwell was rebuilt using the original bricks, salvaged after its bombing in 1940.

Many of the air-raid shelters constructed throughout the Hospital's estate were repurposed after the war, with those beneath the Great Hall converted into public toilets, while part of the super-shelter complex beneath Burton Court was transformed into an electricity substation as inner-city power stations such as Battersea were replaced by large generating stations situated in remote coastal or rural locations. These super-stations were connected to city centres via the high-voltage power lines of the National Grid which, in turn, required a network of substations strategically located in local neighbourhoods, for which abandoned air-raid shelters often proved to be ideally suited.

Throughout this period of physical rebuilding, In-Pensioner numbers were also steadily rebuilt, although over time the establishment strength has reduced as accommodation has been updated and improved. Long Ward berths have been modernised to improve their accessibility for veterans who may have survived injuries which, a generation ago, could well have proven fatal.

Today, the Royal Hospital remains home to some 300 In-Pensioners, who are once again a regular sight on the streets of Chelsea as the institution continues to deliver its mission of providing a home for old soldiers who are broken by age or war, and does so on the same site and in largely the same buildings as it has for over three centuries.

# Notes

## Introduction

1. Captain Charles G.T. Dean, *The Royal Hospital Chelsea* (London: Hutchinson, 1950) pp.15–35.
2. Dan Cruickshank, *The Royal Hospital Chelsea: The Place and the People* (London: Third Millennium, 2003) pp.20–22.
3. Margaret L. Kekewich, *An Anthology of Primary Sources: France and the British Isles 1620–1714* (Manchester: Manchester University Press, 1995).
4. Giles Milton, *White Gold* (London: John Murray, 2015) p.11.
5. Dean, *The Royal Hospital Chelsea*, p.43.
6. The Great Hall at the Royal Hospital Chelsea lists on its wood-panelled walls all the Battle Honours awarded since the Hospital's foundation, with Tangier as the first.
7. Dean, *The Royal Hospital Chelsea*, p.23.
8. *Ibid.*, p.23.
9. Andrew Cormack, *These Meritorious Objects of the Royal Bounty* (London: privately published, 2017) p.44.
10. Royal Hospital Chelsea Archives (hereafter RHC), LDRHC/CAB2: Report of Committee of Chelsea Hospital, 1882.
11. See Major General Arthur Balfour, 'On the Military Conscription of France', *Journal of the Statistical Society of London*, Vol. 30, No. 2 (June 1867), pp.216–92, for a description of the evolution of French Army recruitment after the French Revolution and its impact on army funding. See also, RHC, LDRHC/18/0049: 'Les Invalides', p.29 (in French), for a description of the fall in numbers of veterans at Les Invalides because of changes in army funding. Resident numbers fell from 3,375 in 1863 to only 127 by 1900 in buildings originally designed to accommodate up to 5,000.
12. Sean Murphy, *Bully's Acre and Royal Hospital Kilmainham Graveyards: History and Inscriptions* (Dublin: Oivelina Publications, 1989) p.6.

## Chapter 1

1. Hansard, Debate on International Affairs: Stanley Baldwin – 10 November 1932, Vol. 270.
2. John Keegan, *The First World War* (London: Hutchinson, 1998) p.3.
3. Alan Bullock, *Hitler* (London: Odhams Press, 1952) p.79.
4. Ian Castle, *The First Blitz – Bombing London in the First World War* (Oxford: Osprey, 2015).
5. Dean, *The Royal Hospital Chelsea*, p.294.
6. Castle, pp.176–77.
7. Brett Holman, *The Next War in the Air: Britain's Fear of the Bomber, 1908–1941* (London: Routledge, 2016) p.57.
8. Niko Gartner (2010), 'Administering Operation Pied Piper – how the London County Council prepared for the evacuation of its schoolchildren 1938–1939', *Journal of Education Administration and History*, 42:1, pp.17–32.
9. Gartner, p.20.
10. *Ibid.*, p.20.
11. J. Anderson, *Report of Committee on Evacuation with a Covering Memorandum by the Secretary of State for the Home Department*, X, 607, p.6, Section 24 (Oxford: Bodleian Library, 1937) (hereafter Anderson Report).
12. Anderson Report, p.7, Section 26.
13. Anderson Report, p.24, Section 97.
14. Richard Titmuss, *Problems of Social Policy: History of the Second World War* (Basingstoke: Palgrave MacMillan, 1950) pp.32.
15. *Ibid.*, pp.32–34.
16. Anderson Report, p.14, Section 57.
17. *Ibid.*, p.14, Section 57.
18. *Ibid.*, p.14, Section 60.
19. In 1940 the Office of Works became a ministry in its own right, with John Reith, the 1st Baron Reith appointed Minister of Works and Buildings in October 1940.
20. John M. Robinson, *Requisitioned – The British Country House in the Second World War* (London: Aurum Press, 2014), p.8.
21. Titmuss, *Problems of Social Policy*, pp.4–6, 12–14.
22. Anderson Report, p.18, Section 77.
23. Gartner, p.22.
24. Anderson Report, Section 23.
25. London, London Metropolitan Archives (hereafter LMA), LCC/CL/CD/01/089: General Evacuation Plans, May 1939–July 1939.
26. Titmuss, *Problems of Social Policy*, p.102.
27. LMA, LCC/CL/CD/01/089.
28. *Ibid.*
29. Anderson Report, p.24, Section 99.
30. Roy Porter, *London: A Social History* (London: Hamish Hamilton, 1994) p.372.
31. Anderson Report, p.24, Section 99.
32. Gartner, p.21.

## Notes

33  Anderson Report, p.24, Section 99.
34  Gartner, p.24.
35  *Ibid.*, p.24.
36  Raymond M. Douglas, *Orderly and Humane* (New Haven: Yale University Press, 2012) pp.7–10.

## Chapter 2

1   The National Archives (hereafter, TNA), WO 250/353: Royal Hospital Chelsea, Board Minutes and Papers: Weekly Board Proceedings, 26 May 1938.
2   TNA, WO 250/353: 26 May 1938, folio 1426.
3   *Ibid.*
4   Anderson Report, p.7, Section 26.
5   TNA, WO 250/353: 26 May 1938, folio 1426.
6   *Ibid.*
7   Ben Pedroche, *London's Lost Power Stations and Gasworks* (Stroud: The History Press, 2013) p.80.
8   TNA, WO 250/353: 26 May 1938, folio 1426.
9   TNA, WORK 14/1387: Evacuation Arrangements 1938–1952: 16 June 1938.
10  TNA, WO 250/353: 7 July 1938, folio 1432.
11  TNA, WO 250/353: 18 August 1938, folio 1438.
12  *Ibid.*
13  *Ibid.*
14  Anderson Report, p.24, Section 99.
15  TNA, WORK 14/1387: Evacuation Arrangements 1938–1952.
16  *Ibid.*, 20 August 1938.
17  *Ibid.*
18  *Ibid.*
19  LMA – CL/CD/01/089: Letter to Sir George Chrystal, 18 May 1939.
20  TNA, WORK 14/1387: Evacuation Arrangements 1938–1952, 20 August 1938.
21  *Ibid.*, 5 September 1938.
22  Gartner, p.25.

## Chapter 3

1   TNA, WORK 14/1387: Evacuation Arrangements 1938–1952, Letter from Office of Works to the Royal Hospital, 17 September 1938.
2   TNA, WO 250/353: 18 August 1938, folio 1438.
3   *Ibid.*
4   TNA, WO 351.025 LIS: War Office list of established civil staff members up to 1958.
5   TNA, WORK 14/1387: Evacuation Arrangements 1938–1952, 17 September 1938.
6   TNA, WORK 14/1387: Evacuation Arrangements 1938–1952.

7   TNA, WO 250/353: 26 May 1938, folio 1426.
8   TNA, WORK 14/1387: Evacuation Arrangements 1938–1952.
9   *Ibid.*
10  *Ibid.*
11  Santi Corvaja & Robert Miller, *Hitler and Mussolini: The Secret Meetings* (New York: Enigma Books, 2008), p.71.
12  *Ibid.*, p.72.
13  TNA, WO 250/354: folio 1443, Note 10.
14  TNA, WO 250/354: folio 1443, Note 11.
15  Royal Borough of Kensington and Chelsea (hereafter, RBKC): Metropolitan Borough of Chelsea, Minutes of Proceedings (year ending 31 March 1939), 28 July 1938.
16  *Ibid.*
17  RBKC, Council Minutes – 4 August 1938.
18  *Ibid.*
19  *Ibid.*
20  Frances Faviell, *A Chelsea Concerto* (London: Dean Street Press, 2016), p.17.
21  TNA, WO 250/354: 29 September 1938, folio 1444, Note 9.
22  Neville Chamberlain, *In Search of Peace: Speeches 1937–1938* (London: Hutchinson, 1939), p.393.
23  TNA, WO 250/354: 29 September 1938, folio 1444, Note 9.
24  John Keegan, *The Second World War* (Pimlico: London, 1997) p.32.
25  TNA, WO 250/354: 29 September 1938, folio 1444, Note 9.
26  *Ibid.*
27  *Ibid.*
28  Robinson, *Requisitioned*, p.10.
29  Anderson Report, p.14, Section 60.
30  Robinson, *Requisitioned*, p.8.
31  TNA, WO 250/353: 26 May 1938, folio 1426.
32  TNA, WO 250/353: 29 September 1938, folio 1444.
33  TNA, WO 250/354: 29 September 1938, folio 1444, Note 8.
34  *Ibid.*
35  Keegan, *The Second World War*, p.32.

# Chapter 4

1   RHC, LDRHC/14/0310: RHC War Diary 1939–45 (hereafter RHC War Diary), 23 August 1939.
2   TNA, WO 250/354: 20 October 1938, folio 1447.
3   Dean, *The Royal Hospital Chelsea*, p.304.
4   *Ibid.*, p.305.
5   *Ibid.*, p.294.
6   TNA, WO 250/354: 20 October 1938, folio 1447.
7   TNA, WO 32/21175: Emergency Evacuation and Maintenance of Grounds, 27 May 1941.
8   *Ibid.*, Letter to Fry from Fitzgerald, 27 May 1941.
9   TNA, WO 351.025 LIS: War Office list of established civil staff members up to 1958.

*Notes*

10 TNA, WO 250/354: 17 November 1938, folio 1451.
11 J. Nye, *A Long Time in Making – The History of Smiths* (Oxford University Press, Oxford 2014) p.99.
12 TNA, WO 250/355: 12 January 1939, folio 1458.
13 TNA, WO 250/357: 9 June 1939, folio 1478.
14 RHC, LDRHC/15/0022: Agreement with Major Morland of Rudhall, 1939.
15 *Ibid.*
16 TNA, WO 32/21175: Emergency Evacuation and Maintenance of Grounds, 27 May 1941.
17 TNA, WORK 14/1387: Evacuation Arrangements 1938–1952, 1 June 1939.
18 TNA, WO 250/354: 6 October 1938, folio 1445.
19 RBKC, Council Minutes, 12 July 1939.
20 *Ibid.*
21 RBKC, Council Minutes 1939–40, p.254.
22 TNA, WO 250/355: 21 December 1938, folio 1456.
23 LMA, EO/WAR/1/23: Test Evacuation, Chelsea Borough, 19 June 1939.
24 RHC, LDRHC/18/0019: Agreement to construct permanent air-raid shelter in Burton Court, June 1939.
25 LMA, EO/WAR/1/23: Test Evacuation Chelsea Borough, 19 June 1939.
26 Faviell, *A Chelsea Concerto*, p.12.
27 TNA, WO 250/357: 20 April 1939, folio 1471.
28 Dean, *The Royal Hospital Chelsea*, p.31.
29 TNA, WO 250/357: 25 May 1939, folio 1476.
30 TNA, WO 250/357: 9 June 1939, folio 1478, Note 9.
31 RBKC, Council Minutes, March 1939.
32 TNA, WO 250/357: 3 June 1939, folio 1478.
33 RBKC, Council Minutes, 12 July 1939.
34 TNA, WO 250/357: 3 August 1939, folio 1486.
35 LMA, LCC/CL/CD/01/003: Air Raid Precautions – General Papers, January–August 1939.
36 TNA, WO 250/357: 18 May 1939, folio 1475.
37 *Ibid.*
38 LMA, EO/WAR/1/23: Test Evacuation Chelsea Borough, 19 June 1939.
39 *Ibid.*
40 Faviell, *A Chelsea Concerto*, p.6.
41 RBKC, SR 272: ARP Scrapbook 1 – Article in *Morning Advertiser*, 20 June 1939.
42 RHC War Diary, 23 August 1939.
43 RHC War Diary, 23–24 August 1939.

## *Chapter 5*

1 RHC War Diary, 3 September 1939.
2 RHC War Diary, 23 August 1939.
3 TNA, WO 250/358: 20 December 1939, folio 1489.
4 RHC War Diary, 24 August 1939.

5   Ibid.
6   RHC War Diary, 25 August 1939.
7   RHC War Diary, 26 August 1939.
8   Faviell, *A Chelsea Concerto*, p.11.
9   RHC War Diary, 27 August 1939.
10  RHC War Diary, 28 August 1939.
11  D.J. Wheal, *World's End – A Memoir of a Blitz Childhood* (London: Random House, 2006), p.75.
12  *Ibid.*, p.75.
13  Gartner, p.17.
14  Faviell, *A Chelsea Concerto*, pp.14–15.
15  RHC War Diary, 1 September 1939.
16  RHC War Diary, 2 September 1939.
17  Ibid.
18  TNA, WO 399/14899: Directorate of Army Medical Services and Territorial Force, Nursing Service Records: Edith Taylor.
19  RHC, LDRHC/20/0013: Alphabetical Notebook of Instructions – E for Evacuation.
20  RHC War Diary, 2 September 1939.
21  Faviell, *A Chelsea Concerto*, p.17.
22  RHC War Diary, 3 September 1939.
23  Ibid.
24  Ibid.
25  RHC, LDRHC/18/0002: Townsend, *Memories of a Captain of Invalids*, p.9.
26  RHC War Diary, 3 September 1939.
27  Ibid.
28  Ibid.
29  RHC War Diary, 4 September 1939.
30  Ibid.
31  LMA, CL/CD/01/090: General Evacuation Plans, August 1939–September 1939: Education Office Papers, 4 September 1939.
32  RHC War Diary, 6 September 1939.
33  Ibid.
34  TNA, WO 250/358: 7 September 1939, folio 1491. There is a minor discrepancy in the figures, with the board minute referring to '44 invalid In-Pensioners' accompanied by '2 Infirmary Orderlies'. The total number of evacuees is consistent, however.
35  Ibid.
36  RHC War Diary, 7 September 1939.
37  N.J. McCamley, *Saving Britain's Art Treasures from the Nazis* (Barnsley: Pen & Sword, 2003), p.285.
38  RHC War Diary, 7 September 1939.
39  RHC War Diary, 9 September 1939.
40  RHC, LDRHC/19/0001.1: Call-Up letter for Dr Howell, 7 September 1939.
41  RHC War Diary, 8 September 1939.

42 RHC War Diary, 9 September 1939.
43 *Ibid.*
44 RHC War Diary, 11 September 1939.
45 RHC War Diary, 12 September 1939.
46 Faviell, *A Chelsea Concerto*, p.20.
47 RHC War Diary, 13 September 1939.
48 Faviell, *A Chelsea Concerto*, p.17.
49 RHC War Diary, 14 September 1939. Earl Winterton was the Paymaster General and therefore an *ex officio* Commissioner of the Royal Hospital.
50 TNA, WO 250/358: 14 September 1939, folio 1492.
51 *Ibid.*
52 *Ibid.*, (LEE) AA Bn RE – London Electrical Engineers, Anti-Aircraft Battalion, Royal Engineers, a Territorial Army Volunteer unit.
53 John Keegan, *The Second World War*, p.33.
54 *Ibid.*, p.33.
55 RHC War Diary, 20 September 1939, addendum.
56 RHC War Diary, 21 September 1939.
57 *Ibid.*
58 Regimental war diaries were often the responsibility of a number of officers. However, the adjutant was in many cases the most likely author. In the case of RHC, this would have been Captain Charles Dean.
59 RHC War Diary, 23 September 1939.
60 *Ibid.*
61 RHC, LDRHC/18/0002: Townsend, *Memories of a Captain of Invalids*, p.9.

## Chapter 6

1 RHC, LDRHC/18/0002: Townsend, *Memories of a Captain of Invalids*, p.15.
2 Faviell, *A Chelsea Concerto*, p.16.
3 *Ibid.*, p.26.
4 TNA, RG 101/110G: 1939 Register, Chelsea Metropolitan Borough.
5 TNA, RG 101/110G: 1939 Register, Registration District 336/2 – Ross-on-Wye.
6 Keegan, *The Second World War*, p.35.
7 Brett Holman, *The Next War in the Air: Britain's Fear of the Bomber, 1908–1941* (London: Routledge, 2016).
8 Philip Ziegler, *London at War 1939–1945* (London: Pimlico, 1995) pp.4–20.
9 Titmuss, *Problems of Social Policy*, p.109.
10 *Ibid.*
11 *Ibid.*
12 Barry Turner, *Waiting for War: Britain 1939–1940* (London: Icon Books, 2019), p.130.
13 Titmuss, *Problems of Social Policy*, p.102. Titmuss estimated the unofficial private evacuation figure could be anything up to 2 million.
14 RHC War Diary, 11 September 1939.

15  Wheal, *World's End*, p.93.
16  *Ibid.*, p.94.
17  Penny Starns, *Blitz Families: The Children Who Stayed Behind* (Stroud: The History Press, 2012), p.36.
18  RHC, LDRHC/20/0013: Notebook of Alphabetical List of Instructions, listed under E for Evacuation.
19  Martin Parsons, *I'll Take That One: Dispelling the Myths of Civilian Evacuation 1939–45* (Peterborough: Beckett Karlson, 1998), p.68.
20  RHC, LDRHC/15/0022: Agreement with Major Morland of Rudhall, 1939.
21  RHC, LDRHC/18/0002: Townsend, *Memories of a Captain of Invalids*, p.15.
22  Faviell, *A Chelsea Concerto*, p.34.
23  RHC War Diary, 19 November 1939.
24  RHC War Diary, 1 December 1939.
25  TNA, WO 250/358: 24 August 1939, folio 1489.
26  TNA, WO 250/358: 7 September 1939, folio 1491.
27  RHC, LDRHC/20/0100: Records of Deaths 1900–60.
28  TNA, WO 250/358: 21 December 1939, folio 1506.
29  RHC War Diary, 31 December 1939.
30  Titmuss, *Problems of Social Policy*, p.101.
31  TNA, WO 250/359: 1 February 1940, folio 1511.
32  TNA, HO 250/447: Royal Hospital Chelsea Minute Book, 1 July 1938–28 February 1941, p.304, Note 7.
33  Naomi Clifford, *Under Fire: The Blitz Diaries of a Volunteer Ambulance Driver* (London: Caret Press, 2021) p.36.
34  *Ibid.*, p.21.
35  *Ibid.*, p.36.

# Chapter 7

1  Hansard, War Situation Report, Winston Churchill – Tuesday, 4 June 1940, Vol. 361.
2  The spelling 'Chillianwallah' appears in RHC War Diary, but is spelt on the war memorial as 'Chilianwalla'; RHC War Diary, 20 April 1940.
3  *Ibid.*
4  Anthony Beevor, *The Second World War* (London: Weidenfeld & Nicolson, 2012), p.95.
5  *Ibid.*, p.103.
6  Faviell, *A Chelsea Concerto*, p.37.
7  Hansard, House of Commons Debate, Winston Churchill – 13 May 1940, Vol. 360.
8  Faviell, *A Chelsea Concerto*, p.38.
9  RHC War Diary, 22 May 1940.
10  *Ibid.*, 23 May 1940.
11  TNA, WO 250/360: 23 May 1940, folio 1526.
12  Faviell, *A Chelsea Concerto*, p.39.

13 TNA, WO 250/360: 30 May 1940, folio 1527, Note 7.
14 *Ibid.*, Note 8.
15 Arthur Marwick, *The Home Front: The British and the Second World War* (Wallop: BAS Publishers Ltd, 1976) pp.32–40.
16 Norman Longmate (ed.), *The Home Front: An Anthology of Personal Experience 1938–1945* (London: Chatto & Windus, 1981) pp.52–55.
17 Titmuss, *Problems of Social Policy*, p.355.
18 Clifford, *Under Fire*, p.38.
19 Cecil Beaton, *The Years Between: Diaries 1939–44* (London: Weidenfeld & Nicolson, 1965) p.23.
20 *Ibid.*, p.23.
21 *Ibid.*, pp.23–30.
22 Hansard, War Situation Report, Winston Churchill, Vol. 361 – Tuesday, 4 June 1940.
23 TNA, WO 250/360: 20 June 1940, folio 1530.
24 *Ibid.*, Note 12.
25 RHC War Diary, 28 May 1940.
26 RHC, LDRHC/16/0839: Army Estimates.
27 TNA, WO 250/360: folio 1530, Note 12.
28 RHC War Diary, 15 July 1940.
29 TNA, WO 250/360: folio 1530, Note 12.
30 *Ibid.*, Note 12.
31 Rebecca Manley, *To the Tashkent Station: Evacuation and Survival in the Soviet Union at War* (Ithaca: Cornell University Press, 2009), p.38.
32 RHC War Diary, 17 June 1940.
33 TNA, WO/250/360: 20 June 1940, folio 1530.
34 *Ibid.*, Note 6.
35 Clifford, *Under Fire*, p.40.
36 Keegan, *The Second World War*, p.75.
37 RHC War Diary, 15 July 1940.
38 *Ibid.*, 15–23 August 1940.
39 Basil Liddell Hart, *A History of the Second World War* (London: Pan Macmillan, 2014) p.131.
40 RHC War Diary, 24 August 1940.
41 *Ibid.*, 25 August 1940.
42 *Ibid.*, 26 August 1940.

## Chapter 8

1 RHC War Diary, 11 September 1940.
2 Geoffrey Wellum, *First Light* (London: Viking, 2002).
3 Tim Clayton & Phil Craig, *Finest Hour* (London: Coronet Books, 2001).
4 RHC War Diary, 28–29 August 1940.
5 RHC, LDRHC/18/0002: Townsend, *Memories of a Captain of Invalids*, p.10.

6   TNA, WO 250/358: 14 September 1939, folio 1492, Note 8.
7   TNA, WO 250/353: 26 May 1938, folio 1426.
8   Faviell, *A Chelsea Concerto*, p.117.
9   Ben Pedroche, *London's Lost Power Stations and Gasworks* (Stroud: The History Press, 2013).
10  Constantine Fitzgibbon, *The Blitz* (London: Coronet Books, 2010) p.222.
11  RHC War Diary, 29 August 1940.
12  *Ibid.*
13  *Ibid.*, 30–31 August 1940.
14  *Ibid.*, 4 September 1940.
15  *Ibid.*, 3 September 1940.
16  Liddell Hart, *A History of the Second World War*, p.134.
17  *Ibid.*, p.125.
18  *Ibid.*, p.135.
19  RHC War Diary, 7 September 1940.
20  *Ibid.*
21  Theodora Fitzgibbon, *With Love: An Autobiography 1939–1946* (London: Century, 1982), p.72. The two drinking partners of Fitzgibbon were British diplomat Donald Maclean, later exposed as a Soviet spy, and the poet Dylan Thomas.
22  Clifford, *Under Fire*, p.80.
23  Liddell Hart, *A History of the Second World War*, p.135.
24  RHC War Diary, 7 September 1940.
25  *Ibid.*
26  *Ibid.*
27  *Ibid.*
28  *Ibid.*, 8 September 1940.
29  *Ibid.*
30  Clifford, *Under Fire*, p.86.
31  RHC War Diary, 9 September 1940.
32  *Ibid.*, 9–10 September 1940.
33  Faviell, *A Chelsea Concerto*, p.95.
34  Liddell Hart, *A History of the Second World War*, p.135.
35  Clifford, *Under Fire*, p.83.
36  Liddell Hart, *A History of the Second World War*, p.136.
37  RHC War Diary, 11 September 1940.
38  *Ibid.*
39  TNA, WO 250/353: 26 May 1938, folio 1426.
40  RHC War Diary, 11 September 1940.
41  Faviell, *A Chelsea Concerto*, p.101.
42  RHC War Diary, 11 September 1940.
43  Liddell Hart, *A History of the Second World War*, p.136.
44  RHC War Diary, 12 September 1940.
45  *Ibid.*, 13 September 1940.
46  *Ibid.*
47  TNA, WO 250/361: 19 September 1940, folio 1543, Note 7.

48 RHC War Diary, 13–14 September 1940.
49 *Ibid.*, 14 September 1940.
50 *Ibid.*
51 *Ibid.*
52 *Ibid.*, 15 September 1940.

# Chapter 9

1 TNA, WO 250/361: 19 September 1940 – Comment by Lord Croft, Under-Secretary of State for War.
2 Liddell Hart, *A History of the Second World War*, p.137.
3 TNA, WO 250/361: 19 September 1940, folio 1543, Note 8.
4 RHC War Diary, 17 September 1940.
5 Anderson Report, p.7, Section 26.
6 TNA, WO 250/361: 19 September 1940, folio 1543, Note 10.
7 Marwick, *The Home Front*, pp.68–70.
8 Tom Harrisson, *Living Through the Blitz* (London: Collins, 1976), pp.65–66.
9 RHC War Diary, 20 September 1940.
10 Dean is the most likely candidate to be the author of the Hospital's War Diary.
11 Note of email correspondence with Chelsea Coroner's Office, 25 April 2019.
12 TNA, WO 372/20: Medal Index Card.
13 RHC, LDRHC/20/9999: In-Pensioners Admissions Register from 1 January 1934.
14 Ralph Barker, *Children of the Benares: A War Crime and Its Victims* (London: Avid Publications, 2003).
15 Clifford, *Under Fire*, p.116.
16 RHC War Diary, 26 September 1940.
17 *Ibid.*, 27 September 1940.
18 *Ibid.*
19 *Ibid.*
20 *Ibid.*, 5 October 1940.
21 *Ibid.*, 1 October 1940.
22 *Ibid.*, 11 October 1940.
23 *Ibid.*, 12 October 1940.
24 *Ibid.*, 14–15 October 1940.
25 Faviell, *A Chelsea Concerto*, p.118.
26 RHC War Diary, 15–16 October 1940.
27 *Ibid.*
28 *Ibid.*
29 RHC War Diary, 16 October 1940.
30 *Ibid.*
31 TNA, WO 250/361: 17 October 1940, folio 1547, Note 7.
32 RHC War Diary, 21 October 1940.
33 *Ibid.*, 26 October 1940.

34　TNA, WO 250/373: Letter from Mayor to Governor, 23 October 1940.
35　*Ibid.*, 24 October 1940.
36　TNA, WO 250/373: Letter from Assistant Secretary to Town Clerk, 29 August 1945.
37　RHC War Diary, 26 October 1940.
38　TNA, WO 250/353: 26 May 1938, folio 1426.
39　RHC War Diary, 26–27 October 1940.
40　*Ibid.*
41　*Ibid.*
42　RHC War Diary, 27–28 October 1940.
43　Faviell, *A Chelsea Concerto*, pp.120–21.
44　*Ibid.*, p.118.

# Chapter 10

1　TNA, WO 250/361: 7 November 1940. The title of a Ministry of Information propaganda movie about the Blitz. The Royal Hospital participated in the associated press campaign.
2　RHC War Diary, 1 November 1940.
3　Faviell, *A Chelsea Concerto*, p.139.
4　*Ibid.*, p.141.
5　RHC War Diary, 2 November 1940.
6　TNA, WO 250/361: 7 November 1940, folio 1550.
7　*Ibid.*
8　RHC War Diary, 4 November 1940.
9　*Ibid.*, 28 November 1940.
10　RHC, LDRHC/20/0100: Record of Deaths 1900–60.
11　*Ibid.*
12　RHC War Diary, 18 September 1940.
13　*Ibid.*, 20 October 1940.
14　*Ibid.*, 3 November 1940.
15　*Ibid.*, 7–8 November 1940.
16　*Ibid.*, 8–9 November 1940.
17　*Ibid.*, 12 November 1940.
18　Faviell, *A Chelsea Concerto*, p.161.
19　RHC War Diary, 21 November 1940.
20　*Ibid.*, 29 November 1940.
21　Peter Roach, *The 8.15 to War – The Memories of a Desert Rat* (London: Secker & Warburg, 1982) pp.15–17.
22　Clifford, *Under Fire*, pp.116–20.
23　RHC War Diary, 8 December 1940.
24　Faviell, *A Chelsea Concerto*, p.175.
25　RHC War Diary, 9 December 1940.

26  During this recovery process the bomb was discovered to be 100kg.
27  Faviell, *A Chelsea Concerto*, p.179.
28  RHC War Diary, 25 December 1940.
29  Philip Ziegler, *London at War 1939–1945* (London: Pimlico, 1995) p.143.
30  RHC War Diary, 29 December 1940.
31  *Ibid.*
32  *Ibid.*, 31 December 1940.
33  Dean, *The Royal Hospital Chelsea*, p.259.
34  Anjali Bulley (ed.), *Cadogan & Chelsea: The Making of a Modern Estate* (London: Unicorn, 2017) p.53.
35  *Ibid.*
36  TNA, WO 250/361: 2 January 1941, folio 1557.
37  RHC War Diary, 3 January 1941.
38  *Ibid.*, 11 January 1941.
39  Faviell, *A Chelsea Concerto*, p.185.
40  RHC War Diary, 16 February 1941.
41  *Ibid.*, 22 February 1941.
42  Faviell, *A Chelsea Concerto*, pp.157–58.
43  RHC War Diary, 8 March 1941.
44  *Ibid.*, 19 March 1941.
45  TNA, WO 250/362: 20 March 1941, folio 1568.

## Chapter 11

1  ARP Incident Reports 16–17 April 1941.
2  TNA, HO 198/26: Region 5, London, Headquarters, Group 1 Bomb Damage Reports, 18–19 March 1941 to 5–6 May 1941.
3  *Ibid.*, 18–19 March 1941.
4  TNA, HO 198/26: Report 1 – 16–17 April 1941 – Chelsea Old Church. Report states, 'Presumed objective – Battersea Bridge – 200yds'.
5  Patrick Loobey & Jon Mills, *The Boroughs of Wandsworth and Battersea at War* (Stroud: Sutton Publishing, 1996) p.84.
6  Faviell, *A Chelsea Concerto*, p.210.
7  *Ibid.*, p.210.
8  Clifford, *Under Fire*, p.152.
9  RBKC: Local Q 355 23 CHE, ARP Incident Report, – 21.05hrs Air Raid Warning – Red.
10  Chelsea Society, 1941–42 Annual Report: Royal Hospital Chelsea, Governor, General Sir Harry Knox, p.21.
11  Faviell, *A Chelsea Concerto*, p.225.
12  Clifford, *Under Fire*, p.152.
13  Faviell, *A Chelsea Concerto*, p.211.
14  Constantine Fitzgibbon, *The Winter of Bombs: The Story of the Blitz* (New York: W.W. Norton, 1957) pp.229–30.

15 Barbara Nixon, *Raiders Overhead: A Diary of the London Blitz* (London: Scolar Press, 1980) p.109.
16 RHC War Diary, 16–17 April 1941, and LDRHC/19/0104.1: Letter to Mrs Veldon from Lt-Gov – 25 April 1941.
17 *Ibid.*
18 RHC War Diary, 16–17 April 1941.
19 Faviell, *A Chelsea Concerto*, pp.211–12.
20 ARP Incident Report.
21 TNA, HO 198/26: Report 5 – 16–17 April 1941.
22 Faviell, *A Chelsea Concerto*, p.212.
23 *Ibid.*
24 RHC War Diary, 16–17 April 1941 – this would lead to some confusion when trying to pinpoint the exact time at which the infirmary bombing took place.
25 Faviell, *A Chelsea Concerto*, p.213.
26 *Ibid.*, p.215.
27 TNA, HO 198/26: Report 6 – 16–17 April 1941.
28 Faviell, *A Chelsea Concerto*, p.216.
29 ARP Incident Report.
30 Faviell, *A Chelsea Concerto*, p.216.
31 *Ibid.*
32 *Ibid.*, pp.216–17.
33 *Ibid.*, p.217.
34 *Ibid.*
35 TNA, HO 198/26: Report 7 – 16–17 April 1941. The Bomb Damage Report completed on 29 April 1941 treats this bombing as one incident.
36 RHC War Diary, 16–17 April 1941.
37 *Ibid.* Frederick George Marrable, born in 1890, served as an ambulance driver with the Royal Army Medical Corps in the First World War. He was awarded the Military Medal in 1914 for rescuing wounded soldiers while under fire during the retreat from Mons. He became an In-Pensioner in 1961 and died in 1962.
38 *Ibid.* (There is an explanation in the Bomb Damage Reports [HO 198/26] about why this incident is referred to as a 'Land Mine'. Most of the staff members seconded to the Bomb Damage Report teams were Royal Air Force personnel and a flight lieutenant who inadvertently used the phrase 'Land Mine' was corrected by his Commanding Officer. '"Land Mine" is something peculiar to the army. We use, up to the present, "parachute mine" for these missiles.')
39 TNA, WO/250/362: 17 April 1941, Note 8. Minutes refer to Ward No. 7 taking the main force of the blast. However, LDRHC/20/0100: Record of Deaths 1900–60 also records the deaths of In-Pensioners in the adjacent Ward No. 8.
40 ARP Incident Report.
41 *Ibid.*
42 RHC, LDRHC/19/0106: Letter from Governor Knox to OC 'C Flight' 905 Squadron, Royal Air Force – 25 April 1941.
43 TNA, HO 198/26: Report 7 – 16–17 April 1941.
44 RHC War Diary, 16–17 April 1941.

45 *Ibid.*, 11 September 1939.
46 RHC, LDRHC/15/0084: Citations for Gallantry – Infirmary Bombing.
47 *Ibid.*
48 ARP Incident Report.
49 *Ibid.*
50 RHC, LDRHC/19/0106: Letter of thanks from Governor Knox to Major R. Abercromby MC, OC Guards Chelsea – 18 April 1941.
51 ARP Incident Report.
52 RHC, LDRHC/19/0104.3: Letter from Fitzgerald to Reverend Mallaher, regarding Infirmary Bombing – 4 May 1941.
53 RHC, LDRHC/15/0084: Citations for Gallantry – Infirmary Bombing.
54 *Ibid.*
55 *Ibid.*
56 RHC, LDRHC/19/0102.1: Letter from Ministry of Health Emergency Medical Service, Sector 7 – 29 April 1941.
57 RHC, LDRHC/19/0101: Letter from British Red Cross Society, County Council Emergency Hospital, Old Windsor – 21 April 1941.
58 RHC, LDRHC/15/0084: Citations for Gallantry – Infirmary Bombing.
59 ARP Incident Report.
60 British Library: *War Illustrated*, 13 December 1940.
61 RHC War Diary, 16–17 April 1941.
62 *Ibid.*
63 ARP Incident Report.

# Chapter 12

1 ARP Incident Report.
2 Clifford, *Under Fire*, p.51.
3 *Ibid.*, pp.51–52.
4 *Ibid.*, p.52.
5 ARP Incident Report.
6 Leighton Thomson, *The Rebuilding of Chelsea Old Church* (London: published privately, 1957) p.7.
7 Constantine Fitzgibbon, *The Winter of Bombs*, p.234.
8 Thomson, *The Rebuilding of Chelsea Old Church*, p.8.
9 TNA, HO 198/26: Report 1 – The bomb damage incident report highlights 'human remains' identified as being those of the fire-watchers found in Beaufort Street, 20yds away.
10 *Ibid.*
11 *Ibid.*
12 Theodora Fitzgibbon, *With Love: An Autobiography 1938–1946* (London: Century, 1982) p.90.
13 *Ibid.*, p.90.

14 Constantine Fitzgibbon, *The Winter of Bombs*, p.227.
15 ARP Incident Report.
16 Constantine Fitzgibbon, *The Winter of Bombs*, p.228.
17 *Ibid.*, p.235.
18 *Ibid.*
19 *Ibid.*
20 ARP Incident Report.
21 *Ibid.*
22 RHC, LDRHC/15/0084: Citations for Gallantry – Infirmary Bombing.
23 ARP Incident Report.
24 RHC War Diary, 16–17 April 1941.
25 *Ibid.*
26 TNA, WO/250/362: 17 April 1941, folio 1509.
27 RHC War Diary, 16–17 April 1941.
28 RHC, LDRHC/19/0099: Letter to Mrs Troup, Pretoria, Cape Town.
29 RHC, LDRHC/19/006.19: Letter to Gov. Knox from Admiral Evans.
30 TNA, HO 198/26: Report 125.
31 RHC War Diary, 16–17 April 1941.
32 ARP Incident Report.
33 Clifford, *Under Fire*, p.154.
34 *Ibid.*
35 ARP Incident Report.
36 RHC War Diary, 17 April 1941.
37 *Ibid.*
38 RHC, LDRHC/15/0084: Citations for Gallantry – Infirmary Bombing.
39 ARP Incident Report.
40 *Ibid.*
41 *Ibid.*
42 Clifford, *Under Fire*, p.154.
43 *Ibid.*
44 Constantine Fitzgibbon, *Winter of Bombs*, p.238.
45 *Ibid.*, p.239.
46 *Ibid.*, p.240.
47 TNA, HO 198/26: Report 13.
48 *Ibid.*
49 TNA, HO 198/26: Report 14.
50 RHC War Diary, 16–17 April 1941.
51 ARP Incident Report.
52 TNA, HO 198/26: Report 10.
53 ARP Incident Report.
54 *Ibid.*
55 RBKC, Council of the Metropolitan Borough of Chelsea: Minutes of Proceedings, Year Ended March 1942, p.17.
56 TNA, HO 198/26: Report 9.
57 RHC War Diary, 16–17 April 1941.

58   ARP Incident Report.
59   *Ibid.*
60   *Ibid.*

# Chapter 13

1   RHC, LDRHC/19/0102.1: Letter from Commandant of Winkfield Place convalescence home to the Royal Hospital.
2   Faviell, *A Chelsea Concerto*, p.223.
3   *Ibid.*, p.224.
4   *Ibid.*, p.221.
5   RHC War Diary, 17 April 1941.
6   *Ibid.*
7   *Ibid.*
8   RHC War Diary, 18 April 1941. Four casualties were taken to Brompton Road Hospital.
9   RHC, LDRHC/19/0099: Letter from Admiral Evans to Governor.
10  RHC War Diary and LDRHC/19/0106: Letters of thanks for assistance during Air Raid.
11  RHC War Diary, 18 April 1941.
12  *Ibid.*
13  *Ibid.*
14  *Ibid.*, 19 April 1941.
15  Jeffreys, *London at War*, pp.82–83.
16  RHC War Diary, 20 April 1941.
17  RHC, LDRHC/19/0026.17: Report of injuries to Sister C.E. May.
18  RHC, LDRHC/19/0101: Letter re: evacuated patients, 21 April 1941.
19  RHC War Diary, 20 April 1941.
20  Philip Ziegler, *London at War 1939–1945* (London: Pimlico, 1995) p.177.
21  *Ibid.*
22  RHC War Diary, 21–22 April 1941.
23  *Ibid.*, 21 April 1941.
24  *Ibid.*, Addendum, 16–17 April 1941.
25  RHC, LDRHC/19/0096.1: Nurse Olive Jones – Killed Through Enemy Action.
26  RHC, LDRHC/19/0096.1: Nurse Olive Jones – Killed Through Enemy Action; LDRHC/19/0096.2: Nursing Sister McMullan – Killed Through Enemy Action; LDRHC/19/0096.3: Ward Master James Hutchins – Killed Through Enemy Action; LDRHC/19/0097.1: Nursing Sister Nicholson – Killed Through Enemy Action; LDRHC/19/0098: Nursing Sister Edith Taylor – Killed Through Enemy Action.
27  RHC, LDRHC/19/0104.1: Letter from Major General Morgan-Owen, Lieutenant Governor, to Mrs Veldon of Didcot, Berkshire (daughter of one of the In-Pensioners who died), 25 April 1941.
28  TNA, WORK 14/1387: Evacuation Arrangements 1938–52: Letter from Office of Works to the Treasury, 3 June 1941.

29  RHC, LDRHC/19/0113: Letter from Governor to Regimental HQs – 22 April 1941.
30  RHC War Diary, 23 April 1941; correct spelling is 'Foot'.
31  *Ibid.* All those killed were buried in the RHC plot at Brookwood, except for Sister Edith Taylor, who was buried alongside family members at a cemetery in Birkenhead.
32  TNA, WORK 14/1387: Evacuation Arrangements 1938–52: Letter to RHC, 14 May 1941.
33  TNA, WORK 14/1387: Evacuation Arrangements 1938–52: Sanitary Engineer's Report, 7 May 1941.
34  RHC, LDRHC/19/0101: Letter from Red Cross Society, 21 April 1941.
35  RHC, LDRHC/19/0101: Letter to Red Cross Society, 23 April 1941.
36  RHC, LDRHC/19/0102.1: Letter from Commandant of Winkfield Place, 28 April 1941.
37  *Ibid.*
38  RHC, LDRHC/19/0102.1: Letter from Ministry of Health Emergency Medical Service, Sector 7, 29 April 1941.
39  RHC, LDRHC/19/0110: List of I/Ps in Medical Evacuation Hospitals, 31 May 1941.
40  TNA, WO/250/353: 18 August 1938, folio 1458.
41  RHC, LDRHC/19/0104.2: Letter from Rev. H.T. Malaher to Assistant Secretary Fitzgerald, 4 May 1941.
42  RHC, LDRHC/19/0104.3: Letter to Rev. H. T. Malaher from Assistant Secretary Fitzgerald, 6 May 1941.
43  RHC War Diary, 30 April 1941.
44  *Ibid.*
45  TNA, WORK/WO32/21775: Note from Fitzgerald to Fry, 23 May 1941.
46  TNA, WORK 14/1387: Evacuation Arrangements 1938–52: Note from Treasury, 18 July 1941.
47  *Ibid.*, Letter to Fitzgerald, 23 May 1941.
48  *Ibid.*, Sanitary Engineer's Report, 7 May 1941.
49  RHC War Diary, 4 May 1941.
50  *Ibid.*, 26 April 1941.
51  *Ibid.*, 5 May 1941.
52  RHC, LDRHC/19/0026.18: Nurses Deasy and Howard Gazetted, 25 July 1941.
53  Ziegler, *London at War 1939–1945*, pp.160–61.
54  RHC War Diary, 10–11 May 1941.
55  Faviell, *A Chelsea Concerto*, p.234.
56  TNA, WORK 14/1387: Evacuation Arrangements 1938–52: Letter from Ministry of Works to Treasury, 3 June 1941.
57  TNA, WO/250/363: 22 May 1941, folio 1576, Note 8.
58  RHC, LDRHC/19/0001.23: Petrol ration claim for visit to Ascott House re: its occupation as an infirmary, 22 May 1941.
59  Constantine Fitzgibbon, *The Blitz*, p.266.

## Chapter 14

1. RHC, LDRHC/19/0103.3: Letter to Princess Christian Home.
2. *Ibid.*, 10 September 1942.
3. TNA, WORK 14/1387: Evacuation Arrangements 1938–52: Notes on telephone conversation, 23 May 1941.
4. *Ibid.*, Letter from Fitzgerald to Miller, 23 May 1941.
5. TNA, WORK WO/32/21175: Letter from Fitzgerald to Fry, 23 May 1941.
6. TNA, WO/14/1387: Letter from Fitzgerald to Miller, 23 May 1941.
7. *Ibid.*
8. *Ibid.*, Letter from Miller to Fitzgerald, 23 May 1941.
9. RHC, LDRHC/19/0115.1: Letter from Knox to Mrs Foot, 21 April 1941.
10. RHC, LDRHC/19/0115.2: Letters re: I/P Cox admission to local hospital, May 1941.
11. RHC, LDRHC/19/0115.2: Letter from Fitzgerald to Mrs Foot, 24 May 1941.
12. RHC War Diary, 26 May 1941.
13. Liddell Hart, *A History of the Second World War*, pp.480–82.
14. *Ibid.*, pp.485–87.
15. RHC War Diary, 29 May 1941.
16. RHC, LDRHC/19/0115.2: Letter from Mrs Foot, 30 May 1941.
17. *Ibid.*
18. TNA, WORK/14/1387: Evacuation Arrangements 1938–52: Letter to Treasury from Mr Miller, 3 June 1941.
19. RHC War Diary, 7 June 1941.
20. *Ibid.*, 9, 15, 20 June 1941.
21. RHC, LDRHC/19/0113: Letter from Knox to various regiments, 22 April 1941.
22. British Library, Newspaper Archives, *The Times*, 16 June 1941.
23. TNA, WO/250/363: 19 June 1941, folio 1580.
24. *Ibid.*, folio 1580.
25. RHC War Diary, 23 June 1941.
26. *Ibid.*
27. *Ibid.*, 9 July 1941.
28. *Ibid.*, 19 July and 22 August 1941.
29. TNA, WO/250/363: 28 August 1941, folio 1590, Note 7. The three In-Pensioners in civil hospitals had each been admitted for routine operations and were not air-raid casualties.
30. TNA, WORK 14/1387: Letter from Miller to Gatliff, 15 July 1941.
31. *Ibid.*, Note from Gatliff to Miller, 18 July 1941.
32. TNA, WO/250/363, 28 August 1941, folio 1590, Note 8.
33. TNA, WORK 14/1387: Letter from Miller to Gatliff, 27 August 1941.
34. *Ibid.*
35. *Ibid.*
36. TNA, WORK 14/1387: Letter from Gatliff to Miller, 1 September 1941.
37. RHC War Diary, 17 and 24 September 1941.

38  TNA, WO/250/363: 18 September 1941, folio 1593.
39  TNA, WO/250/364: 25 September 1941, folio 1594.
40  RHC War Diary, 20 October 1941.
41  TNA, WORK 14/1387: Letter from Fry to Wilcox, 18 December 1941.
42  *Ibid.*, Letter from Treasury to Ministry of Works, 24 January 1942.

# Chapter 15

1  TNA, WO/250/365: Letter to the Royal Hospital re: Demolition of the Infirmary ruins.
2  Liddell Hart, *A History of the Second World War*, p.485.
3  *Ibid.*, p.488.
4  RHC War Diary, January, February, April 1942.
5  TNA, WO 250/365: 19 March 1942, folio 1618.
6  RHC War Diary, 28 March 1942.
7  RHC, LDRHC/19/0017.4: Letter from F. Boultwood & Son, 14 May 1942.
8  RHC, LDRHC/19/0017.5: Letter from Ministry of Works re: Infirmary ruins, May 1942.
9  TNA, WO/250/365: 14 May 1942.
10  *Ibid.*
11  RHC War Diary, 29 May 1942.
12  *Ibid.*
13  *Ibid.*, 1 and 3 June 1942.
14  *Ibid.*, 30 June and 1 July 1942.
15  Keegan, *The Second World War*, p.182.
16  TNA, WO 169/5062: 1st Battalion Sherwood Foresters War Diary, 1 Jan 1942–31 August 1942.
17  TNA, WO 250/365: 18 June 1942, folio 1630.
18  TNA, WO 250/366: 16 July 1942, folio 1634.
19  RHC, LDRHC/18/0002: Townsend, *Memories of a Captain of Invalids*, p.15.
20  *Ibid.*
21  RHC War Diary, 10 August 1942.
22  RHC, LDRHC/16/0839: Royal Hospital Chelsea, Army Estimates. By December 1945, the Pensions Secretariat would be 195 strong (TNA, WO 250/373, 13 December 1945, folio 1801).
23  RHC War Diary, 10 August 1943.
24  *Ibid.*
25  *Ibid.*, October 1942.
26  *Ibid.*, 30 June 1943 – Fourteen In-Pensioners returned from Moraston House; 1 July 1943 – Draft of thirteen In-Pensioners sent to Moraston.
27  RHC, LDRHC/19/0103.2: Letter to Princess Christian Hospital, 21 July 1942.
28  RHC, LDRHC/19/0103.3: Letter to Princess Christian Hospital, 10 September 1942.
29  RHC War Diary, 15 November 1942.

30  TNA, WO 250/366: 17 September 1942, folio 1643.
31  TNA, WO 250/366: 10 December 1942, folio 1655.
32  TNA, WO 250/367: 28 January 1943, folio 1661.

## Chapter 16

1   RHC, LDRHC/18/0089.1: Lieutenant Governor's comments on plans for post-war reconstruction.
2   RHC War Diary, 17 January 1943.
3   *Ibid.*, 19 January 1943.
4   Anthony Beevor, *Stalingrad* (London: Penguin, 1999).
5   Anthony Beevor, *Berlin: The Downfall 1945* (London: Viking, 2002).
6   Liddell Hart, *A History of the Second World War*, p.492.
7   *Ibid.*, p.494.
8   TNA, WO 250/367: 18 March 1943, folio 1668.
9   *Ibid.*, 17 June 1943, folio 1680.
10  RHC War Diary, 29 May 1943.
11  *Ibid.*, July 1943.
12  RHC, LRHRC/19/0026: Series of letters 1941–42 re: Recommendations for Gallantry.
13  RHC, LDRHC/18/0089: Series of Plans re: Post-War Reconstruction 1943–44.
14  TNA, WO 250/368: 19 August 1943, folio 1689, Note 11.
15  Faviell, *A Chelsea Concerto*, p.185.
16  RHC, LDRHC/18/0089.2: Captain Dean's memorandum re: Post-War Reconstruction, 4 October 1943.
17  RHC, LDRHC/20/0100: Record of Deaths 1900–60.
18  RHC, LDRHC/18/0089.2: Captain Dean's memorandum re: Post-War Reconstruction, 4 October 1943.
19  Dean, *The Royal Hospital Chelsea*, p.290.
20  *Ibid.*, pp.290–91.
21  *Ibid.*, p.290.
22  *Ibid.*, p.291.
23  RHC, LDRHC/18/0089.1: Reply from Lieutenant Governor to Dean's post-war plans memo, 12 November 1943.
24  *Ibid*.
25  TNA, WO/250/368: 21 October 1943, folio 1698.
26  RHC War Diary, November 1943.
27  *Ibid.*, 25 December 1943.
28  TNA, WO/250/369: 18 November 1943, folio 1706.
29  *Ibid.*, folio 1702.
30  TNA, WO/250/369: 21 January 1944.
31  RHC War Diary, 21 January 1944.
32  *Ibid.*, 22 January 1944.
33  *Ibid.*, 25 and 26 January 1944.

34  TNA, WO/250/369: 27 January 1944, folio 1711.
35  TNA, WO/250/369: 24 February 1944, folio 1715.
36  RHC War Diary, 18 February 1944.
37  *Ibid.*, 20 February 1944.
38  *Ibid.*, 22 February 1944.
39  Wheal, *World's End*, p.326.
40  *Ibid.*, p.321.
41  *Ibid.*, p.325.
42  *Ibid.*, p.329.
43  RHC War Diary, 22 February 1944.
44  *Ibid.*, 31 May 1944.
45  TNA, WO/250/370: 4 May 1944, folio 1724.
46  *Ibid.*, 25 May 1944, folio 1727.
47  *Ibid.*, 8 June 1944, folio 1729.
48  RHC, LDRHC/18/0002: Townsend, *Memories of a Captain of Invalids*, p.17.
49  RHC War Diary, 15–16 June 1944.
50  *Ibid.*
51  *Ibid.*, 17 June 1944.
52  *Ibid.*, 18 June 1944.
53  *Ibid.*, 19 June 1944.
54  *Ibid.*
55  *Ibid.*, 3 July 1944.
56  *Ibid.*, 9 September 1944.
57  TNA, WO/250/371: 28 September 1944, folio 1745.
58  RHC, LDRHC/18/0089.5: Memo from Lieutenant Governor re: return of evacuated In-Pensioners to Chelsea, 12 October 1944.
59  TNA, WO/250/371: 12 October 1944, folio 1747.
60  *Ibid.*, 19 October 1944, folio 1748.
61  *Ibid*, Note 8.
62  TNA, WO/250/372: 1 February 1945, folio 1762.
63  *Ibid.*

# Chapter 17

1  TNA, WO 250/372: Governor's comments to Chelsea Council re: use of RHC grounds, 1 February 1945.
2  Anthony Beevor, *Berlin: The Downfall 1945* (London: Viking, 2002) p.2.
3  *Ibid.*, p.1.
4  Madhusree Mukerjee, *Churchill's Secret War: The British Empire and the Ravaging of India During World War II* (New York: Basic Books, 2010) p.215.
5  Hansard, Parliamentary Debates, Commons, col. 1653–4, 10 November 1944.
6  TNA, WO 250/371: 7 December 1944, folio 1755.
7  RHC, LDRHC/20/0013: Alphabetical list of Instructions – W.
8  TNA, WO 250/371: 14 December 1944, folio 1756.

9 *Ibid.*, 4 January 1945, folio 1758, Note 8.
10 Dean, *The Royal Hospital Chelsea*, p.295.
11 The memorial erected in Ross-on-Wye to In-Pensioners who died during the war records Lockley's date of death as 30 December 1944.
12 TNA, WO 250/371: 4 January 1945, folio 1758, Note 6.
13 RHC War Diary, 3 January 1945.
14 *Ibid.*
15 *Ibid.*
16 RHC, LDRHC/18/0002: Townsend, *Memories of a Captain of Invalids*, p.16.
17 RHC War Diary, 3 January 1945.
18 *Ibid.*
19 *Ibid.*
20 TNA, WO 250/372: 1 February 1945, folio 1762 – Note 6.
21 *Ibid.*
22 *Ibid.* The Office of Works was upgraded to Ministry status in 1940.
23 *Ibid.*
24 *Ibid.*
25 *Ibid.*
26 Max Hastings, *Armageddon: The Battle for Germany 1944–45* (London: Macmillan, 2004) p.396.
27 *Ibid.*, p.437.
28 Antony Beevor, *Berlin: The Downfall 1945* (London: Viking, 2002) p.24.
29 Hastings, *Armageddon*, p.437. There were no figures available for Russian losses.
30 TNA, WO 250/372: 12 April 1945, folio 1771 – Note 6.
31 RHC War Diary, 20 April 1945.
32 Beevor, *Berlin*, p.366.
33 RHC War Diary, final entries 1945.
34 Dean, *The Royal Hospital Chelsea*, pp.295–96.
35 TNA, WO 250/372: 31 May 1945, folio 1777.
36 RHC War Diary, 3 June 1945.
37 TNA, WO 250/372: 7 June 1945, folio 1778, Note 7.
38 TNA, WO 250/373: 28 June 1945, folio 1781, Note 2.
39 *Ibid.*, Note 5.
40 *Ibid.*, Note 8.
41 *Ibid.*
42 *Ibid.*
43 *Ibid.*
44 *Ibid.*
45 TNA, WO 250/373: 12 July 1945, folio 1782, Note 8.
46 RHC, LDRHC/18/0090.4: Post-War plans for the Royal Hospital's infirmary.
47 TNA, WO 250/373: 19 July 1945, folio 1783.
48 *Ibid.*, 6 September 1945, folio 1789 – Letter from Assistant Secretary to Town Clerk, 29 August 1945.
49 *Ibid.*, Letter from Town Clerk to Fitzgerald, 31 August 1945.

50 *Ibid.*, 30 August 1945, folio 1788, Note 8 and 11 October 1945, folio 1793, Note 11.
51 *Ibid.*, 11 October 1945, folio 1793, Note 6.
52 *Ibid.*, 8 November 1945, folio 1796, Note 10.
53 *Ibid.*, 15 November 1945, folio 1797, Note 9.
54 *Ibid.*

# Bibliography

## *Manuscript Sources*

### *London Metropolitan Archives*
EO/WAR/1/23: Test Evacuation – Chelsea Borough, 19 June 1939.
LCC/CL/CD/01/002: Air Raid Precautions – General Papers, January–December 1938.
LCC/CL/CD/01/003: Air Raid Precautions – General Papers, January–August 1939.
LCC/CL/CD/01/089: Evacuation Scheme – General Papers, March–July 1939.
LCC/CL/CD/01/090: Evacuation Scheme – General Papers, August–September 1939.

### *Royal Borough of Kensington and Chelsea Archives*
Metropolitan Borough of Chelsea: Minutes of Proceedings, 1939–46.
SR 272: ARP Scrapbook 1.
Local Q 355 23 CHE: *Chelsea Civil Defence Warden Service Souvenir Magazine* – Published for New Year 1945.

### *Royal Hospital Chelsea Archives Held in Chelsea*
LDRHC/CAB2: Report of Committee of Chelsea Hospital, 1882.
LDRHC/14/026 Series: Agreements for Construction of Air-Raid Shelters, 1939.
LDRHC/14/0310: War Diary, The Royal Hospital Chelsea, 1939–45.
LDRHC/15/0022: Agreement with Major Morland of Rudhall, 1939.
LDRHC/15/0084 Series: Recommendations for Bravery Awards, 1941.
LDRHC/18/0049: Guide to Les Invalides.
LDRHC/18/0089 Series: Plans for Post-War Reconstruction, 1943–44.
LDRHC/19/0001 Series: Letters of Captain Howell RAMC, Medical Officer of RHC.
LDRHC/19/0026 Series: Correspondence re: Bravery Awards after Infirmary Bombing.
LDRHC/19/0096–0098 Series: RHC Staff Members Killed Through Enemy Action, 1941.
LDRHC/19/0104 Series: Correspondence After the Infirmary Bombing, 1941.

LDRHC/19/0106–0115: Further Correspondence After the Infirmary Bombing, 1941.
LDRHC/19/0117–0118: Site Clearance After Infirmary Bombing, 1942.
LDRHC/19/6002–6030: Manuscript Notes for C.G.T. Dean's Book, *The Royal Hospital Chelsea*.
LDRHC/20/0013: Notebook of Alphabetical List of Instructions.
LDRHC/20/0100: Record of Deaths, 1900–60.
LDRHC/20/9999: In-Pensioners Admissions Register from 1 January 1934.

## *Royal Hospital Chelsea Archives Held at The National Archives, Kew*

WO 32/21175: Emergency Evacuation and Maintenance of Grounds.
WO 246 Series: Royal Hospital Chelsea Letter Books.
WO 250 Series: Royal Hospital Chelsea, Board Minutes and Papers. Weekly Board Proceedings.
WO 250/447: Minute Book, 1 July 1938–28 February 1941.
WO 351/025 LIS: List of established civil staff members up to 1958.
PMG 74/251: Paymaster General's Correspondence, 1941–45.
WORK 13/1380: Repair of Wartime Bomb Damage at RHC, 1947.
WORK 14/1387: Evacuation Arrangements, 1938–52.
WORK 14/1489: Reconstruction Work, 1943–53.
WORK 14/2362: Reconstruction Work, 1940–46.
WORK 14/2363: Tenancy of Ascott House, Wing, near Leighton Buzzard, for Wartime Transfer of Chelsea Pensioners, 1941–48.
HO 250/35/1381A: Recommendation for Gallantry – Florence Howard.
HO 250/35/1381B: Recommendation for Gallantry – Hannah Deasy.
HO 250/42/1643A: Recommendation for Gallantry – William Alfred Williams.
HO 250/42/1643B: Recommendation for Gallantry – Bertie James Grant.
HO 250/447: Royal Hospital Chelsea Minute Book – 1 July 1938–28 February 1941.

## *Other Archives Held at The National Archives, Kew*

HO 198/26: Region 5, Headquarters, London: Group 1, 18–19 March 1941 to 5–6 May 1941 – Bomb Damage Reports.
HO 198/39: Air Warfare Analysis Section, London BC 4's – Group 5 – 16–17 February 1941 to 5–6 May 1941.
RG 101/110G: 1939 Register, Chelsea Metropolitan Borough.
RG 336/2: 1939 Register, Ross-on-Wye.
WO 169/5062: 1st Battalion Sherwood Foresters War Diary, 1 January 1942–31 August 1942.
WO 372/20: Medal Index Cards.
WO 399/14899: Directorate of Army Medical Services and Territorial Force: Nursing Service Records.

# *Primary Sources*

Anderson, J., *Report of Committee on Evacuation with a Covering Memorandum by the Secretary of State for the Home Department*, X, 607 (Oxford: Bodleian Library, 1937).

*Bibliography*

British Library Newspaper Archives.
Chelsea Society – Annual Reports.
Royal Hospital Chelsea, LDRHC/18/0002: Townsend, Captain C., *Memories of a Captain of Invalids* (Printed privately, 1980).

## Secondary Sources

Addison, Paul, & Jeremy A. Crang (eds), *Listening to Britain: Home Intelligence Reports on Britain's Finest Hour – May to Sept 1940* (London: The Bodley Head, 2010).
Balfour, Major General Arthur, 'On the Military Conscription of France', *Journal of the Statistical Society of London*, Vol. 30, No. 2 (June 1867), pp.216–92.
Barker, Felix, & Ralph Hyde, *London as it Might Have Been* (London: Murray, 1982).
Barker, Ralph, *Children of the Benares: A War Crime and Its Victims* (London: Avid Publications, 2003).
Beaton, Cecil, *The Years Between: Diaries, 1939–44* (London: Weidenfeld & Nicolson, 1965).
Beevor, Anthony, *Stalingrad* (London: Penguin, 1999).
Beevor, Anthony, *Berlin: The Downfall 1945* (London: Viking, 2002).
Beevor, Anthony, *The Second World War* (London: Weidenfeld & Nicolson, 2012).
Briggs, Susan, *Keep Smiling Through: Home Front 1939–45* (London: HarperCollins, 1977).
Bulley, Anjali (ed.), *Cadogan & Chelsea: The Making of a Modern Estate* (London: Unicorn, 2017).
Bullock, Alan, *Hitler* (London: Odhams Press, 1952).
Calder, Angus, & Dorothy Sheridan, *Speak For Yourself: A Mass Observation Anthology 1937–49* (London: Jonathan Cape, 1984).
Calder, Angus, *The Myth of the Blitz* (London: Jonathan Cape, 1991).
Calder, Angus, *The People's War: Britain 1939–1945* (London: Pimlico, 1996).
Cassin-Scott, Jack, *Women at War, 1939–45* (Oxford: Osprey, 1980).
Castle, Ian, *The First Blitz: Bombing London in the First World War* (Oxford: Osprey, 2015).
Chamberlain, Neville, *In Search of Peace: Speeches 1937–1938* (London: Hutchinson, 1939).
Churchill, Winston, *The Gathering Storm: The Second World War, Volume 1* (Boston, MA: Houghton Mifflin, 1986).
Churchill, Winston, *Their Finest Hour: The Second World War, Volume 2* (London: Penguin, 2005).
Clayton, Tim, & Phil Craig, *Finest Hour* (London: Coronet Books, 2001).
Clifford, Naomi, *Under Fire: The Blitz Diaries of a Volunteer Ambulance Driver* (London: Caret Press, 2021).
Cockett, Frank B. & Dorothy, *The War Diary of St Thomas's Hospital 1939–45* (London: Starling Publishers, 1991).
Cohen, Deborah, *The War Come Home: Disabled Veterans in Britain and Germany, 1914–1939* (Berkeley: University of California Press, 2001).
Cormack, Andrew Edward, *These Meritorious Objects of the Royal Bounty: The Chelsea Out-Pensioners in the Early Eighteenth Century* (London: published privately, 2017).
Corvaja, Santi, & Robert Miller, *Hitler and Mussolini: The Secret Meetings* (New York: Enigma Books, 2008).

Croall, Jonathan, *Don't You Know There's A War On? The People's Voice 1939–45* (London: Routledge, 1989).
Crosby, Travis L., *The Impact of Civilian Evacuation in the Second World War* (London: Croom Helm, 1986).
Cruickshank, Dan, *The Royal Hospital Chelsea: The Place and the People* (London: Third Millennium, 2004).
Curnock, George C., *Hospitals Under Fire: But the Lamp Still Burns* (London: Allen & Unwin, 1941).
Dean, Captain Charles G.T., *The Royal Hospital Chelsea* (London: Hutchinson, 1950).
Douglas, Raymond M., *Orderly and Humane: The Expulsion of the Germans after the Second World War* (New Haven: Yale University Press, 2012).
Faviell, Frances, *A Chelsea Concerto* (London: Dean Street Press, 2016).
Fitzgibbon, Constantine, *The Winter of Bombs: The Story of the Blitz of London* (New York: W.W. Norton, 1957).
Fitzgibbon, Constantine, *The Blitz* (London: Faber and Faber, 2010).
Fitzgibbon, Theodora, *With Love: An Autobiography 1938–1946* (London: Century, 1982).
Garfield, Simon, *We Are At War: The Diaries of Five Ordinary People in Extraordinary Times* (London: Ebury Press, 2006).
Gartner, Niko, *Operation Pied Piper: The Wartime Evacuation of Schoolchildren from London and Berlin 1938–46* (Charlotte, NC: Information Age Publishing, 2012).
Gosden, Peter H.J.H., *Education in the Second World War: A Study in Policy and Administration* (London: Methuen, 1976).
Grayzel, Susan R., *At Home and Under Fire: Air Raids and Culture in Britain from the Great War to the Blitz* (Cambridge: Cambridge University Press, 2012).
Harrisson, Tom, *Living Through the Blitz* (London: Collins, 1976).
Hastings, Max, *Armageddon: The Battle for Germany 1944–45* (London: Macmillan, 2004).
Higginbotham, Peter, *The Workhouse Encyclopaedia* (Stroud: The History Press, 2012).
Holman, Brett, *The Next War in the Air: Britain's Fear of the Bomber 1908–1941* (London: Routledge, 2016).
Inglis, Ruth, *The Children's War: Evacuation, 1939–45* (London: Collins, 1989).
Jackson, Ashley, *Churchill* (London: Quercus, 2011).
Jeffreys, Alan, *London at War 1939–1945: A Nation's Capital Survives* (London: IWM, 2018).
Keegan, John, *The Second World War* (London: Pimlico, 1997).
Keegan, John, *The First World War* (London: Hutchinson, 1998).
Keeling, Clinton H., *They All Came into the Ark: A Record of the Zoological Society of London in Two World Wars* (Guildford: Clam Publishers, 1988).
Kekewich, Margaret L., *An Anthology of Primary Sources: France and the British Isles 1620–1714* (Manchester: Manchester University Press, 1995).
Kent, William, *An Encyclopaedia of London* (London: Dent, 1951).
Kynaston, David, *Banker and Philanthropist: A Portrait of Anthony de Rothschild* (London: Hurtwood Press, 2022).
Liddell Hart, Basil H., *A History of the Second World War* (London: Pan Macmillan, 2014).
Longmate, Norman (ed.), *The Home Front: An Anthology of Personal Experience 1938–1945* (London: Chatto & Windus, 1981).

## Bibliography

Longmate, Norman, *Hitler's Rockets: The Story of the V2s* (London: Hutchinson, 1985).

Longmate, Norman, *How We Lived Then: A History of Everyday Life during the Second World War* (London: Pimlico, 2002).

Loobey, Patrick, & Jon Mills, *The Boroughs of Wandsworth and Battersea at War* (Stroud: Sutton Publishing, 1996).

McCamley, Nick J., *Saving Britain's Art Treasures from the Nazis* (Barnsley: Pen & Sword, 2003).

McKibbon, Ross, *The Ideologies of Class: Social Relations in Britain 1880–1950* (Oxford: Oxford University Press, 1991)

Manley, Rebecca, *To the Tashkent Station: Evacuation and Survival in the Soviet Union at War* (Ithaca: Cornell University Press, 2009).

Mann, Jessica, *Out of Harm's Way: The Wartime Evacuation of Children from Britain* (London: Headline, 2005).

Marwick, Arthur, *The Home Front: The British and the Second World War* (Wallop: BAS Publishers Limited, 1976).

Mason, Francis K., *Battle over Britain* (London: McWhirter Twins Ltd, 1969).

Matthews, Leslie W., *Old Church: Bombing and Rebuilding Chelsea* (London: Industrial Arts, 1957).

Mears, Robin, & Randall Smith, *From Poor Law to Community Care: Development of Welfare Services for Elderly People, 1939–71* (Bristol: Policy Press, 1998).

Miller, Edward, *That Noble Cabinet: A History of the British Museum* (London: Deutsch, 1973).

Milton, Giles, *White Gold* (London: John Murray, 2015).

Mosley, Leonard, *Backs to the Wall: London Under Fire 1939–45* (London: Weidenfeld & Nicolson, 1971).

Mukerjee, Madhusree, *Churchill's Secret War: The British Empire and the Ravaging of India during World War II* (New York: Basic Books, 2010).

Murphy, Sean (ed.), *Bully's Acre and Royal Hospital Kilmainham Graveyards: History and Inscriptions* (Dublin: Oivelina Publications, 1989).

Neate, Alan R., *St Marylebone Workhouse and Institution, 1730–1965* (London: St Marylebone Society Publications, 1967).

Nixon, Barbara, *Raiders Overhead: A Diary of the London Blitz* (London: Scolar Press, 1980).

O'Brian, Terence H., *Civil Defence: History of the Second World War UK Civil Service* (London: HMSO, 1955).

Orr, Sir John, & David Lubbock, *Feeding the People in Wartime* (London: Macmillan, 1940).

Orwell, George, *The Lion and the Unicorn* (London: Secker & Warburg, 1941).

Osborne, Mike, *20th-Century Defences in Britain: The London Area* (Market Deeping: Concrete Publications, 2006).

Parker, Harold M.D., *Manpower: A History of Wartime Policy and Administration – History of the Second World War UK Civil Service* (London: HMSO, 1957).

Parsons, Martin L., *I'll Take That One: Dispelling the Myths of Civilian Evacuation 1939–45* (Peterborough: Beckett Karlson, 1998).

Parsons, Martin L., *I'll Take That One Too: Evacuees, the Invisible Generation* (Peterborough: DSM, 2013).

Pedroche, Ben, *London's Lost Power Stations and Gasworks* (Stroud: The History Press, 2013).
Ponting, Clive, *1940: Myth or Reality* (London: Hamish Hamilton, 1990).
Porter, Roy, *London: A Social History* (London: Hamish Hamilton, 1994).
Postan, Michael M., *British War Production: History of the Second World War UK Civil Service* (London: HMSO, 1952).
Roach, Peter, *The 8.15 to War: Memories of a Desert Rat* (London: Secker and Warburg, 1982).
Robinson, John M., *Requisitioned: The British Country House in the Second World War* (London: Aurum Press, 2014).
Smith, Harold L., *War and Social Change: British Society in the Second World War* (Manchester: Manchester University Press, 1986).
Starns, Penny, *Blitz Families: The Children Who Stayed Behind* (Stroud: The History Press, 2012).
Starns, Penny, *Blitz Hospital: True Stories of Nursing in Wartime London* (Stroud: The History Press, 2018).
Stewart, Andrew, *The King's Private Army: Protecting the British Royal Family during the Second World War* (Solihull: Helion & Company, 2015).
Stewart, Geoffrey, *Dunkirk and the Fall of France* (Barnsley: Pen and Sword, 2008).
Sweet, Matthew, *The West End Front: The Wartime Secrets of London's Grand Hotels* (London: Faber & Faber, 2011).
Thomson, Leighton, *The Rebuilding of Chelsea Old Church* (London: published privately, 1957).
Titmuss, Richard M., *Problems of Social Policy: History of the Second World War* (Basingstoke: Palgrave MacMillan, 1950).
Turner, Barry, *Waiting for War: Britain 1939–1940* (London: Icon Books, 2019).
Turner, Ernest S., *The Phoney War on the Home Front* (London: Faber & Faber, 1961).
Waller, Jane, & Michael Vaughan-Rees, *Blitz: The Civilian War 1940–45* (St Albans: Optima, 1990).
Wellum, Geoffrey, *First Light* (London: Viking, 2002).
Wheal, Donald James, *World's End: A Memoir of a Blitz Childhood* (London: Random House, 2004).
Wicks, Ben, *No Time to Wave Goodbye* (London: Bloomsbury, 1990).
Ziegler, Philip, *London at War 1939–1945* (London: Pimlico, 1995).

## *Unpublished Secondary Sources*

Cawthorne, Martin J., 'Soldiers of Empire: Broken by Age or War? The Failure to Evacuate the Royal Hospital Chelsea on the Outbreak of the Second World War' (unpublished postgraduate certificate dissertation, University of Oxford, 2019).
Cawthorne, Martin J., 'How and Why did Evacuation Strategies for the Royal Hospital Chelsea Evolve During the Second World War?' (unpublished Master's dissertation, University of Oxford, 2020).

# Acknowledgements

The process of writing and publishing this book has required the help of many people. At the Royal Hospital Chelsea, I would particularly like to thank John Rochester, who first recruited me as a volunteer to join his heritage team in 2014. Since his retirement from the Royal Hospital, John has continued to offer tremendous support and encouragement as I have worked on successive drafts. John's successor as heritage manager, Tina Kilnan, has in turn provided invaluable support and continued access to the archives in Chelsea. I would also like to thank Gary Lashko OBE, CEO (until his retirement in March 2024) and Martin Field, Director of Public Engagement, without whose steadfast support this project may well have floundered.

At Oxford, my special thanks go to my academic supervisor, Professor Ashley Jackson, who first encouraged me to think about framing the Royal Hospital's story against the background historiography of wartime evacuation, from which point everything about the Hospital's wartime experience started to make sense.

My research has also benefitted enormously from the enthusiastic support of numerous archivists and librarians. I would like to thank the staff of the Bodleian Library, the National Archives, the London Metropolitan Archives and the Royal Borough of Kensington & Chelsea Archives for their expert guidance in helping me to navigate my way through the wealth of material contained within their collections. I would also like to thank the Imperial War Museum for letting me use images of a searchlight located in the Hospital's grounds, and the staff of Historic England Archives for helping me select amazing aerial photographs to complement the ground-level shots of the Royal Hospital Chelsea at war.

This book would not have come about were it not for the support, encouragement and expert guidance of my commissioning editor at The History Press, Amy Rigg.

Finally, my wife and our children have, as ever, been my greatest supporters.

All reasonable efforts have been made to ensure that, where necessary, permission has been obtained to quote relevant source material and appropriate references have been made. In particular I would like to express my thanks and gratitude to the Royal Hospital Chelsea for permission to use the Hospital's archives.

All and any errors and omissions in the book are, of course, entirely my own responsibility.

# Index

Note: *italicised* page references denote illustrations, and the suffix 'n' denotes notes.

3rd London Scottish Anti-Aircraft Battalion 101
5th Dragoon Guards 191
7th Panzer Division 103
10th Royal Hussars 88
24th Regiment of Foot 88, 191
97th Anti-Aircraft Regiment 65
905 Squadron, RAF 205

Acts of Parliament
  Claim of Right Act (1689) 14
  Emergency Powers (Defence) legislation 53, 68, 131, 221, 248
  Local Government Act (1929) 25
  National Registration Act (1939) 83
  Poor Law legislation 25
  War Damage Act (1941) 239
aerodrome construction programme 249, 250, 254, 259, 281
Air Raid Precautions (ARP) 20, 29
  Chelsea 50–1, 70, 74, 100, 136, 146, *160*, 179, 184, 189, 194, 200, 205, 207, 209, 273–4, 278
  Post K 64, *162*, 181, 186, 199, 201, 204, 205, 209, 285
  Royal Hospital 49, 52, 63, 71, 109, 119, 136, 146, 254, 255, 285
air-raid shelters
  Cadogan Place Gardens 62, 120–1
  Chelsea Borough Council 50–1, 61–5
  and the infirm/aged 24–5, 26
  Paultons Square 62
  Royal Avenue 65
  super-shelters 62, 63, 64, 65, 126, 205, 300
  surface shelters 64, 65, 140, 187
  trench shelters 50–1, 61–2, 64, *167*, 245
air-raid shelters in Royal Hospital 46, 50, 64–5, 67, 70–1, *159*, *161*, *164*, *165*, *166*, *167*
  Artificers Yard 64, 179, 187
  Beer Cellar 70, 150
  Burton Court 50, 61, 62, 63, 64, 75, 80, 126, 205
  Chapel Crypt 64, 70, 76
  difficulty in reaching 30, 35, 54, 71, 116–17, 120, 121–2, 141
  East Wing 76, 77, 141, *166*
  Great Hall 64, 300
  inadequacies 145–6, 244–5

Infirmary Court 63–4, 70, 120, 223
Light Horse Court 70, 125
North-East Wing 70, 125
North Front 70, 155
North Grounds 54
sleeping in 277, 279
Albert Bridge 31, 115, 155–6, 177
Aldershot 266, 272
Amery, Leo 102
Anderson Report 20–1, 23–5, 29, 30, 31, 32, 38, 53, 78, 108
 ad hoc outsourcing of evacuation 26, 33, 54, 55
 evacuation of priority groups 21, 23, 47, 67, 84, 108, 130
Anderson, Sir John 20, 66, 68
anti-aircraft units 81–2, 112, 117–18, 121, 126, 133, 143, 203, 278
 Battersea Park 133–4, 135, 148, 177, 179, 191, 194, 261
 Clapham Common 112, 118
 *see also* barrage balloons; searchlight units
Artificers Yard 64, 179, 187
artworks evacuated 78–9, 296
AS22 (Ambulance Station 22) 110, 120, 193–4, 196, 202
Ascott House *170*, 214, 215, 228, 229, 231, 237, 253, 265
 costs and funding 228, 229, 231, 237, 242, 244
 infirmary, use as 215, 225, 228, 239–40, 243–4
 Ministry/Office of Works 222, 229, 230, 231, 232–4, 235, 242
 In-Pensioners arrive 230, 239–40, 243–4, 295
 In-Pensioners leave 282–3, 286, 292–3, 299
 Red Cross Medical facility at 214, 225, 235
Atlantic War 149, 227, 235–6, 239, 247, 249, 258, 262
Australia 249, 290
Austria 27, 41–2

Auxiliary Ambulance Service (AAS) 109–10, 132, 178, 193, 198, 209
Auxiliary Fire Service (AFS) 125, 126, 181, 186, 189, 200, 201, 203, 206

Bailey, Geoffrey 251, 283, 284
Baldwin, Stanley 19
Barbary pirates 14
barrage balloons 20, 31, 80, 120, 209
 Burton Court ('Blossom') 80, 101, 126, *170*
 South Grounds ('Flossie') 80, 101, 134, 187, 209, 213
Barry, Henry 89
Battersea Bridge 115, 121, 177
Battersea Park 118, 177, 261, 277
 anti-aircraft units 133–4, 135, 148, 177, 179, 191, 194, 261
Battersea Power Station 31, 115, 126, 135, 139, 155, *164*, 177, 265, 300
BBC *169*, 219, 292
Beaton, Cecil 106
Beaufort Street 120–1, 195, 196
Beer Cellar 70, 122, 150
Beezley, James 190
Belgium 102–3, 107, 109, 117
Beneš, President 32, 44
Berlin 28, 111, 261–2, 271, 291
Birdwood, Field Marshal Lord 263
black market 155
blackouts 70, 79, 82, 146
Bomb Disposal teams 116, 137, 138, 144, 150–1
Bomber Command 96, 111, 251–2, 259
Borough Control Room 105, 179, 209
 incidents logged 125, 181, 183–4, 186, 188–9, 190, 192, 193–4, 197, 199, 201–2, 204–5, 285
Bourne, Captain 72, 79
Boyle, Lieutenant Colonel S. 66–7
Braithwaite, General Sir Walter 35, 52, 61
Breda, Declaration of 13–14
Bridges, Margaret 194, 202
Britain, Battle of 110–12, 113–28

*Index*

British Expeditionary Force (BEF) 90–1, 102–3, 107, 109, 131
British Legion 51
British Red Cross Society 211, 214, 225, 228, 230
Brooke, General Sir Alan KCB, DSO 137–8
Brookwood, Surrey 81, 95, 213, 215
Burial Ground 81, 125, 147, 248, 256, 278
Burke, Albert 72, 73–4, 79, 83, 89–90, 94, 95, 225, 228, 243, 253
Burma 249
Burton Court 80, 181, 248, 289
   air-raid shelter 50, 51, 61–3, 64, 75, 80, 119, 126, 205, 300
   barrage balloon ('Blossom') 80, 101, 126, *170*
   bombed 114, 115, 125, 126, 136, 137, 140, 144, 201, 204, 205, 224
   prefabricated houses *173*, 279–80, 282, 283
   tennis courts 136, 137, 140, 144, 286
Burton Court Mansions 125, 204, 256, 285

Cadogan Estates 62, 66, 154
Cadogan Place Gardens 62, 120–1
Cadogan Square 200, 287
Cambridge, Duke of 267
Canada 106, 132
Canadian Army 110, 178, 183, 184, 189, 208, 290
Carlyle Mansions 196
Castillo, Dr Richard 120–1, 124, 206, 208
Caversham Street 181, 184, 192
Chamberlain, Neville 44, 49, 51–2, 55, 61, 74, 102
Chandler, Emma 206, 208
Chapel 74–5, 109, 151, 155, 156, 209, 251, 258, 284
Chapel Crypt 64, 70, 76
Charles I, King 14
Charles II, King 13–14, 15–16, 104, 234, 297

Charles III, King 297
Charles, General Sir Ronald 293
Chelsea Barracks 65, 101, 103, 119, 133, 189, 192, 209, 240, 286
Chelsea Bridge 31, 115, 147, 177
Chelsea Bridge Road 65, 189, 202, 209, 256, 289
Chelsea Flower Show 289
Chelsea, heavy bombing of 115, 129, 143–4, 147–8, 210, 274–5
Chelsea Old Church 121, *169*, 176, 180, 193–207
Chelsea Park Gardens 201, 206
'Chelsea Pensioners,' origins of 17
Chelsea Square 203, 204
Cherwell, Lord 281–2, 293, 294–5
Cheyne Hospital 104
Cheyne Place 51, 74, 179, 181–4, 187, 189, 192
Cheyne Walk 110, 178, 193, 194–5, 196, 204
China 20
Christmas at Chelsea 151, 153, 155, 258, 270
Chrystal, Sir George 38
Church Parades 70, 211, 276–7
Churchill, Winston 102, 103, 106, 109, 282
Clapham Common 112, 118
Cobrey Park, Herefordshire 215–17, 221, 222, 229, 230, 231
Coldstream Guards 236
Commissioners of Royal Hospital 65–6, 98, 138, 218, 234–5, 242, 250, 258, 269
   air-raid shelters 62, 64–5
   Chairmen 70, 106–7, 282
   Chelsea Borough Council 49, 51, 64–5, 139, 270–1, 288–9, 295–6
   evacuation planning 32–4, 44, 48, 52–5, 56–60, 69, 72, 78, 84–5, 99, 100, *160*, 216–17, 228, 233, 238, 241–4
   post-war planning 264, 269, 271, 273, 280, 282, 288–90, 294

supply problems 158, 244, 248–9, 252, 270
Committee of Imperial Defence 20, 30, 222
commutations 17, 58, 77, 97, 98, 132, 153, 193, 220, 231, 293
Connaught Rangers 88, 131–2
Corps of Military Police 286
Cranborne, Lord Robert ('Bobbety') 106–7
Cranmer Court 203
'crash raids' 270
Creedy, Sir Herbert 269
Crimean War 295
Croft, Lord 130–1
Crosby Hall 104–5, 196
Cuthbert, Sydney 178, 179, 199, 200–1, 202
Czechoslovakia 27–8, 32, 40, 42, 44, 51, 55

D-Day 275–6, 283
Danvers Street 110, 120, 193, 194, 195, 196, 197, 202
Danzig 63
de Normann, Mr 45, 46–8
Dean, Captain C.G.T. 57, 70, 96, 212, 213–14, 236, 251, 264–9, 271–2, 292
Dean, Kenneth *161*, 284
Deasy, Nurse Hannah 188, 190, 197, 201, 219, 223
Delano-Osborne, Major General O.H. (Lieutenant Governor) 29, 35, 57
delayed action bombs 115, 119, 209, 261
demolitions 249–52, 256, 257, 268, 284
Denmark 100, 101
Deverell, Field Marshal Sir Cyril 275
Docklands 118, 157, 176, 210
Doley, Francis 187
Doley, Quartermaster Sergeant 92
Dönitz, Admiral 235–6, 239, 248, 258, 262
Duke of York's Barracks 70, 125
Dunkirk 104–5, 109

East End 63, 118, 119, 157, 176, 210, 280, 287
East Wing 131, 153, 156, *174*, 255, 282, 291, 300
   air-raid shelter 76, 77, 141, *166*
   bombed 140–2, *166*, 284, 285, 300
Eastern Front 90, 226, 252, 258
Ebury Bridge Road 151
Ebury Street 199
Eden, Anthony 107
Edgcumbe, Piers 109
Egypt 252, 254, 258
El Alamein, Battle of (1942) 258
Elizabeth II, Queen 300
Elliot, Walter 71, 93
Elms Garage 183, 184, 189, 194, 208
endowment funds 241, 279, 297
evacuation
   children 71–2, 75, 77, 92, 94, 105–6, 132
   Dunkirk 104–5, 109
   in numbers 55, 71, 75, 77, 92, 105–6
   overseas 106, 132
evacuation of Royal Hospital
   artworks 78–9
   to ITC and Regiment training centres 238–9
   threatens Hospital's existence 267–8
   *see also* out-stations
evacuation planning 20–7, 91–2, 94–5, 99–100
   children 21, 23, 27, 67, 91–3, *160*
   evacuation zones 21, 25, 36, 78, 93
   reception areas 21, 34, 36, 94, 104, 270–1
   *see also* requisitioning
evacuation planning for Royal Hospital 29–41, 43–9, 52–5, 56–61, 81, 83–6, 94–5, 99–100, 107–8
   during Blitz 211–22, 228–34, 237–8, 242–5
   confidential report, May 1938 135, 140
   schedule of requirements 33–6, 43
Evans, Admiral Sir Edward 198

## Index

Faviell, Frances 51, 72, 74, 80, 114–15, 121, 123, 134, 143–4, 155, 178, 265
   First Aid Post/Volunteer Aid Detachment 63, 67, 96, 143, 148, 150
   Fitzgerald family 105, 123, 142, 156
   home bombed 179, 181–5
   refugees, aid for 104, 105
Faviell, Richard 51, 156, 178, 179, 181, 182–5, 208
Figure Court 75, 131, 142, 255, 276, 284
finances *see* funding
First Aid Posts (FAPs) 96, 143, 144, 148, 150, 183, 184, 188, 190, 191, 197, 219, 273–4
First World War 19, 87, 96, 105, 110, 124, 269, 295
   participants in 44, 73, 88, 131–2, 187–8, 198, 223, 262, 275, 283, 314n37
Fitzgerald family 45, 142, 156
Fitzgerald, Denise 45, 63, 179, 181, 204, 205
Fitzgerald, Elizabeth 45, 105
Fitzgerald, Lieutenant Maurice 45, 252
Fitzgerald, Maurice (Assistant Secretary) 44–9, 61, 70, 108, 125, 156, 218–19, 255, 283, 292
   post-war 295–6
   Rudhall 58–9, 73, 83, 232
   steers evacuation plans through Whitehall 220, 221, 222–3, 225, 227, 228–34, 238, 243–5
   supply issues 252
Fitzgerald, Paul 45, 105
Fitzgerald, Suzanne 45, 105, 123–4, 151, 156, 252
Fitzgibbon, Theodora 118
flares 135, 147, 149, 179–80, 181, 186, 274
football 64–5, 101–2, 115, 205
Foot, Mrs 215, 234, 237, 240, 257, 318n30
Forth, James 89
Founder's Days 104, 105, 234, 236, 237, 250–1, 263, 275, 292
Fox, Sir Stephen 15–16

France 17, 44, 51–2, 63
   allies liberate 276, 278–9
   Atlantic coastline 149, 235–6, 247
   Second World War 82, 90, 96, 104, 106, 109, 149, 180, 207, 225–6, 235–6, 247
   V1 launch sites 275, 276, 278–9
Fry, Herbert (War Office) 58, 220, 228, 231, 244–5
Fry, Richard (Office Keeper) 70, 110, 125, 255
Fulham 175
funding 16, 96–7, 220, 231, 237–8, 239, 241, 243, 244–5, 253, 263, 266–7
   Ascott House 231, 237, 241, 244
   Chelsea Flower Show 289
   compensation for war damage 239
   endowment funds 241, 279, 297
   public air-raid shelters 61, 64, 65
   rental properties 241–2
   Rudhall 58, 73–4, 94, 97, 98, 220, 244
furlough 152, 153, 240, 258, 285–6

gas leaks 183, 186–8, 196, 282
gas masks 50, 70, 71, 75, 156, *161*
gas supplies cut 120, 130, 148, *165*, 196, 199, 224, 274
Gatehouse, Reverend 275
Gater, Sir George 38
Gatliff, Herbert 241, 243
George VI, King 102, 250–1
Gilliat-Smith, Sybil 132
Gingell, Major 284
Gladstone, William 267
Goldsmith, George 181, 182
Gordon Highlanders 70, 89
Gordon House 201, 240
Göring, Hermann 110, 111, 116, 118, 127
Gort, General Viscount 102, 104
Gough, General Sir Herbert 107, 292
Governor's House 251, 276
Great Hall 30, 64, 79, 270, 279, 284, 297, 300
Greenwich, Royal Hospital 13, 16, 17, 266–7, 268

Grenadier Guards 89, 189, 212, 290
Grice, Alfred 187, 198
Grimm, Stanley 202
Guinness Trust Buildings 71, 92, 273–4
Gummer, E. 284
Guy's Hospital 242, 245

Hampshire Regiment 239
Hampton Court Palace 37
Hans Town 126, 180, 184, 187, 189, 192, 199, 205, 206–7
Harewood House, Hereford 229, 230, 237
Harington, General Sir Charles 105
Harrison, Sergeant Frederick 189, 190, 219, 263
Hartnell, Lady Clare 107, 139
Hastings, In-Pensioner 79
Haylen, Alfred 181, 182
Heavy Rescue Squad 121, 188, 189, 197, 199, 206, 208, 275, 277
Henlein, Konrad 28
high-explosive bombs 126, 129, 140, 157, 180, 199, 203, 274
Hitler, Adolf 19, 27, 28, 40, 41–2, 44, 49, 51–2, 54, 61, 63, 69, 74, 90–1, 262
    Britain, turns attention to 110, 115, 127
    Eastern Front 226, 240, 249, 261
    faces defeat 271, 281, 291
    speeches 42, 96
Hogg, Reverend *165*, 219
Holmes, Ray 127
Home Front 19–20, 256
Home Guard 107, 109, 152, 224, 255, 263
Home Office 20, 50, 71, 220
    Burton Court trenches 61, 62, 64
    evacuation planning 21, 26, 33–4, 39, 41, 92
    evacuation planning for Royal Hospital 29, 32, 33–4, 40–1, 43, 47, 52, 53, 56, 78
'Homes for Heroes' 279–80
Hore-Belisha, Leslie 269
Horton, Admiral Sir Max 262

Howard, Nurse Adela 188, 190, 197, 201, 223
Howell, Dr Trevor 79, 225, 228
Huddleston, Major General H.J. (Lieutenant Governor) 35, 49, 57, 59

identity cards 83, 88, 89
Imperial Defence Committee 22, 23, 53
In-Pensioners, definition 17
In-Pensioners, in numbers 35
    Ascott House 225, 239–40, 244
    Cobrey Park 216–17
    Moraston House 251
    Princess Christian Home 213
    Royal Hospital 30, 152–3, 280, 286, 288, 293, 294, 300
    Rudhall 57, 60, 72, 78, 240, 244, 253
    training centres 238–9
    White Hill Farm 215, 234
incendiary bombs 124–6, 130–1, 201, 224, 273, 291–2
Incorporated Soldiers, Sailors & Airmen's Help Society 213, 296
India 73, 249
Infirmary 77, 119, 134, 139, 155, 158, *168*, 210, 251, 263–4, 270, 295
    bombed (1940) 135–8, *165*, 257–8
    bombed (1941) *168*, *169*, *172*, 175–92, 197–200, 206, 209–19, 223–5, 229, 257, 263, 283
    demolition *172*, 250, 254, 257
    evacuation planning 35, 59, 222–3, 229, 231–4, 245
    evacuations 72, 211, 213, 214–18, 224–5, 232, 235, 240, 243–5, 254, 279
    post-war planning 263–4, 282–3, 286, 293, 294, 299–300
    requisitioning 30–1
Infirmary Court 134, 136, 185, 275
    air-raid shelters 63–4, 70, 120, 223
influenza 269–70
Inglis, Major Frederick 70
Invalides, L'Hôtel des 13, 15, 17, 97
Italy 49, 51–2

*Index*

James II 16
Japan 20, 246, 249, 259, 295
*Jervis Bay*, HMS 149
Jolliffe, Captain 70

Kesselring, Field Marshal 225–6, 239
King's Own Royal Regiment (Lancaster) 223
King's Road 86, 104, 121, 143, 149, 157, 197, 200–1, 203, 224, 273, 274
King's Shropshire Light Infantry 89
Knox, General Sir Harry (Governor) 49, 52, 61, 75, 212, 215, 234, 263, 269
Knox, Lady 115
Kriegsmarine (German Navy) 96, 101, 128, 148–9, 226, 227, 235–6, 247, 262

Lend-Lease agreement between Royal Hospital and Council 139, 295–6
Liddell, General Sir Clive 269
Light Horse Court 70, 125, 140, 151, 152, 204, 224, 255, 284, 300
Lime Tree Avenue 102, 273
Lloyd, Robert 88, 190, 211, 217, 218
Local Defence Volunteers (LDV) 107–8, 110
Lockley, Captain William 70, 75, 108, 136, *165*, *174*, 187–8, 223, 283
London Auxiliary Ambulance Service (LAAS) 109–10
London County Council 26, 27, 38, 133
London Necropolis Company Ltd 81, 95
Long Wards 17, 116, 122, 125, 133, 136, 137, 140, 142, 145, 146, 244, 251, 300
    bombed 140, 141
    evacuation planning 35, 43, 232, 242
    evacuations 72, 244
Lots Road Power Station 31, 155, 177, 180, 265, 273
Louis XIV 13, 15
Loyd, Captain 255, 296
Ludlow, Ernest 19
Luftwaffe 59, 96, 102, 104, 105, 129, 130, 134, 147–51, 180, 212, 216, 223–4, 261, 275

bomb types 175, 272
Britain, Battle of 110–12, 113–28
Eastern Front 226, 246
1944 raids on London 271, 272–3, 275
targets of interest 31, 147, 148, *164*, 177
Lundy, Island of 14

Maclagan, Sir Eric 78
McMullan, Sister Edith 180, 200, 209, 213
Malaher, H.T. 218–19
Mallett, Arthur 194–5, 197
Manchester Regiment 89
Marrable, Frederick George 185–6, 198, 219, 314n37
Marshall, W.D. 222, 233
Marshman, Kathleen 178, 181, 183, 208
Martin, Colonel 255, 272
Mary, Queen 296
Maxwell-Hyslop, A.R. 196
May, Sister Christabel 180, 185, 186, 190, 198, 209, 211
May, Captain G.C. 70, 114, 283, 285
Miller, A. 222–3, 225, 227, 228–31, 232, 233–4, 238, 241, 242, 243
Milne, Lord 236
Ministry of Health 84, 210, 218, 219, 228–9, 230, 237
    East End evacuees 280, 287
    evacuation planning 21, 24, 26, 30, 33–4, 38–9
    evacuation planning for Royal Hospital 59–60
    post-war planning 288
Ministry of Information 144–5, 191
Ministry of Transport 22, 33, 46, 47, 53–4
Ministry of Works 220, 221–2, 255, 256, 285, 293, 296
    aerodrome construction programme 250, 251, 254
    Ascott House 225, 228–31, 241, 242
    evacuation planning for Royal Hospital 221–2, 228–32, 233, 238, 242–3, 245
    post-war planning 279–80, 282, 288, 289, 292–3, 294, 299

339

prefabricated houses 279–80
Rudhall 58, 221, 229, 230
*see also* Office of Works
Molotov–Ribbentrop Pact (1939) 68, 69, 82
Monmouth, Duke of 15
Montacute House 78–9, 296
Moraston House *171*, 242–3, 245, 248, 251, 252–3, 256, 265, 299
Morgan-Owen, Major General Llewellyn Isaac Gethin (Lieutenant Governor) 213, 268, 269, 271–3, 279, 292
Morland, Major Walter Edward Thomson and Mrs Dulcie 57, 58–60, 61, 78, 79, 83, 89, 95, 97, 99, 213, 216, 296
Munich crisis 43–55, 61, 69, 117
Mussolini, Benito 49, 51–2

Napier, Major W. 275, 283, 284
Nash, Colonel 136, 197, 219
Nash, Rachel 188, 190, 197, 219
National Army Museum 300
National Fire Service (NFS) 256, 285
National Trust 78
Nazi Party 19, 27, 41–2, 242
Netherlands 102, 104
New Model Army 13, 14
New Zealand 290
Nicholson, E.W.T. 296
Nicholson, Sister Elizabeth 180–1, 200, 209, 213
Normandy landings 276, 278–9, 283
North Africa 252, 254, 258, 259
North-East Wing 283, 300
  air-raid shelters 70, 125
  bombed 19, *159*, 172, 283–4, 285
North Front 70, 115–16, 155, 278, 283, 284, 286, 291
North Grounds 54
North Terrace 51, 125, 150, *159*
Norway 101, 102, 117

Oakman, Jo 121, 273–4
Office of Works 22, 77, 136, 141–2, 220
  air-shelters at Royal Hospital 64, 121–2

evacuation planning for Royal Hospital 29, 32–4, 36–41, 43–9, 52–4, 58, 60–1
  requisitioning powers 22–3, 30, 31, 32, 53, 78–9, 220
  *see also* Ministry of Works
Old Church Street 179, 193, 194–6, 199, 208
Out-Pensioners 17, 267
  *see also* commutations
out-pensions 97, 107, 153, 231, 266, 267, 293, 295
  Royal Navy 266, 267
out-stations 227–46, 256–7, 266, 270–1, 292–4
  expansion of scheme 217, 221, 240, 253
  remoteness 59, 293–4
  rotation system 253, 255, 256, 265
  Rudhall blueprint for 216
  *see also* Ascott House; Cobrey Park; Princess Christian Home; Rudhall; White Hill Farm
Oxfordshire & Buckinghamshire Light Infantry 239

Pacific War 246, 254
parachute mines 136, 175–6, 181–6, 188, 191, 194–5, 197, 199, 203, 204
Paradise Walk 183, 201, 202, 209
Paultons Square 62, 194
Paulus, General 257, 259
Paymaster Generals 70, 106, 282, 293
Pearl Harbor 246
Pearson, Mr 216
pensions 16–17
  *see also* In-Pensioners; Out-Pensioners
Pensions Secretariat 33, 44, 45, 70, 73, 107, 254, 255, 259, 293, 295
Petyt Place 194, 195–6
The Phoney War 87–100
Pile, Lieutenant General Sir Frederick 116, 121
Pimlico 125, 136
Poland 63, 68, 69, 71, 74, 80, 81, 82, 87–8, 90, 91, 225–6

*Index*

Portugal 14
Post B 197, 201, 204
Post D 194, 197
Post E 204
Post K (Air Raid Warden Shelter, Royal Avenue) 64, *162*, 181, 186, 199, 201, 204, 205, 209, 285
post-war planning 260, 261–80, 282–98
prefabricated houses *173*, 279–80, 282, 283, 287–8, 289
Princess Christian Home 213, 240, 256, 257
propaganda 144–5, 191
Public Assistance Institutions 25–6, 98, 153
   evacuation planning 25–6, 31–2, 34, 36–7, 38, 39, 40, 53, 60

Queen's Own Cameron Highlanders 89

Raeder, Grand Admiral 226, 227
Ranelagh Gardens 65, 102, 103, 289
   bombed 147, 150, 157, 202, 209, 224, 273
   prefabricated houses *173*, 279–80, 289
rationing 83, 88, 100, 149, 154, 244, 248, 252–3, 258, 270
Rattrey, Henry Augustus 88, 190–1, 213
Red Army 261–2, 291
refugees from Europe 104–5, 108, 151
registration night (29 September 1939) 83, 88
requisitioning 81, 105, 193, 221–2, 248
   on behalf of Royal Hospital 37–8, 218
   Office of Works 22–3, 30, 31, 32, 53, 78–9, 220
   Royal Hospital considered for 30–1, 32, 65–6, 114
Rhyl (Ministry of Works) 221, 222
Ribbentrop, Joachim von 68
Ring, Cyril 259
road traffic accidents 80, 82, 146
Roman, Sacha 242
Rommel, General Erwin 103, 252, 254, 258, 259
Ross rifles 110

Rothschild, Anthony de *170*, 214, 225, 230, 240, 241, 282–3, 299
Rowley, George 211, 217, 218
Royal Air Force (RAF) 80, 82, 96, 101, 110–11, 113–27, *170*, 209, 235, 249, 259, 271, 278
   *see also* barrage balloons
Royal Armoured Corps 109
Royal Army Medical Corps 72, 79, 314n37
Royal Army Pay Corps 285
Royal Artillery 117, 190, 278
Royal Avenue 49, 64, 65, 126, 181, 248, 256, 289
   *see also* Post K
Royal Canadian Army Service Corps 178
Royal Engineers 81, 83, 89, 103, 137, 139, *164*, 177, 272
Royal Horse Artillery 89
Royal Horticultural Society (RHS) 289
Royal Hospital Greenwich 13, 16, 17, 37, 266, 267, 268
Royal Hospital Kilmainham, Dublin 13, 15, 17, 37
Royal Hospital Road 67, 143, 146, 178, 193, 256, 278, 286
   bombed 181–4, 186, 189, 192, 201, 206
Royal Munster Fusiliers 44
Royal Navy 14, 16, 71, 96, 101, 104, 149, 176, 227, 235–6, 262, 266
Royal School for the Blind, Leatherhead 299
Royal Sussex Regiment 239
Royal Tank Corps 117
Royal Victoria Patriotic Building, Wandsworth 295, 299
Rudhall, Ross-on-Wye 56–60, 82–3, 95, 98–9, *160*, *163*, 243–4, 265, 283
   blueprint for out-station model 216
   closed 296
   evacuation commences 72–3, 78, 79
   funded through Royal Hospital budget 73–4, 94, 97, 98, 152–3, 220, 221
   Ministry/Office of Works 57, 220, 221, 230, 232

341

numbers of In-Pensioners 57, 60, 72, 78, 240, 244, 253
In-Pensioners' final postings at 83, *174*
registration details and national identity cards 83, 88–90
returnees 96, 98, 99
Russia (Soviet Union) 68, 82, 90, 108, 226, 239, 240, 246, 249, 252, 254, 257, 259

St Luke's Hospital 143, 146, 198, 209, 210–11, 214, 217, 224–5
St Mark's College 104
St Mary's Church, Ross-on-Wye 95, *174*, 283
Sandhurst 300
'The Saturday' (19–20 April, 1941) 210–11
Scots Guards 240
Scott, Harold 66
searchlight units 31, 82, 103
   South Grounds *12*, 81, 103, 112, 113, 114, 118, 140
Secretary's Office 77, 85, 107, 108, 125, 126, 204, 255, 278, 284, 285
Shawfield Street 143–4
Sheean, Vincent 212
Sherwood Foresters 151, 252
Singapore 246, 247
Sloane Court East 277
Sloane Gardens 285
Sloane Square Underground Station 148
Smith, Tony 274
Soane Stable Yard 137, 156, 157, *165*, 179, 254
Somerset Light Infantry 239
South Grounds 51, 65, 80, 81, 102, 105, 137, 138
   barrage balloon ('Flossie') 80, 101, 134, 187, 209, 213
   bombed 201
   searchlight unit *12*, 81, 103, 112, 113, 114, 118, 140
South Terrace 125, 130, 134, 148, 224, 277
South Wales Borderers 239
Soviet Union *see* Russia (Soviet Union)

Spanish Civil War 20, 50
Spencer, June 100, 106, 109–10, 118, 120, 121, 132, 149, 178, 193, 199, 200–1, 202
Stainton, Anne (*née* Marshman) 178, 181, 182–3, 208
Stainton, Cecil 178, 181, 183
Stalingrad 249, 254, 257, 258, 259, 261
State Apartments 139, 295
State Drawing Room 139, 296–7
Station 6W (AFS Station) 181, 186, 189, 200, 201
Steward, Arthur 154
Suez Canal 254
super-shelters 62, 63, 64, 65, 126, 205, 300
supply difficulties 109, 149, 153–5, 157–8, 239, 244, 247–9, 252–3, 258, 262, 270
surface shelters 64, 65, 140, 187

Tangier 14–15
taxis 200
Taylor, Sister Edith 72, 73, 83, 89, 95, 99, 180, 186, 214, 318n31
tennis courts (Burton Court) 136, 137, 140, 144, 286
Territorial Army Nursing Service (TANS) 73
Tite Street 143, 144, 157, 181, 183–4, 186, 191, 201, 209, 287
Tobruk 252
Townsend, Captain Cecil 75, 85–6, 114, 180, 223, 224, 236, 256, 276, 285
Treasury 220, 231–2, 237–8, 239, 241, 242, 243, 244, 245
trench shelters 50–1, 61–2, 64, *167*, 245

U-boats 96, 149, 235–6, 247, 248, 258, 262, 271
unexploded bombs (UXBs) 115–16, 119, 136, 137, 144, 150, 195, 210, 257, 272, 292
United States 106, 145, 212, 247, 254, 262
   Lend-Lease agreement 139, 247
   mortality statistics 290

*Index*

United States Army 178, 254, 278
United States Army Air Forces (USAAF) 249, 271, 281
United States Navy 246, 247, 254
Universal Aunts 106

V1 doodlebugs 271, 275, 276–9
V2 ballistic missiles 271, 281–2, 283–4, 286
Vaughan Thomas, Wynford *169*, 219
Vaughan-Williams, Sister 285
VE Day 291
Versailles, Treaty of (1919) 19, 63
Victoria & Albert Museum (V&A) 78–9
Victoria Children's Hospital 150, 184, 209–10, 214
Victoria Station 127, 177, 180, 199
Vincent Square 277
Volunteer Aid Detachment (VAD) 63, 67, 143

Wallis, Tommy 184
War Cabinet 79, 102, 106
War Comforts Depot 138–9, 295
War Diary 68, 84–5, 92, 98, 109, 127, 141–2, 152, *162*, 223, 235, 248–9, 263, 292
   Ascott House 235, 240, 244
   deaths of In-Pensioners 131, 155
   East End bombings 118, 157, 210
   evacuation planning 81, 83–5, 107–8, 211, 213
   evacuations 215, 234, 235, 240
   fire watching 254, 255
   influenza 269, 270
   London bombed 119, 121, 123–6, 130–6, 143, 147–8, 149–50, 152, 238, 261, 272–3, 276–7
   post-war 291
   propaganda visit 144–5
   rotation system 256, 265
   Royal Hospital, air-raid alerts 75–6, 111–12, 118, 120, 124, 132, 139, 261, 272, 276
   Royal Hospital, air-raid shelters 122, 145–6, 279

   Royal Hospital bombed 125, 132, 135–6, 138, 140–2, 152, 156–7, 185, 198, 201, 204, 213, 275, 284, 291
   Royal Hospital, normal life continues 74, 153, 211, 248–9, 251, 270
   Rudhall 79, 83, 244
   summary of wartime casualties 291
War Office 44, 68, 69, 110, 115, 134, 228, 237, 241, 254
   commutations 77, 97, 98
   evacuation planning for Royal Hospital 32–4, 39, 43, 45–7, 56–8, 78, 215, 220–1, 231–2, 238–9, 244
   funding for Royal Hospital 58, 97, 220–1, 231, 241, 244–5, 258
   personnel issues at Royal Hospital 269, 272–3
   post-war planning 272–3
   requisitions 65–6, 114
   War Office Detachment, Home Guard 224, 255
water supply 109, 120, 130, 133, *165*, 206–7, 216, 224, 256
Watts, Herbert 190, 211, 217
'The Wednesday' (16–17 April, 1941) 175, 211, 263, 283
Weir, Margaret 198–9
Wellington Barracks 277
West Road 125, 130, 133, 156, *165*, 191, 192, 255
West Wing 130, 150, 157, 254
Westminster Hospital 223
Wheal, Donald and Keith ('Kit') 71, 92–3, 274, 275
Wheal, Phylliss 93
White Hill Farm, Berkhamsted 215, 234, 237, 240, 256
Winkfield Place Convalescent Home, Windsor Forest 217
Winterton, Earl 70, 84
Witts, Major General (Lieutenant Governor) 279, 283
Woman's Voluntary Service (WVS) 71–2, 93

workhouses 25–6, 31–2, 39, 53, 98, 267
*see also* Public Assistance Institutions
World's End district 71, 92, 273–4

Wratten, Victor 181, 182
Wren, Christopher 15–16, 22

York and Lancaster Regiment 284